ABOUT THE AUTHOR

Ed Bethune grew up in Arkansas. He joined the Marines when he was eighteen years old and rose to the rank of sergeant. He received an honorable discharge in 1957 and then earned two degrees from the University of Arkansas at Fayetteville, a bachelor of science from the School of Business Administration and a juris doctorate from the School of Law. He served four years as a special agent of the FBI and then became a prosecuting attorney in his hometown of Searcy, Arkansas. As a private attorney, he was lead counsel in the trial of many important cases, both civil and criminal. In 1978, against all odds, he won a seat in the United States House of Representatives, the first Republican to hold that seat in 104 years. He served three terms in Congress and then lost a campaign for a seat in the United States Senate. After Congress, Bethune joined the law firm of Bracewell & Giuliani in Washington, D. C. and became a high profile ethics lawyer, representing Speaker Newt Gingrich, Majority Leader Tom DeLay and others. He and his wife Lana reside in Little Rock, Arkansas. They have two children and eight granddaughters.

JACKHAMMERED

A LIFE OF ADVENTURE

ED BETHUNE

ISBN: 1463753462
ISBN-13: 9781463753467
LCCN: 2011913137
Createspace, North Charleston, SC

For further information: www.jackhammered.com

Cover: *The Snotgreen Sea*, oil on canvas, by Lana Bethune

I dedicate this book to all who have had to deal with shame or embarrassment of one kind or another. Take heart! Live out your dreams! God loves you and has a wonderful plan for your life.

Acknowledgements

Writing is a lonely endeavor, but eventually you turn to friends and family for support and this is the place to thank them for their good counsel and encouraging words.

Huey Crisp, a retired professor of writing and rhetoric at the University of Arkansas in Little Rock was the first to read my completed manuscript and his good counsel inspired me to press on with the hardest part of the project, editing and revising. Joel Anderson, chancellor of the University of Arkansas at Little Rock was one of my earliest political supporters and he introduced me to Huey. Jim and Mel Barden, classmates of mine at Pocahontas High School gave me a boost of confidence at an important moment. Sally Meredith, cofounder of Christian Family Life with her husband Don, took time out of her vacation on Bald Head Island to read my book and then gave me some good suggestions. Jerry Climer, my chief of staff when I was in Congress has always been a good sounding board for me and he was again, as was his wife Mary Ann. Jessica Tiahrt, a new young friend, read a number of lengthy excerpts and offered a perspective my older friends could not give. Danny Harris, a fine photographer in Little Rock took the photograph of me that appears on the About the Author page and the one of Speaker John Boehner and me just before Election Day in 2010. Elliot Berke, a fine ethics lawyer I worked with when I represented Tom DeLay, has always been a good advisor to me. My brother-in-law, Bill Hastings, my nephew Scott Hastings, his wife Kim and their daughter Lindsey validated my recollections about my sister Delta Lew and gave me valuable feedback on my writing style. Two longtime friends from the legal community, David Fuqua and Judge Morris "Buzz" Arnold, generously volunteered to read my manuscript and their reviews were timely and insightful. My longtime supporter, Doyle Webb, now chairman of the Republican Party of Arkansas confirmed my recollections about the party's growth over the last quarter-century. Steve Barnes, a well-known Arkansas television personality with an encyclopedic memory, recalled the details of my near-death experience in Conway County, Arkansas, and I am grateful for his help. I am also grateful for French Hill's fine article on the history of the Arkansas Wilderness Act, most of which I incorporated into this memoir with his permission. Finally, I thank my former colleague, Congressman William Whitehurst of Virginia, who captured an extemporaneous speech I made during the ABSCAM scandal and reported it in a diary he published in 1985.

My children, Paige and Sam, have patiently listened to my stories for years. In spite of that, they read the manuscript and gave me their unique perspective. I love them.

My wife, Lana, read what I wrote all along the way and she read and reread the finished manuscript. She has been my constant advisor and encourager from the beginning. Her painting, *The Snotgreen Sea,* adorns the cover of this book. I love her.

Table of Contents

PREFACE

History will be kind to me for I intend to write it.
Winston Churchill

On our life journey, we see right and wrong, good and evil, fair and foul, love and hate. Sometimes the path is easy to see, sometimes not. We struggle, we succeed, we err, and we go on. Eventually, we encounter an inescapable truth. We are not the center of the universe. Our destiny hinges upon acceptance of that truth.

Winston Churchill's comment is fair warning. I am the author of a tale that is about me. I wrote what I believe to be the truth, but I doubt my work is perfect. I am human; therefore, I seek your indulgence. I may have misstated an event or mischaracterized my role in something, if so I apologize. However, I make no apology or equivocation for my absolutist view that God in Heaven loves us and has a wonderful plan for our lives.

My overarching purpose has been to show how events and relationships affected me, how I struggled, how I denied and how I learned.

I traveled a complicated path. I had an uncomfortable secret to keep throughout my childhood in a broken family. The good people of a small town saved me, an incorrigible child. I served three years in the United States Marine Corps, four years as a special agent of the FBI, three years as a prosecutor, six years as a congressman, and decades as a trial lawyer representing everyone from the poorest of the poor to the speaker of the United States House of Representatives.

My memoir recalls those experiences, but it also tells about the ill-starred attempt my wife and I made to sail across the Atlantic Ocean in a thirty-one-foot sailboat.

A jackhammer is easily the most annoying, distracting racket-making device known to man. It creates a noise level of 130 decibels—equal to a rock concert—according to the Occupational Safety and Health Administration. Rock concerts occasionally produce a discernible melody. Jackhammers do not. Sometimes it takes such a racket to get our attention.

Shakespeare wrote, "Life is all sound and fury, signifying nothing." I understand the point he was making because my life has involved much sound and a lot of fury. Nevertheless, I hope to defy Macbeth's lament that the sound and fury signifies nothing. If but one man, woman, or child profits from the lessons I have learned then that will be something.

In writing this memoir, I mentioned my children and grandchildren only when it was necessary to complete the narrative. I have not told the full story of our children, Paige and Sam. Such a work would be much longer and they are surely happy that I decided against such an exposition.

I shared opinions about other members of my family, especially my mother and my father, only to explain how I came to be me, and my thoughts about the beliefs of the Vermilyes and Bethunes pertain solely to my lineage.

I reconstructed my family history from conversations with relatives and from my own recollection. When possible I squared my conclusions with public and private records, but some of the events I wrote about—particularly those from long ago—rest solely on what my grandparents, parents, and other relatives told me before they died.

Finally, I give tribute and thanks to my wife, Lana, for what she has made of me, for her tolerance of me and for her unwavering love and support.

1

HARD HEADS: THE VERMILYE WAY

Obstinacy is the result of the will forcing itself into the place of the intellect.
Arthur Schopenhauer

My riddle begins on a summer day in 1941. Before the sun got too high, my mother, my sister, and I caught the Missouri Pacific bus from Little Rock to Pocahontas, Arkansas. We were on our way to visit my grandmother, Mama Lewallen, and the rest of Mother's clan. I was almost six years old.

We made this trip every August. I do not know that on my own because my life before then is mostly a blur of kids and things happening at Miss Mary Dodge Hodge's kindergarten—wispy images of singing, crying, laughing, and looking up at big people, big cars, big houses, big trees, and big skies.

This day was different. The vivid sights, sounds, and smells of the day come in loud and clear to me, even now, as I whiz through my seventh decade of life. The general hubbub in the station reached code red levels as our bus pulled into the angled loading spot where we would board. Mother had me by the collar, but I kept squirming and giggling. I could not help myself.

The snout-nosed Missouri Pacific bus, one of the delicious red ones, made a *ppffishhhhhing* sound as it air-braked to stop mere inches from where I stood. I felt the warmth of the engine and can still smell the weird mixture of grease, gas, tobacco smoke, and traveling people.

It is the first day of my life that I remember from beginning to end.

Mother was holding a full-fare ticket for herself and a half-fare for my sister as she herded us to the head of the line so that we could be the first to board. The other ticket holders gave her the small-eye as she jockeyed for position, but it did not slow her down. She needed to get a seat up front to carry off her plan and she was not going to be outmaneuvered. It was my first outing as a player in one of Mother's pinchpenny operations, but I still rank it as her all-time best effort.

This was her plan: The snout-noses had a luggage compartment by the door, just across from the driver's seat. So, as we climbed the big steps leading up into the bus Mother quickly lifted me up and over the stainless steel rails and sat me down in the luggage area. She then announced to the driver and everyone within earshot, "He gets to ride free. See, he's so little that he takes up no more room than a teeny-weeny piece of baggage." She coupled that with her patented stare of defiance; no one, least of all the driver, challenged her claim that I did not need a ticket. Score one for Mother.

I hated this part of the operation because everyone was getting a good snicker at my expense, but I absolutely loved riding in the luggage compartment. It was my special place, set apart from everyone with a good view of the road. I dreamed I was a real bus driver wearing the perfectly creased grey gabardine uniform of an official MoPac motorman, complete with a shiny lapel pin. The pin looked just like the wings of gold that Navy pilots wear, except for a logo in the center of the pin that said MoPac. I kept squirming and giggling, forever it seemed, but finally our bus pulled out. We were underway.

The first high point of my excellent adventure as a make-believe bus driver came about an hour out of Little Rock, in the little town of Cabot. There were passengers to pick up, but the most important thing that happened at this stop was the coming of the Popcorn Man. To me he looked old and used up, like a rickets or beriberi survivor. Groaning, he pulled himself up into the bus and sidled down the aisle selling greasy paper bags brimming full of hot, smelly popcorn. Some passengers could not afford to pay ten cents a bag but many of them could, or at least they could not resist.

Mother, in character, at first refused to buy a bag saying that we had just finished breakfast. Then, seeing the look on our faces, she painfully fished a dime out of her purse and bought one bag for the three of us to share. The bus took on the smells and sounds of the Roxy Theatre. The other passengers rattled the bags and munched the corn, but by careful rationing and urging us to eat one kernel at a time, Mother made our bag last most of the way to Newport, the halfway mark of our trip.

The driver said we would be in Newport for thirty minutes and our fellow travelers went inside a diner for lunch, but we did not. Instead, Mother found us a shady spot outside where she opened a paper sack full of stinky tuna fish sandwiches.

When the lunch break was over, the driver came out massaging his belly and puffing a cigarette. It was time to scramble back to my spot in the luggage rack. Safely ensconced, I dreamed on as we pulled back onto the two-lane road to Pocahontas. It was good to get going because we needed a breeze to sweep out the heat that had everyone fanning. On and on we went, stopping in all the little towns, picking up passengers and letting them off.

Then, as I was busy driving, passing slow cars, and occasionally beeping that magnificent horn, Mother woke me from my dream. It was just in time for me to see our real bus driver speeding across the Black River Bridge, making a beeline for the bus stop in Pocahontas. The long, 136-mile all-day trip and my dreamy day as an official MoPac driver was over. We collected our stuff out of the luggage compartment and walked by the old courthouse on the town square. The Lewallen Café, owned and operated by my grandmother, was a local favorite. It sat kitty-cornered from the courthouse on the northeast corner of the square.

As we neared Mama's café, a dozen men, fighting and yelling, came barreling out of a tavern on Everett Street just across from where we stood. The tavern was on the corner by an alley that fell sharply downhill and away from the café. They were shouting words I had not heard before and the two men that seemed to be the main attraction were on the ground rolling toward the alley. One of them was biting the other one's ear and right before our eyes the ear came off and that pretty much ended the fight.

I wanted to get closer to find out what the earless man was going to do, but Mother hurried my sister and me into the café. The last thing I saw was the man holding his bloody hand over what I figured was now an ear-hole instead of a sure-enough ear. I do not know what became of the ear itself. The people in the café watched the fight through a big solid glass window that had LEWALLEN CAFÉ hand-painted on it in big black letters outlined in gold. By the time we got through the front door most of the customers had returned to their tables, but some were gathered at the long mahogany-topped bar that was on the right as you entered the café.

My grandmother, Thema Lewallen, was behind the bar drawing a beer for an old man with a white beard and they were laughing and talking about the fight. No one else seemed to be worrying about the fight or the man's ear and the thing I remember most was that Mama's laughing revealed her big gold tooth. It was right up front, so in addition to being good for biting it served as a piece of jewelry. Back then, it was a sign of prosperity to have a gold tooth. Mama was extremely proud of hers.

She was tall, trim, and very tough; exuding the unmistakable air of a no-nonsense businesswoman, which is exactly what she was. My mother, Delta Odessa Lewallen, barely five feet tall, was not nearly as big as Mama, but she was prettier and had a shapelier figure. Mama had the straight up and down look of a hard-labor woman, whereas my mother was more ladylike, at least she seemed so to me. Nevertheless, what Mother had, by then, that was identical to Mama was personality. They were both hard as nails and had no time for sluggards or fools. The hardness and toughness came naturally to them as it did to most folks raised in that era in the hill country of Arkansas.

I count that day in 1941 as the starting point of my memory but my story, a riddle, began long before my birth. It began in 1919 when my mother was a little girl. A terrible thing happened when she was nine years old. It changed her and the change in her, later on, affected me.

That year, 1919, was a boom year for Pocahontas. When Arkansas seceded and joined the Confederacy in 1861, the town was destined to suffer but after Reconstruction things picked up. Newcomers to Pocahontas outnumbered those who were leaving. Many came by road or rail, but most still came on the fleet of steamboats that had been working the river and hauling timber, crops, and people up and down it for almost a hundred years. On most days, you could see a cluster of them: Passenger boats, snag boats, barges, and freight boats tied helter-skelter to each other and to deep-set mooring posts that lined the riverbank high above the river's whirl-pooling current. To get off or on the boats people made their way, sometimes from boat to boat, over a series of narrow, wiggly gangplank boards. From there they hauled themselves and their belongings uphill to the town square, set well above the high-water mark of the river.

The arrivals were an odd lot. All year long men staggered home from the battlefields of World War I, a conflict that ended when Germany agreed to a ceasefire on November 11, 1918. Some returned in pine coffins, others with god-awful wounds. A few wore the World War I doughboy uniform, or at least a piece of it. The veterans looked older than they must have been. Others who came in 1919 wore the plain clothes of working people. Friends or family met some of the arrivals, but there were many newcomers, mostly from the East, who did not know anyone. They intended to sink roots and live in or near the town. Germans, Scots-Irish, Welsh—you could pick them out because they came with luggage, gunnysacks and boxes stuffed full of belongings. They were families for the most part. The rest—a parade of whores, roughnecks, toughs, drummers with big sample bags, itinerate sailors, deckhands, snag-boat crews, gamblers, and ne'er-do-wells—came just to make a quick buck or let off steam in the taverns and saloons.

Those with the gumption to stay would quickly learn what those who had come before already knew: There was nothing easy about life in Northeast Arkansas in 1919. The rocky clay soil in the hills west of Pocahontas was scratch-poor and the low-lying farmland east of town flooded in rainy months and was unbearably hot and buggy in the summer. The Current River comes out of Missouri and flows into the Black River, which runs generally from northeast to southwest, and together they make up the fault line between the hill country and the lowlands of Randolph County. In both places, the hills to the west and the lowlands to the east, people had to deal with wounds and prejudices stemming from the Civil War, World War I, and other human conflicts. These issues ran deep and like the scab of a putrid wound they would, from time to time, reopen and ooze pus. There were other perils too, diseases, natural disasters, and accidents. These came with little or no warning. They had nothing to do with war, hatred, or prejudice and they struck indiscriminately.

My grandmother, Mama Lewallen, belonged to one of the families that had come before. She was born in 1885 on a hardscrabble farm in Warm Springs, a tiny outpost in the hill country twenty miles north of Pocahontas. The town had a reputation in the early days as a rough-and-ready place. Fistfights, knife fights, and wrestling matches were commonplace because the local toughs, for some reason, felt compelled to boast of being the "best man" in the community. It was no place for the fainthearted.

Mama was the oldest in a farm family of nine girls and one boy, the boy being the next-to-youngest child born to Mark and Etta Vermilye. Mark, my great-grandfather, was the son of rugged Dutch émigrés and he had made his way to Arkansas via Pennsylvania shortly after the Civil War. It was not his nature to whine about anything, especially the minor setbacks of farm life. The Vermilyes were good people; strong-willed people who had learned, through years of hard knocks and forced relocations, to deal with whatever came along. The girls absorbed the hard, independent edge of their father; they were good-looking but they brooked no foolishness or softness. On rare occasions, the Vermilyes might discuss their fears or foibles with each other, but they never opened up to outsiders whom they always bunched together and considered with the utmost caution as "them" or "they." I remember Grandpa Vermilye coming to the Lewallen Café every morning just as the breakfast crowd was thinning out. He was in his eighties but he walked the two miles from where he lived to the café. He always brought a basket of eggs and garden vegetables he had gathered that morning. Mama would buy them from him, and then she would feed him a good plate of ham and eggs with biscuits and gravy. He was a tough old bird, wiry and short of stature. I was a little scared of him because he did not say much and he smelled like wood smoke and he did not smile or laugh, ever.

Mama Lewallen (far left) with eight younger sisters and a brother, the only boy born to Mark and Etta Vermilye. Circa 1902

Mama told me a lot about the old days but I learned more, things that I will never forget, by just watching her. She was a great cook although most every dish she made dripped fat. Lard, bacon grease or simply fried fat meat were the staples of her diet. Her favorite dishes were wilted lettuce and onions, biscuits and gravy, fried squirrel and gravy, fried rabbit and gravy, brains and eggs, and blackbird pie.

Waste not; want not—that was Mama's motto. At the end of a fulsome squirrel dinner Mama would fish the squirrel heads out of the pot and crack them open with the handle of her knife. With great fanfare and a narrow smile, she would spoon out the brains and spread the goo onto a gravy-covered biscuit—the ultimate poor man's canapé. I was not shocked because the appetite for such things was part of the Vermilye family culture and I realized that country people throughout Northeast Arkansas ate such things. Even so, I always looked away when Mama put it in her mouth.

Thinking about diet and cooking is a good way to appreciate the hard life lived by rural Arkansans in the early part of the twentieth century. People used wood cook stoves that they stoked up before every meal. They had no running water, indoor plumbing, or electricity. They made big gardens every year and canned all the surplus vegetables and fruit so that they would have something to eat during the cold months. They raised and slaughtered chickens, hogs, goats, and cattle in order to have meat on the table. They cured hams, slabs of bacon, jowls, and made chunks of salt pork they could eat and cook with in the winter. Nothing was wasted. Pig's feet were pickled and put up in jars or used as the main ingredient in a souse. People managed, but they were strictly on their own. In the case of the Vermilyes, the urge to be ruggedly independent became stronger day by day, as they adapted to the hardships of life in rural Randolph County, Arkansas.

Mama had a sense of humor, but you had to search for it. Once, when we walked in the woods just down the hill from the café, Mama gave a false alarm. She cried out that she had spotted a "blue-racer snake." It scared me and I ran like a bat out of Hell until I realized she was tricking me. She laughed like crazy, her gold front tooth shining like a light. Mama did not laugh often because that would have been out of character, but when she did, it was something to behold.

Mama met and married George "Papa" Lewallen from Missouri, a Welshman by heritage. He was as tough as she was and together they saved enough to open a wholesale grocery that was a mainstay in Pocahontas for years.

In the first years of their grocery business Papa delivered groceries in a wagon pulled by two old mules that his daddy gave him. Papa's daddy had named the mules Grover and Adlai because he despised President Grover Cleveland and Vice President Adlai Stevenson. They were for the Gold Standard and hard against the idea of Free Silver, a position supported by Papa's daddy and most farmers. Papa did not share his daddy's radical ideas, but that did not matter because it was not long before he and Mama got rid of the mules. They had found a better way to make their deliveries.

The *Star Herald*, a local newspaper, revealed their progressive thinking as merchants with this news story in 1916: "George Lewallen is the first merchant in Randolph County to purchase an auto truck for delivery of merchandise." Shortly thereafter, Papa decided it would be good advertising to put a gaudy red-and-white-checkerboard paint job on the delivery truck. The paint job had the desired effect. Everyone who saw it said, "There goes Lewallen's truck."

They prospered in the grocery business, but unfortunately Papa had a taste for liquor and it began to consume him as their business and family grew. He managed to control his alcoholism with sheer willpower for quite awhile, but it got the best of him during the hard times of the Great Depression.

By the time I came along Papa was a lost cause. I think that is why Mama talked mostly about *her* childhood and building up the grocery and café business, but she *seldom* talked about her marriage and she *never* said anything good about Papa.

In particular, Mama did not talk about my mother's time as a little girl. She did not, that is, until I was thirty-three years old and Mama was near death. Then one day she gave in to my persistence and opened up. She told me things that my mother never, to the day she died, revealed. What she told me helped me to understand how my mother came to be the strongest, sternest, toughest woman I ever knew.

Mother was Delta, named so because Mama liked the sound of it. She was the only girl in a family of five children. She was born in 1909, the same year Mama and Papa opened Lewallen Grocery, their new store on the town square. A younger brother, Gerle, was born two years later. There was an older brother, Herschel, but it was natural that Mother latched on to "Little Gerle"—that is what she *always* called him—as her special charge. Mama said she mothered him like little girls are wont to do, and her gentle ways made it plain to everyone in the family that she was going to be a different kind of Vermilye. With every day that passed Mother showed less interest in her favorite baby dolls. Her attention shifted to her little brother. She was an open, loving, and carefree little girl and it showed the most when she was watching over Little Gerle. Mama said, "They played together, fought over silly things, shared secrets, slept in the same room, and got in the same messes." They were, she said, "inseparable." Mother also felt responsible for Little Gerle. She would blame herself for failing him even when there was no reason to feel that way. She believed Little Gerle was hers to protect.

Mama centered on the end days of September 1919, a glorious moment in America and Pocahontas. World War I, the "war to end all wars," was over and the boys were coming home. The town was growing and the Lewallen Grocery was a success. A sense of prosperity was seeping through the town and optimism was building day by day.

There were chores to do and school to attend, but there was still plenty of time for children to play outside before it got dark. Mother and Little Gerle were the "ringleaders" of playtime, according to Mama. They would meet up with other children at Marr Creek, a tributary of the Black River that carried various kinds of runoff and an assortment of trash through Pocahontas. At a place where the creek deepened and made a small sandbar, their favorite spot, the children would swap stories, fish interesting things out of the water and push, shove, and playfully hit each other when they could not think of anything to say. I imagine they, like kids everywhere, also exchanged peeks at their private parts.

Little Gerle with his pet raccoon, Mother with her pet chicken, and older brother Herschel with his raccoon. Circa 1919.

Mama said the town was abuzz. The war had taken its toll, but it was fall and everyone was feeling good, feeling upbeat.

Northeast Arkansas was enjoying an Indian Summer, that wondrous weather phenomenon that brings perfect temperatures and the clearest skies one can imagine, and—Hallelujah—word had it that a carnival was coming to town.

The carnival people would set up their rides and tents in the holler south of the town square that was reserved for tent meetings, rodeos, big revivals and such things as that. Mama, trying to lower expectations, told the kids it was not a big carnival such as you would see in St. Louis or Memphis, but Little Gerle and Mother could have cared less. The carnival was coming!

Finally, the Chicago White Sox were getting ready to play the Cincinnati Reds in the 1919 World Series. Mama loved baseball and had a weakness for gambling on the games. She made ten-cent bets on the White Sox with a bookie she called, "Baseball Man." He came by the grocery several times a week during baseball season.

Mama's fondness for the White Sox came from a favorite uncle of hers who had worked in Chicago before the war. He talked endlessly about Shoeless Joe Jackson and Eddie Collins and the team heralded to be the best team in baseball. For Mama, a rabid fan and no shrinking violet, the White Sox could do no wrong, and she stuck with them even though the nearby St. Louis Cardinals were the local favorite. Cardinal fans regarded Mama's allegiance to the Sox as apostasy. They were cheering for the National League team, the Reds, to win the Series.

With all that was taking place the little town was about to implode. The rumors about the carnival spread like wildfire. A makeshift World Series scoreboard rigged up just off the square was the place where people could get inning-by-inning results of the games. Baseball Man planned to post the scores as quickly as he received the details from the telegraph office.

Automobiles were still a novelty, but various brands—Ford Model T, Maxwell, and Oldsmobile to name a few—were beginning to show up in Pocahontas, and it was common to see one or two around the town square. Even so, the occasional signs of a new era and a promising future were in sharp relief to the dominant signs of the past. Horses, mules, oxcarts, wagons and carriages easily outnumbered the new-fangled automobiles. People ignored the ever-present smell of livestock droppings, but they paid a lot of attention to where they were about to step. The stores were still featuring old-time hand tools, dry goods, seed and feed, and various farm implements. Only occasionally could you see an ad for a radio, a washing machine, or some other newfangled gadget. The background noises—the blacksmith's hammer, the clopping of hooves—were those of yesteryear.

The burst of new activity was almost too much for the children. The grownups were thrilled too, but they pretended not to be. Finally, the excitement reached its peak. The World Series was underway and the carnival trucks and wagons paraded into town and around the square. A huge man dressed in a fine white costume with gold braid and epaulets led them. He was riding a spirited white Arabian horse with red and yellow plumes. Close behind the rider came a small band in full parade dress, playing Souza-like march music. The parade, with scores of screaming kids in tow, wound its way onto the street that led to the holler where the carnies would unload the wagons and set up. Little Gerle and Mother climbed halfway up a high bank on one side of the holler so they could see it all and watch the carnies work. They were not about to miss anything. The colorful, showy banners told of freaks, wonders of the world, and wrestling champions who offered to take on all comers. There were games of chance, and for the grown men there were whispered reports of a hootchie-cootchie show featuring a star performer who, for an extra dollar, would "smoke a cigarette with it." Little Gerle and Mother were not privy to the whispers about the hootchie-cootchie show, but the rest of it astounded them.

On the afternoon before the first night of the carnival Little Gerle and Mother were acting silly, giggling and running aimlessly in every direction. From time to time, they would fall in a heap and lie there trying to stop laughing so they could get their breath. Little Gerle was especially wide-eyed and full of wonder. It was his nature to get that way when he was about to learn something new. He was a bright boy and Mama said it was impossible to ignore him when he smiled and looked at you with his "big brown eyes." He had one question after another and the closer they got to the carnival grounds, the faster his questions came.

He wanted to know about the wrestlers, the barkers, the carnies, and the freaks, especially the freaks. When Mama told him about the freaks Little Gerle winced and said he did not want to see them because he felt sorry for them. Finally, when they got into the carnival the smells of frying onions, popcorn, cotton candy, candied apples, hot dogs and hamburgers overtook their conversations, catapulting the children into a fit of ecstasy. Little Gerle and Mother took off, holding hands and running wild. All Mama could do was stand back and watch them skip playfully from one concession to another. They were not about to miss a single sight, or the slightest smell or sound, and they stayed until the barkers stopped barking and the carnies started closing down the concessions.

In a few days, it was all over. The carnival folded its tents and was gone as quickly as it had come. The Indian summer fizzled out and Pocahontas was getting a deluge of rain and colder weather. The Cincinnati Reds won the World Series. They beat the Chicago White Sox in eight games (in the period after World War I, the World Series was a best-of-nine series). For the record, Mama did not budge from her support of the White Sox then, or a year later, when she learned that eight players, including Shoeless Joe Jackson, had thrown the 1919 series. Mama lost her bets, and the 1919 White Sox were forever after known as the Black Sox, but until she died, she held fast to her belief that they were the best team in baseball. That was Mama, through and through. When she died in 1971 the preacher, commenting on her renowned stubbornness and bluntness, said, "One thing about it: You never had to ask Mrs. Lewallen what she said." Those attending her funeral chuckled and gave each other knowing glances.

Meanwhile, in the midst of the carnival and the World Series, the chores had piled up. It was time for things to get back to normal. Mother was back to helping Mama around the house and in the kitchen, but Little Gerle fell behind with his chores. The trash baskets filled up and he did not bring the kindling for the kitchen cook stove, two easy jobs that fell to him as the youngest in the family. Mama kept after him to get his work done, but he was listless and said he did not feel good. The day after the carnival left town, he went to bed without eating anything for dinner. Mama figured it was a hangover from "too much carnival."

Mama and Mother tried everything they could to perk him up, but they did not have much luck. When they read to him and talked to him about school, they expected him to show some interest because he was a promising student, but that did not work. Nothing worked.

Little Gerle was very sick, but Mama still believed it was a case of too much carnival. He was sweating and hot, but Mama had seen fevers that were higher. Later on, his neck puffed up, he had labored breathing and a sore throat that got so bad that he could not swallow. That bothered Mama. She tried the usual home remedies for sore throat and congestion such as sipping hot tea with lemon and honey and setting up a jury-rigged vaporizing tent over his bed, but nothing seemed to work and Little Gerle was getting worse by the hour. It was then that Mama sent for the doctor. When he got there late in the day, she told him that Little Gerle had no interest in school, or anything, and that he had gotten worse day by day.

The doctor took one look into Little Gerle's nose and throat and told Mama he feared the boy might have diphtheria. The thick fuzzy coating, a sort of blackish membrane that the doctor found in his nose and throat was a telltale sign of the disease.

Diphtheria! No one, least of all a mother, wanted to hear the word. The hill people called it the "strangling angel of children." For ages, there was no known treatment to reverse the rapid spread of diphtheria. The poisonous disease could race through an entire community as quickly as it could spread though a child's body. An anti-toxin to fight the infection discovered twenty-five years earlier in France was saving lives, but in rural Arkansas, there was a general distrust of such cures. It would be many years before doctors would discover a vaccine to prevent the disease before infection.

The doctor told Mama that he needed to inject the anti-toxin into Little Gerle. She said she wrestled with the idea but he convinced her that it was an emergency. He said the anti-toxin was the best, perhaps the only, chance to save the child.

The doctor also told her they would need to quarantine Little Gerle because diphtheria is highly contagious. It spreads easily by coughing, sneezing, and even laughing. The doctor and Mama sealed off the room and took away all the used handkerchiefs, drinking glasses and dishes that Little Gerle had used.

Mother had been caring for Little Gerle throughout the week and she could not understand why, all of sudden, the bedroom where the two of them had slept for years was off limits to her. She was too short to see into the room through an outside window so she stacked up several boxes and climbed up on them to look in. She could see her brother in his bed and hear him gagging, but she could not make out what Mama and the doctor were saying. She yelled for them to let her in, and when they did not she began sobbing and pecking on the window. Finally, the doctor came out and told her, "Little Gerle is real sick and you must not go near him until he is well."

Mama said Mother stayed outside the house near the window to the bedroom and would not leave even though it turned cool when the sun went down. Eventually her yelling turned into a whimper with her repeating, prayer-like, "Little Gerle, please … please … get well." She kept saying it and nothing could move her from her post. Later that night, Mama picked Mother up from where she had curled up in a corner. She had pulled a horse blanket up around her neck to keep warm but she was still shivering and whining. Mama carried her inside and put her to bed in a room far away from Little Gerle's room.

The doctor put the anti-toxin into the boy, but it was too late. As the sun rose on October 11, 1919, the diphtheria had spread to Little Gerle's heart, his kidneys, and his nervous system. The strangling angel of children brought a gruesome death to the little seven-year-old boy.

When Mother woke up, she ran to Mama and asked about Little Gerle. Mama wiped the tears from Mother's face and tried to explain that Little Gerle was not hurting anymore and that he was at peace, but Mother did not understand what she meant. Mama finally told her that Little Gerle was dead, that he was gone forever and would not come back. With that, Mother collapsed on the floor screaming and kicking at anyone who got near her, but after a bit she wore herself out. Mama managed to get her back to her bed and she cried herself to sleep.

The death of a child is always painful, but back then it was a common occurrence. The graveyards were full of little tombstones. The news of Little Gerle's death traveled quickly through the community, but people were scared of diphtheria and the safest thing to do was to stay away from the Lewallen house. This was not the first time, nor would it be the last, that a child had been lost to the strangling angel.

The hurried funeral for Little Gerle was mostly a private, family affair. They needed to bury his body soon after his death to lessen the chance of contagion. A few brave friends did come to offer condolences and say goodbye, so Mama asked a preacher-friend to say some words. Mama and Papa were not religious people, but they were tolerant of those who were strong believers and knew that those who came to the funeral would expect some preaching and praying.

Church and religion were not a part of the Vermilye way. When Mama's father left New York as a child, he also left the Dutch Reformed Church that had been so important to his ancestors. Mark Vermilye was never able to reconcile the biblical obligation to surrender to a higher power with his perceived need to be ruggedly independent and self-sufficient, and that is what he taught his family. The family would have to work through the loss of Little Gerle without the consoling balm of Christianity.

Mama said Little Gerle's death changed Mother. She had started out as the child most likely to break out of the classic Vermilye hill country mindset. In her first years she was warm, loving and engaging but after Little Gerle died, Mama said, "Delta sank into a spell."

Mother returned to school and did her chores, but she was different. She did not have her heart in playtime as she had before her brother's death. She began to build a shell around herself.

At first, everyone thought Mother's spell was just a case of her being lonely and heartsick. They, especially Mama, thought she would soon get over it, but the tragic manner of Little Gerle's death was taking a greater toll than anyone realized. She slid into a state of despair and detachment. She would not let anyone get too close, a fear of intimacy that continued for years.

She would have nothing to do with dolls or other playthings. She devoted herself to the business of being a grownup. She cooked meals for the whole family, adopting Mama's fondness for grease and frying fatty meats. In her teen years, she got interested in fortunetellers, psychics, and clairvoyants. Her interest in the occult would carry on for years. In the late 1940s, Mother subscribed to and read every edition of *Fate*, a new magazine that reported odd stories suggesting the existence of paranormal forces.

As a child, Mother had the Vermilye indifference to religion even though Mama sent her to parochial school at St. Paul's Catholic Church in Pocahontas. She got a good education, which was what Mama wanted, but the nuns were never able to convert Mother or shake her faith in the Vermilye way of life.

If Little Gerle had lived, I believe he and Mother would have been receptive to and greatly influenced by Christianity, but the little girl from the time before his death was gone, buried deep—just as Little Gerle was now deep beneath the ground. The Vermilye philosophy gave her a hiding place. She became a true believer, an outspoken apostle of the hardheaded, self-centered approach to life, the core of which consisted of a few non-negotiable maxims. When adversity strikes, turn inward and redouble your effort to overcome all obstacles by the sheer force of your willpower. That and that alone will protect you from hurt and, when necessary, from "them," and "those who will take what you have." When it came to sickness, hardship, and death, the Vermilye worldview provided a safe harbor. In their view of life, it did no good to mourn overlong the loss of anything, even loved ones.

When she was seventeen, Mother finished high school and started college at nearby Jonesboro. For the first time since Little Gerle's death, it was possible to see a glimmer of the original Delta lying just beneath the hard Vermilye shell. She became a cheerleader and found a safe way, through art, to express the love she had bottled up long before. She began to draw and paint, prolifically. There were landscapes of watermills, dams and buildings, but her best paintings were of dogs, and kittens. She was an enigma. She revealed the love and tenderness that was still in her heart and soul through her paintings, but in her dealings with people, even those who were close to her, she was careful to maintain the Vermilye discipline. She had found a way to love even as she was fending off the cruelties of the world.

I was in midlife when I first learned all this. It was a revelation to me. Common sense taught me that the death must have hurt Mama and Mother and I could always tell that they longed for Little Gerle, but when I was young neither Mama nor Mother talked much about him. They never told me how much they loved him or how it hurt them when he died. The most Mother *ever* said about it was, "Little Gerle died of diphtheria when I was nine years old." After that, she would just clam up or change the subject.

I feel bad now that I did not understand the dramatic impact that Little Gerle's death had on Mother, but when I was young his death was nothing more than ancient history to me. It was only after Mama opened up that I began to understand my mother and appreciate how the tragedy affected her.

Mother had a life-long need to stay busy and be productive. As she aged, the need became an obsession that led to an endless array of focused, time-consuming projects. She crocheted. She knitted. She sewed. She gardened. She cooked. She read and she kept records, records of everything. In 1984, when I was running for the United States Senate I happened to pick up her copy of the Little Rock telephone directory. I noticed that there were hundreds of names highlighted throughout the book and asked why that was. She stunned me when she said it was something she did each year when the new telephone books came out. Mother would spend days, every year, going through the entire book, page by page, highlighting the names of all the people she knew. In the 1984 directory, the one I happened onto, there were more than six-hundred names highlighted. It was a treasure-trove for my campaign, but it showed me how much Mother valued and needed friendships even as she struggled, throughout her life, with the Vermilye requirement to keep her distance from people.

Talking about my mother's early life is a delicate issue because it is not my intent to be critical of someone so dear to me. My thoughts are merely an attempt to explain how she, a loving little girl, adopted the Vermilye worldview after Little Gerle's death, a way of thinking that stayed with her for decades. It dominated her and thus affected me.

Mother's life was further complicated when she was twenty years old by the onset of the Great Depression. The economic troubles that Americans face in today's world are in stark contrast to the grim reality Americans confronted between 1929 and 1933. The Great Depression lasted forty-two months with an unemployment rate that reached twenty-five percent in 1932. In those days, the only safety net was the soup line. Mother's personality and character were pretty well set by then, but if there had been any hope of pulling her back from the stoic Vermilye philosophy of life to what she was before Little Gerle's death, the Great Depression washed it away. A square meal and a job, any job, were hard to come by. People were frightened and their fears were justified. There was every reason to stick with her hard-shell, self-sufficient persona.

Mother did not have a split personality or schizophrenia, or anything that serious. Nor was hers a case of developing the kind of hard heart often mentioned in the Bible, because when she was little she did not learn much about Christianity, or any religion for that matter. That was not the Vermilye way. Mother was not fighting with God, as is the case with many who are nonbelievers. She was simply protecting herself from the pain she felt when she lost the little brother she loved so much.

To get by during the hard times of the Great Depression, Mother worked full-time at the Lewallen Café. The whole family was living pretty much hand to mouth. They spent long hours working and managed to stay in business by offering inexpensive meals that would stick to the ribs. In the midst of the rough economic times, they opened a dance hall in the café building. People were hurting, so the dance hall was a big hit. They needed an escape from the pain of everyday life in a depressed rural Arkansas. Nevertheless, the church folks were unhappy with the dance hall and many think that was the beginning of a move, later successful, to vote the county "dry."

What was in store for this enigmatic young woman? The Lewallen Café and Dance Hall was the hot spot in Pocahontas and Mother was right in the middle of the excitement.

2

SOFT HEARTS: THE BETHUNE WAY

Are we not like two volumes of one book?
Father's Day Quote: Marceline Desbordes-Valmore

In the summer of 1932, a thirty-five-year-old, good-looking crippled man from Little Rock happened into the Lewallen Café. He had been in before, and Mother had noticed that he was always the center of attention. His infectious laugh and friendly countenance drew people to him. Mother was attracted to him for those reasons, but he also stirred something in her that she had not felt since the days when she showered Little Gerle with love, a fresh chance to comfort and love someone.

Thus, providence led Edwin Ruthvin Bethune, the man who would become my father, to my mother.

He, like Mother, had lived through a terrible experience when he was a small child.

Daddy was born and raised in Ashley County, a fertile, swampy part of Southeast Arkansas. Steamboats came to this inland county in the old days just as they did in Pocahontas, but they did not come on a river. They came on the Bayou Bartholomew, a shallow body of still water infested with snakes, alligators, alligator gar, big snapping turtles, and other abominations common to the lowlands of Southeast Arkansas. The steamboat captains hauled goods and people in and out, but they had to negotiate a lot of snags, fallen trees, and other hazards endemic to the swamps. Many boats went aground before making it through. Once the steamboats tied up to the town dock the scene looked a little bit like the docks of Pocahontas, but the resemblance ended with the steamboats. Life in Ashley County was considerably different from life in the hill country west of Pocahontas.

Growing cotton and cutting hardwood were the main ways to make a living, and for that reason a sizeable number of black people lived in Ashley County. Their ancestors had come to the country and the county as slaves.

The Bethunes were more fortunate. They came freely to America and thence to Ashley County. Exactly why they came to America is lost to history, but thousands of Scots, like the Bethunes, fled the hardships of their homeland in the early to mid-19th century. A number of the emigrants of this period were facing eviction from the land because of the Highland Clearances that converted large agricultural estates to sheep farms. Others, displaced by the Industrial Revolution, simply hoped to find better opportunities for their skilled industrial or professional talents.

The earliest records of my father's family tell how Barbara Bethune of Scotland sailed from a secret departure point in 1820 to South Carolina with her two boys, John and Roderick. Her husband, the father of the boys, had died a few years before. The best record of the family's early years in America was a handwritten letter from Uncle Roderick Bethune in 1894. He wrote that the family first settled in Camden County, S.C. and lived there for several years.

These Bethunes came from Markinch (mark-ineh') Parish, in County Fife near Edinburgh, but the lineage traces to the Isle of Skye.

For over a hundred years before Barbara Bethune arrived, Scots by the thousands settled in South Carolina. It was, for that reason, a welcoming place for the family to get started on their American adventure. Soon after they arrived, young John Bethune married Frances Shaw, and they had two boys, Samuel McBride, and Roderick Alexander, and a daughter, Rebecca.

By and by, the family was enticed to move to Bullock County, Alabama because of their friendship with the McKinnon family. The senior McKinnon was a physician. His influence inspired both Bethune boys to go to Tennessee Medical School. Upon graduation in 1859, shortly before the outbreak of the Civil War, Dr. Samuel McBride Bethune, my great-grandfather, moved to Ashley County, Arkansas. He established a medical practice in Snyder, and it was there that he met and married Sarah Jane Herren.

On March 15, 1862, he enlisted in the Confederate States Army. There is no record telling why he joined so it must have been a sense of duty. Whatever the reason, it turned out to be a lousy decision. He enlisted as a private in Company G of the Eighth Arkansas Infantry Battalion, also known as the Ashley Light Infantry. His unit immediately deployed to Mississippi to cover a bloody Confederate withdrawal from the railroad crossing at Corinth shortly after the monumental battle at Shiloh. They suffered significant losses at Corinth, and after that rearguard action, the unit marched to Port Hudson, Louisiana where they joined 6,000 Confederates who were trying to keep Admiral Farragut and the Union Navy from controlling the Mississippi River. The Union Army encircled the garrison at Port Hudson and commenced a siege that lasted forty-eight days, the longest in American military history. During the siege, the Confederates suffered heavy casualties and had to eat mules, horses and rats. When the Confederates at Vicksburg surrendered to General U. S. Grant on July 4, 1863, the commander at Port Hudson had no reason to continue the defense of the Mississippi. He negotiated surrender terms that included a parole for all enlisted Confederate troops. Private Samuel McBride Bethune headed home to Snyder, Arkansas to resume the practice of medicine. His star-crossed service in the CSA was over, but it would be almost two years before General Robert E. Lee would surrender at Appomattox.

The Reconstruction of the South after the Civil War brought hardship and persecution, particularly for those who had served in the Confederate forces. The impact of Reconstruction was greater in Ashley County than in Randolph County, because there were few black people in Pocahontas and Randolph County. Another factor lessening the impact of Reconstruction in Pocahontas was its proximity to the Missouri border, thirty miles, and a history of townspeople interacting and intermarrying with people from the North before and after the Civil War.

The turmoil of Reconstruction, and the difficulties faced by hungry Southerners after the war could have hardened the gentle Bethunes, but it did not. They were an open, loving, God-fearing, and sharing sort of family. In spite of their experiences in Scotland, the Civil War, and Reconstruction, they did not withdraw unto themselves and wind up distrusting outsiders and people in authority, or anyone for that matter. In that respect, they were polar opposites of the Vermilye family.

Dr. Samuel McBride Bethune and Sarah Jane Herren had six children, one of whom was Samuel Warren Bethune, my grandfather. He was born April 6, 1862, just one month after his father joined the Ashley Light Infantry and left for the fighting at Corinth.

Samuel Warren Bethune married my grandmother, seventeen-year-old Alice Leonora Brymer in 1885 and soon their first child, my Aunt Delle, was born.

Alice Bethune was a homemaker, not a businesswoman like Mama Lewallen, and Samuel Warren Bethune, a well-read man, made a living as a Jack-of-all-trades during his early years. Later on, when his children were young, he served a few years as a deputy sheriff for Ashley County.

Aunt Delle and her younger sisters, Jeffie, and Lillian were, according to most, the sweetest little girls in Ashley County. It surprised no one that they were that way because Alice Bethune was a gentle southern woman, soft-spoken and the picture of grace. The family was poor in money, but they prided themselves on being honest and upright. Samuel Warren Bethune was a gentleman's gentleman.

My grandmother, Alice Bethune. Circa 1900.

The young family was Christian, but they did not wear their religion on their sleeves. They were tough, you had to be to stay alive in rural Arkansas in the late 1800s and early 1900s, but like their ancestors, they were open, trusting and loving people. They trusted that they would get by, that God would provide. They took the scripture that they should be anxious for nothing literally.

My grandparents, Alice and Sam, finally got a boy, Samuel McBride Bethune, in 1893. Three years later, my father, Edwin, was born. Alice took to him right away. Her girls were old enough to help around the house, and that gave Alice time to dote on little Edwin. He was the love of her life. His sisters made over him too, and so did his brother. Little Edwin loved being loved, all babies do, but few would ever need love as much he would.

Ugly sounding diseases—smallpox, croup, scarlet fever, pneumonia, diphtheria—were commonplace in Southeast Arkansas in 1898. The swampy environment made it so. Swamp fever was a catchall name that Ashley County people used when they were not sure what was causing a sickness. There are many Bethune headstones in the local cemeteries—big ones and little ones—marking the graves of those who died of swamp fever.

The scorching, sultry heat of summer also brought a disease that was never mistaken for swamp fever. It was called morning paralysis, a crippling viral disease that targeted children more than grownups. The disease, later known as polio, can strike quickly.

The poliovirus enters the body by nose or mouth and travels to the intestines. There it incubates and after a few days, victims will feel flu-like symptoms: headache, nausea, vomiting, and fever. In the early stages, victims can pass the virus to others because the disease spreads through contact with infected feces or through an infected mist that travels through the air, getting into food or water. Once the virus enters the bloodstream, the victim begins to make antibodies against it, and in most cases that stops the virus and the antibodies create a lifelong immunity against the disease.

One person in ten who gets the poliovirus will develop symptoms, but only one out of a hundred will develop the paralytic form of polio.

Daddy was one of the unlucky ones. The virus found its way into his bloodstream when he was an infant. His sister, my Aunt Delle, remembered the time as if it were yesterday. She said little Edwin was sick for days, crying and crying as the disease spread through his body. Toward the end of the attack he squirmed uncontrollably, racked with pain. His baby neck and baby back stiffened to rock hardness. The disease was attacking his spinal cord. Paralytic polio was busy destroying the nerve tissue in little Edwin's right leg. When the morning paralysis was finished with him, he lay still. Polio had not taken his life, nor had it attacked his lungs, but it had contorted and paralyzed his right leg and stunted the development of his left leg.

Daddy never walked a step in his life without a crutch, a cane, or an artificial leg.

The polio could have twisted Daddy's mind too, but it did not. His family, especially his brothers and sisters, protected him and showered him with love. Sister Delle was eleven, Jeffie was nine, and Lillian was seven when Daddy got polio. Grandmother Alice and the girls spent hours and hours with him, playing games, teaching him to read and write long before he started school. Uncle Mac, the oldest boy, told me how the entire family included little Edwin in play and work. They did everything they could to keep the focus on what he could do instead of what he could not do.

No one in the family blamed anyone, especially God, for what had happened to Daddy, and neither did Daddy. They reconciled how bad things happen to people, even those with a steadfast belief in a good and powerful Supreme Being. They lived one day at a time, with as much love as they could muster and held nothing back as a protection against further hurt. They preferred to believe that God did not cause Daddy's suffering, that He did not single out Daddy and cripple him with polio. Instead, they believed God stood ready to help them cope with the tragedy, and they were open and willing to let him help. It was not a case of them standing independently against the world and against a harsh God.

There was an old photograph of my dad, now lost, that makes this point better than words. In the picture, Daddy, looking to be about eight years old, is playing baseball. He is sitting on his bottom on the ground behind home plate, his tiny diseased leg askew, and he has a catcher's mitt on his left hand. The batter is in the box and the pitcher is on the mound. Daddy is actually playing the position of catcher in a sandlot game of baseball. He was wearing knickers, one pant leg folded and pinned up high, and a country cap that made him irresistibly cute. He looked like a Norman Rockwell paperboy who had just stopped by to play an inning or two.

From that one image, you could sense the pride, satisfaction, and sheer happiness Daddy was feeling. He was playing one of the most important positions, catcher. He could not move, but he could catch and throw. He was doing what he could and not worrying about the rest of it, which is, basically, the story of his life. The brotherly and sisterly love found its way into my father's heart and stayed there for the rest of his life. He was, by any measure, entitled to be bitter, but he was the gentlest, happiest, most softhearted person I have ever known.

Aunt Delle, who became a rock-solid Baptist, told me that Daddy spent a lot of time thinking about miracle cures that might let him one day know the joy of running to first base, kicking a football, riding a bike, or dancing. When he was a little boy, he often asked her about the miracles Jesus had worked, but he also asked her about mystics, snake handlers, and healing preachers. Aunt Delle said they talked often about such things, but in the end, Daddy gave up on expecting a miracle and settled for the idea that God would and could work in his life in other ways to make him an extraordinary person. He consoled himself by excelling in things that he could do: writing, penmanship, speaking and reading. He had physical limitations, but he did not let that erode his extraordinary ability to learn, and to deal kindly and fairly with people. About the only thing that bothered my father was when some thoughtless fool treated him as a case, a problem, or a curiosity. This he always deeply resented.

The men in the Bethune family began leaving Ashley County for Little Rock in 1910. First, it was Grandaddy Bethune, then Uncle Mac, the oldest boy. They went to the big city to find work so they could send money home to Grandmother Alice. They took Daddy with them when he was seventeen years old. My father was quite literate and personable by then; no surprise to those who knew him. He always worked hard to be the best at things that did not require two good legs. Grandaddy, who had learned to make money by selling insurance door to door in Little Rock, taught my father how to peddle the cheap debit policies that were so popular in the early part of the last century. Daddy learned how to find customers, make the pitch, and close the sale. It was hard for him to get from place to place, particularly in the days when there were few automobiles and good roads were nonexistent. Nevertheless, he did it and became good enough at it that selling insurance became the thing he always turned back to on the many occasions in his life when he would "go bust."

The debit insurance team. Daddy is at bottom left and my grandfather, Samuel Warren Bethune is at top right. Circa 1920.

"Going bust" was a regular part of my father's lifecycle because he was a world-class dreamer. He always tried to live out his dreams no matter how lofty, or goofy, they might have seemed to others. It was as if he had decided early on that he was not going to let the polio limit him anymore than it had. The wonder is that his failures never seemed to bother him or change him. His dreams were his secret weapon. They outdid the elixirs peddled by the ever-present snake-oil salesmen of that era, and he sipped that inexhaustible source of hope for the entirety of his life. When things did not work out for him Daddy did not let it get him down. He just kept on dreaming, cheerfully going about the business of living.

In 1923, when Daddy was twenty-six, his insurance business was prospering but his good fortune was not to last. Grandaddy Sam's Model T car broke down and Daddy tried to fix it. He opened the hood and bent over the motor to see what was wrong. When he tried to adjust the spark and fuel-flow the fan belt broke, whipping up and hitting Daddy in the face with great force. The impact knocked his right eye askance. It was beyond repair when he got to a doctor's office. They just pushed it back into the socket and covered it with a patch. It was useless for seeing, and after some time it turned a different color.

There is an old saying that perfectly explains Daddy's lot in life: When it rains, it pours. Just as he was recovering from the loss of his right eye, he fell down a flight of stairs shattering the bones in his withered right leg, the one paralyzed by polio. The doctor that treated him said there was no alternative; he amputated the shattered, paralyzed leg.

Six months later Daddy slipped and fell when getting out of a car and broke his hip. The president of the insurance company he was working for wrote a newsletter article calling Daddy, "an everyday hero." The article told how everyone was "impressed by his happy and optimistic attitude while lying helpless in bed in a plaster cast ... amusing himself by playing his banjo and reading books."

Now, at age twenty-eight, Daddy had only one good eye and one partially good leg. In those days, before the era of Social Security disability, Medicaid, or legally imposed accommodations for the disabled, the path to success for those with disabilities was a long road. To make matters worse, the country was nearing the time of the Great Depression. Any one of the hardships Daddy suffered would have crushed a lesser man but I never heard him complain about his disabilities. Instead of whining, my intrepid dad found ways to overcome his disabilities, or at least live with them.

Daddy in his Model T. Circa 1925.

Selling debit insurance was his mainstay, but in his youth, Daddy fortunately managed to learn the fine art of government bureaucracy. He got his first experience near the end of World War I when many young men were gone to war and that opened up several clerical and administrative jobs in state and county government. The ministerial jobs—all short-term—were just right for my father when he first entered the workforce. Selling insurance worked for him, but there were slow times when he first started and the government jobs came in handy, particularly after he got hurt and the doctor amputated his leg. It was a way to earn a living and put food on the table; a way to "keep body and soul together," Daddy was fond of saying.

For the next few years, Daddy drifted between an assortment of jobs in state government and selling debit insurance. The routines of working for the government came easily to him, and that experience, coupled with what he learned selling insurance, led him to a job with the Arkansas Revenue Department in 1928, just as the Great Depression was about to strike. It was his job to collect or workout ways for people to pay overdue taxes, not an easy task when so many businesses were failing and people were out of work.

Daddy's territory as a tax collector was Northeast Arkansas, and his travels frequently took him to Pocahontas, and to Lewallen Café on the town square.

3

HARD HEAD MEETS SOFT HEART

Let the ideas clash but not the hearts.
C. C. Mehta

It was in Pocahontas in the late summer of 1932, that Mother fell for the good-looking, highly personable man regaling everyone in Lewallen Café with one funny story after another. He only had one leg and one good eye and he walked on crutches but that didn't bother Mother, actually it seemed to attract her, and I now believe that she saw it as a chance to love and mother someone as she had done with Little Gerle.

Seven months later, on March 20, 1933, they married and moved to Little Rock. Daddy was a good man and Mother knew it but he was also her ticket out of Pocahontas, a chance she was not about to miss.

The marriage became a ten-year attempt to mix oil and water. Daddy and Mother had two entirely different perspectives of how life should be lived. Daddy had enjoyed the blessing of growing up in a family of loving caregivers, a family that met his needs. He learned to trust and thought of the world as a trustworthy place. Mother's family did not neglect her or mistreat her, but the Vermilye worldview coupled with the death of Little Gerle had turned her inward and taught her to distrust. To be vulnerable was a sign of weakness. A Vermilye should be strong and independent. Unfortunately, the ability to trust and bond with others will not develop if we do not have the ability to need others. If we do not learn that lesson early in life, then when we are older our inability to trust becomes a barrier to living fully, to relating to others.

Could such a marriage survive?

There were other, more apparent differences. Could a disabled man—a softhearted dreamer—partner with a young, beautiful, physically active woman who had little tolerance for foolishness or wishful thinking? How could that work?

No one dared discuss it, and perhaps it was too early for anyone including Mother and Daddy to see, much less admit, the inevitable conflict of beliefs and lifestyles. I suppose it was a case of opposites hoping that their attraction for each other would overcome their differences.

Daddy was a Bethune, through and through—soft-spoken, willing to yield and accommodate, and forever trusting. Mother, on the other hand, was a rock-solid Vermilye. She had started out with a view similar to Daddy's, and she kept some soft traits and beautiful artistic qualities that surfaced from time to time—she loved to paint and enjoyed a good laugh—but the loving heart of her youth was hard to find. At this point in her life she preferred the hard, protective edge, especially when she felt vulnerable or at risk to be hurt.

They did agree on one thing as soon as they found an apartment in Little Rock. Mother would not take a job outside the home. She knew nothing but waitressing and café work, and in 1933, it was hard for a woman to find another kind of work. It was a good decision because Mother was soon to have her first child.

On December 19, 1933 my sister, Delta Lew (short for Lewallen), was born in Pocahontas. Mother decided as she neared her time of labor with Delta Lew that she wanted to be in Pocahontas so Doc Baltz could attend to the delivery. At that time, and for many years to come, Pocahontas had several chiropractic doctors. Local people, for clarity, called them "chiropractors" and they called the medical doctors "real doctors." Doc

Baltz was a real doctor that Mother trusted. He delivered my sister in the house where Mother had grown up and Little Gerle had died.

It was the deepest point of the Great Depression. People were out of work and there was little cause for hope. My parents told me later that they had it "easier, but not better than most Americans." For one thing, Daddy had a government job but more significantly, both of them had grown up in families that had experienced hard times for years, long before the onset of the Great Depression. In their mind, the rest of the world was just now learning to live with the shortages and deprivations their families had lived with for years.

Shortly after meeting Mother, Daddy managed to shift out of the tax-collecting job he disliked at the Revenue Department to a better job at the Arkansas Department of Welfare. There, doing work for which he was better suited, he made many friends and drew the attention of the political leaders in Arkansas. Daddy impressed them with his people skills, which by then were finely tuned. He knew how to work within the bureaucracy and he knew how to make it work for those who needed help.

It was fortuitous that Daddy got the transfer to the Welfare Department, for in 1933 Franklin Delano Roosevelt took office as the thirty-second president of the United States, and one of the first programs he put in place was the Civilian Conservation Corps, better known as the CCC. The Welfare Department took on the job of selecting boys to join the CCC. The program would house, clothe, and feed them and it put thousands of young boys to work building roads and public projects throughout the United States. There were a number of CCC camps in Arkansas and Daddy got a job for which he was particularly suited. He became the director of selection for the CCC. He would find and select young boys who really needed help.

In 1935, Daddy was busy traveling the state recruiting boys for the program, and Mother was pregnant again. As she neared labor, she headed back to Pocahontas and on December 19, 1935, with Doc Baltz in attendance, Mother gave birth to me in the same bed, and in the same room where my sister had been born exactly two years earlier.

Sheriff Marlin Hawkins of Conway County, a notorious figure in Arkansas politics who played an important role in my life in 1968, wrote a book about his years as sheriff and titled it *How I Stole Elections.* The sheriff made glowing references to my father and the good work that he did for the CCC. He referred to Daddy as "director of the state CCC" and talked about how they, together, would choose boys for the program. Daddy was not the overall director, but he was the man in charge of selection. It was an important job because the CCC gave hope to young men by giving them a chance to work and break out of poverty. The government paid the boys a small stipend of $30 a month, and most of them sent $25 of that home to their parents. I remember going with Daddy and some other men to visit one of the camps when I was five years old and can still see the boys in their work clothes and the uniformed officers in their campaign hats. I can still smell the fragrance of sauerkraut and weenies cooking in the mess hall. I also remember Daddy telling me when I was six years old that the camps were closing and how sad he was about that because the boys were getting ready to go off to fight in World War II instead of working on the CCC projects. I remember a big ceremony at the Little Rock camp the day it closed when all the boys were in formation and the officers were making their last reports. Daddy's good work for the CCC was over.

About the time his job with the CCC was petering out, Daddy got the political bug, or at least he saw political office as something that might work for him. It was not his first try for political office. He had run unsuccessfully for state treasurer in 1932, and lost a race for land commissioner in 1936. In that era there were no special programs to protect the disabled, so men with disabilities frequently sought jobs in government, elected or appointed. The voters intuitively understood the need to support disabled candidates. My dad, ever the optimist, entered the race for state auditor in the spring of 1942. I do not remember all the details, but I do remember a political speaking event at the Old Band

Shell in MacArthur Park in Little Rock. Political rallies in the days before television were like modern-day rock concerts. There were good crowds and the adults stayed for and paid attention to all the speeches, even those of the lesser candidates. I remember the rally mostly because it lasted through sunset and the mosquitoes were eating me alive. I was miserable, but Mother would not let us leave until after Daddy made his speech. He was running against a powerful incumbent, Oscar Humphrey, and they were among the last to speak because the position of state auditor was an important statewide office. I remember crying and hating the fact that we had to hang out at the band shell after dark. There was absolutely nothing for little kids to do and the grownups kept telling us to be quiet, even at the high point of the mosquito assault.

Daddy lost that race and it was his last. He maintained to his death that he might have won but his opponent, Oscar Humphrey, had an unfair advantage. The campaign ended in a landslide for the three-term incumbent, and Daddy loved to joke about it. He would say, always with a chuckle, "I never had a chance. Oscar had an unfair advantage. He has no arms. Hell, I've still got one fairly good leg, both arms, and one eye that works pretty good." With that, Daddy would crack up laughing, but then wince as he explained how Oscar had lost both his arms in a cotton gin accident when he was a boy.

I learned from Daddy's willingness to see things in the best light. He was a man of good cheer; not easily offended by references to his physical limitations. Once, around 1940, the Little Rock Travelers, a double-A professional baseball team, were struggling to stay out of last place in the old Southern Association. Their miserable showing toward the end of the season provoked an *Arkansas Democrat* sportswriter to propose a dream lineup for the Travelers. The dream team consisted of disabled persons, mostly well known Little Rock politicians. The writer published a tongue-in-cheek column that had Secretary of State "Crip" Hall as catcher, my dad at shortstop, and of course, Oscar Humphrey, as the starting pitcher. I do not remember anything, ever, that tickled my dad, a huge baseball fan, more than being in the lineup for the make-believe Little Rock Travelers. Nowadays, the newspaper would fire the sportswriter, and lawsuits would follow a noisy outcry by the politicians.

In early 1942, after the Japanese Empire had attacked Pearl Harbor on December 7, 1941, our federal government rounded up people of Japanese descent, citizens as well as aliens, who were living in the United States. The government sent them to euphemistically named War Relocation Centers. Daddy's campaign for state auditor was over, so he applied for and got a job at the new War Relocation Center in Rohwer, Arkansas. The center was over a hundred miles from Little Rock in Southeast Arkansas, and the only way to get there was over a dusty, rough gravel road.

Daddy took me with him to Rohwer during the summer when school was out, and it was there that I saw my first real-life Japanese people. The theatres in Little Rock never missed a chance to show newsreels portraying "Japs" as evil people. Our government told us through posters, news stories, and radio shows that "Japs" were mean—not much better than a bunch of wild monkeys. One movie—maybe it was a newsreel, or maybe it was my childlike imagination distorted by wartime propaganda—showed a Japanese soldier tossing a Chinese baby into the air and catching it on his bayonet. Another poster challenged us to, "Stay on the job until every murdering Jap is wiped out!" That poster had a picture of a Japanese soldier torturing an American soldier on the Bataan Death March. Everywhere I looked, with the exception of school where the poster-focus was on pure, positive patriotism, there was someone or something teaching me to hate and fear the "Japs." I came to believe they all had buckteeth and wore big, round horn-rimmed glasses.

My visits to Rohwer gave me a chance to see the Japanese in a different way. They were living in tarpaper barracks divided into small cubicles, but each family had a door to the outside. You had to step up to get into the living space, and the ground outside was hard and dusty except when it rained, then it was soggy and muddy. The Japanese made well-kept vegetable gardens all around the compound, and there were occasional flowerbeds. I was glad that I did not have to live there. At first, I was surprised to see the internees laughing and joking with my father; they obviously liked him even though he had power over them. Daddy taught me they were good people, and that they were just like us, except for their looks. I could see that he respected the internees. He said they were "good Japanese" unlike the "bad Japanese" from the other side of the world, the ones who attacked Pearl Harbor. Daddy said our government, thinking it best for national security and the safety of the good Japanese, wanted to get them off the streets and out of sight.

I had some playtime with the Japanese kids when I visited Rohwer. We quickly forgot our surroundings, or at least I did, and I do not think we saw each other as different. The one exception came when they tried to teach me how to use an abacus, the toy-like computing gadget that Asians have used for centuries to calculate numbers. I could not figure out how to use it, and my confusion made me feel different because it made me feel dumb.

The conflict between wartime propaganda and real life was troublesome because of another, similar experience. On several occasions, I saw truckloads of German prisoners of war on the streets of Little Rock. The U. S. Army hauled them to worksites and back to the prisoner of war compound at Camp Robinson. They were always in blue overalls with a big white P on their back. I learned they were "bad Germans" because our soldiers captured them in Europe when they were fighting for the Nazi regime of Adolph Hitler. Hitler, with a moustache and evil look, was the poster-boy for the Nazis. The posters about the Nazis, unlike the posters about the "Japs," seldom indicted all people of German extraction. That made sense to me because many "good Germans" lived in Pocahontas, Arkansas. The DeClerks, Blissenbachs, Gschwends, Junkersfelds and many other German immigrants had helped settle the little community. They founded St. Paul's Catholic Church and the parochial school that my mother and her brothers had attended when they were older.

Doc Baltz, who delivered my sister and me, was one of the "good Germans." The lesson for me out of World War II: There are good Germans and bad Germans, just as there are good Japanese and bad Japanese. Unlike many children who grew up during World War II, I was fortunate to learn the difference between the prejudice of propaganda and the fairness of truth.

The CCC and Rohwer Relocation Center jobs were perfect for my father. He understood people and cared about them, and people liked him. It gave him great pleasure to find and select poor boys for the CCC where they could get good meals, a new pair of shoes, and clean work clothes. In addition, he did everything he could to make life better for the Japanese-American internees who had lost everything they had, including their freedom. The acts of generosity were natural for a man who did not have a malicious bone in his body. Daddy had suffered all his life with physical disability. It bothered him greatly to see the poor boys of the Depression, the good Japanese, and the good Germans suffer for things beyond their control.

Meanwhile, Daddy and Mother did everything they could to keep their differences hidden from my sister and me. The problem of their conflicting personalities and viewpoints on life paled in comparison to the need to survive the Great Depression and the early years of World War II. Daddy's ability to hold a job and put food on the table during tough times deferred the inevitable.

4

FAMILY LIFE BEFORE THE TROUBLES

The happiest moments of my life have been the few which I have passed at home in the bosom of my family.
Thomas Jefferson

When I was an infant and all during World War II, we lived in Little Rock. First, we lived in an upstairs apartment and then in a small two-story rent house at 216 W. 14th Street, just two blocks from the South Main streetcar line. It was not a high-quality house, but it did have open-flame gas stoves in the main rooms, an important feature in those days. In the early-forties, my mother started renting rooms to make ends meet. She rented mainly to the young women who came from the rural areas of Arkansas to Little Rock to find work in the bomb factory or with some branch of the wartime government. In the war years, there was a shortage of housing and young people coming into the city to work in the war effort needed an economical place to stay.

Daddy was only with us on weekends, and he sometimes missed those. First, it was his job at the CCC, and later it was his job at the War Relocation Center. Mother told Delta Lew and me he had to travel the state when he was finding boys for the CCC. Later, after he got the job at Rohwer, she said he was gone a lot because it was a long way to the War Relocation Center and the roads were terrible. Even so, there were times when I went with Daddy to the CCC camps and on a couple of occasions I spent several days with him at the War Relocation Center.

There was, of course, a more significant reason for his absence from our home in Little Rock that they kept from us. Daddy and Mother were struggling to reconcile their differences and keep their marriage together. In the early days of their struggle, my sister and I had no idea that trouble was brewing.

Daddy hired a black woman named Viola to help my mother. There was not a lot for Viola to do, but Mother used to say it made her feel like the "Queen of Sheba" to have a maid who would clean and cook meals. The arrangement only lasted a few months. I am not sure, but I suspect Viola's disappearance had something to do with the fact that my mother had never been around black people and simply did not know how to treat the woman. There were only a few black people in Randolph County and they pretty much kept to themselves in the area near the little AME Church, which doubled as their school building in the old days when segregation was in full sway.

We lived downstairs in the rent house, crowded into a parlor that Mother converted to a bedroom with one double bed and two baby-beds that my sister and I slept in. Our room-renters shared a bathroom upstairs and we used a half-bath downstairs. When the renters left for work Mother would take us upstairs to use the tub. That is how we managed, and I do not remember it as a hardship—it was just what we had to do.

At bedtime, Mother read to my sister and me until we fell asleep. I especially remember Mark Twain's, *The Prince and the Pauper*. Mother used the story to explain the advantages of living on a shoestring. She was right. The lessons from Twain's classic served us well. Our life before we knew about the trouble was austere but good.

It was my job on cold winter mornings to get up, pull on my clothes, and light the open flame gas stove with a match. As soon as I got it lit, I would back up so close to it that the calves of my legs would turn beet red, partially roasted from just below my corduroy knee-length knickers to my shoe tops. From that vantage point, I had a good view of the waking habits and movements of my sister, my mother, and the most interesting of all, my dad.

My main recollection is how, in the morning, Daddy would sit on the side of the bed and cough, cough, and cough. He coughed so long and loud that I feared one of his vital parts would come up and he would keel over dead. When—after a few minutes—his coughing subsided Daddy would strike a match and light up a hand-rolled cigarette. Then, after the first puff, he would cough some more, even worse than before. Mother always said, "Cough it up; it may be a Ford car." I did not understand that until she explained that the first gas-powered cars, which showed up when she was a little girl, used to backfire a lot. Daddy's coughing meant there must have been a Ford car inside of him that was trying to get out. Gallows humor, but that was her way. When Daddy finally collected himself, he would finish his cigarette and then reach for his artificial leg that was propped against a nightstand. He then pulled the artificial leg, which had spent the night in one leg of his trousers, over the felt sock covering the stump of the leg amputated in 1923. Then he put his good leg in the other leg of the trousers and put on his second shoe matching the one that was already on the foot of the artificial leg. With that, he pulled up his trousers and made ready for the most precarious part of the operation. With the balance of an Olympian, Daddy pulled himself up to a standing position using a triangulation technique—one hand on the bedstead, his good leg on the floor, and one hand on the bedside table. Once erect, he grabbed his canes and off he would go, contorting his way to the bathroom.

Once he had peed, Daddy would sit on the commode and lean over the lavatory to shave. I loved to watch him shave because he had the routine down to a science. Daddy used and reused the new-fangled double-edged razorblades by running them around the inside of a drinking glass that he said, "Sharpened them as good as new." Nevertheless, I noted that Daddy would wince with pain when he shaved and he always cut himself, usually more than once. He sealed the cuts with a styptic pencil that contained a chemical that stopped the bleeding. To a youngster, it was magical, one minute he was bleeding and the next minute he was not. Styptic pencils were an essential part of a man's shaving kit.

I also, for some reason have an early memory of Daddy sitting on a wooden box in the doorway of our kitchen pantry with a hammer in his hand. Mother was demanding that he kill a foot-long rat that had taken up residence there. It took him a good half hour and fifteen or twenty swats with the hammer, but he finally got the rat. He was laughing like crazy throughout the process, and when it ended, he summonsed me into the pantry to see the corpse, a few chunks of rat meat. Daddy could turn anything into a fun project.

An early image of Mother is from the time she took care of me when I was sick with what I later learned was double pneumonia. To this day, I can see and taste the bowl of soft-boiled eggs laced with pieces of buttered toast that she brought to me when I got well enough to eat. She did the same when I recovered from chickenpox, the mumps, and measles. When I was little Mother was always there for me, especially when I was sick, and in my mind's eye she was the most beautiful woman in the world. Even so, there was not a lot of hugging and kissing. Mother drove it into our heads that we were engaged in the serious business of making ends meet. She loved me, I knew that, but she was entirely different from my father. She was all business most of the time. That was her default position. After all, we were in a death-struggle with "them." There was no room for failure or idleness because it led to sloth. Those with sufficient will who were willing to work, according to her, could and would make it to Nirvana. Frugality, focus, discipline, grit, and scores of other hardcore character traits were her hallmarks. Curiously, these qualities coexisted with an artistic streak that produced, in her early life, some wonderful paintings and in later life an abundance of afghans, crocheted bedspreads, and handmade stuffed dolls. Pluto, Mickey and Minnie, and a giraffe came to life at my mother's hand. She sewed and stuffed them and they are still around some sixty-five years later.

Mother made a garden every year, even before the Victory Gardens of World War II were all the rage. She canned food for many years after others had given up such practices. She sewed our clothes, a practice that caused some anguish for Delta Lew and me because we had to wear them instead of "store-boughts." We ate fried tripe (put enough ketchup on it), beans, cornbread, fish caught by neighbors, and anything else that was cheap and available. It was our way of life, before, during and after the war.

My sister and I sat on stools we pulled up to the kitchen table, and we ate the lesser portions of whatever was available. If chicken was the main course, then we ate the back, neck, the gizzard or the asshole, literally. If lucky, we might get a wing or a thigh. Kids ate leftovers. Grownups got first pick of the food so they would have the energy they needed to work and provide. No one questioned this rule of survival. Mother taught us to have good table manners, but we never said grace in thanks for the food; after all, the food was there because of hard work, effort and enterprise. It was not there because of God or anyone else.

Rationing, imposed at the outset of the war, limited our food choices, but lack of money was a bigger problem. Occasionally Mother would splurge. We could not afford to go to a sit-down restaurant, but she would buy delicious hot tamales from a push-cart-salesman who came down our street every Wednesday night hollering "hot tamales" in a singsong way at the top of his voice. The Hot Tamale Man was selling homemade tamales, wrapped in real cornhusks. They were delicious and they were only ten cents apiece, or three for a quarter. Our little family developed a Pavlovian reaction to his melodious call. We were regular customers, once a week, for a couple of years but our feasting ended when we learned the police had jailed the Hot Tamale Man for using cat meat to make his tamales.

By this time in my life, Mother had boiled the Vermilye creed down to a few basics. The goal was to be as independent as possible so "they cannot take what you have." This notion was the product of her life with the Vermilyes, the loss of Little Gerle, growing up during the First World War, and the Great Depression. From my days in the crib, she taught me to follow the creed, mainly because it was "us versus them." "Them, or they," depending upon usage, meant anyone or anybody who had power of any sort and who was in a position to "take what little you might have." The idea, according to Mother was to fight your way up to a place in life where "they had to give you a good lettin' alone."

My mother had a multitude of sayings. Some were just cute and bore no relationship to anything: If you dropped something she would say, "You dropped the set out of your ring." We woke up to her saying, "Good morning, Glory." If we were to hum or sing, you could count on her to say, "Sing before breakfast and you will cry before dinner." She had a saying for every occasion but most of them expressed the fundamental beliefs of the Vermilye family. For instance, there was the polestar, the lynchpin of the creed: "Where there's a will, there's a way."

The one common trait that Mother and Daddy shared was humor. Oddly enough, it seemed to work well with either the Vermilye or Bethune lifestyles. It was the glue linking the two philosophies, making coexistence possible. Mother's humor began with her sayings, whereas Daddy's humor was dry wit and his flair for self-deprecation.

Every summer we took a month-long sojourn to Pocahontas. Mother would put one of the renters in charge to collect rent and take care of the house. Daddy never joined us on our trips to Pocahontas, another clue I missed that trouble was brewing between Mother and Daddy.

The Great Depression forced the entire Lewallen family, Mama, Papa, and Mother's two younger brothers George and Lloyd, to move out of the family home and into a few rooms in the back of the café. They sold the home place to pick up a few extra dollars. When visiting Pocahontas, we bedded down in a tiny alcove near the rooms where Mama and Papa Lewallen stayed. We were like sardines at night, but we dismantled our cramped quarters early each morning. The café opened at 5:00 a.m. and there was plenty to do to get ready for the onrush of breakfast customers.

I was never bored with life at the Lewallen Café because it was a magnet for an unusual cast of characters. There was Uncle John Shively, who ran a store a few doors down from Lewallen Café. He came for lunch most every day and would eat standing up at the bar. Mama would serve him and he usually washed his sandwich down with a mug of cold Griesedieck Brothers beer. Griesedieck was the beer of choice at Lewallen Café because the brewery, located in St. Louis, sponsored the broadcast of Cardinal baseball. Uncle John had white hair and a white beard and took a fondness to me, so I made it a point to lurk around the bar at noon. When he came in, I would climb up on a bar stool next to him and Mama would fill a small, glass coffee creamer with beer for me to sip as I visited with my friend. Everyone thought it was cute and I was the talk of the café, especially when having my beer.

Another favorite of mine was the iceman. He came each morning hauling fifty-pound blocks of ice into the café from his truck. He wore a big thick leather pad on his back and carried the big blocks of ice over his shoulder using a huge set of tongs. It was fascinating to me to watch him hoist the heavy blocks into the ice compartments on a huge bank of frontloading iceboxes that covered an entire wall in the kitchen. He was not a big man, but he was strong, and he had a dancelike technique that helped him leverage the ice into position. As he was swinging the blocks upward, he would grin at me saying, "Upsy-daisy." It was a funny routine, and when he finished I would follow him out of the café, mopping up the trail of water left by the melting ice. He always thanked me for helping and it made me feel very grownup.

The café had one big dining room and the tables of four had red-and-white gingham tablecloths. There were several ceiling fans to circulate the air, and it was easy to see the reach of each fan because strategically placed strips of sticky flypaper hung from the ceiling. Those closest to the fans were in constant motion while the more remote strips were motionless. Oddly enough, the ones in motion seemed to catch more flies than those that were still.

It was at one of the tables near the front of the café that Uncle Leaf Hawkins would encamp. Uncle Leaf—a gnomish man in a soup-stained suit that was too big for him—was the glasses man. He came at least once a week to sell spectacles from a big black leather satchel filled with the latest in optics. People would line up to see Uncle Leaf and I would stand by his table for hours watching and listening to him as he made fittings using a gadget that let him switch from one lens to another. He was a happy little man who kept everyone laughing while he worked. I wondered aloud what it would be like to have bad eyes and Uncle Leaf, sensing my interest, put a pair of glasses on me. The lenses were so thick that it made me dizzy. I pulled them off and everyone around the table had a big laugh on me. Mama let Uncle Leaf use the café as his office so long as he did not interfere with the lunch crowd. She figured he brought people into the café and that was good for business.

Papa Lewallen provided the fireworks, without fail, nearly every day of the summer. He was a hopeless drunk. The day-law, Estle Bramlett and the night-law, Butch Stolt ranked him at the top of their list of "town drunks." His falling-down-drunk excursions around the square landed him in the county jail at least once a week. Mama, a teetotaler, would plead with the lawmen to bring Papa back to the café when they found him wandering around town and sometimes they would. Nine times out of ten they just locked him up until someone in the family came to get him with a promise to take him straight to the café.

The family tried hiding Papa's shoes to keep him from going out but that did not stop him. He just walked around town in his stockings. It was a sad situation, but no matter how drunk he got, the next morning Papa would be sitting at his favorite table in the café as if nothing had happened, eating a serving of eggs on top of pancakes with sausage. It was at that moment, when he was sober, that I could get his attention. Though my time with him each day was short, I remember him as a sad, but loving grandfather.

Soon after the lunch crowd left the café, Papa would start the cycle all over again. The drinking—which near the end of his life included shoe polish, vanilla extract and anything that contained alcohol—killed him in 1944. He died of stomach rot—that is what all the grownups called it—and they displayed him in his casket in a room above the café. A man with a deep voice sang "Asa's Death," a funeral dirge that fit perfectly with the somber mood of all those who came up the stairs and circled through the room where his body lay. I learned later that people liked Papa a lot, which was something of a surprise. I liked Papa, but I never heard much good about him at home.

The Lewallen Café was about 300 yards uphill from the Black River and the place where the River Rats lived on a gaggle of ramshackle, homemade houseboats. The river had once been the center of activity in Pocahontas but the steamboats left when the railroad came. Only a few boats were left to work the river and most of them belonged to the River Rats.

The river was off limits for Delta Lew and me. Its fast, swirling current had claimed many victims but Mother and Mama seemed most concerned with keeping us away from the River Rats—poor people who lived hand-to-mouth on the tarpapered houseboats, eking out a living on the river. They fished and sold their catch to the townspeople, and when the weather was good, the River Rats would dig mussels from the muddy bottom of the Black River. They sold the mussel shells to a button factory situated downstream, not far from the town square. Big piles of mussel shells, each shell pierced with several button-size holes, surrounded the factory. Buttons stamped from mussel shells had a pearly look so they were much in demand before the invention of plastic.

The River Rats did not make much from mussel digging and fishing but it was how they got by. Mama and Mother said they were filthy and uncouth and that I should stay away from such "trash."

I could not restrain myself. I slipped away from the café and headed down to the river as often as I could.

Two of the River Rat families had children my age and I made friends with them. My favorite was Toni who lived on a houseboat with her father and a younger brother. She was a pretty girl my age with long black hair that turned to ringlets when it reached her shoulders. Her eyes were captivating, different from any I had ever seen, steel grey and hard not to look at.

We often sat on the side of her houseboat, dangling our feet in the swift current of the Black River and rubbing our heels against the mossy scum that collected on the side of the boat. It was a perfect setting for swapping stories about the way we lived. Toni and the other River Rat kids were enthralled as I told them about life in Little Rock, about streetcars, traffic lights and other things they had never seen. They, in turn, told me all about their life on the river. I did not want to change places with them, but the simplicity of their lifestyle—working the river and living hand-to-mouth—appealed to me in a Huck Finn sort of way.

When Toni told me about digging for mussels, she said they were always on the lookout for pearls when they opened the shells. Toni liked to explain things and she was good at it. She showed me the fish traps and told me what they had to do to keep the fish alive until they could sell them, but her sharp eyes came afire when she explained to me that Black River pearls had a good reputation and there was a ready market for good ones, especially white ones. She said there were many stories about Black River pearls—black ones, pink ones, and white ones—that were as big as peas and sold for hundreds of dollars to the pearl-buyers who came out of Memphis.

Toni said her family had found a few little pearls, but never a "big-un." It was her dream that one day they would find a big, well-shaped pearl. A windfall like that would change their life forever. She said one of their fellow River Rats had found such a pearl and it sold for $500. As she told the story she got excited, talking faster and louder, especially when she told how the man used the money to buy a piece of land. She said, "That-un got him and his'n off the river." I could see that finding a big pearl—hitting the jackpot—was Toni's dream.

When I asked her what was the best they ever got for a pearl her excitement drained away. She thought a minute and said, "Well, we once got thirty-five for a middlin' black-un, but that's the best we ever done." I felt sorry for her because I suddenly realized how hard it would be for her to find a big, perfect pearl. I think she saw how I felt because she said, "We're not 'bout to quit lookin', or give up." "Besides," she said, "we get a little somethin' for slugs." The slugs were imperfect pearls that buyers shipped to India to be ground-up and burned in incense. Toni said, "They need 'em on account of some religious thing." Looking back, I realize that finding a big, perfect pearl was the only hope she and her family had for a better life.

One day when her father was away, Toni and her little brother took me inside their houseboat so I could see how they lived. There was no electric light of course, but I could see that there were two beds and a cook-stove and table that took up one end of the small cabin. She was not ashamed but she felt a need to say, "It's purty little, but it works OK for us." I figured Toni to be the housekeeper because the place was not messy even though it was full of the stuff that you need on a boat.

I could not imagine myself as a River Rat. Nevertheless, I told her how we squeezed our entire family of four into one room in our Little Rock rent house and that we were living in an alcove in the back of the Lewallen Café that was no bigger than the one room where she and her family lived. It was not much to say but it was a little bit that we had in common.

I was fascinated with the River Rats and I never missed a chance to go down to the river to see Toni, but the grownups in Pocahontas were saying that they and their way of life would soon be gone. The townspeople did not want them, there were problems with school authorities, and the button factories were going out of business.

One day, a few years after I first met Toni, I ran down the trail to the river and her boat was gone. I went back several times, but I knew in my heart that her boat would not be there and that I would never see her again. That was the way of the River Rats, always on the move. I feel fortunate to have learned what I did from such a hardy lot.

Not all my adventures turned out well. Like many boys my age, I had a Daisy Air Rifle. I took my BB gun along on my visits to see the River Rats, and that made me a big hit because they had no money for such things. Then, one day when I was returning from the river, I encountered the Shively girls, tomboys who also had BB guns. A discussion ensued wherein I contended that boys are better shots than tomboys are. Coming to no resolution, the argument led to a challenge for a BB gun fight to settle the matter. The Shively girls positioned themselves about thirty yards away and started firing shots in my direction. I returned fire and, reeking hubris, advanced on the Shively position. I would show these girls a thing or two. I was laughing loud enough for them to hear and running as I had seen the U.S. Marines do in the movies. Everything was working according to plan until a BB hit me in the mouth. More specifically, it hit my big front tooth, the one on my left side. I immediately reached up, just in time to catch a handful of tooth chips. The BB gun war was over. I lost. I ran crying to the café, tooth pieces in hand, and Mother met me at the front door.

Closer inspection revealed that I lost about two thirds of my front tooth. Once I calmed down, I was surprised to find that it did not hurt. There was no pain at all, just wounded pride. I asked Mother if I could get it fixed and she quickly let me know that we had no money to spend for such things. Besides, I did not need the entire tooth and she was mad as Hell at me for getting it knocked out. That was that, there would be no trip to the dentist. I was embarrassed to have a snaggletooth look, so I taught myself how to talk without moving my upper lip. It took hours and hours of practice before a mirror but I succeeded. The broken tooth stayed with me all through my school years and until I was twenty-one years old. Just before my discharge from the Marine Corps a kindhearted Navy dentist, ignoring regulations, put on a porcelain cap that lasted twenty years. My motionless upper lip technique stayed with me long after I got the tooth fixed, but I did learn to show my teeth when laughing. I loved doing that after years of turning my head or covering my mouth when I laughed.

I had a secret place in Pocahontas that was my thinking spot. Mama had converted the floor above the café into a small hotel. There were only twelve rooms available but it turned out to be a reliable source of income, particularly after Papa died and Mama closed the café. My secret place was a cubbyhole just off a small open area that served as a lobby. There were two items in the cubbyhole that never failed to stoke my imagination. One was a stuffed bobcat allegedly killed in the northwest corner of Randolph County when it attacked a hunter. He was big, had a nick out of his ear, and his eyes seemed to always be locked on mine. Next to the bobcat was a two-and-a-half by three-foot lithograph, provided courtesy of Anheuser-Busch Brewery, depicting the last minutes of Custer's last stand at the Battle of Little Big Horn. I spent hours in my secret place. I would lie on the floor between the bobcat and the lithograph. I would stare at the battle scene imagining myself as General George Armstrong Custer. I preferred to be General Custer because he was still alive. The Indians killed him, but in the picture, he was still alive and heroically fighting for his life. I did not like the idea of being one of the men in Custer's command, the famous Seventh Calvary, because they were mostly dead, and the hostile-looking Indians were cutting off their scalps.

My secret place was also the place where I would study the pages of my 1942 *Johnson Smith & Co. Catalog.* Never in recorded history has there been a collection of interesting stuff such as that offered in the *Johnson Smith & Co. Catalog.* Whoopee cushions, magic tricks, a complete Negro makeup kit, an exploding deck of cards—the choices reached to infinity. There were books on Jiu-Jitsu, mysticism, mind reading, fortune telling, and if needed you could order a talking Ouija board for $1.50, or a fortune telling ball for twenty-five cents.

My favorite page offered, for twenty-five cents, a pamphlet entitled "How to Build One & Two Passenger Flying Planes." The write-up promised detailed plans for building a single engine airplane using junk parts and a second-hand motor for power. I fixed on that page for hours, reading the fine print repeatedly looking for a catch and finally concluded it was something I could really do. Besides, the twenty-five-cent price included a free ten-lesson course entitled "How to Fly." Perfect!

My favorite page in the 1942 Johnson Smith & Co. Catalog.

My second favorite page, just in case the airplane did not work out, was an ad for detailed plans for building a midget auto racecar. The promise was that I could use a washing machine motor or an outboard engine to power my racecar, but if I used a motorcycle engine, I could reach speeds up to fifty miles per hour. All this could be mine for twenty-five cents and the price included a pamphlet giving hints on dirt track racing. What a bargain!

For a budding young dreamer my secret place and the *Johnson Smith & Co. Catalog* provided unsurpassable moments of reverie. This well-honed talent for escaping reality would serve me well in the next chapter of my family unhappiness.

5

SEPARATION, THEN DIVORCE

We cannot destroy kindred: our chains stretch
a little sometimes, but they never break.
Marquise de Sévigné

I had no idea of the rift between my parents. The serenity of my first years was not to last. Daddy and Mother agreed to separate. I wish I could remember how the trouble developed, when it started and how it fit into my life. Unfortunately (or perhaps fortunately), I cannot remember the order of events, nor can I explain precisely how it affected my life. I just know that it did affect me. I suppose it is natural and a blessing that I cannot remember such details. Mother and Daddy never wanted to talk about it and neither did I, but I have a slew of recollections stuck in my mind, some in order and some not.

I remember the day the trouble began, at least when it began for me. It was a Sunday afternoon and Daddy was getting ready to leave our house on 14th Street for the long trip back to his job at the War Relocation Center in Rohwer. He had spent the weekend with us and he was waiting for a friend to pick him up.

I was going on eight, sitting on his lap in an easy chair in the small living room of our rental house. Daddy told me his "going away" was different from the other times he had left to go back to Rohwer. He told me he was "not going to be living with us anymore." At first, I did not get it, but then it hit me. I knew something odd was happening because Daddy was crying. He tried to keep me from seeing his tears but I saw them. He kept pointing out the window of our living room trying to get me interested in some pigeons that were roosting under the eve of our neighbor's house. He wanted to deflect my attention but it did not work. I climbed down from his lap and ran to Mother to ask her why Daddy was leaving and why he was not going to be living with us anymore. I cannot remember her answer. I can only remember that it did not make sense to me and that I started crying. My life was changing. I did not understand why my life had to change but I could see there was nothing I could do about it.

Mother downplayed the separation. She said Daddy's job in Rohwer was so far away that we would not see him very often. I could tell there was more to it than that, but Daddy was leaving and Mother would not talk about it.

I did not know the difference between an informal separation, a legal separation, and a final divorce. For kids it does not matter, the practical effect is the same: Daddy is gone. Family life will be different.

After that day, Daddy showed up now and then but he never stayed long. I always hoped they were trying to fix whatever was wrong, and I believe they tried.

This awkward period in my life lasted until the end of World War II and the end of Daddy's job at the Japanese War Relocation Center. I was nearly ten years old. After that, Daddy had to go back to selling insurance because thousands of men were coming home from the war and the good jobs were going to veterans. Daddy was struggling to earn a living. Most of the time he lived with his sister, my Aunt Jeffie, in Little Rock and gave us whatever money he could spare, but it was not enough.

Mother appealed to Mama Lewallen for help. They concocted a plan for Mama to buy a house that was big enough for us to live in, but one that had at least four rooms that Mother could rent. The rental income would cover the cost of taxes and utilities and we would live on the money we got from Daddy. It was a good plan because housing prices were low, particularly for buyers who intended to pay cash. Mama paid $7500 for a two-story brick house at 2309 State Street in Little Rock. It had four good-sized bedrooms upstairs that were suitable for renting. It was a blessing for our little family. We moved there when I was in the fourth grade at Rightsell Grammar School. Delta Lew was in the sixth grade and soon she would be going to East Side Junior High School. Things were looking up. We were in a better neighborhood and we had a house of our own.

Daddy's attempts to reconcile after the war, when he had gone back to selling insurance, always included what Mother called "a screwball idea for making money." Daddy, "The Dreamer," was forever determined to find a way to "Easy Street," according to Mother.

Once he persuaded Mother that he was on the verge of writing the great American novel so she let him come back home. For two weeks, Daddy spent every waking hour perched in front of a typewriter that he had borrowed from a friend. He was vague about the story he was writing, but I do know that it was supposed to be about the war and the relocation of the Japanese. Soon the typewriter noise stopped and shortly thereafter Daddy was gone from the house. I never heard anymore about Daddy's book.

Getting a car was the basis for another reconciliation attempt. According to Daddy, a car would enable him to get around the state and that would lead to more insurance sales. It was big news at our house because it would be our first family car and on the day he parked it in front of our house we could barely contain ourselves. There it was, a blue-grey 1939 Ford, two-door sedan. There was one small problem: The Ford did not have an automatic transmission. How could he, with only one good leg, manipulate the clutch, gas pedal, and brake? Daddy's solution was to rig a receptacle on the gas pedal into which he could put the tip of his cane. That enabled him to push the gas pedal down or lift it up. He used his good left leg to operate the clutch and brake, but that required him to put the car in neutral whenever he wanted to stop. Watching Daddy drive the Ford was an unforgettable experience. Every time I hear someone use the expression that an overly busy person looks like a "one-legged man in an ass-kicking contest," I think of Daddy driving that 1939 Ford.

Getting the car was a good move on Daddy's part. It got him back into the house again, this time for a couple of months, but soon Mother decided the car was more trouble and expense than it was worth. It had not produced the windfall in insurance sales that Daddy had predicted. Once again, Daddy left and that was the last time he lived with us. He got rid of the car shortly after that.

Daddy's final attempt to reconcile was initially promising, at least Mother thought so. Daddy had lined up a job managing a newfangled Time of Day service. It did not get him back in the house, but it did put us together as a family at least for a few weeks because Daddy's plan was for our family, grownups and kids, to operate the telephones at the Time of Day office. The service was dependent on advertising that we would read before telling a caller the correct time. It was a cutting-edge idea but it failed for lack of advertisers shortly after Daddy got involved.

In time, Daddy might have succeeded in the job market and that might have improved the chance for reconciliation. Mother cut him some slack because he had just turned fifty, and it was hard for a disabled, nonveteran in the postwar years to find work. Daddy finally gave up trying to find "Easy Street" and went back to selling insurance.

Eventually, Mother gave up on Daddy. The sporadic attempts to reconcile failed. The separation turned into divorce proceedings. In hindsight, I realize that Daddy was effectively gone from my life when he left for Rohwer that day in 1943 when I sat on his knee and he told me he was not going to be living with us anymore. After that, Mother was the dominant influence in my life. She was there; Daddy was not. It was that simple.

In 1948, the divorce was final and Daddy moved to Clovis, New Mexico. There he got an administrative job in the main office of a New Mexico insurance company. He was physically unable to peddle insurance door-to-door as he had done when he was younger. I was twelve and in the seventh grade at East Side Junior High School.

Daddy may have been gone, but he was not out of my mind. He would send cards, letters, and an occasional photograph. I remember one photo that showed Daddy in a pinochle game with three other men seated around a corner table in the lobby of the fleabag hotel where he lived along with other men who were living on meager incomes. Daddy was obviously playing a card of importance because he was in the act of slamming it down on the table and he had a big smile on his face. The smile reminded me of the satisfied smile he had on his face when he exterminated the big rat in the pantry of our rent house on 14th Street. I kept that photograph near my bed and it always made me feel good to see that Daddy was happy even though he was far away.

Daddy would come back to Little Rock once a year, and once he came twice. I would see him when he came home, but it was parent visitation in the purest sense of the word. Mother would not let him stay at our house, so he stayed in an old hotel on Markham Street, near Main Street. The hotel, like the place where Daddy stayed in New Mexico, had seen better days. The clientele was predictable: Old men and a few couples who had negotiated a cheap monthly rate, transients who could not afford to stay in a better place, and a few painted ladies. The desk clerk was picturesque, old and wrinkled, with a shirt collar that was three sizes too big. He had dandruff all over the shoulders of his coat and his hair was shiny, slicked down with Rose Hair Oil, the stinky treatment of choice for most old men in those days. The old man was always there—year in and year out—and once I got by his front desk I took a rickety elevator up to Daddy's floor. I hated the place, but it was all that Daddy could afford. In bad weather, we visited in his room but in nice weather we would find a nearby café or park bench. Mother always limited my visitation to a couple of hours, and I did not argue with her. It was good to see my father, and I treasured the small amount of time I had with him, but the old hotel on Markham Street was not a fun venue.

6

LIFE WITHOUT DADDY

My mother had a great deal of trouble with me, but I think she enjoyed it.
Mark Twain

The separation and eventual divorce of my parents was a big problem. It plagued me. It would not go away, but life goes on so my sister and I did what we could to make the best of it.

School days at Rightsell Grammar School were easier after we moved to 2309 State Street. With no family car, we walked to and from school. Our new house was only five blocks from Rightsell, much closer than the mile each way we had to walk when we lived at 216 West 14th Street.

Delta Lew and I did well at Rightsell, a public school, because we were alumni of Miss Mary Dodge Hodge's preschool and kindergarten. I am thankful that Mother and Daddy sent us there. It was unique. There were other private preschools in Little Rock but Miss Mary Dodge Hodge had the best one. She gave us a head start on reading, writing, and arithmetic, and we met some of the best kids in Little Rock.

At Rightsell, we used to start each day of school with a prayer. I did not have much experience with religion but I had no trouble with the idea of saying a prayer in school. At least, I had no trouble until Shirley Jo Cudd tattled on me for not having my eyes closed during the prayer. The teacher immediately put her in her place with one of the best lines I have ever heard. She said, "How could Shirley Jo Cudd know that Edwin Bethune did not have his eyes closed during the prayer if Shirley Jo Cudd had *her* eyes closed?" Touché, the teacher's perfect squelch immediately purged my embarrassment. The perfect squelch technique I learned that day served me well later on in my work as a lawyer and congressman.

I learned another technique on the playground at Rightsell. My nemesis was L. W. Clements. He was not a bully but he was bigger and stronger than I was. For that reason, he liked to get me into wrestling matches. After he had pinned me in several fights I learned that even though I was small I had super-strong arms. If I could get an arm-lock around L. W.'s head and not let go, I could at least get a draw because my technique would incapacitate him and someone would eventually come along and break up the fight. My strong arms, which I am convinced I inherited from Daddy, saved me a whipping on many occasions later on when my smart mouth got me into trouble.

Modern child protection advocates would freak out if today's schools had playground equipment like that we had at Rightsell. My favorite was a steel and chain version of the classic Maypole. We referred to our device as the "Johnnies." It had chains hanging from a round revolving cap positioned on top of a huge ten-foot steel pole. On the lower end of each chain was a steel ring, just like the rings used by gymnasts. If you caught one of the rings and ran around the center post, you could get up enough speed to make several revolutions without touching your feet to the ground. There were six rings, so six students could ride the Johnnies at one time. With a minimum of coordination, you could really get the thing going. It was a lot of fun so long as the participants took care when letting go because a free-flying ring without a student attached to it was a lethal weapon. The rings were heavy and if they hit you in the head, the stars would fly and you would bleed like a stuck pig. If the rings had ever hit you in the mouth, you would have lost a bunch of teeth. It is a wonder the Johnnies did not produce a class action lawsuit but I do not remember anyone complaining. We just learned how to ride the Johnnies, and how to duck the free-flying rings.

My years at Rightsell coincided with World War II. Almost all of our programs, even Christmas and Easter, had patriotic themes. There were patriotic songs, patriotic plays, patriotic posters, and patriotic poems. Toward the end of the war I almost got the lead in a patriotic extravaganza about General Douglas MacArthur featuring a new patriotic song entitled, "December 7th, Nineteen Hundred and Forty One," but I lost out to Arthur McAnich. I am convinced to this day that Arthur beat me out of the lead role simply because his surname sounded like MacArthur.

In 1945, the war in Europe finally ended. In May, The Third Reich of Nazi Germany was defeated and one of the monsters I feared, Adolf Hitler, committed suicide in his bunker in Berlin. The official surrender of all German forces came on May 8, V-E Day (Victory in Europe) but the fighting in the Pacific continued.

Three months later, on August 6, 1945, the United States dropped an atomic bomb, nicknamed Little Boy, over the city of Hiroshima. The blast obliterated hundreds of thousands of Japanese and started talk that soon the war would be over in the Pacific.

All through my days at Rightsell, I and other little boys drew pictures of our military fighter planes—Thunderbolts, Hellcats, Corsairs and my personal favorite the P-38 Lockheed Lightning—in dogfights with hostile German Messerschmitts and Japanese Zeros. Our B-17 and B-29 bombers were sketched dropping big payloads on "bad Japs" and "bad Germans." We were getting back at the enemy. They had started the war but we were going to finish it. That was our thinking. I never felt bad pretending to kill the enemy when my friends and I played "war" or when I drew pictures dropping imaginary bombs. Lashing out as we did was probably a defense mechanism. We were scared of the enemy and it was better to be on offense than defense, but the idea that one bomb could destroy an entire city as big as Hiroshima never occurred to us. We knew from newsreels and newspaper photographs that it took thousands of bombs to level Berlin and other German cities. Those were the rules of engagement for our pretend wars and that is what we depicted in our drawings, but the reports of this new atomic bomb were unworldly, almost unbelievable. If true, how could the Japanese keep fighting in the face of such devastation? We were still talking about Hiroshima and stories of a great mushroom cloud when, three days later, news came that the Air Force had dropped a second atomic bomb, Fat Man, on the city of Nagasaki.

Soon thereafter, we began to hear gruesome details. Japanese men, women and children who survived the blast were dying from radiation exposure or extensive burns. There was talk that the few who survived would produce horribly mutated children.

I was nine, going on ten. The mix of information I received all during the four years of World War II made me mad, made me proud, and made me hate, but it also scared the beejeebers out of me. It was a relief, when we heard about the atomic bomb, to know that Hitler and Tojo, the Japanese leader who was responsible for the attack on Pearl Harbor, would not be conquering America as they did in my nightmares. That was good, but now I had to factor in the devastation we had caused with the atomic bomb and what it might mean in the years to come. It was too much for a kid. I reduced the deluge of information and my mix of emotions about the atomic bomb to the practical: Thank God, we had the bomb and our enemies did not.

Mother took Delta Lew and me to the Roxy Theatre on Main Street in Little Rock on August 16, 1945. I do not remember the movie that was playing, but I do remember that I was engrossed in the story and not thinking of the war or anything else. Suddenly, the movie stopped and the usher turned on all the lights and shouted: "The war is over! The war is over! The war is over!"

The theatre was about half full and we all got up and headed for the exit, cheering and jumping up and down until we poured out into the street where we mingled with hundreds who were rushing into the street from other buildings. Soon we were all shouting, "The war is over, the war is over, the war is over!" It was daylight, and I know from today's records that it was around 6:00 o'clock on a hot summer night. But there is one memory in my mind that takes no record to refresh. It is the sense of relief I felt and a wonder of what things would be like without the war.

When I got to the fifth grade in the month after the war ended, most of the cool kids at Rightsell were wearing Levi blue jeans, Converse white tennis shoes, and pullover knit shirts. It was the latest clothing fad. Delta Lew and I salivated for Levi blue jeans and other parts of the outfit. We begged and begged and after about two months, Mother broke down and bought us some blue jeans that were on sale at Woolworths. She also got us some tennis shoes. The only problem was that the blue jeans bore no resemblance to the popular Levi jeans that all our friends were wearing. My sister dubbed them, "Farmer Jones Jeans." They had big, baggy legs, pockets stitched on the outside, and they were made of dark iridescent blue denim. They matched perfectly with the all black, Army surplus tennis shoes that Mother got for us. To make matters worse I had to wear the obviously homemade shirts Mother had sewn for me out of the cheapest material she could find on sale. I looked weird.

We revolted, but Mother gave us a speech on the necessity and value of frugality and made us wear them to school. Delta Lew figured out a way to get out of it after a couple of wearings, but I did not. I was the laughing stock at Rightsell Grammar School for a long time thereafter. It took awhile, but I finally convinced Mother to let me stop wearing the Farmer Jones Jeans. I swore off blue jeans and never wore them again, except to work in our backyard. It was thirty years before I wanted to wear blue jeans, even Levis.

Summertime was special. We were out of school, baseball and swimming were in season but everyone was worried about polio, the disease that showed up every summer and was an epidemic throughout the 1940s. Many kids died or spent months in iron lungs. If they survived, they wound up with distorted limbs, like Daddy's, that would be useless for a lifetime. Polio, of course, had a special meaning in our house because of Daddy's medical history. Mother assured us that it was not hereditary, but Delta Lew and I were scared anyway. I am sure Mother was worried too, even though she maintained her customary, stoic Vermilye approach.

Summer also brought the annual trip to Pocahontas. Now, after the separation, my secret place above Lewallen Café took on greater importance. It was a place where I could spend time thinking, grieving, and crying in private about what was happening to my family. Even though Toni and her River Rat family were gone by the time the war was over, I continued to think about her and their life on the river. This good memory served a special purpose. I compared my family life, as screwed-up as it seemed, to the much harder life the River Rat kids had. It did not fix my problem, but the perspective comforted me.

My Uncle Lloyd, Mother's youngest brother, decided to open a secondhand furniture store as soon as he graduated from high school. He rented an unfinished space in the basement of a building on the corner of the square across from the café building, got himself a used 1931 A-Model Ford truck, and headed to St. Louis to buy his first load of used furniture. A few days later Lloyd returned with his truck piled high with furniture and wood-burning stoves he had bought at auction in the big city. I helped Lloyd by cleaning and painting the stoves—cook stoves and regular ones—with stove-black, a messy liquid that looked and smelled like shoe polish. He cleaned and refinished the furniture, and when necessary he reupholstered it, a skill he taught himself. I liked painting the stoves because I could make them look like new but I got about as much paint on myself as I did on the stoves. My payoff for helping Lloyd was to go along on deliveries. The A-Model truck had no doors, and the trips outside town frequently took us over unpaved roads. What could be better for an adventurous boy?

When I was in the fifth grade, Mother decided that I should learn to play the clarinet, mainly because she liked Benny Goodman, the great clarinetist. She bought me a second-hand metal clarinet at Bean's Music Store. She got the metal one because it was cheaper than the wooden clarinets that produced a higher quality sound. Then in her demanding way, she stayed after me to practice, practice and practice. Her persistence and my willingness to work paid off. I made first chair clarinet in the East Side Junior High School Band as a seventh grader. I was good at it, but I did not like the commitment that was required to be in the band because I wanted to play sports, all sports, any sports.

A motto painted on the wall near the ceiling of the band room proclaimed: A winner never quits, and a quitter never wins. I loved reading that and I liked the band room and the fact that I was the best clarinet player in the band, but I wanted the motto about quitting and winning to work for me in sports, not music.

We had sex education at East Side Junior High School, but it was not part of the official curriculum. It took place during recesses and lunch breaks, usually near a tree in the northwest corner of the playground. It was easy to tell when class was in session because a cluster of fifteen to twenty boys, all whooping and hollering and pushing to get to an inside position, encircled whoever had the latest textbook, one of the two-by-five-inch eight-page booklets of pornographic cartoons. The booklets, commonly known as Eight-Page Bibles, featured the well-known cartoon characters of that era: Moon Mullins, Tarzan and Jane, and Popeye and Olive Oil. Enough said.

My best friend was Billy McMillan who lived just two blocks away. He also played the clarinet, but his instrument was made of wood. I envied him for that, but I would not have traded places with him for anything because he had a terrible stuttering problem. Billy was a nice kid and popular, but nine times out of ten when he tried to talk he would go into a stuttering fit. He would roll his eyes, turn red in the face, and look as if he was about to pass out for lack of breath. It was not funny, but some kids—adolescents can be mindlessly cruel—would mock him, tease him, and laugh at him. It was similar to the way some kids treated my father when they saw him struggling to walk with his canes and artificial leg. Billy and my father never let it bother them. On the contrary, I marveled at how they frequently acknowledged the crudeness with a knowing smile or a wink of the eye.

In the summer months, Billy and I spent hours practicing on our clarinets, playing monopoly, or figuring ways to make money. He did not play baseball or other sports, so our times together coincided with foul weather or days when it was too hot to get out of the shade. Our most productive enterprise was our shoe-shining business. We knocked on doors in the neighborhood offering to shine shoes for twenty-five cents a pair. We made good money doing that and came back to it every time we could not find a yard to mow. I loved my friend. He would do anything for me and I would do anything for him. We played mostly at my house because Billy's mother monitored what we were doing when we played at his house. If Mrs. McMillan thought we were wasting time, which is what we were usually doing, she would try to get us to do something more constructive. I thought she was weird because she fed Billy stuff I had never heard of like egg & olive sandwiches and fruit salads, and she made Billy rest for thirty minutes after each meal so that his food could "settle."

It was about this time in my life that I had my first experience with religion. Mother insisted that my sister and I go to Sunday school. She did not go, but she sent us. To make it attractive she would give us twenty cents apiece that we could use for a Sunday afternoon movie at the Arkansas Theatre. We went first to the Baptist Church, then later on to the Methodist Church.

Delta Lew and I enjoyed church and Sunday school because of the friends we made. I did learn a little bit about God and Jesus when I was a kid. The introduction to the Gospel was a good thing, and it helped me with the pain I was feeling as a child in a busted family. Even so, and I have no guilt about it, I did not understand or accept the Gospel in the way that I would later in life.

My occasional attendance at Winfield Methodist Church led me to join the Boy Scout Troop that met there. Our scoutmaster was an old man, so actual leadership of the troop fell to our assistant scoutmaster, Dick Neal. Dick Neal worked for his parents who operated a luggage shop on Main Street. He was a little peculiar, but we all liked him and he worked hard to be a good scoutmaster. Even though I never got past the rank of Tenderfoot, I won first place in a statewide contest at the annual Boy Scout Jamboree for making the fastest and best blanket roll. It was my high-water mark as a scout.

In my second year, our scout troop took a long hike down Arch Street Pike south of Little Rock. When we took a break, Dick Neal walked through the campsite reporting that he had just heard a radio report that Babe Ruth had died that day, August 16, 1948. We found it hard to accept. How could he, The Sultan of Swat, be dead? I had lost family members, but I had watched them grow old and expected them to die. The death of Babe Ruth was different. I did not think of the Babe as old. We heard he had throat cancer but never thought it or anything else could bring down Babe Ruth. He was invincible. How could he die?

A few months after Babe Ruth died, I experienced yet another shock. Charles Vandament, a classmate and fellow scout, called me at 6:00 a.m. on April 21, 1949, to tell me that the Little Rock Police had found the body of Dick Neal on a lonely road near the Arkansas River. It was murder. An unknown assailant had knifed him several times and left him to die. We learned that same day that Dick Neal was a homosexual. There had been whispers that he was a "queer," but we were not sure what that meant. The police supposed his homosexuality was a cause for his death but they never proved it, and they never caught his killer.

We got a new assistant scoutmaster but scouting was never the same. Shortly after Dick Neal's murder, I dropped out of Boy Scouts and filled my life with other diversions.

I made model airplanes using balsa wood, tissue paper, and glue, lots of glue. It was long before label warnings so, as I bent over my work, I discovered glue sniffing at an early age.

Baseball was my true love as it has been throughout my life. There is nothing like baseball. The struggle between a batter and a pitcher is the ultimate sports challenge. The first organized baseball I played was in the Midget League, run under the auspices of the Little Rock Boy's Club. We called our team the Pirates and, on our own, stenciled our team name on white T-shirts. That was our uniform. Later, moving up, I played for the Rocket 88's, a team my friends and I put together. We found our own sponsor, Balch Motor Company, and Mr. Balch bought us official team jerseys. On the back was the name, Balch Motor Company and on the front, Rocket 88's. That was our uniform and we were proud of it. It was the first real uniform we ever had. We did not have baseball shoes; we just wore our tennis shoes. We played our games at MacArthur Park or Lamar Porter Field. We had no adult coaches or managers and parents did not come to the games. We kids were in charge of and responsible for everything and we won the city championship two years running.

My friends and I would ride the streetcar to Traveler's Field at Fair Park. We would hangout outside the fence and try to catch balls knocked over the fence during batting practice. Willie, a skinny old man from the nearby State Hospital, was usually there, and we teased him for acting funny, as he strung together incomprehensible sentences. We could get a seat in the bleachers for twenty-five cents but most of the time we just looked through the knotholes and cracks in the fence and used our cash for other things.

In my early years, I was smaller than the other kids were, so they called me "Shorty." I was a well-coordinated, savvy ballplayer so most of my coaches and friends figured I would be a good athlete when I got bigger. I was barely above five feet in the seventh grade and I only got to 5' 7" and 120 pounds by the time I was in the tenth grade. Nevertheless, I dreamed as hard as I could about becoming a major league baseball player. My fallback dream was to become a sports trainer for the New York Yankees. I spent every available moment studying the box scores and bios of the big players of the day.

In my unrelenting effort to become the best baseball player in Little Rock, I quit the band and sold my clarinet after I finished the seventh grade. Mother did not want me to quit, but I argued that the effort to blow the horn was busting blood vessels in my eyes and that is why my eyes were bloodshot most of the time. I do not think she bought my argument, but she let me quit the band.

Now free to focus on baseball and other sports, I busted my nose five times, broke my right arm once, and strained my right knee so badly that I could not put any weight on it for two weeks. Mother was furious when I broke my arm because that necessitated a costly trip to the doctor to have it set and cast. The broken noses looked OK after I pulled my nose back into position so I never went to the doctor for those injuries. I paid for that later on when I tried to become a Marine pilot and they rejected me because I had a deviated septum, which meant that one side of my nose was completely blocked. The naval flight surgeon took the position that I needed two holes to be an aviator, so I flunked the flight physical. I asked him if he could fix it for me and he declined, saying I only needed one hole in my nose to be a Marine. When I was next on leave in Arkansas, I got a private doctor to fix it. It cost me $175 that I paid out of my own pocket. A year later, when I was in the middle of my tour of duty in Korea, I got an offer to go to Naval Air Cadet School in Pensacola, Florida. My new nose and I passed the flight physical, but I turned down the offer for NavCads because the program required me to extend my enlistment so that I would have a total of four years to serve. By then I was half way through my three-year enlistment and could see the light at the end of the tunnel. I decided to pass up Naval Air Cadets. To this day, my nose swoops slightly to starboard, but I do have two holes for breathing.

The best way for me to get around town was on my bike. I did not like my bike because it was a girl's bike. Mother bought it for $10, second-hand. She said I would have to get used to it because she could only afford one bike and if she had gotten a boy's bike Delta Lew would not have been able to use it. It took awhile, but my friends finally quit teasing me for riding a girl's bike.

I got quite good at riding, particularly riding without touching the handlebars. Once, all puffed up with pride, I waved to a carload of girls as I was riding with no hands. I ran full speed into the back of a parked car. I learned it is not smart to show off or take your eyes off the road. I broke no bones but it hurt my pride to find myself spread-eagled on the trunk of the parked car.

My young life included ping-pong-ball, a game similar to baseball that my friends and I invented. We played with badminton rackets and a ping-pong ball and the favorite venue was my backyard. It is amazing how much movement the pitcher can put on a ping-pong ball. Curves, sinkers, and sliders are easy. The hardest thing to throw is a straight fastball.

One day, right in the middle of a serious ping-pong-ball game, Elizabeth "Tissa" Wilson and two other girls opened the gate and walked into my backyard just as Edwin Spann was getting ready to pitch to me. We began the nervous chatter common between boys and girls of that age. Tissa, in the midst of that, made a comment that cut to the quick and still rings in my head. She said, "Edwin Spann's voice has changed, but Edwin Bethune's voice is still high and squeaky." The passage through puberty is tough enough without such insults. I was tempted to tell her that my voice was lagging behind the progress I was otherwise making with pubescence. I was tempted to brag about my recently discovered virility, but that would have been bad form.

The truth is I matured later than most of my friends, but my development rapidly picked up steam after I accidently busted in on one of Mother's room-renters. I thought Jo Bell had gone to work, and I wanted to get to an upstairs porch that was unreachable without going through her room. To my great surprise she was not only in her room, she was standing in front of the dresser mirror, admiring her gorgeous, completely naked body. I panicked. I knew I was in trouble so I immediately ran downstairs and told Mother what I had seen. It was my first look at a naked woman, a live one at least, and it stirred me up in ways I had never experienced. I do not know what I expected Mother to say, but she gave me Hell for opening the door without knocking and asking permission. I think she was more worried about losing a tenant and $10.50 a week in rent money than the shock I got from seeing a busty, beautiful woman in her mid-twenties, naked as a jaybird. Soon thereafter, with hard work, I managed to make my voice drop an octave.

7

MY VERY SECRET STRUGGLE

The truth of a matter will always haunt you, no matter how secret the hiding place.
Anonymous

The minor skirmishes I had with Mother were symptoms of a deeper divide that showed up after Daddy left. I was living with her, but like my father, I was a dreamer. My dreaming seemed to drive Mother to the brink of insanity. I think that when I did a lot of big talking about my dreams I reminded her of Daddy. She wanted me to succeed, and she was convinced that dreaming would not get me anywhere.

Fortunately, my sister always took my side. She never faulted me or made fun of my dreams. I could come out with the zaniest ideas and Delta Lew would defend me, arguing to Mother that it was a good thing for me to think big thoughts and dream big dreams.

Mother was not buying. She was frustrated that Daddy's big dreams had not panned out, and she feared I was destined for a similar fate. I know she loved me and cared for me, but she never let up. She was constantly preparing me for the certain battle I would have with "them." I heard her say a million times, "You are going to turn out just like your father; those dreams won't amount to a hill of beans." Mother, a devotee of the Vermilye approach to solving life's problems, believed in practical goals, doing things that were useful, not dreaming.

As a child, I excelled in school, the band, sports, and in my friendships. I was a "cute" kid by most accounts, and people seemed to like me but I had a recurring, dominating sense of shame and inadequacy stemming from a personal problem known only to my mother, my father, and my sister.

Some kids stutter, like my friend Billy McMillan. Others have problems that are just as conspicuous. My polio-stricken father, for instance, could not hide the way he had to walk with an artificial leg that fit over the stump of his amputated leg. Their flaws are out in the open and there is no way they can escape derogatory comments about their appearance, their behavior and their physical limitations. Kids can be cruel, so it was particularly difficult for Billy and my father, but I admired the way they dealt with it.

I, on the other hand, had a problem that I could and did keep secret. If the truth had come out, I would have caught unmerciful ridicule and mockery. The fear of exposure and embarrassment haunted me day and night. I figured my plight would be even tougher than that faced by Billy and Daddy because they had dealt with meanness since infancy. It hurt them, I am sure, but they had learned to deal with it. Exposure of my problem would have been sudden and the meanness would have been unrelenting. If I kept my problem a secret, I would not be humiliated.

What was my secret? I was a bedwetter from the day I was born. I mean, I always wet the bed, not just ever so often, but every night and it was always a soaker that would often seep beyond the protective rubber sheeting on my bed. I do not know why I did it, but I cannot remember a day before I was fifteen that I did not wet the bed. It was not easy to keep my secret, and there were times when I had to be very quick-witted. Once, a friend was visiting and he spotted a pile of dirty linen at the foot of the stairs. Without notice, my friend dove into the pile and spread-eagled himself as if he had just completed a high-dive at the swimming pool. He got up quickly, exclaiming, "That stuff smells like piss!"

I quickly answered, "Our dog pissed on it, she's got a problem." After that narrow escape, I redoubled my security effort.

For a little kid, I accumulated a lifetime of experience and a wealth of understanding about the distinct but related subjects of guilt, shame, embarrassment, fear and secrets. I quickly learned to appreciate the old riddle: If a tree falls in a forest and no one is around to hear it, does it make a sound? That was the crux of the matter, knowledge. If no one heard it then how could he or she know that a tree had fallen?

If I could keep my secret from the world's population, billions of people, I could avoid embarrassment, but I would have to deal privately with shame.

If my secret got out, I would have to deal with shame *and* embarrassment. My classmates were already on my case, calling me "Shorty," or "Edwin Baboon," and the one that I hated the most, "Edwin Bathroom." It did not take a lot of imagination to appreciate what they could do with my secret problem.

Some people argue it is better to fess up to problems than to cover them up. They say there may be taunts and ridicule in the beginning, but those issues will eventually fade into the background. Time, they say, heals all wounds.

That is how the choice framed up to me, from infancy to adolescence. My best friend Billy McMillan was dealing with the embarrassment of being a stutterer. My Dad was dealing with being a cripple. They could not hide their problems and I, in my ringside seat, watched them struggle with taunts and ridicule. I defended them as best I could, but with that firsthand experience, I could not see any advantage to going the embarrassment route.

I chose secrecy and shame. After all, I was not hiding something that was morally or legally wrong. People might see bedwetting as socially unacceptable, but it is not a crime, or a sin.

Shame is a potent emotional state. It is painful and it is hard to work through on your own. I never saw a doctor to learn whether my bedwetting was physical or mental, or to find out if there was a way to fix my problem. My parents assumed, and kept telling me I would "grow out of it" and, besides, we had no money for nonemergency medical advice. Consequently, I will never know for sure why I did it or how it affected me, but I do have some thoughts on the subject. Since I am not a psychiatrist I can only tell what I remember and what I think it did to me.

Short-term shame is not what I had. People with that are lucky. I had a daily dose of shame, the Bill Murray *Groundhog Day* kind of repetitious shame. I needed a strategy, one that I could deploy each day because lying in a wet bed was my first waking thought for the first fourteen years of my life. My default approach was to look forward and dream of big victories, big adventures, and better times. It is a wonder, looking back, that I was able to deal with my problem without sinking into despair. *Au contraire*, I turned out to be an eternal optimist. I also, according to those I love and trust, avoided the polar extremes of being an overly strong or weak personality. Perhaps it is because I fashioned a way to cope.

Nevertheless, I could not escape occasional bouts of insecurity, anxiety, and general consternation. These issues derive from self-criticism and shame. I wrestled them down as best I could with doses of optimism, hope, dreams, and more dreams.

One unique by-product of my struggle was that I learned the first rule for keeping a secret—never tell anyone. My family protected me, because it was in their interest not to tell, but keeping a secret from everyone else in the world is hard and it creates a lot of pressure. Oddly enough, I am convinced the lessons I learned about secret keeping helped me later in life. When I served in the U. S. Marines, I got a top-secret security clearance. I was required to read the Navy Security Manual and made the highest grade ever made on the test. The manual instructed Marines how to keep military secrets. I could have written that manual when I was eight years old. Later, as a special agent of the FBI, I dealt with classified information flawlessly, and my legal clients could never have found a servant with more experience and dedication to the importance of secrecy. I know a lot about secrets, and I know how to keep them.

I did face one other challenge as I dealt with my secret problem—the omnipotent Vermilye pressure to will my way to a cure.

My mother, at the time a staunch disciple of Vermilyeism, vacillated on the subject of my bedwetting. Her reactions ranged from loving and forgiving to giving me Hell for not being able to stop. I am certain she did not mean to make it a bigger problem than it was, but I always felt a little extra shame because I could not find a way to overcome a simple, personal shortcoming. I could not summon the necessary portion of Vermilye willpower to stop wetting the bed and that, in my mind, meant that I was a flawed Vermilye. If I could achieve most any goal by the sheer force of willpower then, with ease, I ought to be able to correct a personal deficiency. Only later did I come to realize that I expected too much of myself. I was not flawed, or if I was flawed it was not my fault. It was the Vermilye way that was flawed, but I was not able to see that when I was young. I was yet to learn that I should be anxious for nothing. I would discover that proposition later on, but in my youth, such teaching escaped me.

Thus, I continued my struggle to reconcile the irreconcilable. Should I be Bethune or Vermilye? Should I dream, and let my dreams make me happy? Alternatively, should I try to find happiness by the sheer force of willpower that would, according to Vermilye doctrine, lead to a lifetime of achievement and independence from "them." To dream, or not to dream, that was the question. Which was wrong, which was right? Can there be a proper mix of dreaming and willing things to happen? Could I do both? I loved my dreamtime, and I know my father loved his. He, I think, used his dreams to escape the foul cynicism that could have possessed him because of polio, a disability that was not his fault. I, similarly, used my dreams to escape the shame that I felt for being an incurable bedwetter. My father's example was a lifesaver, but I knew there was a big difference in my situation and his. It was not his fault that he was crippled.

I was a bedwetter and, in my mind at that time, it was my fault. These monumental forces, Bethune vs. Vermilye pushed me first one way and then the other. I wanted to achieve great things, but my unsettled philosophy of life was not working. I could escape into my dream world, but I could not get away from reality. I had to deal with a wet bed each morning. I could see the wisdom in practicing Vermilye willpower and I wanted desperately to please my mother and stop bedwetting and reach all the goals she had set for me but it was hard—in fact, impossible—for me to let go of my dream world, a place where I was not flawed and could, and did, accomplish marvelous works. There I did not have to deal with my flaws. It was a comfortable place to be but it was getting me nowhere. The harder I tried to reconcile the competing forces the more I knew that something was missing from the equation. The Vermilye approach did not help me fix my bedwetting problems and my dreams only provided temporary respite.

Vermilye had my mind, but Bethune had my heart.

In my senior years, I am convinced that my multifaceted struggle strengthened me more than it weakened me because I learned to work out my own problems. It was a hard lesson for a kid but as I got older, I realized that I could deal with shame, stress, fear, anxiety, and secrecy and in time, the negative effects of bedwetting dissipated.

I also learned later in life, with the help of my wife Lana, that there *is* a way to reconcile the competing forces—Vermilye vs. Bethune. There is a superior worldview, but I was one confused kid, wrestling with what appeared to be irreconcilable forces. It was not a good way to be as I moved into the next, equally complicated phase of growing up.

8

SINKING, SINKING

One father is worth more than a hundred schoolmasters.
George Herbert

After the divorce was final, Mother dated. I once saw her kissing a man in our living room. The image scratched itself deep into my memory. More than sixty years later, it is still there. It will never go away. Mother, as the man held her, was bending her knee and raising one high-heel shoe behind her just like the old-time movie stars did when kissing on the silver screen. I have no contrasting memory of Mother kissing Daddy.

I realized she wanted to have fun, dance, and do all the things she could not do with my father. I do not blame her for it now, but at the time I did not like it. It hurt and confused me greatly. I was angry about the kiss, the separation, and the divorce. I wanted things to be different, but I could do nothing about any of it. My dad, in my mind, was the right man for her and he belonged at home with us. I simply could not understand or forgive Mother for what happened to their marriage and my life. At the time, I did not know how to forgive so I just lived with it.

In May of 1950, I finished the ninth grade and graduated from East Side Junior High School. It was a good school and I did well, academically at least. In the summer of that year, I began to venture beyond home and family. I was fourteen, going on fifteen, and I was searching for something, I did not know what.

I started my summer with the best of intentions.

I was not making much off my paper route, but I had saved enough to buy a car. I was too young to have a driver's license, but that minor technicality did not slow me down. For the grand sum of $25, I bought a worn-out 1929 Ford A-Model Roadster, a two-seat convertible with a trunk that doubled as a rumble seat. It had many dents and the previous owner had painted the fenders with a brush-coat of red enamel. The canvas top was long gone and the main body of the car sported a green paint job that partially hid twenty-one years of rust and corrosion. I did not care that my "new" car looked like a big Christmas ornament, it ran and it was mine.

Mother was definitely upset, but she let me keep the car because I landed a summer job that required me to have a car. I was going to make $75 a month as the groundskeeper of a city ballpark, using my A-Model Ford to drag a heavy, homemade leveling device over the dirt infield. It was a great job because it only took about a couple of hours each afternoon to drag the field, sprinkle down the dust, lime the baselines, put out the bases, and open the field for play. I had no liability insurance, no driver's license, and no one to teach me how to drive, but that did not stop me. I taught myself to drive and simply ignored the other two problems. It was going to be a great summer and it started with another promising enterprise.

My friend, Donny Evans, and I conceived a business venture that would take us to the strawberry fields in White County. We planned to leave Little Rock early in the morning, arrive at the strawberry field around 9:00 a.m., and pick berries for a couple of hours. Then, it was our plan to drive back to Little Rock and sell the strawberries door to door. Donny also had an A-Model similar to mine, but his car was in better shape mainly because his tires still had visible tread. My tires were threadbare and one had a boot in it to keep the inner tube from poking through a hole. We sensibly decided to use his car for the eighty-mile roundtrip. It took a little while to find a farmer who would let us pick, and then it took longer to pick two crates of berries than we thought it would. As a result, we did not start back to Little Rock until 2:00 o'clock, the hottest time of the day. By the time we got to Little Rock our berries, exposed to a heavy dose of hot air and sunlight, were wasting away, fast. I had to be at the ball field by 5:00 p.m. to start dragging the field. There was no way we could sell all the berries before they ripened to mush. We wound up losing a full crate, half of our stock. It was a great disappointment because berry picking is hard work and we had hoped to make some serious money. We barely covered the cost of our trip, but I learned a valuable economics lesson: Merchandising is risky. Oddly, that day is one of my fondest memories.

Shortly after the strawberry fiasco, things started to unravel. I found myself in a downward spiral, getting in one jam after another. It puzzled Mother, but it also puzzled me. I did not know and still do not know why I rebelled or why I began to do dumb things.

Delta Lew and me, just before I began my downward spiral. My thanks to the photographer who touched up my snaggletooth. 1950.

The trouble began one day in early June when I was driving on Broadway. A motorcycle policeman stopped me for dodging in and out of traffic. He asked me for my driver's license and, of course, I had none. I quickly concocted a cover story that I had just bought the car and I was taking it to my mother's house only five blocks away. I told him I was going to park the car and did not plan to drive it until I got a license, but that I was going to do that soon because I needed the car to do my job at the ball field. I could see he was not buying my story so I tuned up and started blubbering about how my folks were divorced and I really needed to make some money. I guess I found his soft spot because he let me go. It was not a good lesson for me because I drove the A-Model, that afternoon, to my job at the ball field. I managed to duck the traffic police for the rest of the summer, but I found other ways to get in trouble.

I played baseball, of course, but I did not hang out with my teammates before or after the games. I fell in with the wrong crowd, kids from the east side of town who specialized in troublemaking. Together, we found every available way to challenge authority, any authority, every authority. We embarked on a summer of pranks, vandalism, and larceny. Mother and Delta Lew figured out that I was up to no good and they did what they could to intervene, but I was determined to rebel and prove that I did not need, or want, supervision.

I became, virtually overnight, an incorrigible child. Edwin was my name, but mischief was my game. It poured out of me like a gusher of oil bursting out of a new well.

The summer continued, I avoided arrest and did my job at the ball field, I played baseball, I spent the nights at home, and I practiced the fine art of driving my mother nuts. My sister lost patience with me and that bothered me, but it did not slow me down. Thankfully, my flirtation with troublemaking took place before the era of drugs, pot, and other vices. I was hard committed to the idea of becoming a professional baseball player so it is unlikely that I would have fooled around with anything that might have hurt my body, but I cannot say that for sure. There were other ways to get in trouble, and I managed to find most of them.

When it came time to start the tenth grade, my first year at Little Rock Senior High School (the name was changed to Little Rock Central High School in 1955), I was invited to join a fraternity, Rho Iota Epsilon. The fraternity went by odd but arguably accurate Greek letter initials, PIE. My sister was a member of a high school sorority and it was her popularity in the Greek community that led PIE to extend a bid to me. I liked the kids in the fraternity but I continued to fool around with my troublemaking friends.

For the first time ever I failed not one, but two courses, biology and plane geometry. I did even worse in the second semester that began in January 1951. I flunked everything I was taking, got universally poor marks for citizenship, and led the entire school in truancy. I skipped thirty-plus days of class, a record so they say. Mother knew I was goofing off, but she had no idea I was skipping school as much as I did. She was furious at me for playing hooky. She conferred with the school authorities and together they devised a plan. Mother's fifteen-year-old wild child would attend summer school. In contrast, my sister Delta Lew graduated from high school on schedule.

I protested as strongly as I could. I argued that summer school was for dummies and it would interfere with baseball, the only thing that mattered to me. They did not buy my argument but they gave me a choice: I could go to summer school or I could play baseball and repeat the tenth grade. I chose summer school, but I had a secret plan that I did not disclose to them. I would go to class, but I would skip out on those occasions when my team was playing.

Mother scheduled me to take English and plane geometry, required courses if I was to move on to the eleventh grade with my classmates. I did attend class, but not on the days when I had a game. It was not long before everyone figured out what I was doing. The truant officer for Little Rock Senior High School came to all my games, but he did not come to watch. He came out onto the field, took me by the arm and led me out of Lamar Porter Field and back to the classroom. I was charged with several unexcused absences, but as it turned out I was in class often enough to get two C's on my final report card. I was now eligible for promotion to the eleventh grade.

Shortly after summer school, my friend Billy McMillan got his driver's license. To celebrate his sixteenth birthday, his parents gave him an almost-new 1949 Chevrolet, two-door sedan. I had not seen much of Billy during my summer of incorrigibility, but he drove to my house as soon as he got the new car. He was not one to gloat, but we had grown up together and he wanted to share his moment of excitement. Edwin Spann was at my house when Billy drove up. We piled into the car and headed out for a test drive. We all sat in the front seat. Billy drove, I was in the middle, and Edwin Spann was on my right. We drove all over Little Rock and as it got dark we were way out west on Markham Street, at least five miles past War Memorial Stadium. That part of Markham was a narrow two-lane road through an undeveloped area. It was pitch-dark and we were racing up one hill and down another, headed east back into town, testing to see how fast Billy's new car would go. I remember hitting ninety miles per hour as we crested a hill near the area that is now the intersection of Markham and University. Back then, University Avenue was Hayes Street, and Hayes was unpaved. To make matters worse, Markham ended abruptly at Hayes. To continue east on Markham a driver would have to make a sharp right turn on Hayes and then a sharp left turn back onto Markham. We were jabbering with excitement about how fast we were going when, all of a sudden, we entered the intersection. It was too late to stop and we were going too fast to make the turn. We plowed into an abutment and the car went sailing into the air and came down nose first in a ditch on the other side of the abutment. The impact was violent and when I realized I was still alive I could not see anything because there was so much dust. The engine was racing and I saw Billy was out cold, his head lying against the steering wheel. Edwin Spann was already out of the car. Edwin found a fruit jar in the ditch and he was holding it under his nose to catch the blood. His nose was flat against his face, but he was walking around and did not seem to have other injuries. My head hurt and so did my left elbow, but shock had set in and the pain was tolerable. Billy was still unconscious.

A man came out of a house across the intersection and said that he had called the police to report the accident. An ambulance arrived and they took Billy to a nearby hospital. Edwin Spann, fruit jar still in place, and I followed in a police car. The Chevrolet was a total loss, and Billy regained consciousness at noon the next day. He had a very serious concussion. The doctors worried about him for several days, but he recovered fully. Edwin Spann had a broken nose. He told the doctors he was catching blood in the fruit jar in case he might need it. The doctors got a kick out of that. I had a serious bruise on my left elbow and two black eyes, including a sizeable bloody area in my left eye. I apparently hit my elbow on the handle of the emergency brake and whacked my face against the dash. It took a full month for my injuries to heal.

We were lucky to survive the car crash, but for Mother the accident was the last straw. My near brush with death led to my removal to Pocahontas. Mother told me she was sending me to live with Mama Lewallen. Delta Lew, just graduated from high school, was going to take a job at Pocahontas High School as a secretary. Mother would stay in Little Rock and go to business school. All this I learned one week before Delta Lew and I caught the bus for Pocahontas. It was a total surprise and it hit me like a ton of bricks. I was mad about it and told various cover stories to my friends about why I was leaving Little Rock. Anger blinded me, but the move to Pocahontas would turn out to be a lifesaving change.

❦

9

NEW TOWN, NEW LIFE

Small boys become big men through the influence of big men who care about small boys.
Father's Day Quote: Unknown

In 1951, 3,700 people lived in Pocahontas. Delta Lew and I got there at the end of August and moved in with Mama Lewallen. Mother stayed in Little Rock to learn how to operate a comptometer machine. Later, she got a job in the bookkeeping department of a Little Rock business. My sister never aspired to go to college, so she stuck with me.

By the time we got to Pocahontas, Mama had long since closed the Lewallen Café and rented out the entire downstairs of her building. She was living upstairs in a small apartment adjoining her hotel, the twelve small rooms that she rented out to itinerants. Delta Lew and I moved into two hotel rooms that overlooked the town square. Austere is not the right word to describe our rooms: white painted walls, gaudy linoleum on the floor, a double bed, a chest of drawers, and a straight chair. That was it, unless you counted the little gas heat stove or the thirty-foot coil of half-inch hemp rope anchored beneath the window that served as a "fire escape." One unisex bathroom served our two rooms and two other hotel rooms that also overlooked the square. There were four rooms in the hotel that had a private bath, but Mama saved those for paying customers. My room was near the front entrance, right next to the room where the funeral man had put Papa Lewallen's casket after he died of stomach rot and the man with the bass voice sang "Asa's Death." I did not like that grim memory, but my thinking spot, the lithograph of *Custer's Last Stand*, and the bobcat with a nick in the ear was just a few steps from the door to my room. My mind wandered from despair to dreams of greatness, but ultimately despair won out. I began to feel sorry for myself. My thoughts were selfish. I should have been thinking about how my sister was sacrificing to help me. She deserved better—I did not.

Delta Lew started her new job as a secretary at Pocahontas High School and she was up and gone every morning by 8:00 a.m. I, on the other hand, would wake up early, strip my wet bed, put on dry bedding and sleep until late morning. I read, I moped, and I spent time at my thinking spot. I had no interest in going out of the hotel. I did not know anyone. I just wanted to be back in Little Rock, back with my friends. I did not like the idea that Mama Lewallen was watching over us, nor did I want to go to a new school where I did not know anyone.

At the end of our first week in the hotel, I was in a deep sleep when at 9:30 a.m. I heard a terrible noise that rattled the window, ricocheted off the linoleum, and shattered a dream of greatness. I sat upright trying to figure out what was causing the noise, and then I went to the window and looked down to the sidewalk below. There a worker was busting up the sidewalk and street with a jackhammer. What a racket! I had seen jackhammers from a distance in Little Rock, but never had I been so close to one. I put on my clothes and hustled down the stairs to get a better look. I could hear the racket all the way down, and it was almost as loud in the stairwell as it was in my room. When I got outside, I saw the man sticking the point into the concrete as it hammered its way deeper and deeper. His entire body was jiggling in time to the beat of the jackhammer and he looked to be hanging on for dear life. The noise was indescribably irritating, but the sight of a man having to make his living doing such work bothered me more than the noise.

I retreated to my thinking spot and after a séance with General Custer and the bobcat, came to my senses. I would give Pocahontas a chance. I was tired of hanging around the hotel and I did not want a future as a jackhammer operator. If Delta Lew was willing to give up two years of her life to help me get through school, it was the least I could do.

A few days later, I left the hotel at 7:30 a.m., made my way through town and then walked out Thomasville Road to Pocahontas High School, a distance of two miles. People in passing cars kept looking at me, obviously a new kid in town. I hated that. Then, I suffered through the awkward business of enrolling and introducing myself to my homeroom teacher. Soon I was a full-fledged eleventh grader at PHS.

The first few days were painful, but then I began to meet the kids and find out a little about each of them. They were an interesting mix. A few, by my standard, were filthy rich but most were from ordinary, low-to-middle-class families. Some lived out in the country, but most lived in town.

The Spikes boys lived in town and they were the first kids to befriend me. We met while walking to school on Thomasville Road, because they, like me, had no money and no means of transportation. We started meeting after school to walk home, and soon we became a threesome.

It was in those first days of my junior year that I learned to shoot pool and play snooker because that is what the Spikes boys—Billy and Bob—liked to do. We played at Suler's Pool Hall or Coconut's Pool Hall when we could bum a ride across the river to East Pocahontas. The pool sharks swam in both places. I learned who they were and how to avoid them, but I studied them and they taught me how to make a three-in-the-side bank shot and shoot for a leave as much as trying to sink the ball that was in play. Coconut, an old man with a bum leg, used to say, "You're playing so much pool you'll rub blisters on your belly walking around the table."

One of the Spikes boys, Bob, was lame and had to wear a built-up shoe. He reminded me of my father because he was always in a good mood, had an easy smile, and never let on that he felt sorry for himself. He, like my father, had learned to steel himself to the stares and comments about his foot. The other, Bill, was a cut-up who was the leader of our little clique. The Spikes boys did not play sports or do other school activities, so in time I began to enlarge my circle of friends.

After a that few weeks at the hotel, Delta Lew and I moved into a small apartment in a house owned by my uncle, Lloyd Lewallen. It had worn-out furniture and slick patches of used-up linoleum on the floor in the center of each room. There was a small bedroom just big enough for a dresser and twin beds. There was another slightly bigger room, which we used as our living room. Those two rooms were bookends to a tiny kitchen that had a sink, a small refrigerator, a two-burner gas cook stove and a small table big enough to seat three people. Delta Lew and I made our little place as comfortable as we could. It would be our home for the next two years.

We didn't have to pay rent at Lloyd's so we lived off Delta Lew's modest salary and what little I could make working for fifty cents an hour doing odd jobs at Promberger's Hardware and at Lloyd Lewallen's second-hand furniture store. Mother would occasionally send a few dollars, and Mama Lewallen would feed us if we really got hungry. Most of the time, we ate a lot of bologna, cheap cuts of pork, chicken, macaroni and cheese, and tuna casserole. Occasionally there would be a windfall: Lloyd Lewallen would kill a deer or catch a lot of fish, or barbeque a goat, and he and Betty, his wife, would invite us to eat with them and their kids. I fondly remember those days—living below the poverty line before there was such a thing—as the turning point in my life.

Several important things happened to me after we moved to Pocahontas. I finally started growing and filling out. In the space of my junior year at PHS, I grew five inches and gained thirty pounds. I now stood six feet tall and weighed 155 pounds, all muscle. Not surprisingly, I made the football team, the basketball team, and the track team. In summer, I played American Legion baseball.

I was fortunate to have two coaches who cared about me. In my junior year, it was Coach Aubrey "Cob" Fowler. In my senior year, Coach Howard "Choo Choo" Powers replaced Coach Fowler. Both coaches were powerful influences in my life because they were good men who came to me at the right time. Coach Fowler was lightning fast. They called him Cob because he was tough as a cob in his days as a track star and scat-back for the Arkansas Razorbacks. They called Coach Powers Choo Choo because he was a powerful running back at Arkansas State. They both saw my potential as a quarterback based on the skills and game sense I had developed as a baseball player.

I became a good passing quarterback and quite adept at working the classic T-formation. When I became the starting quarterback in my senior year, Coach Powers designed a double wing formation similar to the modern wildcat formation that we would run occasionally to confuse the opponent. It included a spinner play where I would take a direct snap from the center, turn my back to the line, fake a handoff to the right halfback and then fake a handoff to the left halfback who was going in the opposite direction; finally, I would complete a 360-degree spin and run the ball off right tackle. It was a tricky play for those days and the first time we tried it I went 84 yards, unmolested, for a touchdown. The play became a staple in our repertoire. It never failed to fool the defense and it always opened a big hole and produced a good gain—except for the night we played Augusta High School. That game found us up against Coach Curtis King, one of the best high school coaches in the state. He had been scouting us and he had a big, tough country boy named Billy Ray Smith playing defensive tackle. Billy Ray later starred for the Arkansas Razorbacks and then played several years with legendary Johnny Unitas and the Baltimore Colt teams. The first time I tried the spinner play against Augusta, I, upon completion of my fancy 360-degree spin wound up in the arms of Billy Ray Smith. He lifted me entirely off the ground and said, "Not tonight little darling," then smashed me to the ground, hard. I tried the play two more times but got the same result. We lost the game to Augusta. Fortunately, the other teams on our schedule were not into scouting, so the spinner play worked well for the rest of the season.

It surprised no one in my family that I did well in sports. What did surprise everyone were my achievements off the athletic field. I had an important role in the Junior Play and an even bigger part in the Senior Play. I made the Honor Roll every semester and I was active in a host of intramural activities.

Jim Barden, a new PHS classmate and a prolific reader who became a writer and national editor for *The New York Times,* turned me on to the works of Frank Yerby. I read a number of his books, but the one that sticks in my mind is the *Saracen Blade,* a historical novel about the Crusades featuring a hero with indomitable willpower. Yerby, an African American, wrote movingly of the human spirit and I often stayed up overnight reading his works. Another book that touched me deeply was *Captain from Castile,* by Samuel Shellabarger. The hero, Pedro de Vargas, was with Cortez on his exploration of the New World. The chaplain of the army, Father Bartolomé de Olmedo preached equality for all humankind and urged Pedro to understand that the zest of life is the quest, the pursuit of dreams—the effort, not the attainment is what really matters. It is no surprise, looking back, that I was attracted to books with high-minded protagonists going against the odds, relying mainly on dreams and willpower. These and similar books shaped my thinking at a time when I was very receptive. I am convinced that the ideas I embraced then influenced the decisions I made throughout my life.

Barden also holds the distinction of catching the last touchdown pass I threw as quarterback for the Pocahontas Redskins. It was Homecoming Day and we were playing the Walnut Ridge Bobcats, our archrival. I burned a bullet to Barden from the five-yard line and that gave us the win. The play worked so well that we tried it again for the extra point. Alas, the Bobcats smeared Barden at the line and sacked me. Later in life Jim—a lucky man—married the homecoming queen, Mel Bradley, the most beautiful girl in school. In 1981, they came to see me in

Washington, D. C. and we had a mini-reunion in my congressional office.

I attended First Methodist Church in Pocahontas mainly because a number of my friends were going there. It was a good thing for me to do even though I still did not see church as much more than another place to meet new people and be with my friends.

I suppose I could have found my place in Little Rock, but I did not. In Pocahontas, the townspeople opened their arms, took me in, and made me feel at home. They kidded me, complimented me, encouraged me, and criticized me. Almost overnight, I had an army of surrogate fathers, mothers, brothers, sisters, and friends. The good feeling I had about the town included a hodgepodge of memories from my childhood visits—BB gun fights, River Rats, Uncle Leaf the glasses man, Papa the town drunk, *Custer's Last Stand,* and the bobcat—but there was more to it than that. In a little town when you meet a stranger on the street, you just keep eye contact, raise your chin a little and they will do the same—that is all you have to do, nothing more—a simple sign of recognition, of brotherhood. In a little town, all eyes are on you, and there are few secrets. People are sharing miseries and living on a shoestring, but they are thankful for what they have. All together, it gave me a sense of belonging that I desperately needed and to top it off, a goodly number of men took a special interest in me because of my achievements on the baseball diamond and the football field. Lloyd Lewallen, Jim Burke, Charlie Promberger, and several others took the time to give me the encouragement and attention that I craved. I was finally getting the mentoring from adult men that I had missed because of my father's absence. In Pocahontas, I was secure; I had found a place I could always come back to when I needed a rock to stand on.

Then, of course, there were my first honest-to-goodness girlfriends. On my first serious date, I did not know what to do. I had played Kick the Can, Spin the Bottle, and other kissing games at house parties in Little Rock, but I was so naive that the first girl

I got serious with told me, "You will make someone a good husband, someday." I asked her what she meant by that and she said, "Because you are so innocent." She meant it as a compliment, but it hurt my pride.

Using the logic of a teenager, I worked hard to fix my innocence problem, as if it were a flaw. Like all teenagers, I was in a hurry to grow up and be an adult. Since my mother was elsewhere, and my father was out west, I no longer had the problem that many kids have when they try to separate from parental control. I did not need independence. I just wanted to be grown up. Pocahontas was a good place to learn such things without getting into a lot of trouble.

Current River flows from Missouri into Arkansas and connects to the Black River just north of Pocahontas. There are a number of sizeable sandbars along the Current River, but the biggest one lies immediately downstream from the Highway 67 Bridge where the sand is nearly a hundred feet in width. Everyone calls that place, "Current River Beach." It is the best swimming hole in all of Northeast Arkansas and on any given day of any summer in the early 1950s, you would find scores of people swimming, sunning themselves, or hanging out in a big, whitewashed wooden pavilion that doubled as a snack bar and dance hall. The pavilion was on the downriver side of the sandbar and it was built-up on stilts because Current River would flood from time to time. Small cabins, owned by "rich people" dotted the riverbank north of the bridge and south of the pavilion. It was the place to go for a good time.

Randolph County was "dry" but it was easy to find a local bootlegger and failing that, it was only twenty miles to the Missouri line where booze and beer were readily available and gasoline was only nineteen cents a gallon. Nevertheless, people who drank alcohol did their best to hide their drinking from others because Current River Beach was a fun place and there was little tolerance for troublemakers.

There was one incident involving a drunk that could have ended badly. One night, after dark, my girlfriend, Margaret

McFall and I were sitting in a circle near the bridge with three other couples. We had spent a wonderful day swimming and sunning ourselves, and we had danced in the pavilion to a number of our favorite tunes, including Johnny Ray's version of "Cry," a song that was number one on all the charts. A large barrel-chested guy, who was quite a bit older, was just a few feet from us bragging and showing off to his friends. Big Shot was obviously trying to impress our dates as well as his friends, so he began to crow about how many times he had dived off the highway bridge that crossed the river. Soon he drew a double-dog dare to dive off the bridge in the dark. That raised the stakes because it was dangerous to dive from the bridge into the river in daylight, but at night there was always the chance of hitting a floating log or other object. The alcohol took its toll on the braggart's judgment and he headed into the shadows, on his way to the highway and the bridge. Big Shot was going to take the dare and make the dive. We were interested, which is what he wanted, but it took him some time to get up onto the highway and walk out onto the bridge. It was a dark, moonless night. He could not see us and we could not see him. He hollered to us several times in an effort to determine where he was in relation to the river. Eventually, he figured he was over water so he said, "Here I go!" We were expecting to hear a splash, but instead we heard a loud thump. Big Shot had not walked far enough onto the bridge. His dive ended on the sand bar about fifty feet from where we sat. It is a wonder he did not kill himself. He got up and with a groan skulked off into the dark to avoid further embarrassment. At first, we were concerned but one of his friends caught up with him and shouted back to us that he was fine. We never saw him again but the story of Big Shot's nighttime dive lives on at Current River Beach.

The pleasures and frustrations of sexual discovery and the attendant heartthrobs and heartbreaks that I experienced at PHS were, as with all teenagers, an essential part of my passage from puberty to early manhood.

Don Cox was in my class and became a close friend for life. His father owned cotton gins, land, and livestock but Don did not act like a rich kid. He had a new car and some other material advantages, but he has always been a regular guy and I have never heard anyone speak ill of him. Another close friend was John "Butch" Stolt. He was a year behind me in school, but he was strong as an ox and a good football player. His father was the night-law in Pocahontas, and his mother, Lucille Stolt, could have been a Bethune. She was warm, friendly, and loving and she opened her arms to me. She seemed to understand that I needed attention and when I was around her, she treated me as if I were one of her own. The girls in my class, Norma Sue, Betty Sue, Betty Lou, Mary Nell, and a long list of other double name sweethearts, were salt-of-the-earth types. All these friends, as well as the Spikes boys, played important roles in my new world.

There was another young man I met because I was on the football team. His name was Clifford, a black youngster who volunteered to serve as our team mascot and helper. Everyone on the team loved Clifford. He was fast and had the potential to be a good player, but he could not join our team or attend PHS. It was 1952 and the country was still following the separate but equal doctrine of *Plessy v. Ferguson,* a case decided in 1896 that provided legal justification for segregation. The United States Supreme Court overruled the *Plessy* decision in 1954 in the landmark case, *Brown v. Board of Education,* but the decision to end segregation came too late for Clifford. He got his high school diploma, but only because he was willing to ride thirty-five miles each way every day to Jonesboro, the nearest school for blacks. I think of Clifford nowadays when I see the disproportionately large number of black athletes playing football for the best college and professional football teams. I lost track of Clifford, but I hope he is satisfied with the way things have changed and that he remembers me as fondly as I remember him.

In the summer, I played as much baseball as I could. When I first got to Pocahontas, I bragged to some of the boys on the American Legion team that Coach George Haynie, the remarkable coach for the outstanding Little Rock Doughboy team (an American Legion baseball team that achieved national prominence) had invited me to try out for the Doughboys when I was in the tenth grade. The word spread to Tom Baker who was the best all-sports athlete at PHS and, as luck would have it, he happened to be pitching batting practice on the day I made my first appearance at the plate. All eyes were on me and Baker said, just before he threw me his best fastball, "Hit this one, Doughboy!" If I had whiffed, the catcalling and joking would have stuck to me like glue. I never wanted to hit a ball as much as I wanted to hit Tom Baker's fastball and hit it I did! My hard line-drive sailed into the gap in left field— easily a double or triple at Camden Yards, the home of the Baltimore Orioles. Redemption is sweet.

It is true that I was an excellent player, and Coach Haynie did want me to play for the Doughboys, even though I was not a particularly fast runner. Raymond Mock, who claimed to have played professional baseball in the minor leagues, first saw me play when I was catching for the Pocahontas American Legion team. He believed I was good enough to make it to the "Bigs" as a catcher. Raymond was in his forties when I knew him, but he was still playing semi-professional ball on the weekends. He was too old to play catcher, the position he played in his early years, but he was still a good hitter so teams would hire him to play outfield. Most every town of any size had a semi-pro team and the games drew good crowds in those days before television. Raymond took me under his arm and when my Legion team was not playing, we offered our talents to the semi-pro teams. There was a team in Corning, about thirty miles north of Pocahontas that liked Raymond and took his word that I could help the team. We played for them several times. To get there we would ride the bus from Pocahontas and the manager of the team gave us cash to cover the cost of our tickets, with a little pocket change left over. Once, on the bus trip from Corning to Pocahontas with Raymond I remember stopping in the little community of Datto, Arkansas. The driver shouted back to a black man in the rear of the bus, "Do you want to get off here?" The black man was sleeping and did not hear the driver. Raymond Mock told the driver: "He doesn't want to get off in Datto, they don't allow niggers here." Everyone on the bus laughed, but I was embarrassed. I thought of Clifford, but to my shame, I did not tell Raymond that I did not like it that he called the man a "nigger" and ridiculed him in public. It reminded me of the way people hated the "good Japanese" and the "good Germans." Still I said nothing. I did not like myself for not saying something, but I took some comfort with the fact that I was uneasy with what had happened.

My semi-pro baseball play probably violated the rules that amateurs were supposed to follow, but I loved to play so much that I really did not worry about it at the time.

In the summer of 1952 my football teammate and friend, Bill Templeton, and I spent several days floating down the Black River in an old fourteen-foot wooden boat that Temp had scrounged from somewhere. The boat was waterlogged and heavy, and it leaked like a sieve but every five minutes or so we bailed it out with old coffee cans we kept at the ready. We fished with cane poles and used worms that we dug for bait. We had no motor so it was a job to get from one side of the river to the other. All along the way, we fished the snags and the treetops keeping the sluggish boat in place with our paddles. We usually caught a good mess of fish—all kinds—but predominately catfish, bream and bass.

Our biggest challenge was logistical. We started our trips by tying the boat on top of Temp's 1940 convertible and driving to a favorite spot upriver where we would put-in. After a lazy day of floating and fishing, we took-out at the Highway 67 Bridge, a distance of ten miles downriver. We secured the boat, hid our catch in the river on a stringer, and hitchhiked back to the spot where we had left Temp's car. Then we drove back to the Highway 67 Bridge to retrieve, clean and dress our catch, pull the boat out of the water and tie it on top of the car. Within minutes, we were home and Delta Lew was frying the fish and making corndodgers. To top it off she would slice some tomatoes from our garden and cut a big onion. The feasting did not end until we were all stuffed.

Most importantly, perhaps because of all the good things that happened to me in this little town, I suddenly stopped wetting the bed. I still had an occasional mishap, one (which I will tell about later) that almost brought me down, but for the most part, I seemed to be through with that particular problem. I now believe, based on all that I have read, that my bedwetting may have been physiological in the beginning, but it was surely aggravated by the separation and divorce of my parents and the battle that raged deep within me to reconcile the conflicting Vermilye and Bethune worldviews. The best evidence that the bedwetting problem was largely in my head was that it went away as soon as I began to find my place and purpose in life in the little town of Pocahontas, Arkansas.

10

OFF TO COLLEGE AND OUT OF COLLEGE

I never let schooling interfere with my education
Mark Twain

As I approached high school graduation, I had to come to grips with what I was going to do next. No one on either side of my family had graduated from college and only a few had graduated from high school. I would have to figure out the business of going to college for myself and that was hard because I had absolutely no idea what college was like and the only thing I knew anything about, other than sports and public school, was the second-hand furniture business.

From the time I was a little boy, it was apparent that we could not afford college, so there was little talk of it. Mother kept telling me the main reason to finish high school was, "You need to get an education because they can't take that away from you." On the rare occasion when I did talk to Mother about college she insisted that if I did go I should learn to be a dentist. In her mind, Dr. "Booge" Spikes, of Pocahontas had it made and that is what I should be, a dentist. Never mind that I had no aptitude for science or the regimented life of a dentist.

Most of my high school classmates did not go to college. A few did talk about it and planned to go. Don Cox, one of my best friends, was one of those and he encouraged me to go with him.

I had no other plans and the only practical alternative was to go into the military. I did not know how I would pay for college, but tuition to the University of Arkansas was only $50 a semester. Maybe there was a way I could do it.

College did not start right away, so my classmate Cecil Keith and I got a job at a lumberyard in Hoxie, Arkansas, about fifteen miles from Pocahontas. We were stacking lumber all day long. I would use a metal jack to hoist the planks to the top of the stack and Cecil would catch them and lay them out. Occasionally, Cecil and I would switch jobs, but I did not like being on top of the stack because it was rickety and the higher it got the more chance there was that it would topple over. This hard labor work experience, coupled with the prospect that I might end up working a jackhammer or something equally as bad, made going to college look better and better.

Mama Lewallen, Mother and Delta Lew came up with the money to pay my tuition and the first couple of months at Pop Gregson Hall, a boy's dormitory. I decided to join Don Cox as a freshman at the university. We enrolled in summer school to get a head start on other freshmen. I made passing grades in English and a required history course, Western Civilization.

Then I enrolled in the fall semester and pledged Kappa Sigma fraternity. I was bleeding my mother and sister dry and the odd jobs I had picking up laundry and cleaning and working on lawns simply did not cover the essentials. More importantly, I was only seventeen years old and I was not ready for college. The undisciplined fraternity house environment did not help. I spent most of my time goofing off and I was using too much of the money I made from part-time jobs for beer and cigarettes, bad habits I picked up after finishing high school and what I thought would be the end of my athletic career. Moreover, because Mother wanted me to be a dentist, I enrolled in the School of Arts and Sciences. I was required to take freshman biology and chemistry, two courses that absolutely mystified my unscientific brain. My fate was sealed. It was easier to duck out than to grapple with those courses. I was well on my way to flunking out of college.

11

SEMPER FIDELIS

The Marines I have seen around the world have the cleanest bodies, the filthiest minds, the highest morale, and the lowest morals of any group of animals I have ever seen. Thank God for the United States Marine Corps!
Eleanor Roosevelt, First Lady of the United States, 1945

It was apparent as I neared the end of the fall semester that I would flunk every science course I was taking, so in late December 1953, I joined the United States Marine Corps. Not knowing any better, I did a dumb thing after I signed the enlistment papers. I just dropped out of the University of Arkansas. I did not go back to school after the holidays. I did not formally withdraw nor did I tell anyone at the university that I was leaving. I just left. I did not appreciate it at that time, but failing to go through the formal withdrawal process put twelve hours of F on my transcript. Later in life, when I returned to college and started making good grades the twelve hours of F were a constant drag on my grade point. My stupid decision was just another example of how I, with my Vermilye hardhead, had to learn the hard way.

On January 20, 1954, I reported to Robinson Memorial Auditorium in Little Rock, where former Governor Sid McMath, a World War II Marine who had just finished his second term as governor, swore me and seventy other Arkansas boys in as recruits in the United States Marine Corps. We spent the night at the YMCA on Sixth and Broadway and early the next morning we met at the Rock Palace Café for breakfast. We boarded buses that took us to Adams Field where we caught an American Airlines flight that would take us to San Diego via Dallas, Texas. It was my first flight in a real commercial airplane and the thing I remember most is the drop-dead beautiful American Airlines flight attendant (she called herself a "stewardess") who was taking care of us and calming our nerves. A photographer for the statewide newspaper boarded the plane and took a picture of me after I buckled into my seat. The flight attendant was helping me settle in so she was in the picture that appeared in the newspaper the next day. The caption noted that I was part of the Arkansas Traveler Platoon that had joined the U. S. Marines. The flight to Dallas seemed long even though we were in a new four-engine airplane, but the trip from Dallas to San Diego was longer and scary because we were plagued with rough thunderstorms along the way. In those days pilots could not detect storms as well as they can today, and the old gasoline motored planes could not fly high enough or fast enough to get around the trouble. The pilot did the best he could but it was a bumpy ride.

When we arrived at Lindbergh Field in San Diego around 1:00 a.m., a sergeant met us and loaded us onto a bus that had no seats. He unceremoniously told me and the other recruits, "Get your dumb asses on the cattle-car."

After a short ride, we passed through the main gate of the Marine Corps Recruit Depot (MCRD) in San Diego, California. I saw the unmistakable gold and red signs of the United States Marine Corps. My new and different life as a brand-new boot camp recruit was underway. I would never be the same.

The sergeant got us off the cattle car and herded us into a barracks. We formed a line to get our fart-sacks and pillows, one each per recruit. We each found an empty bunk, quickly put on the fart-sack and pillow, and collapsed into a deep sleep. At 4:00 a.m., a terrible racket awakened us. One of the Marines was sliding a Coke bottle around the inside of an empty metal, corrugated garbage can. The racket was interspersed with him, in a rude voice, growling to us, "Hit the deck, shitheads." It was a culture shock for me, a boy who had had no parental supervision for several years. I was unprepared for the harsh discipline that began the moment we got off the bus at MCRD. I knew it would be tough, but you never fully understand Marine Corps discipline until you experience it personally. After rousting us from our bunks, they ordered us to "Get outside and fall-in on the grinder." We did not know what they meant by grinder, but we had enough sense to go outside. When we were out of the building, they told us to put our feet on pairs of yellow feet that were painted on the tarmac. That forced us into four rows of seventeen each. The enlisted Marine who would be our drill instructor, Staff Sergeant Lorres, suddenly appeared before us.

He was dressed in starched, freshly laundered dungarees, the pale green fighting outfit that Marines had worn all through World War II and the Korean War. The trousers had a sharp crease and he wore a campaign hat that marked him as a drill instructor. He was not a big man but he was in perfect physical condition. He had an aura of authority that never diminished; in fact, we gained respect for him as we learned more about him. It turned out that he was a survivor of the Chosin Reservoir, one of the great battles in Marine Corps history.

Sergeant Lorres ordered us to snap to attention. I, fortunately, had taken a few classes in ROTC at the University of Arkansas and had marched in the band at East Side Junior High School, so I had at least a working knowledge of what to do when told to stand at attention. I froze, but the boy next to me did not. He and some of the other boys had no idea what to do. They made the mistake of moving and mumbling. Sergeant Lorres repeatedly barked the command, "Stand still and shut the fuck up." He then disappeared behind the four lines and it was still for a moment, except for the faint noise made by those who were still mumbling and moving. Suddenly, out of the corner of my eye I saw a boy near me propelled forward head over heels. Sergeant Lorres had rushed through the ranks and plowed into the hapless recruit from behind. He then reeled off a string of obscenities that made no sense. The stunned recruit jumped up and got back in formation. We did not understand Sergeant Lorres' cusswords, but we all got the message. We were in for a tough new way of life and it was definitely a good thing to do whatever the drill instructor seemed to want.

On our first full day we drew our brand new dungarees, skivvies (underwear), boondockers (boots), covers (hats), toiletries, and 782 gear (a webbed belt on which to attach a canteen, ammunition, etc.). We were "marched" to the barbershop for the famous Marine Corps recruit haircut. The barber made six swipes with large electric clippers and I was, in a blink, a bald recruit with a brand-new cover that was now one size too large. The indignity of that moment is an important part of the Marine Corps technique, tested over the years, to make Marines out of runny-nose civilian kids.

Next we were marched (herded would be a better word) to our assigned quarters, three Quonset huts positioned on the east side of a field containing hundreds of similar huts. A separate shack called the Head (meaning toilets, showers, and sinks) was nearby. This would be our home for the next three months.

The next few days were a mixture of physical examinations, shots, and instructions on how to make a bunk and outfit your footlocker. There were precise methods for doing everything in the Marine Corps and woe unto the recruit that misunderstood or ignored that rule.

By the third day, the drill instructor was managing to keep us in reasonably tight formation. He quickly identified those who were out-of-step, treating their incompetence with a sophisticated blend of ridicule and corporal punishment. Their learning curve took a sharp turn upward and soon we were beginning to look like a military unit, except for the conspicuously dark color of our dungarees and covers, which were still brand new, and unlaundered. We soon learned that the color-shade of a platoon's dungarees was a telltale sign of how long they had been at MCRD. We hungered for the day when our uniforms would have that washed out look.

Marching in the Marine Corps, officially called Close Order Drill, is truly different. The drill instructors each have a unique cadence count and their orders are indecipherable to an untrained civilian ear. Early on, recruits learn that Marine drill instructors want you to dig your heels in on every step. It is how they judge the level of synchronization, and they are never happy until the entire platoon sounds like one big heel hitting the ground. "Heels, heels, heels," the drill instructor will intersperse those words into his cadence count until he is satisfied with what he hears.

It is hard to imitate Sergeant Lorres' cadence count and it is nigh impossible to write how it sounded. Suffice to say, it was musical, singsong in style, and it changed from time to time depending upon his mood, but his base cadence, from which all others evolved, sounded like this: "One, Two, Three—Rite idle Lelf—Rite idle Lelf."

Within a week, we began to get the routine. Up at 4:30 a.m., shit, shower, shave and get dressed—make up bunks, square away the Quonset hut, and fall out for morning muster. All this we did in less than thirty minutes, and at 5:00 a.m., we were marching away from our area, out onto the grinder, and bearing left to the Mess Hall.

Boot camp mess halls work like a precision timepiece. Each platoon forms up outside, waiting for its turn to march into chow. When it was time for our platoon to go in Sergeant Lorres would position us near the front door in a single line, and then he would say, "At a half-step, forward march."

As we shuffled forward, Sergeant Lorres would order us to tighten up the line: "Close it up—close it up—assholes and bellybuttons—assholes and bellybuttons!"

The NCO in charge of the mess hall takes over once recruits are actually in the building and no matter how many times we entered his mess hall his first order was: "Each man will take one knife, one fork, and one spoon."

Finally, our line reached a row of steam tables, a stack of metal trays, and the food. The NCO would then remind us that recruits in the chow line must extend their arms and tray over the steam table if we wanted the server to slop on a serving of a particular food. Oral communication is wasted effort. It does no good to tell the server you want something, if you do not stick out your tray, you will get nothing. This is an important decision point because you are always hungry, but the NCO makes it clear that you must eat whatever you take. A reckless move could result in an unwanted serving of brains and eggs, beef liver, salt mackerel, or tasteless succotash.

Once through the line the platoon sits together. Recruits can talk but there is no time for a casual meal. The drill instructor allows only twenty minutes for the meal because he must empty the tables to make room for the next platoon of hungry recruits. Once outside and in formation the drill instructor may, or may not depending on how he feels, say, "The smoking lamp is lit." It is the only time recruits are allowed to smoke (cigarettes only), and once finished we were required to fieldstrip the butts. That is, we had to carefully tear away the paper and roll it into a tiny ball that we put in our pocket. The leftover tobacco was scattered with the wind.

There was a similar rule against eating candy, known in the Marine Corps as pogeybait. There were no vending machines near our quarters, but pogeybait was available in machines near the Chapel, which we could attend on Sunday mornings. The punishment for unauthorized smoking or the unauthorized eating of pogeybait was a decision left solely to the discretion of the drill instructor.

In the eighth week of our training, our platoon got a new assistant drill instructor, Private First Class Johnson, a real prick. He was nothing like Sergeant Lorres; in fact, he was a sadist. We could tell that Sergeant Lorres did not like Johnson, but he could do nothing about his assignment to our platoon. One night when Lorres was off duty, Johnson overplayed his hand. He caught two of our people, one smoking when the smoking lamp was out, and the other eating pogeybait. He made the smoker put several Camel cigarettes in his mouth, lit them, and then put a bucket and then a blanket over the recruit's head and made him smoke the cigarettes. He damn near suffocated. Then, Johnson made the candy-eater chew up an entire box of Milky Way bars. As he ate them, PFC Johnston hit him in the stomach, repeatedly. The chewed-up candy backed up into the man's nasal passages and caused him to have two black eyes as well as an episode of uncontrollable vomiting. He had to go to sickbay (the Navy Hospital). When the doctors who attended him reported the facts to the commanding officer of our battalion, they court marshaled PFC Johnson. His stupid mistake was one that he could not cover up or deny. In those days, there were not many prosecutions for recruit mistreatment because the Marine Corps tolerated a relatively high level of corporal punishment in the discipline of recruits. Nevertheless, they busted PFC Johnson and he spent the next few months in the brig. The feeling amongst members of Platoon 213 was that the punishment of Johnson could not have happened to a more deserving son of a bitch.

In our second week, the DI marched us to the armory where the armorer issued an M-1 rifle to each recruit. These weapons were the same rifles that Marines had used in World War II and Korea. Sergeant Lorres ordered us to memorize the serial number of our rifle and told us, "A rifle is a Marine's best friend." He told us to keep it clean and treat it as if it were a family heirloom. We learned that every Marine is, first and foremost, a rifleman. Later, we spent two weeks at nearby Camp Matthews where we learned to shoot like Marines. I easily qualified as a sharpshooter, falling just short of the expert medal.

Boot camp is running, running, and more running. Then there are drills and work details. Double-time is the order of the day. The only time they allowed us to stop running or working was when we were eating, sleeping, or sitting still for a class or demonstration. The hardest thing about boot camp was to stay awake during a lecture on military history, or anything for that matter. Sergeant Lorres made it plain that falling asleep in class was akin to unauthorized smoking or candy eating so the pressure was immense. We all nodded off—we could not help it—particularly if we had just come inside from the cold. Sergeant Lorres would rap us on the head with his fist on the first offense, but woe unto the recruit who nodded off more than once.

There was one demonstration where falling asleep was not possible. It was during the afternoon that they marched us into the gas chamber with gas masks on. Once we were inside they unleashed a heavy dose of tear gas. After the chamber was full of gas, they ordered us to remove our masks and sing, as loudly as we could, the entire "Marine Corps Hymn." As soon as we finished the last word of the hymn, we barreled out of the gas chamber and rolled around on the ground trying to restore our respiratory function. It took about an hour to get back to normal. What was the lesson? Gas masks work, but you have to be wearing them.

One day, about a month into boot camp they ordered us to climb a rope ladder to a platform fifty feet above the ground. As I approached the top, the assistant drill instructor up there saw that I was struggling. He stuck his face in mine and growled: "Don't even think about saying you can't make it, where there's a will there's a way." Whoa! I had heard those words all my life. This was like family. I wanted to ask the drill instructor if he was part Vermilye, but of course, he would not know what I meant, so I did not ask him. Hey, I thought, I have a home in the Corps. I scurried over the top and that afternoon I was designated First Squad leader and put in charge of a squad of sixteen of my fellow recruits.

Strangely, that night, for the first time in almost three years, I wet the bed. I do not know why, but looking back, I think it had something to do with my new sense that the Corps was now my home. I guess I just relaxed or something, anyway I thoroughly pissed on myself and soaked the bunk, the blankets and the sheets. How was I going to cover this up? I had two challenges. I had to keep it secret from my fellow recruits, and most importantly, I had to deceive the drill instructor. It was the DI's practice to pass through our Quonset hut each day after we were outside in formation. If he saw one wrinkle in a bunk, he would tear up the bedding and call the offending recruit out before the platoon for an ass chewing. He always found one offender each day, always. If he were to focus on my bunk and tear up my bedding, I would be undone. I would be humiliated and sent to see a Navy psychiatrist.

Fortunately, I was good at keeping all my clothes and equipment in perfect order. The Marine Corps is anal about keeping one's gear in perfect order, and there are all sorts of regulations and inspections to keep the troops from backsliding into a slovenly civilian attitude. The ultimate was the Full Field Inspection, otherwise known in the vernacular as Junk on the Bunk or Things on the Springs. During such an inspection, a Marine must lay out all his possessions, in perfect order, on a perfectly made-up bunk. The footlocker must be open, ready for inspection. It is the pinnacle of personal accountability. Many a recruit underestimated the importance of absolute precision. They paid dearly, but I seemed to have a knack for doing Junk on the Bunk. The DI always complimented me and used my display as a model to teach other members of the platoon.

If Sergeant Lorres, or our company commander had called for a Full Field Inspection there was no way I could have kept my secret. I do not think I have ever been as scared as I was each morning that I awoke to find myself in a wet bunk. I would slip out of the rack, get out of my wet skivvy shorts and make up the bed, wet as it was. I was lucky that the dark olive-drab wool blanket did not show dampness, and the general odor of the hut overcame the slight odor of piss. I pulled the blanket so tight that a quarter-coin tossed down on it would bounce up a few inches. That, I knew, was what the drill instructor was looking for. If he saw a wrinkle or a wave in the blanket, he would tear the bedding right off of the bunk. I might be able to get by for a few more days, but if they called for a Full Field Inspection, I would never make it. They would discover my secret and I would be a goner. I had to get control of my situation, and I had to do it soon.

I worried all day, every day, of this last wet period in my life. I loved the Corps and I wanted to make it through boot camp and become a full-fledged Marine. I certainly did not want the Marine Corps to discharge me as a bedwetter. If that had happened, the public humiliation I avoided for the first fifteen years of my life would become a reality. I do not know what I would have done, or how I would have handled it if they had caught me with my wet bed. My military career, and in my mind, my entire life was at stake. If caught I would have to see the "talking doctor," also known as a "head doctor" in Marine Corps jargon. These were the Navy psychiatrists who discharged all recruits they found to be unsuited for military service, usually because a problem recruit was too immature, a crybaby, or a bedwetter.

Looking back on it, it is now funny, but it was not funny at the time. For three nights, I tried everything from staying awake to not drinking liquids after noon. I thought about sleeping on the floor, but backed out of that plan because it would have created suspicion that might have led someone to check out my bunk. Nothing seemed to work, I kept wetting the bed. On the fourth night, my bunk began to smell. To make matters worse the next day was the day designated for turning in our dirty linens and drawing clean ones. I needed to do something, and I needed to do it right away. I concluded that, somehow, I had to get rid of the soaked mattress and get a clean, dry one. I developed a plan. The Quonset hut next to mine was vacant. A graduating platoon had just left. I looked in and saw that there were dry mattresses in there, but I needed help to make the exchange. It had to be done surreptitiously, in the middle of the night. The close quarters of our hut made it impossible for me to carry a mattress in or out without hitting or at least waking someone. A high school classmate from Pocahontas, Bob Borner, was in my squad thus he was in my hut. In desperation, I decided to take Borner into my confidence and ask for his help. I woke him up and whispered for him to be quiet. Then I whispered to him that I was having a problem and needed to switch my mattress without asking anyone's permission. He was half-asleep, but I think he could see how much I needed him. He did not ask questions, he just slid out of bed and we each grabbed an end of my wet mattress and carried it to the door of our hut. I do not think anyone saw us, at least no one said anything. There was a Fire Watch (Marine Corps terminology for an all night guard) stationed in another hut that was next to the empty hut. It was his job to stay awake and be alert so Bob and I could not talk aloud or make the slightest noise. I would be in the most trouble, but Bob would also catch Hell, just for helping me. There were roaming guards who patrolled the whole area, but we saw no one when we opened the door and peeped out. All was clear so we hustled across the open space and into the vacant hut. We dumped the wet mattress on an upper bunk and started out of the vacant hut with a dry mattress. When we hit the open space we scampered, dry mattress in tow, to our hut and quietly opened the door. We got the mattress through the door and only had a few feet to go when I stumped my toe on a footlocker that someone had failed to push under his bunk. I saw stars and bit my tongue until it bled. God, it hurt, but I could not make a sound.

Finally, we were at my bunk. I got the dry mattress in place and thanked Bob profusely. I pledged him to secrecy and told him I would explain fully at breakfast.

I had managed to dodge a bullet so far. When reveille sounded and everyone was getting up, I was the first to throw my dirty and soiled sheets into the outgoing laundry bin. Ha! The evidence was now out of my hands. I had a dry mattress and later that day I would draw clean linens. I had lived to fight another day. At breakfast, I told Bob a little white lie. I told him I did not know why I had pissed in the rack, but I was sure it would not happen again. I asked him to protect my secret and he pledged that he would. He did.

The emergency midnight maneuver to exchange my wet mattress for a dry one somehow solved my problem. My mysterious episode of bedwetting stopped as suddenly, and unexplainably, as it had started and I never had trouble with it after that. I have often thought how my life would have changed if I had been summarily discharged from the Marine Corps as a bedwetter.

By the third month of boot camp, we were a hardened and competent platoon of recruits. We were still "shitheads" to the enlisted drill instructors, or "recruits" if an officer was in the area, but we were making progress and it was noticeable. It is an amazing experience to see the difference that three months of boot camp can make on a group of teenagers. Our pride and confidence showed up when we marched, singing at the top of our voice. "Lift your head and hold it high, Honey; lift your head and hold it high, Babe; Lift your head and hold it high, 213 is passing by; Honey, Baby, mine." This tune, sung to the cadence of marching, also worked with a variety of other lyrics, for example: "I got a girl in Kansas City, Honey; I got a girl in Kansas City, Babe; I got a girl in Kansas City—she's got a wart on her left titty; Honey, Baby, mine." There were other verses, equally sophisticated, and we sang them repeatedly as we marched.

At the end of our training period our drill instructor congratulated us and told us, "I never thought I would be able to say it, but you shitheads are now United States Marines, welcome aboard." Upon the recommendation of Sergeant Lorres, I received an award as the outstanding recruit for Platoon 213. I saved the certificate and it remains one of my proudest possessions.

That same day, April 13, 1954, I marched with my platoon in the graduation parade. I was in the front rank as First Squad leader. My heart filled with pride and thanksgiving and tears came to my eyes when the band struck up the Marine Corps Hymn and we passed in review. The men in my squad snapped their heads toward the reviewing stand when Sergeant Lorres gave the "Eyes right" command and our commanding officers returned the salute. I was now a United States Marine. Semper Fidelis!

I got orders to report from San Diego Marine Corps Recruit Depot to El Toro Marine Corps Air Station, Santa Ana, California, to work in air intelligence. I had ten days leave that I could take before reporting, so I decided to take the train from San Diego to Little Rock. What an experience. Like most boys, I loved trains. I had never taken a serious train trip, but I was about to take one now.

It took two full days to get from San Diego to Little Rock and I loved every minute of it. In those days, passengers could raise and lower the windows in the coach cars and we took our meals in a sit-down dining car staffed with porters in starched white coats. The meals were fantastic, especially after twelve weeks of boot camp chow.

I stayed two days with Mother in Little Rock and then caught the bus to Pocahontas. On my first day there, I wore my dungarees and boondockers and strutted around town and to the beach at Current River. It was against regulation to wear the dungarees in public, but I was puffed up with pride. It was not long before my old friends teased me for showing off. Since that is exactly what I was doing, it got to me. I took off the dungarees and never again broke that regulation. For the train trip back to California, I followed the rules and wore my dress uniform bearing the single chevron of a newly appointed private first class.

When I got back from Arkansas and reported to El Toro, I got my first liberty, an official pass to go off the base for the entire weekend. A new friend, Technical Sergeant Seimer, invited me to go with him to Long Beach to do what single Marines usually do when they go on liberty; check out the girlie shows and drink. By midnight Saturday I was stinko, a perfect target for the silver-tongued hustlers luring Marines and sailors into an infinite array of brightly lit tattoo parlors. Soon I was next in line to get a three-color globe and anchor with USMC beneath it tattooed on my upper left arm. I would have it today if Sergeant Seimer—a true old salt and a veteran of World War II—had not intervened. He pulled me out of the tattoo parlor and promised that he would bring me back the next day and pay for the tattoo if I still wanted it. Tattoos are all the rage nowadays, but one day those who resist the urge may join me in saying, "Thanks again, Sarge."

On May 2, 1954, I received orders to report to the Intelligence Section of an aviation squadron where I began my work as an intelligence specialist. There I met a number of Marine Corps pilots who encouraged me to apply for the Naval Air Cadet program and become an officer. That forced me to think seriously about my future. I already knew that I did not want to be an enlisted man for the rest of my life, but I was not sure whether I wanted a career as an officer in the Marine Corps.

I was now eighteen years old, but I had never had *one* mentor to replace my father. My idea about how I should develop was a collection of thoughts that I had pieced together from *all* the men who had taken the time to mentor me, at school, in the Corps, in Boy's Club, Scouts, band, and sports. While this can be confusing, and it was to me, it may actually be a good way to develop a worldview and a plan for your life—if you can survive the process, that is. I went through a number of crying spells and painful admissions, but I did mature and wound up with a strong commitment to achieve all I could with the tools I had.

My lofty thinking about becoming an officer and pilot, and my periods of introspection came to an abrupt end in September 1954. My company master sergeant ordered me, a lowly PFC, to serve one month of duty at the El Toro Enlisted Mess Hall. Mess duty is 24/7 because you start at 4:30 a.m. and work until 8:00 p.m. At the end of the workday, you have just enough energy left to shower, fall into the rack, and sleep the sleep of the dead. Outranked by most everyone, I drew the scullery assignment. My job was to scrape leftovers off the metal trays, a yucky job made worse if there was a glob of sticky peanut butter on the tray. The slop went into garbage cans that we carried to the dump. We put the scraped trays through a huge steaming machine and returned the sanitized trays to the mess hall. I hated the scullery. The sights, smells and sounds of clanging metal trays in the small steaming room were borderline sadistic. I cannot stand, to this day, clanging noises or the smell or site of slop. My scullery experience, has led me to a lifelong insistence that any food served to me must have a clear separation from any other food served on the same plate. No slop, thank you very much.

The long month of mess duty ended and in October 1954, I got orders to go to Korea. The armistice, signed July 27, 1953, at Panmunjom, Korea, was in effect, but no one knew whether it would hold. We all hoped it would. I was to leave by troop ship for Korea in late December so I got another leave. On October 22, 1954, I rode the bus from Santa Ana, California to Phoenix to see my dad, who I had not seen in several years. Unannounced, I went to the address he was using at the time and was surprised to find that he was living alone in a little beat-up trailer parked on an otherwise vacant lot. I could not get in so I just waited for him to get home from his job at a fly-by-night insurance agency where he was posting accounts. About 4:30 p.m., a bus stopped a block away and I saw a man get off. Then I saw the unmistakable gyrations of my father walking from the bus stop. He was coming across the vacant lot toward the trailer. He was conspicuously older, had grey hair, and moved much slower than I remembered. It was painful to see how hard it was for him to walk. Images from my childhood and the love he gave me when I was little came back in a rush. I broke down, sobbing and crying big tears. As soon as Daddy saw me, the grimace on his face disappeared and he broke into that old familiar smile. I collected myself and shouted, "Hey, Old Man," and ran to him as a baby would run into the arms of his father. We hugged and cried in the middle of that empty lot, ignoring the litter, the old tires, and the empty cans. For that moment, we were in Heaven.

The few days I spent with Daddy gave us a chance to talk about our lives after the separation and divorce. He had kept up with my activities in Pocahontas and wanted to hear all about my successes in scholarship as well as athletics. He was proud of me for being a Marine and was interested in what I planned to do once I got out of the military. It was the first time I ever had a chance to talk to Daddy, man to man, about grown-up things. I found out what he had been doing during all the years he spent in New Mexico and then Arizona. It was a high point in my life.

The days passed quickly, and then on November 9, 1954, I had to leave for Santa Ana to make ready for the troop movement to Korea. I spent Christmas Day on the base at El Toro and our unit left for Korea on December 29, 1954. We took the train to San Diego where we boarded the troop ship, *General N. M. Walker*, and got underway at 2:00 p.m. on December 30, 1954.

We celebrated New Year's Day on the boat. We got USO packets as a going away memento. There was nothing much in the packets—a deck of playing cards, a comb, and some other stuff—but it meant a lot to me, and to everyone else.

We lived in the ship's hold. In olden days mariners referred to the space below the deck as the hold, especially when the space was used for storage. On the *General Walker*, we called it the "hole." There were rows and rows of triple tiered bunks, situated side-by-side with barely enough room to get in and out. Once you were in your bunk, there was only about ten inches of clearance between your body and the canvas bunk above. For that reason, the top bunk was the prime spot, but it was hotter up there. I had the second, middle bunk and a huge black man was in the canvas bunk that connected to mine. He got sick on the first day and for two days threw up every time he tried to eat. On the third day, he quit eating and dry-heaved most of the time. He lost at least twenty pounds and was so sick that I would have sworn under oath that he got a shade lighter. He was an affable sort and even though he was not in a mood to talk we got along well for two people who were sleeping side-by-side, shoulder-to-shoulder, for twenty days. I often brought him some crackers from the mess hall and urged him to eat. I would say to him, "Man, you are wasting away and turning white, you need to eat." He would grin and eat the crackers but after a few minutes, he was throwing them up.

My black friend was not alone. Sick people were forever running from their bunks to the head hollering: "Hot chow coming through!" It was the same warning that linebackers (the men on mess duty who carried the big hot pots of food from the stoves to the food line) shouted to get people out of their way. It worked pretty well in the mess hall to clear the way for those carrying steaming-hot food. It worked even better, down below, when a nauseated Marine was making a beeline to the head.

I did not get seasick but it is a wonder that I did not. The foul odors down below in the sleeping compartments were indescribable, and they got worse day by day. The ship's captain—praise God—allowed us to go on deck several times a day to get fresh air. The outside deck was not a risk free zone, however. There were powerful vents spaced every fifteen feet to purge foul air from down below. If you walked too close to a vent, the stench would buckle your knees. It was enough to make anyone throw up and several did, which made it important to stay as far upwind as possible.

On January 15, 1955, during the night, we made landfall in Kobe, Japan. I went on deck at first light and got my first view of a foreign country. It looked like "Anywhere, USA," but all the signs were in Japanese. It was just breaking day and there was no one on the dock, not a soul. Then, all of a sudden, I saw a little Japanese boy run to the edge of the dock. He turned his back to the water, dropped his pants, and unceremoniously took a shit off the side of the wharf. Then he wiped his butt with a flick of his finger, pulled up his pants, and ran back out of sight—welcome to the Orient!

The *General Walker* was in Kobe a half-day, and then we left for Korea via the Inland Sea of Japan. Soon, we were well into the Yellow Sea, which is actually yellowish in color. We were heading north, up the west side of Korea to Inchon. The sea off the coast of Inchon is shallow and deep draft vessels cannot get close to land. That difficulty is what made General MacArthur's surprise amphibious landing at Inchon in June of 1950 so successful. Troops, material, and vehicles must move from a ship in deep water over long pontoon docks to a shore that is one mile away. We arrived there on January 17, 1955, disembarked, and marched over the pontoons to Ascom City, a tent camp midway between Inchon and Seoul. There we would spend the night, in tents with no heat, sleeping on cots and doing our best to keep warm. One Marine left his arm outside his sleeping bag and the next day a corpsman treated him for frostbite. It was that cold.

A couple of cold Marines in Ascom City, Korea, January 17, 1955. I am the tall guy.

On January 18, 1955, we boarded a confiscated Korean train for a long, slow ride to Pohang Dong, midway down the east coast of Korea. It was only 180 miles by rail but the trip took twenty-five hours. The seats on the train were unpadded wooden benches so it was a long, uncomfortable overnight trip. Upon arrival in Pohang Dong, we marched to a makeshift airbase designated as K-3 and I reported to G-2, the Intelligence Unit of the First Marine Air Wing.

Our job in Korea was to maintain the recently signed armistice. The serious fighting had stopped, but there were incidents from time to time. For the most part, we Marines did what Marines always do when standing by for a call to duty. We trained, we prepared, and we waited. We were on duty seven days a week. Boredom was our biggest challenge. We certainly did not want the shooting war to start up and counted ourselves lucky to be serving after instead of before the armistice. Nevertheless, it is hard to maintain sanity when you have little to do but to stay prepared for war, and wait. It is even harder when you are nineteen years old and marooned in a backward country for at least sixteen months.

Korea, in 1955, was like stepping back in time. The country, a victim throughout history, never developed and conditions worsened due to the ravages of World War II and decades of Japanese occupation before that. Housing in the villages was a hodgepodge of huts with thatched roofs. Most people wore native costumes, the most conspicuous item being the trademark Papasan Hat, a stovepipe black hat made out of horsetail hair and worn by elderly men to top off their white gowns. Younger people frequently wore blue jackets, buttoned in front, that resembled the Mao jackets of China, but for adults the most common attire was a white robe-like garment. If a young woman was in western dress, it signified that she was a working girl, a euphemism downplaying the fact that for $2 she would give anyone a "short-time." Civilian vehicles were nonexistent. Military vehicles belonging to the USA or the ragtag Korean military had to weave their way over dirt roads littered with oxcarts, the main form of transport for Korean civilians. Each morning there was an antlike stream of men carrying honey-buckets full of fecal matter, one bucket on each end of a pole, to the rice and vegetable fields. Throughout the day, the honey-bucket brigade gave way to men carrying loads on A-frames—ancient backpacking devices the Koreans used for moving almost anything. Smallish Korean men routinely carried A-frame loads that were bigger and heavier than they were.

The odors of Korea were almost unbearable. The villages had no plumbing, no safe water supplies, and no electricity or gas, thus no refrigeration. The Koreans heated their huts with whatever they could find that would burn. In winter, the stench of whatever the Koreans were cooking and burning was the dominant smell, but in summer, the unmistakable aroma of the honey-buckets and rotting things took over.

The Korean people seemed to like us. They were friendly but it was advisable to keep them at a reasonable distance because a staple of their diet was Kimchi, a vegetable concoction that includes a green similar to kale that grows wild throughout the country. The Koreans cook it with a heavy dose of garlic; consequently, you could smell most of the villagers before you saw them.

Most of the time, we stayed within the confines of K-3. On base, there was work and more work. When we were not working, we slept, read, listened to the radio or played softball. There was the Slop Shute where after 6:00 p.m. you could buy a beer for five cents, but otherwise there was absolutely nothing to do. K-3 was boring, but it was safe, it was clean and it did not smell. In spite of its shortcomings, we Marines made occasional forays into the village of Pohang Dong looking for something different to do to break the monotony of our time on K-3.

On one such trip, my friend Sergeant Ackerman found a Korean who claimed to be the town barber. Ackerman, looking for a little excitement and pampering, decided he wanted a real shave from a barber using a straight razor. I suggested the barber might be a communist sympathizer who would enjoy using the occasion to cut Ackerman's throat. He was not about to be deterred. The sergeant stationed me and another Marine on either side of the barber chair with our M-1 rifles at the ready. The barber got the message, gave Ackerman a good shave, and never made the slightest suspicious move.

On February 15, 1955, only one month after arriving in Korea, the company master sergeant assigned me to thirty days of guard duty. It was not a punishment. Guard duty is something every low-ranking Marine has to do, and you usually get it soon after assignment to a new unit. We would walk one four-hour daytime shift and one four-hour nighttime shift. It is definitely better to do guard duty in the summer than in the winter, particularly in Korea. When I reported to the guard company, the quartermaster issued me a huge down-filled parka and a pair of rubber thermal boots, essential gear for the bitter cold of mid-February. The boots were state of the art in 1955. Each boot was essentially a close-fitting inner rubber boot suspended inside a big, tough outer rubber boot. The air space between the inner and outer boot protected the foot from the cold. The boots were enormous so we dubbed them "Mickey Mouse Boots," but they were a godsend for those of us who walked guard duty around the perimeter of K-3. The size and shape of the boots made it clumsy to walk, but they kept our feet warm even though our socks were wringing wet when we took the boots off.

Those of us assigned to guard duty lived in the Guard Shack for the entirety of our thirty-day tour. Our quarters were next door to several Quonset huts, which were home to the Korean Marine Corps, KMC for short. I had never heard of the KMC, but it was not long before I learned to respect them as much as I respected the men in my own unit. They shared responsibility for guarding the perimeter of K-3 and the standard procedure was to post a U. S. Marine for one segment of the fence and then post a KMC Marine for the next segment. KMC guards walked the same four-hour shifts that we did, but there were differences: The KMC troops were not on guard duty for a mere thirty days; guarding the perimeter was their permanent assignment. They did not eat as well as we did, nor were they dressed as well. They wore hand-me-down long wool coats and boots, United States of America surplus from World War I and the early years of World War II. They had no Mickey Mouse boots, and their officers were as tough on them as any boot camp drill instructor in the U. S. Marine Corps.

One day in my second week on guard duty, I saw the KMC troops in formation outside their Quonset huts. The officers were ordering the men to hold their rifles in both hands above their head, parallel to the ground. The officers then instructed the men to bend backwards as far as they could and then hold in that position. I first thought they were doing a callisthenic exercise, but then the officers started hollering at them as they whacked them across the belly with a rifle. Several of the KMC Marines fell to the ground in pain, but the officers forced them to get back in line and the drill went on for a good ten minutes. That night, when I got to the end of my segment of the fence, I saw the KMC Marine who was guarding the next segment so I waited until he got to where I was and then I offered him a cigarette. The KMC troops loved to meet up like that because we Marines would always give them cigarettes. We bought cigarettes for a dollar per carton, so it was nothing to us, but it meant a lot to the men of the KMC. We lit up and exchanged knowing looks as we rubbed our hands together and stamped our feet in mutual recognition that it was cold as Hell. He had only the old wool coat and regular boots, both worn to a frazzle, but he still managed a smile. I was determined to find out about what I saw that morning so I said, "Today … KMC," and I leaned over backwards with my rifle over my head. I then took my rifle and simulated a KMC officer swinging it hard into the belly of the troops. At first, he did not get it but after a couple of tries, he suddenly knew what I was asking. The challenge was for him to tell me in broken English what had occurred. It took awhile but he finally said with full Oriental dialect, "Uh … KMC … uh … inspection … uh … inspection … uh … all fucked-up." Only a U. S. Marine could appreciate the plight of the Korean Marines. I had found a soul mate, a brother in arms, on the other side of the world.

In June of 1955, I finally got the long awaited offer to enter the Naval Air Cadet program. The flight surgeon gave his blessing to my new two-hole nose and everything else checked out. But the hitch was that I would have to agree to serve four years from the time I entered the program. I thought about it for a few days and decided to decline the offer to be a pilot. I would finish my three-year enlistment.

To celebrate the Fourth of July my first year in Korea, we smuggled some beer off the base and went to a nearby beach just a couple of miles from Pohang Dong. There were several Marines there, and for some reason, there was a large rubber raft tethered to the shore. After a few beers, eight of us decided we would launch the raft and paddle around the small bay that led out into the Sea of Japan. It was a beautiful day, not a cloud in the sky, but a big, westerly wind was building to gale force level. We rafters failed to take proper account of the wind that was blowing us steadily out to sea, in the general direction of Japan. We were about a mile offshore before we realized our plight. We paddled as hard as we could but we were no match for the thirty-mile-an-hour wind. We were too far out to swim and there was little hope that the wind would subside. Fortunately, K-3 was a Marine air base and someone on the beach alerted the flight line that eight Marines in a raft were well on their way to Japan. Shortly, a helicopter approached and dropped a cable that we attached to the raft. The helicopter pilot towed us back to shallow water where we jumped over the side, pulled the raft back up on the shore, and then disappeared as quickly as we could. For several days thereafter, we lived in fear that the commanding officer would call us in for summary punishment, but nothing ever happened.

On Christmas day, 1955, I went to the village with some friends, but walked back to the base on my own. I crossed a small creek and saw a Korean family butchering a dog. I could not understand a word they were saying, but they were quite excited. They were going to have meat to go along with their Kimchi. That scene on Christmas day brought back a flood of memories of my life before the Marine Corps. I remembered the clarinet my mother gave me for Christmas when I was in the sixth grade and the holiday tunes I used to play on it. I thought of the hardships that Delta Lew and I faced when we were living alone in Pocahontas, and the separation and divorce of my mother and father. I cried like a baby. I was alone on the other side of the world and there was no Christmas tree, no family, no presents. The Corps was laying out a better meal for us, but as usual it was made from powdered eggs, powdered milk, and canned vegetables. The one treat was that they were going to serve fresh-cooked turkey. As I continued on my way to K-3, I finally stopped blubbering. After all, I was much better off than the Koreans were. It also occurred to me that being in Korea was probably harder for my fellow Marines who did not come from broken families. I learned, at an early age, that family life can be difficult and that you have to make the best of it. I admit I was feeling a little sorry for myself that Christmas day, but I felt sorriest for the young Marines who had come from rock-solid families, the ones who had no experience with family separation.

Twice during my tour in Korea, the Marine Corps sent me to Japan for a week of R&R, short for Rest and Recuperation. In most cases the time off is a weeklong drunken orgy. Throughout the history of the world, military forces, ours included, have implicitly condoned prostitution. The military may declare certain areas and activities off limits, but the troops are encouraged to use condoms and taught the risks of venereal disease. I expect there will always be R&R, it may go by another name, but troops will be troops, now and forever more. The time off is recuperative—troops need R&R to maintain sanity—but it does not have to be all about drinking and sex. My first R&R was to Kyoto where I saw my first Japanese gardens, and many other memorable sights. I thought often of what I had learned from my father about "good Japanese" and "bad Japanese" when I had visited the War Relocation Center in Rohwer. It was educational to be in Japan where the "bad Japanese" lived. I was there just ten years after World War II, but I did not find a single person that I considered a "bad Japanese." As a footnote, the Shore Patrol was everywhere in Kyoto, but I managed to avoid arrest and spent no time in the brig.

My second R&R was to Iwakuni, but a buddy and I made a three-day side trip to Hiroshima. The city was just beginning to recover from the atom bomb that the United States dropped there on August 6, 1945. That strike, coupled with a similar one at Nagasaki three days later, forced the Japanese Empire to surrender, ending World War II. Estimates are that in the first few months after the bombing as many as 100,000 people died, most from flash or flame burns during the explosion. It was strange to be in Hiroshima. I was nine when Hiroshima was bombed, and now at age nineteen I was there in the uniform of a United States Marine. We toured the city and on the last day of our visit, we happened into a movie theatre that was playing *Flying Leathernecks*, starring John Wayne. It surprised me to find a theatre full of Japanese people watching a movie, with Japanese subtitles, showing American Marines shooting down Japanese warplanes and killing Japanese pilots. My buddy and I scrunched down in our seats and then—discretion being the better part of valor—slipped quietly out of the theatre before the movie ended.

As I entered the last month of my tour in Korea, I was entitled by custom to tie a Short-Timer Ribbon in the side vent of my dungaree cap. No one can remember when or why the custom started, but everyone was eager to take the yellow and black ribbon off a bottle of Seagram's Seven and tie it in their cap. It signified the highest standing of all; the wearer of the ribbon was in the last month of his tour and would soon be going home.

On the last day of my tour of duty, I boarded an R4Q transport, also known as a Flying Boxcar, for a flight to Yokohama, where I boarded the troop ship, *General M. M. Patrick*. On February 24, 1956, the *Patrick* set sail and arrived in San Francisco, and docked at Treasure Island, on March 6. I was back in the United States. The crossing ended with a rough two days of up and down as we rode over the San Francisco swells west of the California coastline. The first night ashore, in keeping with Marine Corps tradition, I went on liberty with several buddies. We all got drunk in a nondescript bar somewhere in San Francisco and that night I "got rolled," a new experience for me. I did not know about it until I awoke on my bunk at Treasure Island the next morning and discovered that someone had separated me from the $100 cash that I had stored in the pocket of my blouse.

Getting rolled did not set well with me, but it was a good lesson similar to the gambling lesson I had learned when I was fresh out of boot camp. An old salt by the name of Corporal Sandwich used to run a blackjack game at El Toro after every payday. Sandwich had been in the Marine Corps for eighteen years, and he had tattoos all over his body. He had been up and down in the ranks and was a corporal at the time I jumped into his blackjack game. I had just received two crisp twenty-dollar bills as my pay for a half month as a PFC. It took Sandwich less than ten minutes to take possession of my two twenties. I have not played blackjack a single time since that day at El Toro, and no one has rolled me since that night in San Francisco.

The Marine Corps gave me travel time and a cash allowance to get from Treasure Island to Cherry Point, North Carolina, my next assignment. To save money, I finagled a hop on a military flight to Edwards Air Force Base in California and took a bus to Phoenix, Arizona. I wanted to visit with my dad before heading to Arkansas.

I spent a week with Daddy, and we had a great time. We went to the races every day that Uncle Mac, Daddy's brother who also lived in Phoenix, had a horse running. For a while, Uncle Mac had the best quarter horses in the West. His first big winner was I'll Do It. Later he had I'll Do It Too and Do It for Me. We also took in a Baltimore Orioles spring training game. As I saw one of the players running to first base, I told Daddy, "I know that run." I said, "I'm sure that's Brooks Robinson from Little Rock." I knew Brooks from my days playing baseball in Little Rock and, most importantly, I knew his distinctive running style. I got a roster sheet and confirmed that it was Brooks.

At the end of my week's visit, I caught the train to Arkansas and two days later I arrived at the old Rock Island terminal in Little Rock. Delta Lew, her husband, Bill, and Mother met me. I was in uniform and Delta Lew cried as soon as she saw me stepping off the train. It is a moment I have never, and will never forget.

I spent two weeks in Arkansas, and during that time I made a quick trip to Pocahontas. I told my Uncle Lloyd that I had saved up enough money to buy a car, but I had no experience in car shopping. I asked him to help me. He was a Ford-man so he took me to Million Motors and I bought a brand-new, two-tone white and blue, two-door Ford sedan. I was officially in tall cotton. I drove around Pocahontas showing off my new car. A day later, I drove to Little Rock and did the same thing. I went on a date in Little Rock with Dana Kirkland, an old friend from

Rightsell and East Side Junior High School. We played the radio constantly and Dana kept asking me to tune it to a particular station that played the music of a new singer named Elvis Presley. Dana was raving about Elvis and she was stunned when I said, "Who's that?" We did not get much music in Korea and if we got Elvis, I must have missed it.

On April 1, 1956, while I was still on leave, my promotion to sergeant came through. I quickly got the chevrons sewn on my uniforms. Then I drove to North Carolina and started my last few months in the Marine Corps with the Second Marine Air Wing at Cherry Point. While there, I learned to sail with a fellow sergeant who was from Massachusetts. That planted a seed that would take root years later. As I neared the end of my enlistment, there was a threat that the Marine Corps might extend all enlistments due to a flare-up in the Middle East. It made me nervous for a few weeks, but the situation settled down and I made it to my discharge date. The Marine Corps gave me a series of psychological and vocational tests as part of the discharge process to help me understand what I should do with the rest of my life. Interestingly, the counselors who interpreted the test results did not tell me that I should become a dentist. The testing suggested I should be a teacher.

On January 20, 1957, my three-year enlistment was over and I mustered out of the Marine Corps. In the two days it took me to drive home, I had a chance to think deeply about my time in the Corps, what it would be like to re-enter civilian life, and what I might do with the rest of my life. I had just turned twenty-one.

12

HOME, COLLEGE, AND LANA

One should choose a wife with the ears,
rather than with the eyes.
French Proverb

In 1944, President Roosevelt signed into law the Servicemen's Readjustment Act, commonly known as the G.I. Bill of Rights. It provided educational benefits to veterans. When I signed up for the Marine Corps in December of 1953, I was told that if I served honorably I would be entitled to receive a monthly payment of $110 that I could use to go back to college. I was not sure that I would ever use the GI Bill, but it was definitely an incentive that was on my mind when I joined the Marines. In my second year as a Marine, I considered the idea of going into the Naval Air Cadet program, becoming an officer, and making a career out of the military. If there had been no GI Bill I might have stayed in service, but the bill was an attractive benefit that would help me get an education. I decided to finish my enlistment and go to college.

As soon as I got to Little Rock, I went to see my sister and her husband, Bill Hastings. I told them I was planning to find a job, earn some money, and then start college in the fall of 1957. Bill said I should not wait to get started because I might lose interest and never go back to college. He urged me to enroll for the spring semester that was just starting at Little Rock Junior College. He said I would have plenty of time to work a part-time job, and the early start would put me well on the road to graduation, particularly if I attended summer school. I had twelve hours of credit from the days I spent at the University of Arkansas in 1953 and I could earn at least twenty-five additional credits at Little Rock Junior College between January of 1957 and September of 1957 by going straight through. Bill's idea made sense to me, so I enrolled at LRJC. I met other veterans and discovered that we had a more mature outlook than the kids who came to LRJC straight from high school. I was hungry to learn, and determined to prove to myself that I could get a college education. I attacked my studies energetically and, fortunately, I had good professors for my classes on economics and English history. I made an A in both courses and discovered that I thoroughly enjoyed learning about our Anglo-American heritage and free market economics. I seemed to have a flair for these subjects, unlike the mystifying science courses that had given me so much trouble in 1953. I decided to pursue a degree in business administration.

The monthly stipend from the Marine Corps was not enough to cover all my living expenses, so I shared a cheap apartment with two other veterans. One of my roommates was Lewis Bracy, also a veteran of the Marine Corps. Lewis had a part-time job at Samuelson Cigar Company and encouraged the company to give me a part-time job delivering cigars, cigarettes, and sundries. I made the grand sum of a $1.50 an hour, but I was able to get in thirty hours a week and that gave me enough money to get by. The Samuelsons were nice people and I worked with a number of colorful fellow employees who had been with the company for years. We drivers got a stack of new orders each day when we came to work. It was our job to fill the orders, load them on our truck, and deliver them to drug stores, small groceries and other vendors. I have always liked to drive, so I really enjoyed the job. I drove all over Little Rock and got to know the small business owners and managers who were our main customers.

On September 4, 1957, I punched-in on the time clock at Samuelson and started filling the orders I would deliver that day.

One of the orders was for a drug store on Park Street near Little Rock Central High School. As I drove the delivery truck out 16th Street, I was oblivious to what was going on at the high school. I had no interest in politics, did not take the newspaper or have a television set, and I only listened to music on the radio. Little did I know that I was about to run headlong into a sociopolitical conflict that rocked the nation and dominated world news for days. As I neared South Park Street, I saw crowds gathered and then, to my surprise, I saw troops and Army vehicles. I was just out of the Marine Corps and accustomed to seeing troops and military equipment, but to see them in front of the high school that I attended through the tenth grade was breathtaking. I parked the delivery truck and began asking people in the crowd, "What's going on?"

I quickly learned that Governor Orval Faubus had deployed the Arkansas National Guard in support of those who were protesting the integration of Little Rock Central High School. Some people were saying the governor was not taking sides and that he sent the troops in "just to keep order," but the restless crowd was clearly in favor of what he was doing and they said so in the crudest terms.

The governor's deployment of the Arkansas National Guard was not "just to keep order." The governor was currying favor with die-hard segregationists who opposed the integration of Little Rock Central High School. Governor Faubus was dead wrong to oppose the admission of black children to a public school—that was obvious—but I needed and wanted to know more. I got a newspaper that afternoon and began to learn as much as I could about the conflict.

In the days following, President Dwight Eisenhower tried to calm the situation. He warned Faubus not to interfere with the Supreme Court ruling in *Brown v. the Board of Education,* the landmark case requiring public schools to integrate with all deliberate speed. Faubus did not respond. On September 24, the president ordered the 101st Airborne Division of the United States Army to Little Rock and federalized the Arkansas National Guard, taking it out of the hands of Governor Faubus. The 101st took positions immediately and nine black students—The Little Rock Nine—successfully entered the school the next day, Wednesday, September 25, 1957.

I followed the events closely and drove by the high school as often as I could. I wanted to etch the unpleasant sight of troops at LRCHS into my memory.

My study of the Little Rock school integration crisis would last for years, but I had no idea on that day in 1957 that I would eventually play a part in the struggle to improve racial relations.

The best thing that ever happened to me occurred at Little Rock Junior College shortly after I enrolled. I was talking with my friend, Lewis Bracy, when a beautiful blonde-haired girl walked right by us and into a classroom. I asked Lewis if he knew her and he said, "Yes, that is Lana Douthit. She is very popular, and everyone likes her." I asked Lewis if he would introduce me to Lana and he said he would. The next day we positioned ourselves in front of the classroom so that it would be hard for Lana to come out of her class without acknowledging our presence. Our plan worked. Lewis got Lana's attention and then, being a straight-laced guy, commenced a formal introduction. He said, "Miss Lana Douthit, may I introduce you to Mr. Ed Bethune." I had prepared for the moment by putting on my best outfit, a brown leather bombardier jacket and khaki pants. At the time, I had crew-cut hair and I was not sure I looked my best. Lana, on the other hand, had on a smart grey wool suit with a black velvet collar and trim, and she had on high heels. She was all dressed up for some event she was going to after class. She looked like a million dollars. I was a little nervous, but she was not. As I was about to say my first words to Lana, Lewis cut me off and continued the formal introduction that he must have learned from Emily Post, "And, Mr. Ed Bethune, this is Miss Lana Douthit." It was now my turn to speak, so I told her it was nice to meet her, that Lewis and I were Marine Corps veterans and we did not know a lot of people on campus, and that I hoped to see her around. She smiled and said, "Sure, but right now I have to go downtown." That was it, but it was a start.

It was easy to find out more about Lana because everyone, teachers as well as students, seemed to know something about her. She was the daughter of George Douthit, a longtime reporter for the *Arkansas Democrat.* Her mother, Mary Lou, a beautician, worked in a shop at Stifft Station. Lana was a graduate of Little Rock Central High School and lived with her parents in a small duplex on Monroe Street. She was working her way through college with a job as a nighttime receptionist at Channel 7, the ABC affiliate in Little Rock. I also discovered that Lewis Bracy was a hundred percent right; everyone liked Lana Douthit.

No one can ever explain the magic that causes men and women to be attracted to one another, but I was definitely attracted to Lana. She was good looking, personable, had a good reputation, and she was working her way through college, just like me. I figured out her schedule of classes and "accidently" encountered her often enough that she eventually learned my name, and when she showed a little interest in me I invited her to go to lunch at Sam's, an eatery on Fair Park Boulevard. Sam made a killer meatloaf sandwich and the place was always full of LRJC students and professors.

A couple of lunches at Sam's and a few meetings on campus led to our first genuine date. We went to the Officers Club, a small nightclub in Little Rock. It was there that we first kissed and realized that we really cared for one another. We dated a lot after that. I would pick her up when she got off work and we would do inexpensive things. One of our favorite things was to go to a drive-in restaurant where we could order a drink and just sit and talk. There were several good ones, Granoffs at Tenth and Main, Old King Cole at Fifth and Broadway, and Peck's Drive-In on Markham across from the State Hospital. None of them expected young people to spend a lot of money. The good thing about that kind of dating is that we had plenty of time to talk, to assess each other, and to figure out whether we were right for each other.

As time went by, I realized I not only wanted Lana's love, I needed it. I could see that she knew how to love people, truly love people. Hers was the kind of love the Vermilye worldview could not accept. Lana grew up wanting to serve people. She had no fear of "them" and she was not looking for a "good lettin' alone." When she was in high school, she flirted seriously with becoming a missionary, and she would have been a good one because she is always willing to stop whatever she is doing to put the wants and needs of others first. When we were dating, I would always ask what she wanted to do and she would always say, "I'm with you, whatever you want to do is fine." I have never heard her turn down a person who asked for help. She never says, "I can't, I have to finish what I am doing for myself first." When we first met, I attributed these unselfish traits to her personality, but I learned later that her willingness to love and help others comes from her strong faith.

She loves to laugh and have a good time, but her joyful nature is more than good humor. Her joy is the kind of joy you read about in the Bible. Hers is the kind of joy that does not go away when times are tough.

Most importantly, from the time of our first date, Lana has encouraged me to dream. Deep down inside I wanted to be more like her, more like my father, but I knew it would be a hard business. At the time I met Lana, my mother was aging, and as she did she began a transition back to the girl she must have been before she saw Little Gerle die of diphtheria. She was throwing off the confinements of the Vermilye worldview. I could see the change in Mother, and wanted that for myself, but I knew I had a long way to go and much to learn. It became apparent to me that Lana was the missing ingredient in my life. I intuitively knew that together we could have a wonderful life. Now that we have been married well over fifty years, I shudder to think what I might have become without her.

In May of 1957, Lana graduated from Little Rock Junior College. She was transferring to the University of Arkansas at Fayetteville. I did not have enough money to transfer to Fayetteville, so I stayed in Little Rock for another semester at LRJC.

Midway through the fall semester, I decided I would transfer to Fayetteville so that I could be with Lana. To get money I sold my beloved Ford and bought an old Hudson Jet. The extra cash would pay for my first few months of room and board and give me time to find part-time work in Fayetteville.

In January of 1958, I enrolled at the University of Arkansas at Fayetteville. Lana had pledged Kappa Kappa Gamma, one of the best sororities, so I rejoined Kappa Sigma and moved into the fraternity house on 711 West Dickson Street. I rekindled many old friendships and made new ones that have lasted for a lifetime.

I worked several odd jobs, one was to sell and distribute display racks loaded with a wide variety of TV tubes. In those days, televisions and radios used vacuum tubes instead of modern transistors. If a TV failed, you tried to identify which tube had gone out. If you found the bad tube and replaced it with a good one the TV would work. Our displays contained a tube-testing device. It was a keen idea, but people who bought our replacement tubes would bring them back to the store if their TV still did not work. It was a lot of trouble for the storekeepers. They finally got so upset with the rash of complaints and demands for reimbursement that the whole thing became a big mess. The business failed and I had to find other work.

Lana and I dated for all of 1958. By then we had been going steady for almost two years. She initiated into Kappa Kappa Gamma, and I initiated into Kappa Sigma. As the year ended, we had long talks about what we wanted to do with our lives and how we could best find our place in the world. We both needed money so we decided to drop out of school, go to Little Rock, get married, get jobs, save money, and then go back to school when we were ready.

I got a job at Reynolds Metals as a filing clerk and George Douthit got Lana a starting-level job at the Arkansas Education Department at the state Capitol.

We rented an apartment on North Midland Street near the waterworks and set January 24, 1959 as our wedding date. We asked Dr. Kenneth Shamblin, pastor of Pulaski Heights Methodist Church, to marry us in the small chapel, but first he wanted to have a premarital conference. At the outset of the conference, Dr. Shamblin said he wanted to talk about loyalty. We—our hormones in full bloom—thought he was talking about sexual fidelity to each other. That was not his point. He said the "loyalty" he was talking about was greater than that. He said we should always put each other first and never engage in down talking each other to anyone. He said we should never say a negative word about each other to our parents or friends because that opens the door and gives them a chance to tell what they do not like about your chosen one. That, he said, is a formula for disaster once it gets started. As we left the preacher's office, Lana and I looked each other in the eye and agreed that we had just heard some good advice. We pledged that we would honor each other with our loyalty. We agreed that if we had a problem we would speak about it to each other and not discuss it with others, any others.

We had a little wedding on a Saturday morning in the chapel at Pulaski Heights Methodist Church. My best man was my Kappa Sigma brother, Mike Smith. I borrowed his car for our honeymoon trip to Hot Springs. We could only stay Saturday night because we had to go to work on Monday. George Douthit arranged a room for us in the Lanai Suites at the Majestic Hotel. When we were having lunch on Sunday, Lana developed a horrible toothache and we had to check out early. We drove to her parent's house and when George opened the door, he started laughing and kidding me, asking if I was bringing her back. It did look funny, I admit, but we had only gone by to get the telephone number of the dentist so we could call him to see if he could see Lana first thing Monday morning.

Our wedding at Pulaski Heights Methodist Church in Little Rock, Arkansas. January 24, 1959.

Soon after we settled into our little apartment on Midland Street in Little Rock, we had our first hot argument, and that led us to make another pledge, one that has worked well for us. We fashioned a supplement to the loyalty rule that we had learned from Dr. Shamblin. We agreed that we would never go to bed mad at each other. This rule has caused us to stay up late on a number of occasions, but it is a good rule and we have always worked out our differences before going to bed.

After only three months in Little Rock, we headed to Dallas, because I had landed a better paying job as a book salesman. Lana got a job in a Dallas bank and I started my new job with Prentiss-Hall Publishing Company. I was supposed to make cold calls and sell loose-leaf treatises about tax and labor law to businesses and law firms. We were only in Dallas for thirty days when Prentiss-Hall transferred me to Shreveport, Louisiana. Dallas was too big and too citified for me, so I eagerly took the transfer. Lana quit her job and quickly found another one with a bank in Shreveport. We rented an apartment and our Shreveport experience was fun. There were some nice young couples in our apartment complex and it helped that my sister, Delta Lew, and her husband, Bill, were also living in Shreveport. He was a traveling salesman for Walker Auto Parts.

It took a few months, but I soon established that I was, without a doubt, the world's worst book salesman. I did not like making cold calls and it was hard to convince prospects to pay the high price that Prentiss-Hall demanded for its loose-leaf services. Nevertheless, I stuck with it for the rest of 1959. We managed to put a few dollars away, and in January 1960, we quit our jobs and returned to Fayetteville and the University of Arkansas.

Our plan was for me to enroll in the School of Business Administration, fulltime, because I, as a male in the 1960s would have the best chance to succeed in the job market. In addition, I needed more hours to graduate than Lana did, so we figured we needed to attack that part of our education problem first. I enrolled and Lana took a job as a secretary for the president of a local insurance company, Preferred Risk. Our idea was for me to graduate and get a job and then Lana would get the few hours she needed to complete her degree. About midway in the spring semester, I discovered that if I transferred to the School of Law my first year of law school would count toward my BSBA degree. If I were to go fulltime, summer and winter, we could be out of law school in two years and I would have two degrees, a bachelor of science in business administration and a juris doctorate in law. My chances of getting a good job would be better. We decided to do that.

Law school surprised me. I made good grades at Little Rock Junior College and did well after I transferred to the School of Business Administration in Fayetteville. I expected to do just as well in my study of the law, and I would have except for the fact that law school professors allowed students to type final exams. I was an excellent typist in high school and figured I would make better grades if I typed my finals. That was a bad decision. I almost typed myself out of law school in the first semester. I totally botched the final examination in the class on torts, mainly because I could not think and compose while typing; consequently, I wrote poor answers to the test questions.

There was another problem for me that first semester of law school. I discovered I had no background for the study of law. The professors assumed, logically, that all students had a basic familiarity with the sophistications of commerce in the modern world, but my immediate family had never had a checkbook, a mortgage, or any experience with such things. My mother never talked about deeds, notes, mortgages, check writing, savings, investing, or business of any sort. We had just lived from one payday to the next. So much of the study of law is about that kind of activity, events that were a mystery to me. It had not bothered me in undergraduate school, but my unfamiliarity with such matters—along with my determination to type, type, type—did hurt me in law school. Anyway, I quickly realized that I needed to ditch the typewriter and write my exams. I also spent time learning the things that had befuddled me in my first semester. I did well in the second semester. I made an A in real property, a B in criminal law, a C in contracts and a B in the second semester of torts. My confidence restored, I could see the light at the end of the tunnel. Over half of our freshman class dropped out of law school at the end of the first year but I was on my way to graduation.

I attended summer classes in law school but I also worked the night shift as a weighmaster for the annual grape harvest at the Welch Grape Juice plant in Springdale. The farmers, mostly Italian descendants living in and around Tontitown, brought truckloads of grapes to the plant and I weighed their trucks—first full, then empty—and gave them a receipt for what they had delivered. I made a $1.55 per hour, but I worked seven days a week, and I was able to get in twelve hours for each day of the harvest, which lasted about six weeks. It was a good supplement to Lana's income, and we were still collecting the GI Bill, which was now paying me, as a married veteran, the princely sum of $135 per month. These were our only sources of income.

Austerity, of necessity, was our watchword all during our time in law school. We learned to eat the cheaper cuts of meat, turn the lights off, and take good care of our clothes. We took advantage of every cost-cutting technique known to man. The centerpiece of our financial strategy was our car, Old Black. We had purchased Old Black, a well-worn 1950 Ford from Lana's dad for $100 cash. The oxidized paint and the dents and rust-holes scattered from front to rear made it hard to make Old Black look good, but—aside from using a lot of oil—the old Ford ran good. The worn out accelerator kept falling over on its side, but we fixed that by taping it, repeatedly, in an upright position. That fix, amazingly, worked for us for two years. The falling accelerator became a symbol of how we could cut corners if we tried. We also learned to buy five gallons of used oil from service stations for a dollar. We carried the oil in a big jug that we kept in the trunk. We routinely stopped every fifty to seventy-five miles to "top her off."

We had our first child, Madalyn Paige, on May 17, 1962, as I was finishing my second year of law school. She was a healthy baby, so Lana was able to get back to work in a few weeks. We found an inexpensive day care arrangement that worked for us. We had medical insurance through Lana's employer, but in those days, we were healthy. We used the insurance to cover the birth of our daughter, and we used it to cover our new baby's pediatric examinations. We did have one other medical incident that necessitated a call to the pediatrician. We were having dinner one night in our little one-bedroom apartment when Lana noticed a button missing from Paige's dress. We looked everywhere and, not finding the button, concluded that Paige had swallowed it. We read Dr. Spock's book on baby care to see what to do but found no help. We panicked and called the pediatrician. Lana carefully explained the situation to the doctor and he told us we really did not need to do anything. We insisted that we ought to be doing something and he responded, "Well, you will have to get another button."

I was on track to graduate in a few months, in January 1963. The goal line was in sight and nothing was going to stop us. We were flat broke most of the time but we did not worry about such things in those days. We trusted that we could find a way to make it.

In October of 1962, we got another surprise that forced us to redouble our austerity effort. Lana was pregnant with our second child. Fortunately, the baby was not due until May 1963, and by then, with luck, I would have a law license and be earning money instead of spending it on books, tuition, and other school expenses.

We made it. I finished law school and we did it without having to borrow money, which would have been next to impossible because we had no collateral and there were no student loan programs back then.

It was about here in my life that I, for the first time, realized that I might actually turn out to be somebody. I had a law degree, an undergraduate degree, a healthy baby daughter, and the good fortune to be married to a wonderful Christian woman.

13

ATTORNEY AT LAW

God works wonders now and then—Behold a lawyer, an honest man.
Benjamin Franklin

After graduation, I immediately started studying for the Arkansas Bar Examination, the prerequisite for getting a license to practice law. There were many horror stories about good students who flunked the exam. It happened every time students sat for it. One friend of mine had to take it three times before he passed. The bar examiners scheduled two, and only two, exams each year, so my friend could not get a job as a lawyer for a year and half after he graduated from law school. I could not afford that, emotionally or financially. I studied around the clock from the time I graduated to the date of the exam.

I had a job lined up with Herbert McAdams, a well-known lawyer and banker from Jonesboro. Herbert was a friend of Bill Ritter, the man who owned and ran Preferred Risk Insurance Company, Lana's employer. Herbert was on Ritter's board so he came to Fayetteville often. When he came to the company he would always visit with Lana (I think he had an eye for her). One thing led to another and that is how I got the job with Herbert. He was going to pay me $400 a month but I had to pass the bar exam first.

I learned from one of the examiners that I had made the second highest grade on the examination. That was not official, he said, because the examiners only tell the rank of the student who makes the top grade. It was a joke; he was telling me something that all of us could say without fear of rebuttal. I really did not care. I passed, took the oath, and got my license to practice law in Arkansas. Lana enrolled at Arkansas State to get the last six hours she needed to graduate from the University of Arkansas at Fayetteville.

Herbert McAdams did hire me as promised but he had not told me that he was winding down his law practice and wanted me to be the trust officer at his bank. I was disappointed. I had no interest in becoming a trust officer. I wanted to practice real law, street law, people law, the kind of law you read about and see in the movies. That is what I had in mind and I immediately began to look around for a way to do what my head and heart were telling me to do.

We rented a three-bedroom house in Jonesboro and settled in just in time for Lana to give birth on May 21, 1963, to our second child, Samuel McBride Bethune. A month later, I learned that a young lawyer in Pocahontas, Paul K. Lewis, was going to give up his job as deputy prosecuting attorney for Randolph County and close down his private practice. I cannot begin to describe the magnetism I felt when I learned of the opening. Pocahontas was my rock, my salvation place. It was a mysterious mix of memories and lessons learned. Once again, I needed what Pocahontas had to offer.

Paul was going into the Air Force to make a career as a military lawyer. He had been a few years ahead of me at Pocahontas High School, but I knew him well enough to give him a call to see if I might take over his practice and get the job as deputy prosecutor. He was delighted because, if it worked out, he hoped to sell me his law books. He called W. E. "Wid" Billingsley, the prosecuting attorney to see if Wid would be interested in giving me the deputy job. Wid said he would like to meet me, so I drove to his home in Melbourne, and after a fun interview, he told me the job was mine. It only paid $150 a month, but that would cover the rent and utilities for my private office. The deputy job would give me some exposure and that would lead to a few private legal cases. I made a deal with Paul to take over his practice. He sold me his books for a good price and gave me a couple of cases he was working on, but could not finish. I thanked Herbert McAdams for the opportunity he gave me, but told him I wanted to practice law—not be a trust officer. He understood. We moved out of the rent house we had lived in for less than four months and moved into a two-story rent house in Pocahontas.

After Lana completed her degree, she got a job teaching English at Pocahontas High School. The students loved her. We found a wonderful woman who came to our house to keep the kids. Things were looking up but we had a long way to go.

I dug into the practice of law. Wid Billingsley came to the first session of court in Randolph County after my appointment and told me we were going to try a criminal case. It was a slam-dunk larceny case, but it was my first jury trial and I did not want to screw it up. We got a conviction, but the only thing I remember is that I had a bad case of stage fright. After that first trial, I got a lot of experience prosecuting lesser offenses in Pocahontas Municipal Court. Eventually I gained confidence and began to feel like a real lawyer, but I had an important lesson to learn that would serve me well in the years to come.

My most frequent opponent was A. A. Robinson, an old lawyer who had never been to a real law school. He had a degree hanging on the wall of his office, but it was from a diploma mill in East Tennessee, and I learned later that A.A. passed the bar by reading the law under the supervision of another lawyer. That was a common way to become a lawyer in the old days. I made the mistake of thinking I was better than A.A. and that I could overwhelm him with raw intelligence and the book learning I got at the University of Arkansas Law School. He proved to be a tough customer, and it always made me mad when the judge would rule for him, which was often. "Double-A" was cleaning my clock so often that it was embarrassing. The word was getting around town. I had to do something so I asked the judge, George Steimel, an eighty-year-old man with a droopy, drippy eye, why Double-A was winning and I was losing. He said, "Eddie, you get mad and then Allen has you where he wants you. He gets your goat and you cannot think when you are mad." I resisted this unwelcome information, but Judge Steimel pushed on with his advice and wound up with a short sentence that I have always remembered, "You cannot get a lawyer mad—because if he is mad, he is not a lawyer." I took his advice, learned to control my emotions and started winning almost every case I had with Allen and I quit calling him Double A. He had earned my respect.

My private practice was slow to develop. It is hard for a young lawyer to get rid of the schoolboy aroma and it is particularly hard in a town where everyone best remembers you as Eddie, the high school football star. In my first year, I earned more fees for preparing income tax returns than I did for doing real legal work. The basic charge was $5 for preparing a personal tax return and $7.50 for a farm return. Of course, I charged more if the return was complicated or if I had to compile the basic records before starting the return. Many of my tax return clients would bring in two shoeboxes. One box would be marked "In" and the other "Out." That was the extent of recordkeeping for a typical tax return client. They were counting on me to go through a year's worth of receipts, pay stubs, bills, and cancelled checks so that we could complete their returns. It was hard work, but the meager fees I earned paid my overhead and left a little for me to take home.

I had an instructive experience shortly after opening up my law office. An old woman came in to see if I could prepare a deed for her. I said I could, but she was not so sure about it. She looked at me and said, "You look awfully young, are you sure you can write a deed that will be good?" It hurt my feelings, but I needed the $5 fee that was standard for preparation of a warranty deed, so I replied, "Yes Mam, I can do it." I pointed to the diplomas hanging on the wall behind me and showed her my law license. I was sure that would do the trick, but she did not look convinced. She was about to leave when I said, "The $5 fee includes notarizing your signature." She said, "Are you a notary public?" I said yes and she said, "Well, why didn't you say so?" That is all she needed to know. It did not matter that I had spent three years in law school or that I had passed the bar. What resonated with her was my status as a notary public, a title any nonfelon could have gotten by buying a seal and paying a $10 license fee to the state of Arkansas. It was another good lesson for an overly proud young lawyer.

14

SPECIAL AGENT OF THE FBI

FBI agents are some of the finest people you will find any place in the country or the world, and I'm lucky to have the opportunity to work with them.
Robert Mueller, Director of the FBI

Bill Rapert was sheriff of Randolph County during my time as deputy prosecuting attorney. He was a first class law enforcement officer, and he took a special interest in me. He helped me get started in my private practice and in my role as deputy prosecutor. One day when we were visiting, Special Agent Milford Runnels of the Federal Bureau of Investigation came into the sheriff's office. Bill and Milford got along well, which is not always the case with federal and local law enforcement officers. I liked Milford immediately and over the next year, we had many chances to talk about the FBI. I had heard a recruiting pitch about the Bureau when I was in law school and, of course, I had seen the Jimmy Stewart movie, *The FBI Story*. Milford thought I would be a good FBI agent and he brought it up every time we met. At first I had no interest, but Lana and I started to talk about it. My law practice was not developing as well as we had hoped, and we were a little restless living in Pocahontas. We knew we would have to move out of state if I joined the Bureau, but the starting salary of $9,600 per annum was attractive and I knew that I would like the work. Another factor was the similarity between the FBI and the U. S. Marine Corps. Both are tight-knit, demanding organizations with a high degree of *esprit de corps*. It was a natural fit for me, so in early June of 1964 I filled out an application to be a special agent of the FBI and gave it and a photograph of myself to Milford. He was pleased, but reminded me that the FBI only selects a few applicants and that I should not let my hopes get too high.

Milford called me a couple of weeks later and told me that I needed to go to Little Rock for a written test and an interview with the special agent in charge of the Little Rock Field Office of the FBI. It was a promising development and if I did well the FBI would do a full-field investigation to determine my character, associates, reputation, and loyalty to the United States of America. I had gone through such an investigation when I was in the Marine Corps because I needed a top-secret clearance for the work I was doing as an intelligence specialist. For that reason, I felt I would easily pass the background investigation. Chances were looking up that the FBI would offer me a position as a special agent.

In July of 1964, Milford came to my law office and said things were looking good. He had just received a teletype from FBI Headquarters in Washington with an important investigative lead for Special Agent Milford Runnels. The terse message concerned my application. It said, "Determine if applicant is amenable to a more conventional hairstyle." Milford was breaking up with laughter. He said I was in, but I had to get rid of my crew cut. I told him to tell the Bureau that I was amenable to a more conventional hairstyle. Two days later, I got a personal letter from Director J. Edgar Hoover offering me a GS-10 position as a special agent of the FBI and directing me to report to Headquarters, FBI in Washington, D. C. on Monday, September 14, 1964. I would join a class of new agents, and if I satisfactorily completed the fourteen-week course of training, I would be a special agent of the FBI.

Lana and I had already discussed the need for me to go to Washington for the training period. Milford made it clear that I would not know until the last week of training where the Bureau would send me for my first office of assignment. It did not make sense for us to move the kids or for Lana to quit her teaching job. The best plan was for me to go to Washington, D.C., complete the training, and then we could move as a family to my first office of assignment.

On Friday, September 11, 1964, Lana drove me to Hoxie, Arkansas where, to save money, I caught a bus that would take me to D.C. We had never been apart for more than a day since we got married in 1959, and now we had two little children. It was a painful goodbye followed by a long, overnight bus trip, but I was excited to begin a new chapter in my life. I have always relished the burst of new energy that comes from change. I arrived in D. C. at 2:00 a.m. Sunday morning and checked into the old Harrington Hotel near FBI Headquarters. The next morning I reported to the Old Post Office Building to begin my training, most of which would be at the FBI Training Center on the Marine Corps base in Quantico, Virginia.

The training of a new agent is intense, but it was relatively easy for me because it had been only seven years since I was on active duty in the Marine Corps. I knew how to survive in a militaristic environment, I had background as a prosecutor, I was in good physical condition, and I knew a lot about the weapons and the martial arts maneuvers we would use as FBI agents. Being on the Marine Corps base at Quantico gave me a good feeling and brought back memories of my time in the Corps. I knew I would sail through the training, and I did.

Most of my twenty-five classmates in new agents class (NAC-4) had degrees from law school or degrees with an emphasis in accounting. A few had studied other disciplines, but all of those new agents had previous experience in law enforcement or service as an officer in the military. There were no women in my class, and no blacks.

We studied criminal law and procedure and learned the latest investigative techniques. We learned how to take, read, and classify fingerprints. There were classes to explain the workings of the FBI Laboratory and the importance of collecting and preserving physical evidence. We learned the art of interviewing and reporting, with precision, what a witness or suspect said. Most importantly, we learned to shoot a .38 caliber Smith & Wesson Police Special revolver, the pistol we would carry in our everyday work, and when we shot our qualifying round I almost made a perfect score (one of my fifty shots was just a half-inch out of the best part of the target). Near the end of our training, we had a personal meeting with Director J. Edgar Hoover and spent a week in the Washington, D.C. field office working with veteran agents.

On the firing range, FBI Training Academy, Quantico, Virginia. 1964.

Lana and I wrote letters to each other almost every day, and I would call her when I had free time and access to a pay telephone. She was busy with the kids and teaching high school English, but we longed to see one another. Midway through my training Lana flew to Washington to visit. We got a room at the run-down Willard Hotel where the rooms were not expensive. It was Lana's first trip to Washington, D. C. and we had a great weekend. A few weeks later, my classmates and I got our credentials and graduated. We were now full-fledged special agents of the FBI. On December 18, one day before my twenty-ninth birthday, I headed home to Arkansas. A few days later, we piled Paige and Sam into our Volkswagen Beetle and hit the road for a long drive from Pocahontas to Indianapolis, Indiana, my first office of assignment.

We spent a couple of nights in a motel, and by the time our furniture and belongings arrived, we had located a small, three-bedroom rent house. We moved in around 2:00 p.m. on December 24, 1964. We shoved the furniture into place, made up the beds, and got the children settled. It was dark before we had time to think about getting a Christmas tree and presents for the children so we took turns going to nearby stores, racing up and down the aisles grabbing toys and putting them into the shopping basket. Miraculously, by 10:00 p.m. we had our tree decorated and got the kids in bed. Then Lana and I put the toys and presents under the tree and lay down to rest. The children were up early on Christmas morning and so were we. It remains one of our favorite Christmas days.

My first month on the job in Indianapolis was quite an experience. I was a rookie and the special agent in charge assigned me to a squad working criminal matters. I worked with a senior agent for a while, but soon I learned how to get a bureau car from the motor pool and go out on my own to work leads assigned to me.

On the first day that I worked on my own, the radio operator notified all cars of a bank robbery in a little town outside Indianapolis. I cannot remember the name of the town, but it had less than 5,000 people. When I arrived on the scene, the case agent assigned me to do a neighborhood investigation.

Doing a neighborhood—knocking on doors to see if anyone has seen anything—is a menial but important task given to rookie agents. I began with gusto hoping that I would turn up some valuable information that would lead to the identification of the robbers. I found nothing, but I learned an important lesson about America. Indiana, particularly its rural areas, is the heartland of this great country. When I knocked on a door in that little town, I would show my credentials to whoever came to the door and say, "FBI." Without fail the person who opened the door would say, "Oh, how can I help? What can I do? What do you need?" In every instance, people were friendly and willing to support the FBI. I could have been in Pocahontas or any small Arkansas town where people care about their community and want to do their part.

A year later, after my assignment to Newark, New Jersey, I was working a bank robbery. I was again doing the neighborhood investigation, but this time I was in Jersey City going into brownstone walk-up apartment buildings. When I knocked on an apartment door, the occupant would open it, but only as wide as the security chains would allow. I would show my credentials to the eyeball peeping out at me and say in a loud strong voice, "FBI!" The voice of the eyeball would say, "So?" and slam the door shut.

There is a huge difference between the heartland of America and the inner cities of megalopolis, and the difference is attitude. The people in the inner cities practice anonymity to a fault. They have lost, if they ever had it, the feeling that they are part of a community and that they have a responsibility to help their neighbors. It is sad, but it is true, and it is a problem for our nation.

My first scary moment with an armed and dangerous subject came in my first days in the Indianapolis office. Our squad supervisor sent us out to arrest a man on a warrant for unlawful flight to avoid prosecution for murder. He was a little over six feet tall and well put together. By the time we cornered him, he was in an absolute rage and brandishing a knife. After some tense moments he relented, and we got the handcuffs on him. We took him back to headquarters, and he calmed down enough so that the supervisor said we could take the handcuffs off and get his fingerprints. That was a mistake. As soon as the cuffs were off his wrists, he took off. We tackled him but he fought like a tiger. It took four of us to subdue the man, but as we were wrestling him into submission, he kept trying to get his hands on our weapons, which were still in our holsters. It was a dumb mistake. We should have disarmed and posted an armed agent to cover us when we took the cuffs off the man. I never made that mistake again. If he had gotten his hands on one of our pistols, the scuffle could have turned into a nightmare.

We were not in Indianapolis long. In my second month, the Bureau transferred me to the Hammond, Indiana resident agency. Hammond is a suburb of Chicago, and the work there involved organized crime, gambling, and prostitution. We rented a small house in Schererville, Indiana, a little town ten miles south of Hammond. It was a fun community. The townspeople celebrated Oktoberfest, a new experience for us.

We also had another new experience. Lana was in our front yard talking to a neighbor and forgot that she had left a skillet full of tater-tots frying in boiling oil. In her defense, she had left the house to look for our three-year-old daughter, Paige, who had gone missing. The firefighters put out the fire in record time but it took a month to get the smell of smoke out of our furniture and clothing. Thankfully, our neighbors helped us and the owner of the property had insurance that paid for the cleanup and repairs. Again, we learned the advantages of living in the heartland of America where neighbors care about neighbors.

In early November of 1965, I received orders to report to Newark, New Jersey. We celebrated Christmas, stored our furniture, and Lana, Paige, and Sam caught a train for Arkansas where they would stay with Lana's folks until I could find suitable housing in New Jersey. I drove the VW to Newark and rented a room in an old house close to the FBI office. It was cheap and since I was an armed FBI agent, it worked as a temporary residence, but it was clear that I could not bring the family to New Jersey until I found a safer neighborhood well away from Newark.

It took a month, but I finally located a rent house in Middlebush, New Jersey. It was a crummy house but it was safe and cheap. It was also close to the Pennsylvania Railroad commuter line that I would take to and from work in Newark. My commute took an hour and five minutes each way, a new experience for a country boy from Arkansas. Lana got a job teaching English at a school in Piscataway. She needed the VW to take the kids to nursery school and get back and forth to her job. I needed a car to get to the train station, so I bought an old Ford, much like Old Black, the car we had had in law school. I paid $100 for it. It was blue and pockmarked with rust holes, some the size of golf balls. We had to park it on the street so we told the neighbors that I needed such a car in my work as an FBI agent. I am not sure they bought our story, but they never complained. One of the neighbor children used to say the holes were bullet holes, so I imagine their parents used that line to explain the presence of such an eyesore.

I was on the C-1 squad in Newark. It was our responsibility to investigate all bank robberies and hijackings. There were plenty of bank robberies, but hijackings were out of control in the New York and Newark metropolitan area. Most of our work was in Kearny, Jersey City, Hoboken, Union City, and Bayonne. They all qualified as tough areas.

Hijackings present an interesting investigative challenge because the thugs who steal the trucks and sometimes kill the drivers have to coordinate their activities with the mob. It does no good to steal an expensive load of cigarettes or whiskey if you do not have a ready market for the "swag." The mob, powerful at that time, provided the market and protected the merchants who sold the stolen goods to the public. The best way to solve a hijacking was to develop informants who would find out when the hijackers planned to deliver the hijacked truck or trailer to a storage facility, also known as a "drop," where the goods would be unloaded and transferred to the mob. It was relatively easy to catch the minor players, but it was much harder to reel in the important players, the mobsters and the big merchants who sold the swag to the public. They were wise to the ways of the FBI. Nevertheless, we were good at what we did. We developed a number of good informants, and we spent many hours surveilling hijackers to the drop. There were many days when I got home after a long ride on the commuter train only to discover that the office had called and wanted me to come back in for an all-night surveillance.

One of the first things I heard when I got to Newark was that its city government was corrupt. Hugh Addonizio, a former congressman, was mayor and in the late 1960s a blue ribbon panel appointed by Governor Richard Hughes reported that there was a pervasive feeling of corruption in the city. The panel recommended the appointment of a special grand jury to investigate the allegations of corruption. I had a brush with Newark corruption when I asked the city police to hold a federal prisoner for me. It was customary to use county and local jails to detain federal prisoners since the federal government had no such facilities. When I returned two days later to get my prisoner, a Newark police lieutenant told me he had charged my prisoner with a state offense and that they were not going to give him back to me. I was furious and got into a shouting match with the lieutenant in the presence of my prisoner. The lieutenant stood his ground so I picked up the phone and called our special agent in charge who immediately called FBI Headquarters in Washington, D. C. to report what was happening. In about ten minutes, the lieutenant got a call and left the room. When he returned, he said I could take the prisoner. As we left the building my prisoner, who seemed flattered that we were arguing over him, said: "Man, I thought you guys were going to draw pistols." I had little doubt that the mob was behind the effort to get my prisoner out of federal custody. I had arrested him for hijacking, and there was the possibility that the prosecution of his case might be troublesome for organized crime. A few years later, the mayor was convicted for "delivering the city into the hands of organized crime," according to former U.S. District Judge Herbert J. Stern. In spite of that, corruption continued. Newark was a terrible place to live and raise a family, but it was a good place to be an FBI agent. There was an endless supply of interesting work.

I had one case where a tip led us to set up surveillance on the New Jersey side of the Hudson River. Our information was that the hijacker would be coming from New York to New Jersey in a particular rig. The load was fresh beef, very expensive, but difficult to market because it had to be refrigerated. We waited for hours and our patience paid off. Around noon, the tractor-trailer we were looking for rolled out of the tunnel, and we followed it onto the New Jersey Turnpike, heading south. Usually the drops were in the city, close to the markets, but this load left the metropolitan area and continued south. Surveillance is a tricky business, particularly on the New Jersey Turnpike. You have to avoid detection and that is not easy, because clever hijackers have many tricks they use to "clean" themselves. We had several cars working on this surveillance so we managed to follow the hijackers all the way to an unusual place. They, for some reason unknown to us, had taken the stolen load to a rural area and turned into a large grove of trees protected by acres of open fields. It would be hard to get close enough to see what they were doing, and we needed to get a positive identification of the driver, the vehicles, and some basic idea of what they were doing in order to get authority from the United States attorney to move in and make an arrest. I sneaked up to a tree on a small hill near the grove and climbed up to a perch on the first big branch. Once settled I could see that there were several people and cars in the grove. Typically, hijackers either unload the trailer or just leave it in a hiding place, but these suspects were painting the truck and changing its identifying marks. With that information, we were able to get arrest authority so we converged on the grove from all directions. It was a good bust; we caught several important players and recovered the load of beef. The driver of the rig recognized me from a previous investigation and when he saw me he said, "He's the guy who ought to get the stripes for this one."

Several of the agents on C-1 had been born and raised in the south. Once we surveilled a carload of suspected mobsters from Newark to Philadelphia. We made radio contact with agents from the Philadelphia office as we neared the Delaware River because we were going to transfer the surveillance to them. When it was over we met the Philadelphia agents for a cup of coffee and they said, "Man, you guys sounded like Mississippi coming down the

New Jersey Turnpike." We liked it that we still had our southern drawls.

Lana and I were determined to make the most out of our time in the New York metropolitan area. We were on a tight budget, but we learned to beat the system by taking picnic lunches on day trips. With careful planning there was a lot to do that did not cost much. We took Sam and Paige to every zoo within a day's drive of Middlebush, New Jersey. The Bronx Zoo was a good one, but it was no match for the Philadelphia Zoo. We quickly developed our ability to rate zoos and other low-cost public facilities. We were freebie-connoisseurs; nothing escaped our scrutiny. We saw free events at Central Park, free museum events, and we never missed the Macy's Christmas Parade. F.A.O. Schwartz and other stores had fascinating displays that our kids loved, and we made our way from one place to another on the subway. We tried the Circle Line boat cruise, but it was too pricey. Besides, the cheapest and best boat ride in New York City is the Staten Island Ferry, which gives a great view of Manhattan and passes close to the Statue of Liberty. Lana and I always kept an eye open for bargains on theatre tickets. We managed to see a dozen first-rate Broadway shows. The first one we saw was *Funny Girl*, but the best was *Sweet Charity* starring Gwen Verdon as she was winding down her fabulous dancing and acting career.

In 1966, the Baltimore Orioles won the American League pennant. Brooks Robinson, a native of Little Rock, was the star third baseman for the Orioles. I had played sandlot baseball with Brooks when we were growing up in Little Rock, and we had both made the Little Rock All-Star Team. We were also in the same Boy Scout troop, but Lana had an even closer relationship with Brooks. She had dated him when they were classmates at Pulaski Heights Junior High School and they were in the same graduating class at Little Rock Central High School. In late September, Lana heard that the Orioles were playing one of the last games of the regular season at Yankee stadium. They had not clinched the pennant, but they were close and it was a virtual certainty that they would do it. She picked up the phone, called

Yankee stadium, asked for the visitor's dugout, and when someone answered she said, "I want to speak to Brooks Robinson." The person on the other end said, "Lady, he's getting ready for a game, he can't come to the phone." Lana replied, "You tell him that Lana Douthit is calling." In no time at all Brooks was on the phone. Lana said, "Brooks, we are so excited, we have never been to a World Series." He laughed and said, "Neither have I, Lana." The next day, the Orioles clinched the pennant and three days after that we got a special delivery letter from Brooks. It contained tickets to games three and four, scheduled for Memorial Stadium in Baltimore. Brooks also invited us to his home for a party before and after each game. I was the envy of the Newark FBI office. We attended both games. The Orioles swept four straight games from the National League champions, the Los Angeles Dodgers. For the first time in franchise history, the Orioles were World Series champions. The Dodgers scored only two runs in the entire series and those runs came in the first three innings of the first game, which meant that the Baltimore pitchers shut out Los Angeles for the last thirty-three innings of the World Series. It was a fantastic accomplishment.

In late 1966, the FBI transferred me to the resident agency in Red Bank, New Jersey. It was good news because I was tired of my daily commute on the Pennsylvania Railroad. We bought a house in Middletown, only ten minutes from my new office, which backed up to the Navesink River, and Lana landed a teaching job at Middletown High School. I had just received my promotion to GS-11 and now I would not have the expense of commuting. Things were looking up for the Bethune family. We joined a beach club where the children could learn to swim, and we got a big RCA color TV, our first color television set. We did make one mistake as we were outfitting our new home. We purchased a beagle puppy and named him Beau. He was cute, but he loved to jump up on top of his doghouse and, true to the beagle breed, bay at the moon. His baying did not bother us, but many of our close neighbors left their windows open at night because they did not have air conditioning. It was not long until

I was getting phone calls asking me to put Beau in the house so the neighbors could get some sleep. On the first night Beau was in the house, he chewed the arm off my favorite stuffed chair. My fellow agents laughed when I told them I was so mad that I was planning to take Beau to the dog pound, but softhearted Jim Marley, our most senior agent, could not bear the thought of that. I seized the opportunity by suggesting he should take Beau, and he agreed. Paige and Sam offered little resistance because their neighborhood friends teased them unmercifully about having a dog that bayed at the moon.

In the summer of 1967, I got a radio call to go to a chicken farm near Lakewood to assist in an investigation. It was a one-hour drive from where I was at the time, and when I got there, around 10:00 a.m., I saw backhoes, trucks, and agents with shovels.

The case agent, Thomas Powers, was briefing other agents on the situation. A source had provided information that the chicken farm was a Mafia burial ground and that we would find several bodies there.

The work at the burial ground went on for several days and the digging unearthed several things of interest. I saw the partial remains of one body, a chest cavity with most of the ribs attached. A fellow agent showed me a sixty-gallon drum of fluid that contained a few globules of fat. He theorized it might be the remains of a body stuffed into a drum of acid that neutralized as the body was consumed, leaving only the globules of fat. I—the unscientific dunce who flunked chemistry as a freshman at the University of Arkansas—readily accepted his theory, but I later wondered if my friend was just having some fun with me. The case was big news because it generated sexy headlines and there were good visuals for television—a formula guaranteed to drive the media crazy. For several days, the media treated the entire nation to breathless reports about the FBI digging up a "Mafia Burial Ground." Soon the media grew tired of telling and retelling the same story so they lost interest and moved on to other things. The burial ground case was just one of many episodes involving *La Cosa Nostra* (Mr. Hoover's preferred name for the Mafia) in the late 1960s.

My work in Red Bank was different than it was in Newark. We had an occasional bank robbery, but hijackings were rare. I worked various cases in and around Fort Monmouth and Long Branch, against a backdrop of national political and cultural turmoil. It was early 1967. The country was tearing itself apart over the Vietnam War, a conflict that was not going well. A new counterculture had formed and many organizations espoused socialist and sometimes communist doctrine. Many Americans opposed escalating the U.S. role in Vietnam, believing the economic cost too high, but most disapproved of the counterculture that had arisen alongside the antiwar movement. Those identified with the new movement were called "Hippies." Middle Americans, particularly older Americans were uncomfortable with the youth culture of the period—long hair, casual drug use, promiscuity, and protest music.

The Black Panthers, an extremist group organized in 1966, and Students for a Democratic Society (SDS) had different ways of operating, but they typified the intense protesting that exploded after President Johnson, in early 1965, ordered the bombing of North Vietnam and introduced ground troops to fight the Viet Cong in South Vietnam.

There was so much unrest nationwide that it was no surprise to those of us in the FBI when rioting broke out in the black neighborhoods of Newark. The summertime riots lasted six days, ending on July 17, 1967. The city was ablaze. The governor of New Jersey said it was an "obvious open rebellion." He called out the National Guard and sent large numbers of state troopers in to quell the riot and put an end to the looting, burning and sniping. I had occasion to be in the heart of the riot at the height of the trouble. I will never forget what I saw. It was heart wrenching. It reminded me of the time I saw the National Guard troops and the 101st Airborne surrounding Little Rock Central High School in 1957, only this was worse.

I wondered: Why are these things happening in the United States of America? The black community of Newark was effectively under military occupation. Twenty-six people died, nearly all from police shootings. Hundreds were injured and the police jailed more than a thousand. Official inquiries later concluded that the riot started because black citizens of Newark felt excluded from meaningful political representation and often suffered police brutality. Unemployment, poverty, and issues over low-quality housing also contributed to the turmoil.

All during this time of political and cultural upheaval, those of us in federal law enforcement were on alert for attempts to break into armories. The most virulent protest groups had announced their intention to use force, and later a faction of SDS, the Weather Underground, did exactly that.

It was a difficult time to be an FBI agent, but 1967 was especially difficult for me for a personal reason. My father, after a long illness with lung cancer, died on April 19. Daddy visited us a few months before he died. When he flew into Newark, Lana, the kids, and I met him at the airport. When the flight attendants got him off the plane and into a wheelchair on the tarmac we ran to meet him, but when we got close to him we could see that he was frail, obviously sick. In spite of that, Daddy gave us his trademark smile and managed to keep up a good front for the three days that he stayed with us. I took some time off and we treated Daddy to a complete car tour of our favorite places. When we put him on the plane back to Arkansas I think he knew, as did I, that it was the last time I would see him alive.

Shortly after Daddy got home my sister put him in a nursing home, and he died a few weeks later. I could not be there for the last days of his illness, but my sister told me it would not have mattered because he was in such bad shape that he would not have known I was there. I flew home for Daddy's funeral in Wilmot. Aunt Delle made the arrangements. The undertaker would bury Daddy in the cemetery overlooking a lake near Bayou Bartholomew, but friends and family would have a chance to view him in his open casket at Aunt Delle's house before the burial service. The open casket viewing is an integral part of the Southern Baptist way of saying goodbye to a loved one. My sister and I were so appreciative of Aunt Delle's help that we did not object to the open casket or the huge amount of food displayed and served throughout the house. My Uncle Rod Bethune attended the funeral, but was not too fond of the Southern Baptist way. He said, as the event wound down: "It's OK, but it's a little too picnicky to suit me." Daddy would have laughed a belly laugh at Uncle Rod's remark, but then he would have defended Aunt Delle. He was that kind of man. He lived hard, he died hard, and he did it all with good cheer.

In early 1968, the Tet Offensive in Vietnam turned out to be a military defeat for the communists, but politicians and military leaders had led the American people to believe that the communists were incapable of launching such a massive effort. The offensive proved our leaders wrong and revealed to the American people that the war in Vietnam was in disarray. On March 31, 1968, President Lyndon Johnson announced he would not seek re-election. Just as everyone believed things could get no worse, a gunman assassinated Dr. Martin Luther King in Memphis, Tennessee. The national turmoil reached a new level, and despite the urging of many leaders, the assassination on April 4, 1968, led to a nationwide wave of riots in more than one hundred cities. The worst of these riots were in Washington, D. C., and Baltimore, Maryland.

I was deep into my work but I had come to realize that I was stuck in New Jersey. Senior agents, in a position to know, told me that Mr. Hoover had established a policy in the mid-1960s to the effect that no southern born agent could serve in a southern office until he had been in the Bureau for a long time. He made the rule after Dr. King, who Mr. Hoover never got along with, alleged that FBI agents in the South were unsympathetic to civil rights allegations. If I ever got an assignment outside New Jersey, it would not be in the South. The barrier to serving in the South was a concern. We would have loved a transfer to Arkansas, but it never really bothered us until one day our kids came home from preschool and our four-year-old son, Sam, said in a perfect New Jersey brogue as he was taking a Dr. Pepper out of the refrigerator: "Hey, youse guys want a bottle of pop?" Lana and I looked at each other, knowingly. We wanted our children to have the same kind of early life we had had growing up in Arkansas. We wanted them to know their Arkansas relatives and understand their Arkansas roots.

We started thinking seriously about leaving the FBI. I knew what it was like to practice law because of my experience in Pocahontas. I was confident that I could be a good lawyer and make a good living, especially since I had four years experience as an FBI agent. After much discussion, we decided that if I could find a good opportunity in Arkansas we ought to consider it. It was hard to talk about getting out of the FBI because I loved being an agent and I was good at it. Nevertheless, we decided to take the next step.

15

ARKANSAS LAWYER, ARKANSAS REPUBLICAN

Home is where we love, home that our
feet may leave, but not our hearts.
Oliver Wendell Holmes, Sr.

I typed letters to several of my law school friends to see if they knew of any openings for me in the legal profession. It made me a little nervous to drop the letters in the mail because I did not want the Bureau to find out that I was looking around. Nevertheless, I took the risk. Over the next two weeks, I received responses from every one of my friends. That made me feel good, but it felt even better to learn that there were several promising job opportunities for me to explore. I took a week off and flew back to Arkansas to begin my investigation of the job market. I stayed with Mother in Little Rock, borrowed her Plymouth Valiant, and headed to Harrison, Arkansas for my first interview. In the days that followed, I drove from one side of the state to the other and talked to several lawyers, mostly in small towns. I also interviewed in Jonesboro, Fayetteville, Pine Bluff, and Texarkana. I spent hours on the road, and that gave me what I needed most, time to think.

We were in reasonably good financial shape, thanks to four years of frugality and two steady incomes. The FBI had a policy that allowed agents to pass up vacations and accumulate leave time. I had not taken much leave during my four years, thus I would receive over $4000 from the FBI for unused vacation if I resigned. Other than that, we had about $2000 in savings, and we had all our bills paid. When we were in law school, Lana and I used to dream of the day when we would "have all our bills paid and have a thousand dollars in the bank." We used to laugh and say if we ever reached that goal, we would be rich. In our minds, we were "rich" as we considered taking a new step in our life. We put financial considerations aside and pledged to focus on professional opportunity, finding the perfect community to raise our kids, and being close to loved ones. We were convinced that the financial issue would take care of itself if we based our decision on the other factors.

As I drove from one interview to the next, one thought kept running through my mind, and it dominated all others. I was thirty-two and, for the first time in my life, I honestly felt that I might eventually be a success. I had no particular definition of success, but I had started believing that I would eventually "be somebody." I thought about my personal, material, and professional achievements and measured them against the doubts I had had about myself when I was an incorrigible, bedwetting child in the tenth grade. I had made slow but steady progress, and I was reaching new plateaus with regularity. There were bumps along the road, but overall I was pleased with myself, not overly proud, just pleased. Unfortunately, I gave undeserved credit to the Vermilye worldview. I concluded that my accomplishments—overcoming bedwetting, being a Marine, getting college degrees, marrying the right woman, having healthy children, and becoming a special agent of the FBI—were the product of my will. I had accomplished more than I ever thought I would when I was a young boy. I even had a nice house and a color TV. I could reach any goal and I did not have to take "No" for an answer. Why should I? I was proving the fundamental tenet of the Vermilye worldview: Where there is a will there is a way. As a side benefit, I had "them" on the run so that "they" could not take anything from me. I needed nothing more than what I had.

In the end, Lana and I decided I should take the job offered to me by Odell Pollard, a true country lawyer in Searcy, Arkansas, a small town forty-five miles northeast of Little Rock. Odell, ten years my senior, had just built a new law office, and his general practice was well established. He was a solo practitioner at the time, but Jerry Cavaneau, a young lawyer, was going to rejoin the firm upon completing a hitch in the U. S. Navy. Lana and I knew several people in Searcy. E. D. Yancey, and Jack Gardner and his wife Anne were friends from our days at the University of Arkansas. The proximity to Little Rock made Searcy a perfect choice because in less than an hour we could visit my mother and sister, and Lana's mother and father. We had other relatives living close by, but our biggest incentive was that Searcy had excellent public schools. Our children were ready to enter grammar school, and Lana could get a job teaching English. Little Rock, where we both spent our early years, would have been a good choice. The public schools in Pulaski County were still in turmoil following the 1957 school integration crisis, but that was not the reason we chose Searcy.

We picked Searcy because we liked the town and the people. It reminded me of Pocahontas with flat land east of town and hills on the west side. It would take some time to settle in and create a backlog of shared memories with new friends, but eventually Searcy would be like Pocahontas. It would give us a sense of place and be a rock for us to stand on, one we could always come back to when we needed to get our bearings.

I resigned from the FBI, and on May 4, 1968, we left New Jersey for Searcy, Arkansas. We moved into a little two-bedroom house that we rented from Jim Smith, and I went to work with Odell Pollard. My monthly guarantee of $400 was quite a comedown from my FBI salary, but I was convinced I would do better eventually. I did everything from reading abstracts of title to writing deeds to defending criminal cases. I was busy but I had much more time to spend with my family. Paige and Sam made many new friends, and most importantly, they stopped saying "youse guys," and "bottle of pop."

Settling in Searcy was good for many reasons, but it still impresses us that the first question townspeople ask a newcomer is, "Where do you go to church?" We resolved that question by joining First Methodist Church of Searcy. Several of our old friends were members of First Methodist, and Lana had grown up at Pulaski Heights Methodist Church in Little Rock. I had attended Winfield Methodist Church in Little Rock. It was a no-brainer.

I was not thinking about politics when Lana and I decided to move to Searcy, but Odell Pollard was chairman of the embryonic Republican Party of Arkansas. Because of that, I began to keep up with what he and his allies were trying to do.

I had learned a little bit about Republicans when I was in Pocahontas and Barry Goldwater was running for president. An eighty-year-old doctor who had his office next to my law office, Doc Hamil, kept saying the country needed to get back to basics and get away from the likes of Lyndon Johnson. Doc was a Goldwater man and his constant refrain was, "We need to start new money."

I learned a lot more about the Republican party when I was in the FBI even though, as agents, we had orders to refrain from conspicuous political activity. That was easy for me because I had little interest in such matters. Nevertheless, I met many agents from the North who were life-long Republicans. When riding around in a FBI car, particularly during long surveillances, we talked about sports, girls, and politics. Invariably, they would ask, "What are you Bethune, a Republican or a Democrat?" I always told them I had been "rocked in the Democrat cradle," and said without equivocation, "I'm a Democrat."

They would say, "You don't sound like a Democrat—you sound like a Republican." To that I would respond, "That's impossible; we don't have any of those in Arkansas."

I liked the conservative ideas I heard from my Republican friends in the FBI, and it got me to thinking about the difference between Democrats and Republicans. Even so, I did not change parties. Politics did not matter to me when I was in the FBI, but that was about to change.

Odell Pollard, like me, had been raised a Democrat, but he became a Republican in the early 1960s. Odell switched because he despised what was happening in Arkansas. The Old Guard—a Democrat political machine led by Governor Orval Faubus—controlled state government. The regime prospered because it had no competition. Arkansas was a solid one-party state. Almost all officeholders—local, county, and state—were Democrats. Winning a Democrat primary was tantamount to election. Those affiliating with the GOP must have been out of their minds or they were looking for a federal job (mainly as postmasters), so said the Democrats. For that reason, the Democrats called all Republicans "Post Office Republicans."

Winthrop Rockefeller, one of the wealthy Rockefellers, took up residence in Arkansas after World War II. He was a lifelong Republican and the antics of Orval Faubus mortified him. As he got more involved in Arkansas affairs, Rockefeller decided to challenge the Old Guard by running against Faubus in 1964. He lost that race, but when he announced that he would run again in 1966, Faubus saw what was coming. He stepped down, and the Old Guard machine nominated Justice Jim Johnson, a member of the Arkansas Supreme Court, to be their standard-bearer. Johnson—a colorful figure—used everything from segregation to suspicion in his effort to keep the Old Guard together. He called Rockefeller "Big Daddy Two-Boots" and labeled all who supported him as "Rockefellercrats." It did not work.

Arkansans were not quite ready to be Republicans, but they could see the need for competition in politics. Rockefeller put together a force that included fed-up Democrats and Independents who wanted to change Arkansas for the better. The coalition included a substantial majority of African Americans who had suffered oppression under the Old Guard. Rockefeller won, as did the Republican candidate for lieutenant governor, Maurice "Footsy" Britt, a Medal of Honor winner. Arkansans in the Third Congressional District also elected John Paul Hammerschmidt of Harrison to be the first Republican member of the U. S. House of Representatives from that district since Reconstruction.

It was a new day in Arkansas. The Rockefeller administration was the antithesis of the Old Guard. Decision-making was transparent, an immoral prison system was reformed, illegal gambling and graft in Hot Springs were stopped and most importantly, government was, for the first time, opened up to women and blacks. It was a testament to the power of competition in politics and an important toehold for the Republican party, giving hope that one day there would be a viable two-party system in Arkansas.

Within a few weeks of my arrival in Searcy in 1968, I decided I wanted to be a part of what Governor Rockefeller, Odell Pollard, and the Republican party were doing for the state of Arkansas. In those days, we had two-year terms of office for governor so Rockefeller was running for re-election. The Old Guard, eager to get back in power, handpicked a candidate, Marion Crank, to run against Rockefeller. The Democrats controlled virtually every other office in the state and they, for years, had used their county and district level positions to shamelessly steal votes and distort the election process. Rockefeller and his supporters had worked hard since 1964 to stop the foul practices, particularly the vote stealing, but the reform effort did not get traction until Tom Glaze, a law school classmate of mine, organized The Election Law Institute in 1970.

The Rockefeller team welcomed me and put me to work enforcing election laws. The Democrats were doing everything they could to minimize the black vote, which was sure to go to Rockefeller. There were instances where the Democrats would arrange precincts so that large numbers of blacks would have to vote in one box. The voting in those days was by paper ballot, so by cutting down the number of election judges and clerks the process of voting slowed to a virtual standstill. Blacks desiring to vote had to stand for hours in long lines waiting their turn to get a ballot, and many would do just that. Some dropped out of line because they had to get back to work, while others just got discouraged and gave up.

A few days before Election Day in 1968, the Republican party sent me to Crittenden County to file a *mandamus* action against Democrat election officials. The Democrats were up to their old tricks. They were refusing to appoint a proper number of election officials, and my job was to get the circuit judge to issue a writ requiring the Democrats to comply with the law so that people could vote without standing in long lines. When I got to the courthouse and filed my petition the clerk told me the judge, Todd Harrison, a Democrat, was out of town and that it would be hours before he could hear my argument. The lawyers for the Democrats told me they intended to fight my request and that it would be necessary to call witnesses. Their insistence to have an evidentiary hearing was an obvious attempt to stall. There was no need to call witnesses—the facts were undisputed. I said I would wait for the judge to get there because I was entitled to an immediate hearing on my petition. Eventually the judge showed up and the Democrats said they were ready to go to trial. I noticed there was no court reporter and told the judge I had no intention of proceeding without an official reporter. He said he did not realize I might want to report the proceedings so he had excused his reporter for the day. He said a reporter "would be a waste of time" because the election was only a day away and there would not be enough time for me to appeal an adverse ruling to the Arkansas Supreme Court. I cited cases showing that election law issues are never moot and that I wanted a reporter so that there would be an appealable record. With that, the Democrat officials, their lawyers, and the judge just laughed at me. I asked for a recess and advised the court it was my intention to bring a qualified court reporter from nearby Memphis to make a record of the proceedings. That irritated the judge, but he dared not block my insistent effort to make a record for fear of turning the case into a *cause célèbre*. He granted my request for a recess, and in a couple of hours the reporter I hired showed up and the trial started. The Democrats called several unnecessary witnesses who from the witness stand referred to me as a "Rockefellercrat." They also made a number of absurd arguments to justify what they were doing. The judge, as expected, ruled in their favor. I explained to the large number of blacks who had come to the trial that I would turn the record of the proceedings over to Governor Rockefeller. With that, I left Crittenden County. I was glad to get away from the disgusting environment. It made me sick to see lawyers and judges use our system of justice to keep people from voting.

Governor Rockefeller won re-election. We decided not to appeal Judge Harrison's flawed ruling, but the episode remains a good example of why we must have competition in politics.

A better example of the need for two parties occurred in Conway County. I played a key role in a political drama that was stranger than fiction, a fiasco that nearly cost me my life. A fellow attorney in Searcy, Cecil Tedder, who later became a circuit judge, laughingly said I should have received the "Order of the Purple Navel," for what happened to me in Conway County.

Marlin Hawkins became sheriff of Conway County, Arkansas in 1951, and before that he had held other county offices. He was a classic county-level politician. The people in his home county revered him, but elsewhere he received mixed reviews. Shortly before his death in 1995, he published an autobiography entitled, *How I Stole Elections.* My father and I are in his book: Daddy for the work he and Marlin did during the Great Depression to recruit young men for the Civilian Conservation Corps, and I for the fiasco.

In the mid-1960s, Marlin Hawkins had a running feud with Gene Wirges, the publisher of a local newspaper in Conway County. That dustup produced a number of allegations, one of which was that Marlin Hawkins, as sheriff, was engaged in an unlawful scheme to skim money from traffic ticket collections. A number of taxpayers filed suit contending that the sheriff wrongfully converted to his own use substantial sums of money collected and received as fines and costs. After years of litigation a judge ruled in favor of the taxpayers and ordered the sheriff to pay a judgment of $10,082.

Winthrop Rockefeller was governor of Arkansas at the time and that was an unfortunate development for Sheriff Hawkins.

The governor's lawyers, at the urging of Wirges, found a law saying that a sheriff was disqualified to hold office if he owed such a judgment to the people. In their opinion, the office of sheriff was, *eo instante*, vacant upon entry of the judgment. Having reached that conclusion, the lawyers opined that Governor Rockefeller had the duty to appoint a successor to fill the vacancy. Governor Rockefeller needed no coaxing. He and Marlin Hawkins had been at odds for years. The problem was to find someone with enough courage to take an appointment that would surely infuriate the citizens of Conway County.

It took some searching, but eventually an eighty-three-year-old gentleman, Mr. Ralph Childers, agreed to take the appointment. The paperwork was quickly prepared, and by the time Childers took the oath of office in Little Rock, news of his appointment had already reached Conway County. The governor received reports that Marlin's supporters were gathering around the county courthouse in Morrilton. Some were armed, and they were saying to anyone who would listen that they were not going to let Ralph Childers serve as sheriff of Conway County. They intended to block any attempt by him to enter the courthouse office of Sheriff Hawkins. Mr. Childers was willing to go to Conway County, but everyone agreed he needed an escort to help him navigate his way through hostile crowds and make comments to the press explaining why he was sheriff and Marlin Hawkins was not.

The governor's lawyers nominated me to accompany the new sheriff.

Mr. Childers and I boarded a small single engine Bonanza at Central Flying Service in Little Rock shortly after lunch. After a short flight, we landed on a grass airfield just west of Morrilton. There Gene Wirges met us and drove us to his newspaper office. He told us the streets around the courthouse were full of irate Hawkins supporters, but he said a few people who supported our cause were in the crowd. The director of the Arkansas State

Police called me at the newspaper office and warned me that we were walking into a hornet's nest. He urged us to use extreme caution. Mr. Childers, Gene Wirges, and I debated the situation, trying to decide whether we should go to the courthouse to finish what Governor Rockefeller had started. It would be risky, but it was the right thing to do. The governor was dedicated to clean government and Sheriff Hawkins was the poster-boy for county level corruption. We decided to go.

By the time we got to the courthouse there were well over five hundred Hawkins supporters milling around. Most were on foot and quite a few were armed. They were carrying pistols, rifles, and shotguns and making no effort to conceal the weapons. Many others were sitting in their cars and trucks, armed and ready. Two state police troopers escorted us into the courthouse where a deputy sheriff told us that Sheriff Hawkins was out of town and he did not have a key to the office. He said, "If you want to get in you will just have to wait for the sheriff to return." That was an obvious put-off so we said we would just take a seat on a bench in the hall and wait for Marlin Hawkins to return, or for someone to open the door and let us in.

Meanwhile, the Hawkins supporters were circulating inflammatory stories to keep their people fired up. One of the stories was that Gene Wirges and the state police, operating under the authority of the governor, intended to go to Marlin's home and take the keys to the office from his wife, by force if necessary. To make matters worse, Hawkins, who was in Little Rock, gave an interview to the press alleging that the governor was using gestapo tactics at the courthouse and at his residence.

The mayor of Morrilton, Thomas Hickey, got so upset that he came to the courthouse with a shotgun and pistols holstered on his hip. He demanded that the state police allow his city police officers to enter the building so that they could stop any attempt we might make to take over the sheriff's office. The state police relented because they had no legal right to keep the local authorities out of the courthouse. Once they were in the building the mayor stationed an inexperienced rookie, Gene Price, to stand in front of the door to the sheriff's office and—unbeknownst to me—told Price to use his sawed-off shotgun to shoot anyone who tried to enter the sheriff's office. By then some of the sheriff's deputies were also in the building. The atmosphere had reached boiling point.

Steve Barnes, who later became Arkansas's most revered TV news reporter, was at the time a cub reporter for Channel 11, KTHV-TV, in Little Rock. He was in Morrilton to cover the story and somehow managed to get inside the courthouse. Mr. Childers and I had been sitting on the bench waiting for half an hour. It was nearing the end of the day and Barnes was running out of time to get a story on the evening news. He asked me if Mr. Childers and I would allow him to film a short video of us in front of the door leading into the sheriff's office.

I saw no harm in that so we agreed and Mr. Childers and I started down the hall toward the sheriff's office. Steve followed with his camera up and ready to roll. As we got close to the office the rookie officer, Gene Price, jumped out of the shadows and stuck his shotgun in my stomach, saying, "Halt, I'm fixin' to shoot you." Thank God I had just finished a four-year tour as a special agent of the FBI, otherwise I might have fainted dead away.

The rookie cop was shaking and his voice was squeaky and shrill. His jittery eyes, only a foot or so from mine, told the story. He was the one with the gun, but he was scared to death. As he pushed the gun harder into my belly, I realized that my life depended on the wiring between the rookie's brain and his trigger finger and I did not like the odds.

At that life-and-death moment, a state trooper stepped up beside me and told Price to calm down. The trooper took hold of the barrel of the shotgun and slowly lifted it straight up as he gently continued his effort to soothe Price. I held my breath as the muzzle started its life-long journey upward. It passed my chest, then my Adam's apple, then my mouth, and finally it passed directly between my eyes. My mind was abuzz and I cannot remember what I was thinking—I only remember that it was a prayer.

Once the muzzle of the shotgun was up and out of the way, the confrontation with Price was over, but it was immediately apparent that we should abandon the attempt to install a new sheriff, at least for the moment. I told the state police and Steve Barnes that Sheriff Childers and I were going to Little Rock where I would appeal to the attorney general to seek a writ of *quo warranto,* a legal proceeding that forces an ousted official—Marlin Hawkins in this case—to show by what warrant he continues to serve.

Mr. Childers and I went outside and stood on the courthouse steps where I gave an impromptu interview to others in the media. As we were speaking, a fight broke out. A Hawkins supporter attacked a Rockefeller supporter and bloodied his nose as they rolled down the courthouse steps. I told the media that I would be at the attorney general's office first thing the next day. Sheriff Childers and I got into a state police car and headed for Little Rock. The crisis was over, at least for the day, and I was lucky to be alive.

The next day, I confronted Attorney General Joe Purcell, a Democrat, and urged him to seek a writ of *quo warranto.* He grinned, and said nothing. He knew, and I learned later, that Marlin Hawkins and several friends had paid the judgment that morning by tendering a certified check for $10,082 to the county treasurer.

Thus ended the fiasco for which my friend, Cecil Tedder, awarded me the fictitious Order of the Purple Navel.

It was about this time that Lana and I bought our second house. Jim Baugh Jones, a good friend, was moving to a new home, so we bought the small three-bedroom house at One Meadowlane Drive in Searcy, where he and his family had lived for several years.

Shortly thereafter, I learned that the prosecuting attorney for the First Judicial District, Lloyd Henry, had died of a heart attack while exercising at home. The district included Searcy and White County, and it extended a hundred miles east to the Mississippi River, taking in the Delta counties of Phillips, Lee, St.

Francis, and Woodruff. The governor's people contacted Odell Pollard to see if I would be interested in taking an appointment to fill the unexpired term of one year. I immediately agreed and took to my new job like a duck to water. It was a natural for me since I had previous experience as a deputy prosecutor and four years experience as a FBI agent.

During my year as prosecutor I traveled Eastern Arkansas with Elmo Taylor, the longtime circuit judge of the First Judicial District. Judge Taylor was an old time, conservative judge. He gave no slack to those charged with crime, and he had little use for the lawyers who regularly defended such people. He was especially hostile to a Jewish lawyer from Little Rock, Jack Levy, who often appeared on behalf of indigents facing punishment for serious crimes. Elmo loved to pick on the lawyers and he delighted in making them look incompetent. You never knew whom Elmo would use as a foil, but when Jack Levy showed up for docket call, the rest of us relaxed. Poor Jack, a good guy, was like a lightning rod for Elmo's sarcasm. All the lawyers loved Jack Levy.

The criminal justice process in Eastern Arkansas forty years ago was an embarrassment, and that is putting it mildly. When Judge Taylor came into a county seat for court, the sheriff of the county would bring all the prisoners from the jail to the courtroom for docket call and arraignment. Judge Taylor would summarily appoint lawyers to counsel with the prisoners who had no representation. The lawyer would confer with the prisoner for a few minutes then go into a huddle with the sheriff who would offer a plea negotiation that he had worked out with the local deputy prosecuting attorney. If a plea was agreed to, the prisoner would go before Judge Taylor who would take a plea of guilty from the prisoner and then commence a lecture about the evils of criminal life. When he wound down, Judge Taylor would ask me if I had a recommendation. I would recommend the punishment my deputy had agreed to in the plea negotiation and Judge Taylor would impose sentence. We repeated this scenario for all those who intended to plead guilty, which was usually the majority of the cases on the docket. For those who pleaded not guilty, a date was set for trial and bail was set. The entire process bore close resemblance to an assembly line. On one occasion during Judge Taylor's favorite speech about how the moment was a red-letter day in the life of the defendant, he pointed at me and asked the defendant, "Do you know who that man is?" The defendant said, "Yes sir, he be's The Recommender."

Everyone in the courtroom laughed, but the moment sadly demonstrated the need to reform the criminal justice system. I vowed to use my new position to encourage an upgrade of our antiquated laws of criminal procedure.

Any reform of the system would be complicated because the state of Arkansas had no central authority or repository for criminal procedure law. The pertinent laws were scattered through the constitution, the statute books, and the case reports. It was truly a hodgepodge and no one knew, with confidence, how to proceed when prosecuting or defending a criminal case. The leaders of the Arkansas Bar Association were looking for volunteers to head up a reform effort, and I jumped at the chance to take an important role. I wrote an article entitled "It's Assizetime in Arkansas" that called for all judges and members of the bar to get behind our reform effort. I worked so hard coordinating our state effort with a national reform effort sponsored by the American Bar Association that I became the de facto leader of the reform movement in Arkansas. Chief Justice Carlton Harris asked me to chair the procedures committee of the newly organized Arkansas Criminal Code Revision Commission. Justice John Fogleman, Jack Lessenberry, and Bill Thompson were members of my committee. We planned to base our work on the *American Bar Association Standards for Criminal Justice*, a body of excellent work put together by some of the finest minds in the legal profession. We worked on our own time, mostly on weekends. It was a grand volunteer effort. We got a small, $25,000 stipend from the legislature to hire law students as reporters. That helped our committee finish our work in less than a year.

The rules we wrote were good, but Arkansas, like many southern states, had always let the legislature control the laws of criminal procedure. That is the main reason we had a hodgepodge of rules that no one could understand. I learned in my work with reform leaders in other states that some states had transferred the power to write procedural rules to their state supreme court. Knowing that it would be difficult to get the Arkansas legislature to adopt our proposed rules, I drafted a bill similar to one in Kentucky. It provided for the Arkansas legislature to quitclaim authority for rules of criminal procedure to the Arkansas Supreme Court. I took the draft to Attorney General Ray Thornton who thought it was a good idea, and with the help of many people, the proposal passed and became Act 170 of 1971. Shortly thereafter, the Arkansas Supreme Court adopted the work of my committee as the official *Arkansas Rules of Criminal Procedure* for all courts in the state of Arkansas.

Arkansas became the poster child for a major drive sponsored by the American Bar Association to change and improve the criminal justice system in all fifty states. The American Bar Association dispatched me to tell the Arkansas story to judges and lawyers all across the USA, from Alaska to Washington, DC. I went to more than a dozen states. My mission was to urge other jurisdictions to do what "little Arkansas" had done on a meager budget of $25,000. The unmistakable message: How could supposedly more enlightened states with greater wealth refuse to upgrade their laws?

Governor Rockefeller lost his try for a third term in 1970. He had accomplished a lot, but the Democrats wanted desperately to win the office and return to power. They wisely rejected the Old Guard forces and nominated a clean, wholesome young lawyer, Dale Bumpers, to be their candidate. Bumpers won, but fair-minded political observers gave Governor Rockefeller credit for breaking up the Old Guard and opening up Arkansas politics to a new and better breed of Democrats.

Toward the end of my tenure as prosecuting attorney, the sheriff of White County arrested a young man he caught smoking a marijuana cigarette. He brought him to see me because the young man was a student at Harding University, a conservative Christian school in Searcy. I told the young man that I would not prosecute if he would go back to the campus and tell the dean that he had made a mistake he would never again make. He seemed flustered by my offer, so I said, "Look, they will understand. They will give you a second chance." He shook his head and said, "Hell, Mister, at Harding they kick you out for smoking a regular cigarette." I told the sheriff to let him go and later told the story to a friend at Harding who laughed and said it was good that the students worried that Harding would react sternly to misbehavior, particularly drug use.

In the final week of his governorship, Winthrop Rockefeller commuted the sentences of twenty-three men on death row. He said he did it because he did not believe in capital punishment. I had prosecuted five of the twenty-three and felt the governor had overstepped his constitutional authority to commute prison sentences. I wrote him a letter arguing that he had authority to issue commutations on a case-by-case basis, but the issuance of *carte blanche* commutations was essentially an attempt to change the settled law in Arkansas. My letter created a bit of a flap in the media so the governor's chief of staff, Bob Faulkner, chided me for criticizing the man who had given me my appointment. Governor Rockefeller and I finished our terms of office a few days later and that was the end of the commutation issue.

I rejoined the law firm. Jerry Cavaneau had finished his tour with the Navy, so he was back with us at the firm. I buried myself in the practice of law, working hard on a variety of civil matters and handling an occasional criminal defense, but I was restless. As prosecuting attorney and chair of the procedures committee of the Criminal Code Revision Commission, I had tasted the feeling of accomplishment one gets from public service, and I liked it.

16

DEFEAT, DOUBT, AND SUCCESS

Failure is not falling down but refusing to get up.
Chinese Proverb

The effort to build a viable two-party system in Arkansas suffered a setback in 1970. Orval Faubus and the Old Guard Democrats tried to retake the governor's office, but Dale Bumpers won the Democrat primary. He then turned back Governor Rockefeller's try for a third two-year term. The Democrats, new and rejuvenated, were back in power. The Old Guard was dead, thanks to the mortal blows delivered by Governor Rockefeller and the Republicans in 1966 and 1968. Unfortunately, the urgency to create a competitive two-party system died with it.

As the 1972 presidential election year began, President Richard Nixon was reasonably popular and the national Democrats were imploding. Their nominee-to-be, George McGovern, was running on a platform of ending the Vietnam War and openly advocating a guaranteed minimum income for the nation's poor. His opponents in the Democrat party portrayed him as a radical. They labeled him as the candidate of "amnesty (for draft dodgers), abortion, and acid." Arkansas's own Congressman Wilbur Mills was one of the Democratic candidates who tried, unsuccessfully, to wrest the nomination from McGovern.

It was going to be a good year for Republicans nationally but we needed something to jumpstart our local effort to elect

Republicans. The leaders of the Arkansas Republican party came up with the idea to field candidates for the top five constitutional offices, all of whom would run as a team known as Five for the Future. It was a grand concept, but it was destined to fail. It was too much to ask of the Arkansan electorate. It was one thing to get rid of the Old Guard by electing Winthrop Rockefeller, but once Faubus was gone, there was no compelling need to vote for Republican candidates. If a living, breathing Democrat was on the ballot for state or local office in Arkansas in 1972, a Republican candidate for that office had no chance to win. Arkansas, a reliably Democrat state since Reconstruction, was not about to open the door for Republicans. Nevertheless, we needed candidates to fight the good fight.

I, having achieved a modest level of public notoriety, was a natural to run for attorney general. Lana and I knew it would be hard, if not impossible, to win but we took the leap. After all, we reasoned, how can you build a two-party system if people are not willing to run as Republicans?

Jim Guy Tucker, prosecuting attorney for Pulaski County, and Bill Thompson, who later became the prosecuting attorney for Sebastian County, entered the race for attorney general as Democrats. They had a spirited primary contest and Jim Guy emerged as the Democratic nominee. I would face him on Election Day.

We worked as hard as we could, but campaigning is all about getting your name out, and that takes money, lots of it. We naively assumed when we entered the race that people would contribute because they wanted to have good government and competition in politics, and many contributed for those reasons, but not enough. We managed to raise around $65,000, far short of the amount needed for a statewide campaign. We had a measure of identity in Little Rock where Lana and I grew up and went to school, and in White County where I had just finished my term as prosecuting attorney, but elsewhere we were virtual unknowns.

The race brought out the worst in some people. In August, we went to the Watermelon Festival in Hope, Arkansas and worked the crowd until dark. When we got back to our car there were several pieces of profane and obscene hate mail under the windshield wipers, all making the same point: Republicans are not welcome in Hempstead County! That, unfortunately, was typical of the reception we received in many counties in 1972.

We did get a few good breaks, one in particular. My opponent, Jim Guy Tucker, had incurred the wrath of the Little Rock Police Department for a number of reasons related to the way he handled criminal cases. Since I was a former FBI agent and had been a tough prosecuting attorney, the police naturally gravitated to my candidacy and that, along with ties from our schooldays, helped us immensely in Pulaski County. A defining encounter occurred when the Little Rock Junior Chamber of Commerce held a mini-debate and I challenged Jim Guy to reconcile his newfound advocacy for the death penalty with the fact that he was a charter member of the Arkansas chapter of the American Civil Liberties Union. Tucker, caught off guard, gave an indecipherable response that firmly cast him as a liberal who was trying to sound conservative. Jim Guy carried that burden for the rest of his political career. George Fisher, the noted cartoonist for the *Arkansas Gazette* captured it best, later on, when he depicted Tucker as a liberal, in camouflage hunting gear with a pack of Red Man chewing tobacco in his back pocket.

On Election Day, 1972, Richard Nixon carried Arkansas with sixty-nine percent of the vote. He was the first Republican to win the state since Ulysses S. Grant in 1862. The rest of us did not fare so well.

I won my home county (White) and I won Tucker's home county (Pulaski), where the voters knew us best. I also won in sparsely populated Searcy County, which had a history of voting Republican. In every other county of the state (seventy-two of them), Jim Guy beat me badly simply because he was running on the Democratic party ticket.

In life, there is no rejection as clear or as hard to take as political rejection. When the debates, the speechmaking, and the handshaking are over the voters have their turn. When the officials count the votes, you will have won or lost. There are no draws in politics.

I had plenty of doubts about myself in my early life and I had stumbled many times, but by the grace of God, my screw-ups were private. I had reeled off a string of successes that I attributed to a firm application of the Vermilye worldview, but public rejection was a new experience. To what should I attribute the loss? It was not a lack of will; we had given it all we had. Was it poor messaging? No, it could not have been that because we beat Tucker where they knew us best, and where the voters were listening to us. How do you lose seventy-two out of seventy-five counties in Arkansas? Simple, you run on the Republican ticket.

I was down in the dumps after the loss to Tucker. I liked public service but winning office as a Republican was going to be harder than I ever imagined. President Nixon had won re-election, and he had carried Arkansas but his success was due to a set of unusual circumstances; the Wilbur Mills candidacy, and the emergence of a deep philosophical split in the national Democratic party.

I was puzzled and began to question the workability of my Vermilye theory of life. I was anxious, disappointed, and somewhat confused for the first time since childhood. Fortunately, Lana was not a disciple of the Vermilye approach to life. To the contrary, she is an unwavering Christian. She always does her best, takes winning and losing in stride and does not go into a funk if things do not go her way. I leaned on her, as I would do many times in the years to come.

She was back caring for the kids, and planning what she was going to do with the rest of her life. Her optimism and good cheer should have perked me up, but I was stuck on dysfunctional. Losing is not compatible with the Vermilye way of thinking.

I sulked for days, but my melancholy did not last long, it could not. We were broke—flat broke. Lana had left her teaching job to campaign, I was a defeated candidate with no job, and we had only a few hundred dollars in our personal bank account. We had some equity in our house on One Meadowlane

Drive (no more than $4000), our furniture, and our trusty 1963 Volkswagen Beetle that had been with us since graduating from law school. That was it!

In early December, 1972, after weeks of pondering our options, Lana and I decided I should start my own law practice in Searcy. We considered taking a federal job in the Nixon administration, but it had only been four years since we left a federal job, the FBI, to practice law in Arkansas. To take a federal job now, even a good one, seemed to us to be a step backwards.

I would need an office and a few basics, but we could not afford much. I rented a small two-room office on the first floor of the old Mayfair Hotel for $50 per month. I bought a second-hand IBM Selectric typewriter for $75, and we set it on a second-hand dressing table that we bought from a local auctioneer, Colonel Ivan Quattlebaum, for $10. Lana was going to be my secretary until she could get a job teaching English at Searcy High School starting in September of 1973. I had no law books, but figured I could use the county law library. I needed a desk—every lawyer needs one—so I bought a hollow-core door and laid it on top of cinder blocks. *Voilà*, we had a lawyer's desk for less than $20! We installed a single-line telephone and paid $25 to have a sign (Ed Bethune, Lawyer) painted to hang in front of the hotel. It was getting close to Christmas, but we were in business!

We scraped together a few dollars to buy a Christmas tree and gifts for Paige and Sam, and we invited my mother and Lana's mother and father to come to Searcy for Christmas. Lana and I agreed, for obvious reasons, that we would not exchange gifts, but on Christmas Eve, I gave her a "Bond" that I had typed on the Selectric typewriter. It was a simple pledge that I would work as hard as I could and a promise that better times would come to the Bethune family.

My first client was Dan Dunn, a friend who had a small, but successful roofing business in Searcy. We were so grateful that he came to me, that he trusted me, and that he felt I could help him solve his legal problem. It was not a complicated legal matter, but he did need representation. I jumped on his case like a hungry dog attacks a bone. I am sure my aggressiveness astounded the lawyers on the other side, but I needed to close the case so that I could collect my fee. We desperately needed to collect some money so that we could pay our rent, telephone bill, and utilities. When it was clear that we had resolved Dan's issue, I asked him if he would please write a separate check for my fee, even before we received the money that was due to him from the settlement. I was honest with him, saying, "Dan, you have the right to wait until we get the proceeds from the settlement, but I am struggling to get my practice going and I really need my fee, now." He understood, and wrote me a check for $600. It is and always will be the most important fee for legal services that I ever collected.

My second piece of business came from Ruby Eubanks and Travis Blue at the Farmers Home Administration. They asked me to approve titles and close FHA home loans. The fees were not great but it was a good piece of business and it would pay the overhead. We were making progress!

My unsuccessful race for attorney general branded me as a Republican lawyer, one of the few in the state, certainly in Central Arkansas. For that reason, my name came up as a possible replacement for Bill Smith, one of the state's finest lawyers. He was stepping down from his part-time post as chairman of the Federal Home Loan Bank Board for the Ninth District, which included Arkansas, Louisiana, Texas, and Mississippi. Bill Smith's daughter, Kay, had been a classmate of Lana's at Little Rock Central High School, and I used to play golf with Kay and her husband, Bill Patton, when we were in law school. Bill Smith (the senior partner of the Smith, Williams, Friday, Bowen, and Eldridge law firm) supported me to be his replacement and I became chairman of the Ninth District Federal Home Loan Bank Board in late 1973. The appointment exposed me to the world of high finance, but most importantly, Lana and I made many nice trips to board meetings and I received a much-needed fee for each monthly meeting that I attended. In one of the great ironies in my life, I got the telephone call from Bill Smith to see if I would be interested in the appointment in early 1973. At the time I took the call from Arkansas's most distinguished lawyer, I was sitting on a folding chair behind my $20 hollow-core-door desk in my $50 a month office at the Mayfair Hotel.

After a few months of law practice and collecting more hard-earned fees, I borrowed $5000 cash from Mother (it almost wiped out her savings) and made a down payment on a little house on the corner of 210 East Vine Street in Searcy. We made a loan that covered the purchase of the house and left enough money for us to buy proper furniture and convert the house into a law office. We were glad to get out of the Mayfair Hotel, and our move to the new location sent the right signal to the people of White County. My law practice took off. The business community, long committed to other lawyers, did not hire me, but the ordinary folks trusted me, so I handled a lot of divorce, personal injury, and criminal defense cases. I did well, much better than I ever expected to do.

Many of the people who came to my office did not have a legal problem and they did not need a lawyer. They just needed someone to talk to because they had let their imagination get the best of them. When I was in the FBI, I often took random calls from the public—alligators coming up through the toilets to wreck marriages—Martians stealing government secrets—you name it, I have heard it. Everyone in law enforcement will tell you that the nut-jobs are most active when the moon is full.

The stuff I heard in my law office was less bizarre, but there was one exception: It involved an attractive middle-aged woman, slightly plumpish, who came to my office and told me of her belief that someone was breaking into her house on a regular basis. She had not reported it to the police because she thought the intruder might be her ex-husband and she did not want to make trouble for him. I asked her whether the intruder had taken anything of value and if she had any proof. With a perfectly straight face she said, "Yes, he goes into the attic—I know he has been there because he has made my wedding dress smaller." I thought she was kidding so I cracked a little smile, but I quickly wiped it off with my hand when I realized the woman was deadly serious. We sat there in silence for what seemed an eternity. I tried to think of something to say, but I could not. I was speechless.

The nice woman seemed relieved to have told her story. She thanked me for listening, stood up, smoothed out her dress and left.

We might have lost the race for attorney general, but the attention we garnered in the losing effort was definitely good for business. In September, Lana returned to her teaching job at Searcy High School and I hired a secretary. Our income stream was strong so I made good on the Bond that I had given Lana for Christmas just ten months before. I bought her a brand-new gold 1973 Lincoln Continental Town Car from Duane Treat at Capps Motor Company. Then, in January of 1974 I bought a lot from Kenny Rand and we started building our dream home, a two-story traditional brick home that backed up to the tee on the eighth hole of the Searcy Country Club golf course.

I was back to believing there might be something to the Vermilye way of thinking after all.

In early 1974, less than a year from the date she loaned us the money to buy our law office, I repaid the $5000 that I had borrowed from my mother, in full, with ten percent interest. She was happy for us, and we were happy that we were on a sound footing.

Things were definitely looking up for us, but there was a fly in the ointment. In an unexpected turn of events, the Republican party got a bad name due to the incredibly stupid Watergate burglary that led to the downfall of President Richard Nixon. It was a rough time to be a Republican, particularly in Arkansas. Richard Nixon resigned under pressure and Vice President Gerald Ford became president of the United States. The Democrats picked up a huge number of congressional seats that year, and those members, many of them young liberals, became known as the Watergate Babies. It looked as if the Republicans would never recover, nationally or in the state of Arkansas, so I focused on family, my burgeoning law practice, and living out a host of unfulfilled dreams.

In the late spring of 1974, I was driving by the Searcy Airport and, as if pulled by a magnet, I impulsively turned into the parking lot and went inside to ask Elmo Everett, the aircraft mechanic who doubled as airport manager, if there was anyone there who could teach me how to fly. It was a dream from my youth that stemmed from my reading, repeatedly, the full page of the *Johnson Smith & Co. Catalog* that told how I could build an airplane and power it with a washing machine motor. Why not learn how to fly? I had missed the chance to become a pilot in the Marine Corps because of a deviated septum, and for most of my life I could not think about spending the kind of money that it would take to learn to fly. Now I had some extra cash in my pocket, and by damn, I was going to do it.

Elmo put me in touch with a former Air Force pilot who was giving flying lessons, and within a couple of months I soloed and made the requisite cross-country trip that permitted me to get my private pilot's license. I rented airplanes from Elmo for a year, mostly Cessna 172's, and had the usual number of hairy experiences that new pilots have with bad weather and stupid mistakes. Once when I was taking off, the engine sputtered and I pulled back on the throttle thinking I ought to abort the takeoff but I was already too near the end of the runway so I jammed the throttle to full-on and barely cleared the trees at the end of the runway. It is a wonder I survived but I was determined. I bought a one-third interest in a Cherokee 180 owned by Dr. Cliff Ganus, the president of Harding College, and his sons. It was a good little airplane. We used it to fly to the Cotton Bowl in Dallas and later, we flew the kids to John Newcombe's tennis camp in New Braunfels, Texas.

Those two trips with the family convinced me I needed to get an instrument rating. The Cherokee 180 was a little slow and not a good plane for learning how to fly on instruments, so I parted company with Dr. Ganus and his boys and got into a three-way ownership of a Cessna Skylane with Dr. Jay Bell and Dr. Gene Joseph. It was a great arrangement because neither of them flew very often and the airplane was a perfect platform for learning to fly on instruments. Zearl Watson gave me some introductory lessons, but I finished my work and got my IFR rating with Dave Ridings, who later became a pilot for Harding University.

My law practice continued to grow and I began to use the airplane to travel around the state. The most interesting destination was the grass strip at Cummins Prison. In those days, I could fly right in and a security guard would come out to meet me, check my identification, and then drive me to the administration building where I would put in a request to see a client.

The most challenging trip was to fly into Gaston's fishing resort on the White River near Mountain Home, Arkansas. Unlike the strip at Cummins, the Gaston strip was nestled among rolling hills along the river and it required some good piloting to get in and out.

My thirst for adventure took me to other grass strips, but soon I was so busy with my law practice that I had a hard time maintaining my proficiency as a pilot. On several trips, I made mistakes—not fatal, but stupid—and I convinced myself that the worst thing a pilot can do is to fly when he, or she, is preoccupied with other business. I disciplined myself to focus on flying when I got in the airplane and that worked well, at least for the next few years. Later, when I started my campaign for Congress—the ultimate preoccupation—I stopped flying altogether.

In 1975, I got a chance to strike a blow for competition in politics, and I took it. As general counsel for the Republican Party of Arkansas, I filed a suit to nullify Governor David Pryor's attempt to call a "limited constitutional convention" without submitting the call to the electorate for ratification. The Arkansas Supreme Court agreed with our position. In a 4-3 decision, the court said, "all political power is inherent in the people." It was a solid legal decision that once again proved the need for a two-party system.

Many of the matters I handled in my solo law practice were standard fare for a small town general practitioner. I read abstracts of title and closed hundreds of loans for the Farmers Home Administration. I handled divorces and child custody matters, some were contested and painful, but most were blessedly uncontested and peaceful. I probated estates, did adoptions, wrote contracts, set up small businesses, and worked on a host of other matters. These cases formed the backbone of my practice and paid the bills. They were not glamorous matters, but they were important to the people involved and I took satisfaction that I was helping others get along in life.

One day I was in Diaz, Arkansas looking for a witness that I wanted to depose. Diaz was just a crossroads. There was part of a cotton-ginning operation on one corner and an old country store kitty-cornered from that. I was using tobacco at the time so I went into the store to see if they had any cigars. When I got inside the first thing I noticed was that a fine layer of dust covered everything. The proprietor, an old man wearing well-worn one-strap overalls pointed me to a shelf where I saw a box of Mississippi Crooks, an unwrapped cheap cigar that is actually crooked. I picked one up out of the box. It was so dry that it crumbled in my hands. I was sure it had been there since the Great Depression. If I had tried to light one it would have caught fire. I decided to ask the storekeeper if he had any other cigars. I knew it would be useless to ask for a fancy cigar so I downgraded my request. I asked him if he had a Roi-Tan or a King Edward—popular, but cheap cigars that were selling for around eight cents each at that time. He gave me a puzzled look and said, "Naw, Mister, we don't get much call for them good cigars."

There is nothing like working in the backwoods of Arkansas.

17

HIGH PROFILE CASES

Celebrity is the advantage of being known to people who we don't know, and who don't know us.
Sebastien-Roch Nicolas De Chamfort

I was establishing a reputation as a good, all-around country lawyer but my work on the Criminal Code Revision Commission, my time as prosecuting attorney, and my background as an FBI agent led people to see me as a criminal defense attorney. I handled two cases in early 1973, my first full year of practice after the race for attorney general that enhanced that image.

In February of 1973, Federal Judge G. Thomas Eisele, a friend from the days when we were both helping Governor Rockefeller, assigned me to represent a young man from Memphis charged with robbing a bank in Cherry Valley, Arkansas. The FBI and the media referred to him as Billy the Bank Robber, because he was a suspect in a string of bank robberies in and around Memphis and Eastern Arkansas. Billy had an alibi, saying that he was elsewhere at the time of the robbery, and that was his main defense. The case came to trial in Little Rock in March 1973 and, being a former FBI agent, I picked holes in the testimony of the FBI agents who investigated the case and testified against Billy. I doubt I would have known how to do that effectively if I had not been an agent myself. After five days of trial the case went to the jury, and after hours of deliberating, it was apparent that they were hopelessly deadlocked. Judge Eisele declared a mistrial.

As counsel appointed by the court, it was my duty to defend Billy to the best of my ability. In my early days, I worried about defending someone who might be guilty, but I came to understand that it was not my duty to get an accused off, free and clear. It was my duty to see that they got a fair trial and fair treatment. That included the obligation to challenge the testimony of all witnesses. The prosecuting attorney has a duty to present, as vigorously as he or she can, all legitimate evidence of guilt. If the testimony can stand the light of day, so be it. On the other hand, if the testimony is weak and questionable, then the jury ought to know that too. Our adversarial system for finding the truth is not perfect, but it is the best that man has ever devised.

All's well that ends well, Shakespeare says, and that was true in the case of Billy the Bank Robber. It was not long before the FBI had Billy again and soon thereafter, he helped them clear up a rash of bank robberies that had plagued state, local, and federal authorities for years.

The second case in the spring of 1973 that attracted some attention involved Franklin Ray, a poor farmhand from Bald Knob. Franklin was locked up in the White County jail for fifty-eight days on a charge of burglary and grand larceny. The prosecuting attorney moved the court to deny bail and put Franklin's case off for four more months alleging that other cases, civil and criminal, deserved priority. Franklin's family came to me to see if I could do anything to help Franklin who was about to spend another one hundred and twenty days in jail.

As it turned out, I had just finished my work on the Criminal Code Revision Commission, and I knew that the Arkansas Supreme Court had just adopted two new procedural rules regarding the right of an accused to a speedy trial. The rules said jail cases have precedence over bail cases, and criminal cases have precedence over civil cases. There was no excuse for holding Franklin without bail in the county jail. He was entitled, as a matter of law, to a speedy trial. When I filed a petition demanding the state to either try Franklin or let him out on bail, it upset the prosecutor and the judge. It was a new wrinkle for them. They did not like someone telling them how to run their criminal docket. Arkansas was leading the nation in the effort to implement new and better standards for criminal justice, but the reality of everyday practice in our rural state lagged far behind our national reform effort.

I filed a petition for extraordinary relief in the Supreme Court of Arkansas on March 16, 1973 and a few days later the court granted my request and directed the trial court to try the defendant in thirty days or release him on his own recognizance. A few weeks later, April 4, Franklin got his trial. The jury found him guilty and the judge sentenced him to two years in the state penitentiary. As it turned out, Franklin got an early parole and release from prison before the date he would have gotten to trial if I had not filed the petition.

The case was a garden-variety burglary and grand larceny case. The prosecutor had evidence that Franklin had stolen things that did not belong to him but this little case, otherwise unremarkable, became a benchmark in Arkansas legal history. It was the first case decided after the Arkansas Supreme Court began adopting the new rules of criminal procedure that I had worked on in 1970 and 1971. It also recognized that the court, having adopted the two rules on speedy trial, would henceforth use its new authority (Act 470 of 1971) to promulgate rules of procedure. Gone forever was the anachronistic and antiquated notion that the legislature would establish rules of procedure based more on political pressure than logic. I never made a dime for representing Franklin, but I remember the experience fondly because in my mind, it justified all the days and weekends I gave to the volunteer effort to upgrade the criminal procedure law of our state.

My handling of the bank robbery case and the speedy trial case led to several other high profile cases.

In August of 1973, twenty-three men charged with the crime of nightriding hired me to represent them. It turned out to be the most unusual case I would ever handle.

The events giving rise to the nightriding charge began a few years earlier. In the midst of the rebellious wave that swept the nation in the late 1960s, a group of young people committed to a communal lifestyle moved into the very small community of Greer's Ferry, Arkansas. Their leader was Dixon Bowles, an accomplished musician who got his start with the Dan Blocker singers in Hollywood. The newcomers bought a big commercial chicken-house, converted it into living quarters for members of the commune, and began to find odd jobs in and around beautiful Greer's Ferry Lake, a Corps of Engineer's project dedicated in 1963 by President John F. Kennedy.

Their arrival created a stir among the local residents, most of whom were descendents of traditional, conservative Arkansans who settled the area in the early 1800s. They did not want a commune in their area, and their reaction to it was as hostile as the reaction they had when the federal government, by the power of eminent domain, took their lands and dammed up the Little Red River to create the lake. Most longtime residents did not like what was happening to their little community. Since there was very little they could do about it they consoled themselves with grousing about the federal government, and suffering the commune to exist.

The new lake and the area surrounding it became a haven for weekenders from Little Rock, Memphis, and other nearby places. Soon thereafter tourism surpassed agriculture as the economic base for the county.

Dixon Bowles wisely took advantage of the upsurge in tourism. The members of the commune organized themselves into a legal unit with a perfectly descriptive name, The Group, Inc., and opened a dinner theatre that became quite popular, particularly with the outsiders who flooded into Greer's Ferry every weekend from late March to early November.

In a short while, The Group, Inc. was succeeding financially. They expanded their influence by starting a popular ambulance service, and as the population of Greer's Ferry grew, a number of new and longtime Greer's Ferry residents began to side with The Group, Inc. on local political issues. That development, coupled with festering hate or fear of the commune—it is hard to tell the difference sometimes—triggered the events of August 25, 1973. Twenty-three men, longtime local residents, gathered near the commune after dark.

They had had a bellyful of the commune and the members of The Group, Inc.

At 9:00 p.m. a large number of pickup trucks rolled onto the property next to the chicken house. The men and women inside the commune were just finishing dinner and putting their children to bed. They knew the old-timers of Greer's Ferry were restless and that there was growing discontent with the commune, particularly their recent political activities, but they assumed the animosity would eventually subside. They were mistaken.

The first thing they heard inside the commune was the sound of rocks bouncing off the metal roof of the chicken-house. Next, they heard a string of obscenities, followed by several gunshots. A few personal confrontations took place when the men of the commune dared to go outside to see what was going on. Shouting matches ensued and word spread throughout the commune that they were under attack. The women and children were scared to the point of crying and they were huddled in a corner.

Someone called the Arkansas State Police, but it took an hour for the troopers to get to the scene. By the time they arrived, the assault was over but there was damage to vehicles and other commune property. The troopers checked on the people in the commune, and then persuaded the men gathered outside to get in their trucks and leave.

The prosecuting attorney, Kenneth Smith, a law school classmate and good friend of mine told the media that night: "The local boys were in the wrong." The next morning he announced that he was planning to charge the men with nightriding, a law passed in 1909 to deal with vigilantes who unite at night to terrorize and commit unlawful acts against select groups, most frequently African Americans. The last prosecution for nightriding—a serious felony—had taken place decades before, but the law was still on the books and it provided a hefty prison sentence for violators.

A few of the local boys contacted me a few days later to see if I would represent them. They said they were going to reassemble that night on the property adjoining the commune. I urged them to stay away from the commune, but they said they were determined to go back to the commune and I could meet them there, that night.

By the time I got to the meeting place at Greer's Ferry, it was dark. I parked my car about fifty yards away and walked into the center of a bunch of trucks and a cluster of men wearing an assortment of ball caps. I shook hands all around and even though the light was poor, it was easy to see the look of frustration on their faces.

There were several police cars and state troopers on hand, ready to take action if it became necessary.

As the men took turns telling me what they had done, and what they had not done, I heard every conceivable justification, every possible excuse. Their arguments lacked reason and were understandable only if one accepted their one-sided perception of things. It did not take long for me to see that their conduct was legally inexcusable, but I also saw their frustration with the twenty-year chain of events that had changed their community and their way of life. They needed my help. The prosecutor, the larger community, and the media needed to calm down so that they could view the case with perspective.

I told the men that I would represent them, but only if they would agree to cool off, disband, and stay away from the commune. Most importantly, I conditioned my agreement to represent them upon their staying out of trouble, any kind of trouble, and following my advice without question. They agreed.

The prosecuting attorney formally charged all twenty-three men with the felony of nightriding. They made bond, and we entered a cooling off period, waiting for Circuit Judge Joe Villines to set a trial date.

The statewide media had a field day comparing The Group, Inc. with the "nightriders." Their coverage included the events of the night I met my clients near the chicken house and carried through the trial, which started on November 10, 1974.

Two distinctly different cultures were clashing. What can man do to protect his way of doing things, his way of thinking? At what point should we, and to what extent can we, redress damage resulting from such clashes by resort to the criminal process? To what extent, if there is no personal injury, should we excuse conduct driven by hatred or fear of change? These questions I raised for the jury, a little more than a year after the date of the wrongdoing. The prosecutor objected to every attempt I made to get the jury to think in the larger sense, and I objected to every attempt he made to show what good citizens the victims were. We both knew such references were inappropriate. At one point, when the prosecutor started asking about the ambulance service that The Group, Inc. had started, I just leaned back in my chair, threw up my hands and said, "Oh, Boy!" Judge Villines, one of the best trial judges I ever knew quickly said, "Sustained."

The trial lasted four days. Of the twenty-three defendants, the jury found three men guilty of the misdemeanor of disturbing the peace. One received a directed verdict of acquittal, and the prosecuting attorney dismissed charges against the other nineteen. Judge Villines sentenced the convicted defendants to fifteen days in the county jail and each of them had to pay a $200 fine. A corresponding civil suit against the twenty-three defendants settled out of court for $900.

The clash of The Group, Inc., and the Greer's Ferry defendants ended that day. Most people, even the alleged nightriders, agreed that the process was fair and that the trial was a good thing for the community. Everyone had a chance to vent and heal the unfounded fears that each faction had for the other. By and by, The Group, Inc. moved away from Greer's Ferry, but most people in Cleburne County remember this little case for the good lesson it taught.

Shortly after the nightriding trial, I got into an odd case that also involved hate speech and terroristic conduct against innocent victims.

Throughout the early 1970s, Joe Weston, an infamous figure in Arkansas, published a scandal sheet known as the *Sharp Citizen.* The state tried him twice for criminal libel because he constantly wrote articles trying to connect local people with organized crime, the Communist party, and various other unsavory entities. In 1974, he announced his intention to run for governor as a Republican. Those of us in party leadership were aghast at the prospect of having Weston as a candidate on our ticket. I filed a suit to bar him from filing as a candidate in our primary. We did not have a good legal case and I knew it, but the party needed to show that we did not want the likes of Joe Weston carrying our banner. The trial court ruled against us on April 10, 1974 and I immediately announced that I would appeal to the Arkansas Supreme Court. The case was the lead story in newspapers all across the state, which is what we wanted. We got wide coverage when we argued against Weston's candidacy and when the court ruled against us as we expected. It was the one time I tried a lawsuit knowing that the facts and law were against me and that I was going to lose the case no matter what I said or did. We were willing to lose, and I was eager to get coverage of losing the case, just so we could show the people of Arkansas that we did not want Joe Weston in our party. Fortunately, Ken Coon, a fine man and good Republican, clobbered Joe Weston in the Republican primary. Ken got eighty-two percent of the vote. The whipping Weston took underscored the point we were making in the lawsuit: There is no room in the Republican Party of Arkansas for bigots and demagogues.

All criminal cases are sad, but some are sadder than others are. I had two such cases. The first involved an intelligent young lawyer who lost his bearings, and then his life. The second was the sad case of an old doctor who worked hard all his life and did much good, but lost his way and died in prison.

Troy Wiley was a lawyer in Searcy who fell on hard times. He was deeply in debt and began drinking too much. Soon he quit taking care of his legal business, and then he quit filing his income tax returns. The United States attorney charged Troy with two counts of failing to file his federal income tax returns, serious felonies. Troy asked me to defend him and I told him it was hard to defend a failing-to-file case when the accused had actually failed to file. Even so, Troy was a friend who needed a glimmer of hope and there was always the chance that a jury might refuse to convict him. When it came time to discuss the instructions that would be given to the jury, I urged Federal District Judge Tom Eisele to give a jury nullification instruction, telling the jury that they could disregard the proof and the law and acquit if they so desired. Judge Eisele said it was the first time anyone had requested such an instruction in Arkansas. I could find no current authority on the subject so I cited the 1735 case of Peter Zenger, a journalist charged with seditious libel. The case is famous for several reasons, but in the course of defending Zenger, Alexander Hamilton argued that the jurors enjoyed the prerogative to ignore the judge's instruction and render a verdict according to their collective conscience and the interests of justice. Judge Eisele was amused with my ingenuity, but the best I could get him to do was to begin his instruction to the jury with the phrase, "Although you may decide to the contrary …." The jury found Troy guilty on one count, but they acquitted him on the other. It was a small victory, but Troy appreciated it immensely, and the judge considered the jury's reluctance when he sentenced Troy. I think the jury was trying to give Troy hope and a chance to get his life together. I know that is what I was trying to do by defending him. Alas, it did not work. Two years later Troy committed suicide. His widow asked me to lead a secular memorial service for Troy in the courtroom of the White County Courthouse. She said that was what Troy wanted, so I did it. Troy's friends, former clients, fellow attorneys, and court officials filled the room. It was an emotional farewell for a bright, lovable young man.

In 1974, the State of Arkansas accused Dr. Porter Rodgers, Sr., a seventy-one-year-old prominent physician, of conspiring with his twenty-year-old secretary-girlfriend to hire a co-conspirator to murder the doctor's wife. Dr. Rodgers had a significant degree of organic brain syndrome so I defended him on the grounds of insanity and diminished responsibility, contending he was not responsible for the plot because of his mental condition. The proof against him consisted of a questioned confession and the testimony of the secretary-girlfriend who fully implicated him in the plot. The trial, which started February 13, 1975, lasted six weeks. The jury found him guilty of first-degree murder, but not capital murder. In a later proceeding in Federal District Court, Judge Tom Eisele took judicial notice that the doctor's capital felony murder trial was "the most notorious and lengthy criminal case in modern Arkansas judicial history." Indeed, it was and when it was over, I was exhausted. I appealed the decision to the Arkansas Supreme Court, but the court affirmed the conviction, and Dr. Rodgers died November 4, 1980, a prisoner of the state. It was a sad ending for a man who had done a lot for his community. He had delivered thousands of babies, built the first real hospital in White County, and saved many lives. Everyone in the county knew Dr. Rodgers. His fall from grace, and the tragic death of Mrs. Rodgers, was a bitter pill for their daughter, and for their son who has been my good friend for almost fifty years. The old doctor's death came on Election Day in 1980. I had just won re-election to my second term in Congress with seventy-nine percent of the vote. A television reporter stuck a camera in my face, told me of his passing, and asked for my comment. I said, "It was the longest, hardest, and saddest case I ever handled," and it was.

18

ALMOST A JUDGE

For everything you have missed, you have gained something else and for everything you gain, you lose something.
Ralph Waldo Emerson

In early 1976, President Gerald Ford nominated me to be a federal district court judge for the Eastern District of Arkansas. At the time it was standard practice for the American Bar Association (ABA) to conduct a background investigation of all nominees, and if a nominee was declared unqualified or the bar association failed to make a recommendation, the nomination was dead on arrival in the United States Senate. Liberals, mostly Democrats, dominated the ABA investigative committee. I was rated "A v," the highest rating a lawyer can get in the Martindale-Hubbell legal directory, but there was still some concern that the committee might torpedo my nomination. Those fears were unfounded. My overall record was good and I had worked hard to promote the *American Bar Association Standards for Criminal Justice* in Arkansas and all across the country. The committee gave me a "qualified" rating. My fate was in the hands of the United States Senate, controlled by Democrats.

I had worked with Senator John McClellan when I chaired the Criminal Code Revision Commission. He asked me to come see him in Washington, D. C., and when we met, he told me that he appreciated what I had done to upgrade the criminal process and that he intended to fully support my nomination. Senator Dale Bumpers, our junior senator, would not declare whether he was going to support me or not. The nomination languished as the 1976 presidential campaign—Jimmy Carter versus Gerald Ford—heated up. Soon it was apparent that Dale Bumpers was delaying the confirmation process, and finally he admitted he was holding it up until after the presidential election. If Ford won, the Senate would confirm me, but if Carter won, he would select a new nominee.

My law practice suffered during the waiting period. For the best part of 1976, prospective clients took their business elsewhere; after all, I was about to become a federal judge. There were several news stories about my nomination during the presidential campaign. Political observers were saying I, if confirmed, would be one of the youngest, if not the youngest federal judge in the country. Lana did not care about setting such records. On the contrary, she was concerned that the judgeship would not be a good thing for me. She kept telling me, "If you get it you might become a pontifical son of a bitch, like all the rest of them." Her concern was premature. President Ford lost the presidency to Jimmy Carter and my nomination to be a federal judge died on the vine.

We received hundreds of calls and letters from people who felt I had gotten a raw deal and that it was uncharacteristic for Bumpers to do what he did. I appreciated their support, but I never saw it that way. Dale Bumpers did a partisan thing, but it was well within his prerogative as a United States senator.

Once again I buried myself in my law practice. The publicity about the judgeship hurt my law practice, but things picked up when people realized that I was not going to be a judge after all.

19

RUNNING FOR CONGRESS

One person can make a difference and every person should try.
John Fitzgerald Kennedy

In 1974, Judy Petty, a dynamic young woman who had served as Winthrop Rockefeller's administrative assistant when he was governor, decided to challenge Congressman Wilbur Mills for the Second District congressional seat. It was an uphill battle, but Judy ran an extraordinary campaign and made a good showing for a Republican running in a solidly Democratic district.

She focused on contributions that Congressman Mills received during his brief run for president in 1972, specifically an illegal $75,000 contribution he received from the Associated Milk Producers. Judy began referring to Wilbur as "Wilbur Milk," saying he was "standing with his feet planted in sour milk." An Old Guard veteran, state Senator Guy "Mutt" Jones of Conway was so putout with her that he refused to let Judy ride in a car in the Faulkner County parade. Judy—a gutsy woman—defiantly walked in the parade and there was nothing Mutt could do about it. She made him look like a fool.

It was a terrible year to run as a Republican. President Richard Nixon resigned the presidency on August 9, 1974 because of the Watergate scandal. Judy was running hard, but she was not making much progress.

Then, on October 9, a news story broke that shocked the political world. The U. S. Park Police in Washington, D. C. stopped Wilbur's car at 2:00 a.m. because his driver had not turned on the car's lights. When the police approached the car, Fanne Foxe, a thirty-eight-year-old stripper also known as the Argentine Firecracker bolted from the car and jumped into the nearby Tidal Basin in an attempt to escape. Wilbur was intoxicated and his face appeared scratched. It later developed that Wilbur frequented The Silver Slipper, a Washington nightclub where Foxe performed.

On Election Day, November 5, 1974, Mills won all nine counties of the Second District, as he had always done. Petty got around forty-six percent in Saline and Pulaski counties, but overall she only got forty-one percent of the votes cast district-wide. Wilbur had easily defeated his Republican opponent, but his political career was over and he knew it.

In late 1975 Wilbur Mills announced his retirement, and Jim Guy Tucker, who had been attorney general for three years, floated a trial balloon that he was going to run for the Second District seat. He called me to see if I had any plans to run because in our race for attorney general in 1972, I had carried Pulaski and White counties. Tucker knew that I might beat him in a race confined to the nine counties comprising the Second District. I had not thought about politics since losing the race for attorney general, but his call made me realize that I might do well in a race for the Second District congressional seat. Whoever carried Pulaski and White counties—the two largest counties in the district—would most likely win the seat. The other counties were Cleburne, Arkansas, Lonoke, Saline, Conway, Faulkner, and Prairie. Even though I might have done well, I did not want to run. It was that simple. I told Jim Guy I had no intention to get into the race, and wished him well. Shortly thereafter, Jim Guy announced his candidacy. He easily won the race and took his seat in Congress in January of 1977.

On November 28, 1977, Senator John McClellan died at age eighty-one after having served thirty-four years in the United

States Senate. Governor David Pryor appointed Kaneaster Hodges, Jr. of Newport to fill the vacancy. According to the Arkansas Constitution, Kaneaster, an appointee, could not run to succeed himself. Jim Guy Tucker, still in his first year in the U. S. House of Representatives, announced that he was going to run for the U. S. Senate. He would face Governor David Pryor and several others in the Democrat primary. The Second District congressional seat would be open in the 1978 election cycle.

The leaders of the Arkansas Republican party sought me out. They argued that it was going to be a good year for Republican candidates. Jimmy Carter was in the second year of his presidency. The economy was suffering and liberal Democrats were complicating things for Carter, a mild-mannered Southerner. The Arkansas Republicans, led by Joel Anderson who later became chancellor of the University of Arkansas at Little Rock, cited the vote totals I had accumulated against Tucker in 1972 in White and Pulaski counties. They theorized that I could use that base to win the Second District seat.

Lana and I started weighing the pros and cons of entering the race for Congress. My law practice was successful. Robert Edwards, a young lawyer in Searcy who had served as deputy prosecuting attorney during the Rodgers murder trial, had joined me in the practice of law, so I had someone to keep the law office going should I decide to get in the race. Lana was teaching high school English, but she would be through with that in June. Our kids were stable and doing well in school. We put out the word that we were seriously considering the race and our telephone began to ring. Most of our friends and political supporters encouraged us to do it but some said they did not believe a Republican could win in the Second District.

We enjoyed the encouragement, but the negative comments began to take their toll, which was normal given our hard-fought losing effort for attorney general just six years earlier. We started thinking about the good life we had in Searcy. Our kids were doing fine and we were in our dream home on the golf course. Who needed the pain and anguish that was likely to come from an attempt to win a congressional seat, one not held by a Republican for a hundred and four years, since Reconstruction?

We backed out. I called Joel Anderson and told him our decision. He asked if I had put out a news release to that effect and I said no. It was a Friday night, but Joel asked me if I would at least extend him the courtesy of letting him drive to Searcy to visit with me about my decision. I owed him that much, so I agreed to keep our decision private for a few days. Meanwhile, Joel and the party leaders got out the heavy artillery. They called Washington and got Congressman Guy Vander Jagt, chairman of the National Republican Campaign Committee (NRCC), to give me a call. He promised that his committee would fully support my campaign if we changed our mind and decided to run. Next, they asked President Ford to give me a call, which he did. When his call came, I was at home with Lana. I was taken aback to be receiving a call from President Ford, but I was ready with my best lines. After he made the pitch for me to run, I gave him all the reasons we had decided not to run. I told him how we had built our new home, how we had scratched our way through college and law school, and how comfortable our kids were in Searcy. He listened patiently but I could tell I had not persuaded him. Having saved my best line for last, I said, "Besides, Mr. President, what can one man do?" President Ford did not hesitate, he said, "Now Ed, what if everyone said that?" It was at that moment that I knew I was going to get in the race for Congress. When I hung up, I asked myself what is it about a call to duty that has always cut through my selfishness, overriding the Vermilye notion that all I should ever strive for is a "good lettin' alone."

A few days later, I announced that I would be a Republican candidate for the United States House of Representative in the Second District of Arkansas.

Shortly after I entered the race, the NRCC conducted a thorough benchmark survey to determine the thinking of voters in the Second District of Arkansas. We learned that my name identification was only in the high teens, but that did not surprise us. It had been six years since my campaign for attorney general.

What did surprise me was the response when the pollsters asked people to say what they expected of their congressional representative. The survey posed two choices: "Should a congressman go to Washington to study and vote on the great issues of the day? Or, should a congressman go to Washington and do what he can to take care of his constituents?" By a five to one margin, the respondents in the benchmark survey said a congressman should take care of his constituents.

I had lived my life believing that the government, "they" and "them" in Vermilye parlance, was the enemy. Now I learned that, if elected, my constituents would want me as their main link to the government to take care of them. Was I the right person to do that? I rationalized—of necessity—that the people were not saying that I should get money or benefits for them, but that I should protect them from the heavy hand of government. For that role, I was perfectly suited.

We rented an old grey-stone house on West Third Street in Little Rock for our campaign headquarters. Lana and I had a number of friends—Democrats and Independents—who promised to help. We did not want to scare them off so we decided to purge the office of all partisan signs. Unfortunately, the word did not get to my longtime political ally and friend, the feisty redhead, Phyllis Kincannon. On the day we moved into the headquarters, Phyllis arrived at 9:00 a.m. sharp with a dozen hardcore Republican women in full battle dress, ready for action. They were wearing GOP elephant earrings, elephant bracelets, elephant necklaces, and a wide assortment of Republican apparel and campaign paraphernalia from battles past. There were "Nixon-Agnew" buttons, "I Like Ike" pins, and Goldwater "In Your Heart You Know He's Right" badges. It took some real diplomacy to get out of that mess, but Phyllis helped me do it.

The Democrats had an all-star cast running for their nomination. Cecil Alexander of Heber Springs was the speaker of the state House of Representatives; Stanley Russ of Conway was an important state senator representing Faulkner County; Dale Cowling of Little Rock was a well-known Baptist preacher, and

Doug Brandon of Little Rock chaired the Revenue and Taxation Committee of the Arkansas House of Representatives. Cecil and Doug led in the preferential primary, and, since neither got fifty percent of the vote, a runoff was required. The runoff was a spirited contest with Doug Brandon emerging victorious, but Cecil's supporters, particularly those from Cleburne County, his home county, were upset that Cecil had lost. Many Alexander and Russ supporters decided to back me. They felt that Doug had an unfair advantage because he was from heavily populated Pulaski County.

The NRCC took another poll after the Democratic runoff to see where we stood. It came back showing Doug Brandon, Democrat, from Little Rock at seventy-two percent. Ed Bethune, Republican, from Searcy was at sixteen percent. It was early June. There was plenty of time, but we had a lot of ground to make up and we were campaigning in a district that had no Republican officeholders at any level of government, not even a constable or a justice of the peace. The political ground was hard and Democrats gleefully used their power to make life miserable for Republicans.

One night after the Democrat nomination, I went to a well-attended North Pulaski County political event. My opponent, Doug Brandon, had a scheduling conflict so he was not present. The master of ceremonies, a big time Democrat, did everything he could to ignore my presence. He invited every Democrat candidate, even those running for justice of the peace, to speak. Finally, when there were no other Democrat candidates, he called on me. Almost as an afterthought, he said, "Oh, we also have a candidate for Congress here tonight." The event had gone on for hours and everyone was tired. People just wanted to go home, but I could not afford to pass up such an opportunity. When I rose to speak I heard a faint groan, so I said, "I'm Ed Bethune from Searcy and I'm running for Congress. I want you to remember me for two things: First, I never thought I would live to see the day when a head of lettuce would cost $1.25. Second, I made the shortest speech here tonight!" As I sat down,

I got a rousing round of applause, cheers, and a standing ovation. The next day my speech was the only speech mentioned in the statewide newspapers.

Political campaigns are always collective efforts. From the outset we worked as hard as we could, but after a few weeks, it was apparent that the campaign was destined to fail for lack of leadership. I was an experienced candidate but I was also busy winding down my law practice. Lana needed to finish the spring term at Searcy High School. She would not be free to work full time on the campaign until June. She was doing all she could and I was giving it my all, but every campaign needs a polestar and if we didn't find one soon our campaign would be so screwed up by June that we would never be able to put it together. I invited my longtime friend E. D. Yancey to lunch and told him that I could and would win the seat if I had someone like him to chair my campaign. To my surprise he did not say no. He said he felt the race was important and that he would think about it. The next day he called me and told me he was going to take a leave of absence from his job as a vice president of First Security Bank in Searcy, without pay, and that he would do everything he could to help me win the race.

E. D. called every friend either of us ever had to raise money and gain support. It was slow going at first, but he was just what we needed, particularly since Lana could not campaign full time until June and I, the candidate, could not also manage the campaign. Together with E. D., we persevered and by the time we got to September, we had laid a good foundation. Throughout the summer months, we gained traction but struggled to convince the pundits that we could win. Then, magically, our campaign took off about the time everyone was sending their kids back to school. We raised a total of $200,000 in September and October, and a goodly amount of that was from groundwork that Joel Anderson had done months earlier as my Political Action Committee fundraiser. The late influx of money was exactly what we needed to pay our bills and buy the all-important last minute television ads. Doug Brandon had more money, but we had enough. We closed the gap and even though we never led in any poll (even our own internal calling showed us down by at least eight percent), we could sense that things were going our way.

Early in the campaign I embraced the Kemp-Roth tax cut proposal, and the new theory of supply side economics. In every speech I hammered home why we needed to cut spending and reduce taxes. Kemp-Roth was a dramatic proposal that would cut marginal tax rates by thirty percent. The country needed economic growth, jobs, and more jobs. It was the perfect message at the perfect political moment.

As we got into the last week of the campaign, I put out a radio ad that featured a recording of my opponent saying he did not want to discuss the issues for fear of making voters mad and losing votes. In my mind, the words he spoke supported my ongoing contention that he was saying different things to different groups. I had accused him of political doublespeak and this was a chance to prove my point. I offered proof that he was talking about the need to have a moratorium on federal spending even as he was sending direct mail pieces to special interest groups saying that he would support more spending for their programs. There were many other examples, but I was particularly concerned about conflicting comments he had made to black and white voters on the volatile school busing issue.

As soon as the radio ad with his voice in it started running, Doug Brandon claimed that I had taken him out of context and that it was unfair to run the excerpt of his voice in a political advertisement. He said I should release the entire tape recording because it would prove that I took him out of context. It developed into quite a controversy so I called a news conference to deny his allegation and made a big scene of giving the entire tape recording to John Brummett and Steele Hays, reporters for the liberal *Arkansas Gazette.* I said I wanted the tape reviewed by the newspaper that was against me. Brummett and Hays wrote a lengthy front-page story about the issue, complete with pictures. Their story did not say that I had taken Brandon out of context, nor did it report that I had not taken him out of context. In my judgment, the inconclusive story vindicated me but the next morning I saw Cliff Jackson, a longtime political friend, who disagreed. He said, "Ed, you have blown the race for Congress."

As it turned out, the tape incident worked to my advantage, primarily because it was fair to make Brandon explain what I thought were contradictory statements about a number of issues. It also signaled to my supporters that I was willing to fight and speak out on hot issues of importance to them. A burst of publicity that gets voters to arguing about the candidates is usually a good thing for the underdog. The story was front-page news and the intense coverage helped me to victory.

Good television ads are a rarity in politics, but Mangan, Rains, and Ginnaven made one in the last month of the campaign that set our people on fire. Lana and I were sitting with our kids at our kitchen table and I looked up into the camera and said, "I'm Ed Bethune and it was right here at this kitchen table that my family and I decided—we'll run for Congress." Then after touching on a couple of issues I ended the TV spot saying, "You see, I'm a strong believer in the family, and God, apple pie, and the American flag. If you feel as I do then I'd like to represent you in Congress." The ad struck a nerve. Within minutes of its first appearance on TV, the workers in our campaign headquarters received hundreds of calls from people wanting to help us win. The ad also set off a flurry of helpful parodies. One supporter produced a batch of apple pie lapel pins. The ad and the parodies branded our campaign, in a good way.

Provincialism is a key factor in political campaigning. Lana and I developed a rule right after I announced that if we engaged in a conversation with a voter that lasted more than fifteen seconds, we would say, "Lana and I (or Ed and I) grew up and went to school in Little Rock." We committed ourselves to say those words regardless of what the other person wanted to discuss. By working those words into every conversation, we would constantly build the case that we had roots in Pulaski County, Doug Brandon's home and the largest county in the district. During the last week of the campaign, we ran a television ad that showed us, hand in hand, walking toward the camera with Little Rock Central High School in the background. I said, "Hi, I'm Ed Bethune. You know, Lana and I grew up and went to school in Little Rock, and I am concerned about what is happening in our country. If you feel as I do, then I'd like to represent you in Congress."

In the last three days of the campaign, people began to say, "Hey Ed, you are going to carry Pulaski County—you and Lana grew up and went to school in Little Rock." There is nothing to match the power of advertising and a disciplined message.

We won. We received 65,288 votes (51.2 %) to Brandon's 62,140 (48.8 %). We won only three of the nine counties in the district, but our margins in Pulaski, White, and Cleburne counties were sufficient to provide a 3,148-vote win over Brandon.

I always say "we" won the race for Congress because I would never have won had it not been for Lana, everybody knows that. She is the best politician I ever met and she never meets a stranger. On top of that, she is a tireless campaigner and a good fundraiser.

Every campaign produces vignettes worth repeating. Early on, I made a promise that I would campaign in every corner of the Second District. Therefore, two weeks before the general election, I drove into Prim, Arkansas, the northernmost community of Cleburne County. There was not much there, just a crossroads and an old country store. I saw only one person, an old gentleman in his eighties. I had been going strong for almost eight months, and on that day I was particularly tired. I told the old man that I would really appreciate his vote. He studied me carefully and then allowed as how he would vote for me. I was glad to hear that, but then he said, "Now, young feller, when are you going to get started?" Two weeks to the election and I was unknown in Prim, not a good sign.

On election night, we used our headquarters for our watch party. We could not afford to rent a hotel meeting room, but it did not matter. When the pundits began to report that we had won the seat our supporters were jubilant. They had worked hard and we had made history. I was the first Republican to win election in the Second District in 104 years (and the last until 2010 when Tim Griffin won the seat).

I expected to see my photograph on the front page of the statewide newspapers, but the *Arkansas Democrat* sent a photographer to Mount Holly Cemetery to take a picture of the tombstone of the last man to hold the Second District seat as a Republican, in 1874. That picture, not mine, was on the front page of the *Arkansas Democrat* the day after I won the seat.

Our friends in Searcy arranged a welcome home rally at the White County Courthouse for the day after we won. Lana, Sam, Paige, and I headed for Searcy in the campaign car, and just as we got on the north side of Beebe, we ran out of gas. Within minutes, a man in a truck recognized us, stopped and took me to get a can of gas. We were about forty-five minutes late for the rally, but I had a great opening line, "We apologize for running late. Many people said our campaign would run out of gas, and it did. Fortunately, it was after the election and not before!"

My opponent, Doug Brandon, was so certain of victory that he had already been to Washington to look for housing. Our upset victory caused him to collapse at his headquarters the morning after Election Day. He was in the hospital for two days. He was exhausted, shocked, and depressed.

Doug was one of the first people to visit me in Washington after I took the oath of office. We were friends before and after the election. I think it said a lot about Doug that he was willing to lay aside the campaign rhetoric, the disappointment of defeat and make the effort to come calling. He died a few years later of cancer.

20

POST ELECTION FUNK, THANKS ABE

Doubt whom you will, but never yourself.
Christian Nestell Bovee

After winning you would think I would have been euphoric, and I was, at least for a day. I fielded calls from well-wishers, happy supporters, and colleagues-to-be. Within twenty-four hours of winning, we filled three big cardboard boxes with résumés from job seekers. It was an amazing swirl of events, but then a curious thing happened to me.

I became anxious. I realized I knew very little about how Congress works, much less how I would approach my new and awesome responsibilities. I was like the dog that caught the streetcar.

I went into an unexplainable funk, not the depressive kind that I was in after I lost to Jim Guy Tucker, but a funk nonetheless. I had reached a new level, but I had no sense of where life was taking me. More importantly, I did not have a clear sense of how I should conduct myself as a congressman for constituents who believed that I should take care of them. That thought was anathema to a disciple of the Vermilye worldview.

On the third day after winning, my funk intensified to the point where I told Lana I had to get away. I needed to be by myself. I needed to get my head together. When I was a little boy, suffering from one funk or another, I would hustle off to my thinking spot in Mama Lewallen's hotel lobby to settle myself. There, I could enter the scene depicted in the lithograph, *Custer's Last Stand*, rub the stuffed bobcat with the nick in its ear, and dream the endless dreams triggered by the pages of my *Johnson Smith & Co. Catalog*. I needed such a place, but Mama Lewallen was dead, and my childhood thinking spot was gone. Where could a grown man go to do some serious thinking?

I packed a small bag, got in my car and headed to Pocahontas, the site of my teenage salvation. I am not sure what I expected to find there, but along the way, I impulsively decided not to stop in Pocahontas. Drawn by a mysterious force I headed north to Springfield, Illinois to consider the life of Abraham Lincoln. The Lincoln memorials in Springfield, New Salem, and Sangamon County would be my thinking spots. There I would sort out the odd streams of thought running through my head.

I spent three days in the Land of Lincoln and did not miss a single place of interest. I was not thinking in a religious way, but studying and evaluating the life of Lincoln was the next best thing I could have done. My thinking then was largely secular, but I did notice how Lincoln drew on scripture to explain so many of his actions. I visited his home, his law office, and the state legislature where he served. And I read everything I could find about the one term he served in the United States House of Representatives. Lincoln opposed the Mexican-American War when he was in the House. His stand was unpopular with his constituents and spoiled any chance he might have had to serve a second term. In the end, I decided that I should not worry about public opinion or try to figure out what might be popular with the people of the Second District of Arkansas. I would model myself after Lincoln. I would go to Congress, vote the way my heart and head told me to, and let the chips fall where they might. My time in Illinois was time well spent.

On the long drive home I began to look back. My Lincoln time was about looking forward and resolving how I should act as a congressman. My look back, on the other hand, led me to the inescapable conclusion that my strong will—the Vermilye worldview—was not the only thing at work in my life. Willpower is important and man cannot succeed in life without goals and a high degree of determination and perseverance, but man needs more than willpower and independence. Man needs faith in a higher power.

I was filling my need for something more through Lana. Simply put, I was leaning on her. I was getting the benefit of her way of thinking without giving up my own independence. We were a good team, but my reliance on her allowed me to paper over a fundamental issue. My Vermilye creed fostered self-centeredness and its natural corollary, worry. Anxiety is the flipside of the self-centered man because he focuses on life experiences and worldly things. He sees everything as being within his control or will. If things are not working out as planned, a self-centered man will be disappointed, anxious, and frequently angry. I was a better man for having Lana to lean on, but I was still a top-notch worrywart.

For me, life continued to be an ongoing struggle against any force I might encounter on the road to success. Lana had a leavening effect, but I could not find the inner joy that she and other Christians seemed to have. My mother and my father did not go to church, but in my youth my sister and I started going to Winfield Methodist Church. A few of our friends went there, and Winfield was the place of our baptism. When the Sunday school teachers talked about Heaven and the joy of being a Christian, I was sure there was a way for me to get there if I but had the will to live a good life and do a lot of good works.

21

CONGRESSMAN BETHUNE

One of the standing jokes of Congress is that the new Congressman always spends the first week wondering how he got there and the rest of the time wondering how the other members got there.
Anonymous

Just before we moved to Washington, the public relations firm that handled all our advertising held a private celebration for us. Our television ads always ended with a picture of my signature writing itself in white on a blue field as Bob Ginnaven said in his double-bass voice, "Bethune! And, you've got it in writing!" As a memento of our victorious campaign, the firm gave me a bronze replica of our campaign bumper sticker. It was in script with the words "Ed Bethune for Congress." We all had a good laugh, then Bob Ginnaven pulled out a second bronze plaque that said, "Lana Bethune for Congress." We cracked up. Everyone in the room knew the indispensable role that Lana had played in our winning campaign.

We bought a house on 37th Street in Arlington, Virginia and arranged to rent our home in Searcy. Our new house was close to Yorktown High School, the school we wanted our kids to attend. We shipped our belongings from our house in Searcy, and Lana flew to Washington in late December, 1978, to get the new house ready for the movers.

We had two cars that we wanted to take with us: Lana's Lincoln Town Car, and my 1974 BMW-2002. Paige was old enough to drive, but Sam was not, so I decided that we would go in tandem. I would drive the Lincoln and Paige would drive the BMW. We left early and everything went according to plan until we got into the hills of eastern Tennessee. Then two things happened that led to an encounter with a Tennessee state trooper. First, the heater in the Lincoln quit working, and it was cold, bitter cold. Second, it got dark, real dark. I was freezing. We had packed all my winter coats in the moving-truck, so I asked Sam to let me wear his Searcy Junior High School letter jacket. The sleeves were too short by four inches and I could not get it zipped up, but I was glad to have it. Because it was so dark, I told Paige to keep the BMW as close behind the Lincoln as she could, so that I would know if she and Sam were to have car trouble. Things went well for a couple of hours. I was smoking cigars at the time and I had a three-day growth of beard. Paige, following my instruction, was right on my tail when we passed the state trooper. He fell in behind us, turned on his lights and pulled Paige over to the side of the road. I saw the lights, so I stopped and went back to the trooper's car as quickly as I could. It was so cold that the trooper stayed in his car and rolled the window down as I approached. I asked him why he stopped Paige. He said he stopped her because she was following me too closely.

At that moment, the state trooper was looking at a middle-aged man with bloodshot eyes and a three-day growth of beard who had a short cigar stub sticking out of his mouth. I was wearing a kid's letter jacket that was too small and telling the trooper that I was a newly elected member of Congress from Arkansas. I explained to him that those were my kids in the BMW, and we were on our way to Washington, D. C., and that I had told my daughter to follow me as closely as she could.

The trooper was stunned. He looked at me as if I were crazy, a fully justified point of view considering my appearance. After a pregnant pause, the trooper told us to be on our way. He never even asked for identification. My story was so bizarre the trooper must have decided that it had to be true.

As soon as we moved into our new house, the Washington metropolitan area suffered the biggest snowstorm it had seen in years. The snow was so deep I could not get out of our driveway. It had banked to depths of three feet on our street. I was so eager to start work that I spent two days studying the *Rules of the House of Representatives,* the only official reading material available to me. I doubt if any other member of Congress has ever done that.

One of the best decisions I made as a congressman-elect was my first decision. I chose my old friend, Jerry Climer, to be my chief of staff. We were two of the Five for the Future candidates in 1972, and even though Jerry had taken a job in the Nixon administration, we had kept in touch through mutual friends. At the time of my election, Jerry was working for Congressman Tom Coleman of Missouri and knew his way around Capitol Hill. I wanted to focus on substantive issues and political matters at home and in Washington, and I wanted to have as much family time as possible. I did not want to deal with administrative or personnel issues, so I turned all that over to Jerry. I gave him the power to hire, fire, and set salaries—including his own. I, of course, retained the right to veto, but I never exercised it. Jerry stayed with me throughout my congressional career, and I never spent a moment worrying about the minutiae of office management.

Jerry's first recommendation was that I should make an effort to be president of the new class of freshman Republican members. There were thirty-six of us in the new class, and we met for the first time at the Dulles Marriott hotel in early December after the election. Little did we know that the class would produce several congressional chairpersons, a governor, a speaker of the U. S. House, and a vice president of the United States.

In my speech to the new members, I said we Republicans had the right philosophy, but we needed to do a better job of explaining it to the voters. It was not an earthshaking revelation but it struck a chord. I won on the first ballot.

I was quite proud to be president of the freshman class, but Lana upstaged me. The spouses of all the newly elected members of the House—Democrats and Republicans—elected her president of their organization. Since that time, she has been a leader in other spousal groups such as the Congressional Club, and the Republican Congressional Spouses.

On the day of my election to the House of Representatives, two of my law school classmates also won federal offices. Beryl Anthony of El Dorado won the Fourth District congressional seat, and David Pryor of Camden won the U. S. Senate seat vacated by his appointee, Kaneaster Hodges, Jr. They also moved their families to Washington, and that proved to be a good thing, particularly for the children who became good friends and spent a lot of time together when we first got to Washington. They did not go to the same schools, but they got together as often as they could.

22

FIRST DAYS, FIRST ISSUES

When we got into office, the thing that surprised me most was to find that things were just as bad as we'd been saying they were.
John F. Kennedy

On the day that I took the oath of office, my mother was in the gallery alongside Lana, Paige, and Sam. I wish my father could have been there, but I am sure he was beaming as he looked down from Heaven. I sat next to John Paul Hammerschmidt, on the second row from the front, in the seat by the center aisle that divides the House. We took the oath of office and then voted to select the speaker of the House. I voted for John Rhodes of Arizona, our nominee. We only had 176 members in our Republican caucus, so John lost to Tip O'Neil of Massachusetts. It was my first lesson on the importance of party control. The Democrats were in control of the House, and I was a member of the minority party. I could never chair a committee meeting until we, the Republicans, managed to elect at least 218 members out of the 435 members of the House. The Democrats would control the agenda. In the House of Representatives—unlike the Senate—there is no right to filibuster and the Rules Committee can limit the right to offer amendments. That makes it difficult to accomplish anything if you are a member of the minority party.

I held an open house in my office in the Longworth Building after the swearing-in ceremonies. Former Congressman Wilbur Mills came by to pay his respects. That to me was a high honor. He had fallen from grace, but he was a legend for the good work he had done as the longtime chairman of the House Ways and Means Committee. We were in different political parties, but as fellow Arkansans, and fellow White Countians, Wilbur and I struck up a friendship. We visited frequently because he was always in or near the Ways and Means Committee room that was on the first floor of my office building, the Longworth. The most memorable conversation I had with Wilbur Mills took place in the first month of my first term. He was lamenting the notorious episode with Fanne Foxe that was his undoing and told me to watch out for four things: money, booze, women, and power. It was sage advice that I have passed on to countless young politicians. We remained friends until his death in 1992.

Shortly after my open house, we attended a gala event at the Kennedy Center. J. William Fulbright, who served Arkansas as our United States senator from 1945 to 1975, was on the Kennedy Center Board of Directors and when we came to him in the receiving line, he beamed. I was surprised that he recognized me, but perhaps a staff member tipped him off. Then, Senator Fulbright got out of the receiving line and led Lana and me around the room introducing us to his many friends. Each time he introduced us he said the same thing, "This is my friend, Ed Bethune and his wife. He is a new congressman from Arkansas." Then he paused for dramatic effect and added in a louder, slightly incredulous voice, "And, he is a Republican." After each introduction the senator would chortle and pose theatrically until he approached the next friend, then he repeated the process word for word, inflection for inflection. Eventually, I got as big a kick out of it as he did.

I also met former Arkansas Congressman Brooks Hays in my first week as a member of Congress. He was a delightful man who distinguished himself during the 1957 school integration crisis in Little Rock by trying to find a way to moderate the crisis. A segregationist opponent twisted what Brooks was trying to do and defeated him with a write-in campaign. Brooks Hays loved the House of Representatives and after he lost his seat, he co-founded the United States Association of Former Members of Congress, a nonpartisan, educational organization chartered by the United States Congress. The organization originally began as an alumni organization to keep former members connected on a social basis, but it now offers a number of important domestic and international educational programs. Brooks referred to his wife, Marion, as "Little Manager," and he began all of his speeches with an admonition to himself to adhere to a directive he attributed to her, "Don't overegg the pudding." He also founded the Close Up Foundation, an organization that brings high school kids to Washington, D. C. to learn about government. He died in 1981.

In 1949 fifteen young Republican members of the House, including Richard Nixon of California, formed a small group that they later named, The Chowder and Marching Society. The founders of C&M were opposed to monthly bonuses for war veterans, which they considered too costly, so they started meeting once a week to discuss their plan to block the legislation. The men soon realized that the meetings welded them together as friends, not just fellow politicians. To enlarge and perpetuate C&M they selected, after each election, two newly elected congressmen to join the group. In time, the organization became a power matrix that produced two presidents, several governors and senators, and many leaders of the House of Representatives. C&M has never had a formal structure—no bylaws, no rules, and no officers. It exists spontaneously. It was an honor that the members asked me to join the group in 1978, and I have faithfully attended the weekly meetings since that time. Nowadays, C&M meets in the Capitol every Wednesday night with an active member of the House serving as host. It is a great way to maintain friendships and keep up with what fellow members are trying to accomplish.

President Gerald Ford and I celebrate a Chowder & Marching anniversary at a gala in Washington, D. C. in 1979. The crazy get-up—a chef's hat and an apron over black-tie formalwear—is traditional but no one can remember how it got started.

I had barely settled in as a new congressman when thousands of farmers converged on Washington from four directions. On the morning of February 5, 1979, there were nearly nine hundred tractors and other farm vehicles in the city. The farmers, members of the American Agriculture Movement were belligerent because many were losing their farms. They refused to park peacefully at a local stadium, and they were tying up traffic. Finally, the police confined them to the Mall area. Many members refused to meet with the farmers but all the members of the Arkansas delegation showed up for a hostile meeting in the Senate Caucus Room. Beryl Anthony and I had it the easiest since we had just arrived as newly elected members, but the farmers gave the other members of the delegation a hard time. Our two senators and Congressman Hammerschmidt were courteous listeners but Congressman Bill Alexander gave as good as he got. He chewed the farmers out for messing up the Mall and told them they were hurting their own cause. I was impressed with his show of political courage and when I saw him in the House gymnasium later that day, I told him so.

The National Republican Congressional Committee is a political organization dedicated to electing Republicans to

Congress. The Democrats have a comparable organization, and both spend a lot of time teaching newly elected members the art and science of winning re-election. Through orientation sessions and mentoring arrangements, the parties urge new members to issue endless press releases, newsletters, and other communications to insure re-election. These mailings are free of postage under the congressional franking privilege. The quintessential advice is that a new member should go home each weekend during the first term to be sure that constituents get a good first impression. The incessant focus on re-election, and how to engineer it turned me off. I had an irreverent notion that we ought to focus on substance, not politics. Nevertheless, I did work hard in my first year, and I did go home every weekend. At the end of my first year, a friend came up to me after I made a speech to students at Catholic High School in Little Rock and told me that I needed to get some rest and lose some weight. He was right. I embarked on an exercise program that included going to the gym early each morning and then running a couple of miles on the Mall. My friend's simple advice was better than all the political advice I got about how to win re-election.

The House of Representatives is a reflection of the country. The people are not looking for angels to represent them. They want their congressional representatives to be honest, and they want them to work hard and do the right thing.

There will always be one or two rotten apples in the barrel; nevertheless, I was thoroughly impressed with most of the Democrat and Republican members I met when I got to Congress. They were well educated; many were from Ivy League and other prestigious schools. Some had served in high political office. Dick Cheney, for instance, was President Gerald Ford's chief of staff and Claude Pepper, a Florida Democrat, had served in the U. S. Senate.

To be perfectly honest, I was slightly intimidated when I first arrived. I did not know as much as I needed to about the various bureaus and departments of government, and I had no previous legislative experience. I wondered if I could play in that league, but after a few weeks, I realized that I had unique skills and experience that others did not have. Congress, by design, is a diverse body that profits from the uniqueness of its members. From that time forward, I never doubted myself but I did begin to gorge myself with information. I read constantly—on the airplane, in bed, on the House floor, and in my office. I asked my new colleagues to recommend their favorite authors, and wound up reading several books that influenced me greatly. My study did not change my basic philosophy, but it did provide a deeper and better understanding of the conservative principles that had settled into my head since childhood.

The first two books I read in 1979 challenged me to compare the planned economy advocated by socialists with the free market economy of capitalism. Michael Harrington, a noted socialist, argued in his book, *Twilight of Capitalism* that the United States was headed to socialism and we could do nothing about it. Bill Simon, a conservative and former Treasury secretary, used the same facts as Harrington and agreed with him that the United States was doomed to be a socialist nation. However, in his book A *Time for Truth,* Simon said we could stop the slide to socialism if we were willing to stop deficit spending, get control of our national debt, and stop creating new entitlement programs. The dilemma framed by Harrington and Simon is still unresolved.

I read works by Eric Hoffer, Friedrich Hayek, Karl Marx, John Stuart Mill, Hannah Arendt, Norman Podhoretz, Milton Freidman, and many others. My thirst was unquenchable. Someone said that each year spent as a member of Congress is equivalent to getting a master's degree, and I agree with that.

My consternation over the Harrington-Simon dilemma came to full bloom in early 1979, shortly after I became a member of what is now the Financial Services Committee. The Chrysler Corporation was in serious financial trouble, contemplating bankruptcy, and there was a move afoot to get a $1.5 billion federal bailout. Lee Iacocca, the Chrysler CEO, argued that he could fix the company and that all the stakeholders—unions, shareholders, banks, and dealers—were willing to share the sacrifices necessary for the survival of the company. The bailout, in the form of loan guarantees, was coming just three years after the federal government had bailed out New York City. I was appalled at the idea of bailouts. Cities, states, and private companies should solve their own fiscal problems. Bailouts, in my judgment, do not lead to efficiency or profitability; they only lead to more bailouts. The Chrysler bailout went through. Chrysler repaid the loans in 1983, but in 2009, the company (along with other carmakers, and several financial service companies) was back before Congress asking for another bailout at a time when the national debt was nearing $13 trillion. I am convinced I took the right stand, but my decision to stand on principle led to my discovery of a larger problem. Many, in fact most congressional representatives actually believed loan guarantees are cost-free and have no impact on the deficit, the national debt, or the economy.

I began to study the lending practices of the Rural Electrification Administration (REA), Fannie Mae, Freddie Mac, and a host of other agencies that used the federal loan guarantee concept to create low interest loans. Congress authorized such programs with no regard for how such favoritism might affect the allocation of credit or the national economy. I introduced a bill that would require Congress to pass a "credit budget" as well as the customary tax-and-spend budget and I repeatedly offered amendments to cut the guarantees for REA, Fannie Mae, and Freddie Mac. My efforts were not popular. On one occasion, Majority Leader Jim Wright, a Texas Democrat, and Congressman Bill Alexander, an Arkansas Democrat, challenged my thesis in a vigorous debate with me on the floor of the House. Wright said, "Loan guarantees are cost-free." I responded by saying, "If that is so then let's give low interest loans to all Americans." Bill Alexander hammered my amendment to cut the REA subsidy by saying, "The gentleman is trying to turn out the lights in rural Arkansas." The harder I fought the more I discovered that almost no one in Congress or the government cared about the credit issue. There was a sense that government could do whatever it wished to do with loan guarantees and low interest rates for favored constituencies. My bill to establish a credit budget and thus force Congress and the executive branch to consider the economic impact of such programs never passed the House. The *Arkansas Democrat* editorialized in favor of my credit budget, calling it "Bethune's Baby." If it had become law, our nation might have averted the great credit problems that surfaced for all to see in late 2008.

My conservatism and refusal to want to take anything from "them" also led me to refuse to take the obscene retirement benefit that was available for members of Congress. This, coupled with my refusal to take a pay increase for members of Congress that passed in my first term, caused me some heartburn at home. Lana was keeping the family checkbook and we were having a hard time living on the $65,000 per year salary, not to mention that we were not saving much for college expenses that were right around the corner. The decision to reject the retirement program was a good one in my mind, but I left millions of dollars, literally, on the table.

In 1979, America was in the midst of a nationwide gasoline shortage that stemmed from federal controls on oil and adverse international developments, not the least of which was the fall of the Shah of Iran. Long lines formed at service stations. People were furious. They demanded federal action to fix the problem, and that triggered a yearlong debate about energy policy that produced a number of bad ideas. Congress passed and President Carter signed a law creating the Synfuels Corporation, an ill-starred plan to make synthetic fuels. Congress also tried to pass a gas-rationing plan similar to the rationing plans used in World War II, but cooler heads prevailed and the rationing idea was limited to the preparation of an emergency rationing plan. President Carter put solar panels on the roof of the White House and a wood-burning stove in his living quarters. He also ordered all government agencies to turn down thermostats to conserve energy. Congress, at the president's insistence, also imposed a windfall profit tax on oil companies to show its willingness to punish someone for the shortages. Taken together, the policies proved the incompetence of government, but did little to improve supplies of energy.

I conducted a series of town hall meetings throughout the Second District of Arkansas all during the gasoline crisis. My constituents were universal in the belief that we should all practice energy conservation as best we could. That is when I decided I needed to lead by example. I sold Lana's gas-guzzling Lincoln Town Car and bought a Plymouth Arrow, a lightweight two-door sedan.

Lana eventually forgave me for my decision to turn down the retirement benefits and the congressional pay increases but she has never forgiven me for selling her gold, 1974 Lincoln Continental Town Car, the one I bought for her when my law practice took off in 1973.

23

TROUBLE ON THE POTOMAC

Power corrupts; absolute power corrupts absolutely.
Lord Acton

On Friday, February 1, 1980, Lana and I headed to a retreat for Republican House and Senate members at the Tidewater Inn in Easton, Maryland. The retreat, a weekend session to plan our legislative and political agenda for the upcoming presidential and congressional elections, turned into something altogether different.

The Saturday meetings focused on our economic ideas and troubles in the Middle East, not the least of which was the Iranian hostage crisis. We intended to think about our discussions overnight and then make some resolutions before adjourning on Sunday afternoon. As was customary, we ended our Saturday sessions with a reception and dinner.

Elizabeth Taylor was there with her then-husband, Senator John Warner of Virginia. Her eyes were as beautiful as they appeared to be in the movies so I was mesmerized. Lana thought Liz was rather shy, but up against Lana most folks appear to be shy.

The festive mood at the reception was disturbed when word spread like wildfire that a major scandal was breaking that would involve a United States senator and several members of the House. The word was that the FBI had conducted a sting operation, code named ABSCAM. The media were saying that FBI agents, posing as associates of a mysterious Arab sheik, had secretly videotaped members of Congress taking cash in exchange for favors promised to the sheik. It was a stunning bit of news. The reception turned into a quest for information about the scandal, and the newspapers were full of it the next morning.

We learned to our dismay that a Republican colleague, Dick Kelly of Florida, was one of the suspects. The other suspects, four House members, and one U. S. senator, were all Democrats. It was a disgusting turn of events that worsened with every new revelation.

Over the next few days, information about the videos began to surface. We heard there was a clip showing United States Representative Dick Kelly, our Republican colleague, stuffing $25,000 worth of bribes into his pockets and then turning to an FBI agent saying, "Does it show?" Kelly, during an interview by David Brinkley on NBC, admitted taking the money but made the ridiculous claim that he was "conducting his own investigation." He said he put the money in the glove compartment of his car and spent some of it for meals and incidental expenses before turning it over to the FBI after the story broke.

The members of the Republican House Conference were livid. The honor and integrity of our conference was on the line. One of our leaders drafted a resolution stripping Kelly of financial assistance from the National Republican Campaign Committee and suspending him from membership in the Republican Conference.

On February 21, 1980, the Republican Conference met to consider the draft resolution. Some members expressed concern for Kelly's due process rights, and others were concerned that we were moving too quickly. I had a chance to wind up the debate, and unbeknownst to me, William Whitehurst, a fine member from Virginia who kept a detailed diary of his congressional service, memorialized my remarks in a book he published in 1985 entitled *Diary of a Congressman, ABSCAM and Beyond*:

> This is not a criminal trial; it is not a court. We are not levying a fine nor are we taking away his committee assignment. It is a process to suspend him from this conference and take away his campaign funds. Kelly has said that he would not offer a defense, but the proof of his guilt is in what he has said publicly. The nature of his offense is obvious, and his public defense of it reflects a reckless disregard of House procedures. Due process is not at stake here. What we are talking about are privileges, not rights. It is a privilege to sit in this conference, not a right. You speak of precedents being set. You are right; it is time to set precedents.

Congressman Whitehurst called my remarks a "ringing statement that defined the debate in a way that no one else had." We did not have to vote on the resolution. Dick Kelley resigned from the Republican Conference. We had done all we could do. The rest was up to the Ethics Committee and the Justice Department.

24

SAVED BY SAILING

The sea! the sea! the open sea!
The blue, the fresh, the ever free!
Bryan Waller Procter

In the spring of 1980, Lana, ever wise, realized that serving in Congress is hazardous to family life. I had finished my first year in Congress, and we were settling in to life in the fast lane. Many marriages of congressional representatives, mostly those that are fragile to begin with, collapse under the pressure of official and political duty. In most cases the wreckage includes one or more of the things Wilbur Mills had warned me about: money, women, booze, and power. Lana was not worried about Wilbur's no-no's. I did not take a drink during my time in Congress, and money had never been a driving force in my life, so I was not likely to fall prey to either of those. I was lucky to have Lana. I knew it from the beginning of our relationship, and she knew that I felt that way about her. We have never questioned our commitment to each other or the lifelong loyalty we pledged when we had our conference with Dr. Kenneth Shamblin, the pastor who married us. Power was another thing. We had never had it so we were not sure how it could be a problem. In any event, we figured the best antidote for power and outsized egos would be to have time alone doing something that would keep us from taking ourselves too seriously. That "something" was sailing on the Chesapeake Bay.

Lana heard about a sailing course at the Annapolis Sailing School. Sailing is the heart and soul of Annapolis, Maryland, and there is no finer place to sail than the Chesapeake Bay. The beginner's sailing course takes one weekend, and successful completion qualifies graduates to rent a sailboat. We signed up and on the first day the school surprised us by putting us in separate boats. The sailing instructors knew from experience that husbands and wives do better when they learn the fundamentals independently of one another. It prevents what they call "Captain Bly Disease." We had a good time, learned a lot, earned our certificates, and rented a boat the next weekend.

It was our intention on our first sailing trip to spend the night on the boat at anchor, so we provisioned the boat with food for lunch, dinner the first night, and breakfast the following morning. We raised full sail, headed into the Chesapeake Bay, and, with some nervousness, charted a course for the Wye River, a tributary on the other side of the bay. We spent a beautiful night on the Wye River listening to Canadian geese honking their way north, and watching the watermen put out crab traps. There is nothing like the sights and sounds of the Chesapeake. On the way home we sailed around in the mouth of the South River, so named because it is south of Annapolis. We were under full sail, heeled over, strutting our stuff. All of a sudden, we learned that the bay is a shallow estuary, with many shoals. We hit bottom and for the first time in our sailing career we were hard aground. Ironically and fittingly, we were just off Turkey Point. I felt like a turkey as I tried to get the boat unstuck. As luck would have it, the wind piped up and in short order we were in a bit of trouble. The wind was blowing us toward the shoal and if it had not been for a gentleman in a powerboat, we would have spent an uncomfortable second night on the water. He pulled us off and we headed back to port. Chastened, we turned the boat in and headed back to D.C.

In spite of going aground off Turkey Point, we loved our first taste of sailing. We pledged to go at least once a month, and we kept that pledge. Sailing was, at first, a simple way to escape the pressures of high office but soon we began to notice and discuss the difference between sailing and serving in politics. Politics is artificiality writ large. It is a necessity, for we must have a means to manage the messy business of government, but the endless posturing, fund-raising, deal-making, and ever-recurring elections, lie in stark contrast to the natural forces at play when you are on a sailboat on the Chesapeake. At sea, there are no artificialities. The wind, the waves, the currents, the tides, and the question of whether you have enough water and food are dominant. One might overcome, on occasion, the forces that permeate politics but in sailing, as King Canute proved when he was trying to get people to realize his limitations, you cannot order the tide to go out or in, and there is nothing you can do to change the weather.

Sailing is, therefore, the antithesis of politics. We soon were addicted and that led us to consider the next step, blue water sailing. It is one thing to sail in the Chesapeake or other protected waters; it is another to venture into, or across an ocean.

Jim Ford became chaplain of the House of Representatives in 1979. In 1976, when he was chaplain of the United States Military Academy at West Point, he and three friends flew to England, bought a thirty-one-foot Golden Hind sailboat and sailed from Plymouth to New York Harbor to celebrate the 200th anniversary of the Declaration of Independence. When Jim got his congressional appointment, he sailed his boat to Annapolis, and it was not long before we met him and became fellow sailors. Jim enthralled us with stories about his thirty-day crossing of the Atlantic Ocean. My favorite was his explanation that neither he nor his comrades knew anything about sailing or navigation, so when they left Plymouth Harbor they just headed out into the English Channel and "turned right." Jim guffawed when he told that story, but then he explained that one of his comrades was a professor of math who quickly mastered the tricky business of celestial navigation. Totally hooked, I began to read books about blue water sailing, particularly those written by married adventurers, the Hiscocks, the Roths, and the Pardeys. Lana did not read about blue water sailing as much as I did, but we talked endlessly about it. Our responsibilities had us tied down, but that did not keep us from dreaming about sailing away into the blue water.

In January of 1981, I was scouring the *Washington Post* classifieds and saw an ad for a thirty-one-foot Golden Hind sailboat. I called the owner and within thirty days, Lana and I were the proud owners of a boat just like the one that Jim Ford had sailed across the Atlantic. We named her *Salute* and every time we got a chance we would go out for a day sail, but we especially enjoyed the times when we would anchor out for the night. We gained experience and soon began planning a trip to Maine, which would take us from the Chesapeake to the Delaware Bay and then into the blue water between Cape May, New Jersey and Block Island, Rhode Island.

25

SAVED IN ANOTHER WAY

Skepticism is the beginning of Faith.
Oscar Wilde

Sailing, and our dreams of blue water voyaging helped us to see the distinction between natural forces and the artificiality of politics, but how did God fit into the picture? How did God fit in with the Vermilye creed? These great puzzles, lifelong quandaries for me, began to clarify soon after I got to Congress.

Once we settled into our house in Arlington, we started looking for a church home. We considered several churches that were close by, but then we realized that the National Methodist Church—the representational church for the Methodist denomination—was only a twenty-minute drive just across Chain Bridge, in the District of Columbia, near American University.

We were married in the Methodist Church, raised our children in that denomination, and I had served a term as chair of the Administrative Board of the First United Methodist Church in Searcy. The pastor at the National Methodist Church was Dr. William A. Holmes, an Arkansas native who graduated from Hendrix College in Conway, Arkansas. It was a natural for us—or so we thought.

We attended regularly for six months, but it did not take that long to realize that, too often, the church seemed to be teaching and preaching about human philosophy, science, or Supreme

Court decrees. I have the utmost respect for Dr. Holmes; he has a good heart. He exalts Christ and points people to Him but we needed to go elsewhere.

Lana heard about a new church that was meeting in a nearby junior high school. It was nondenominational, started by Don and Sally Meredith, the couple who planted Fellowship Bible Church in Little Rock. On our first day at Potomac Chapel, I knew we were in the right place. There was a period of singing and praise, then a period of sharing, followed by a lesson. The lesson was always about scripture not current events, political, or social issues. We were also pleased to see that several congressional colleagues attended the new church. Mickey Edwards of Oklahoma was a regular as were Senator Bill Armstrong of Colorado and his wife, Ellen, a good friend of Lana's. Several Democrats also found a home at Potomac Chapel. Congressmen Tony Hall of Ohio and Marvin Leath of Texas were regulars. Marvin's wife, Alta was also a good friend of Lana's.

It was at Potomac Chapel that I first heard about *The Four Spiritual Laws.* Bill Bright's little tract teaches us to put God—not man—in the center of our life. It was a simple revelation that enabled me, for the first time in my life, to see the Bible as entirely consistent and understandable. Before then, I saw the Bible as a beautiful, poetic collection of magnificent stories. To me it was a good guide for a busy man making his way through the challenges of life, but that was about it. I did not see the Bible as the inviolate word of God, and I certainly did not know how to put God in the center of my life. Man was in the center of my life, and it was my Vermilye will—not God's will—that mattered most.

I still had a long way to go, but at least I was now on the right road.

26

THE 1980 CONVENTION, MY HIGH WATER MARK

Success is not measured by the position one has reached in life, rather by the obstacles overcome while trying to succeed.
Booker T. Washington

In 1980, I attended my first Republican National Convention. I was on the platform committee, so I needed to arrive in Detroit, the site of the convention, before most delegates. Lana and the kids left a few days later, driving our BMW. When they got to Detroit, we stayed with the Arkansas delegation at the Holiday Inn in Windsor, Canada, on the banks of the Detroit River, just across from the Joe Louis Arena.

Ronald Reagan was the nominee-apparent, having turned back a serious bid by George Herbert Walker Bush. The national economy was in the tank. Interest rates and inflation rates were nearing twenty percent, unprecedented levels. The memory of gasoline shortages, closed filling stations and long lines at the pump, was fresh. The American people were furious, and as an added insult, fifty-three United States citizens were in their eighth month as hostages of the rogue state of Iran. They had been in captivity since militants seized the U. S. Embassy on November 4, 1979. The country was desperate for leadership.

Reagan asked Congressman Guy Vander Jagt to deliver the keynote speech for the Republican National Convention. Guy was a renowned public speaker. President Richard Nixon called him the "best ever." President Reagan said, "Some call me the great communicator but if there was one thing I dreaded during my eight years in Washington it was having to follow Guy Vander Jagt to the podium."

The stage was set. Expectations were sky high; it was going to be a good year for the Republican party. Ronald Reagan was almost certain to turn back President Jimmy Carter's bid for a second term, and it appeared that we would gain several seats in the House and Senate.

I had no idea that the historic confluence of events would lift me as high as I would ever get in national partisan politics. A few days before I left for Detroit, Congressman Guy Vander Jagt asked me to introduce him as the keynote speaker. He wanted me, as president of the freshman class, to make the point that a new force was moving in America, a force built on Republican principles. I would only have ten minutes, but it was a rare opportunity for a rookie.

I, of course, thought my speech was perfect. I showed it to Vander Jagt before I gave it and he liked it too but as I read it three decades later, I realize any national politician, of any party, could say the same thing, in any year. I am a little disappointed in myself for that reason, but bearing in mind that my main job was to whip twenty thousand people into a frenzy, here is part of what I said when the chairman introduced me:

> Thank you, Mr. Chairman. My fellow Americans, tonight I am excited about introducing the keynote speaker because something good is happening in America, something that is long overdue.
>
> There is a new force building in this country. I felt it in 1978 when I got close to the good people of Arkansas in my race for Congress …
>
> This year, people in and out of government, politicians, businessmen, workers, farmers, homemakers, everyone—the young, the old—tell me that they feel the

same force building in this country. Everyone can sense that something is happening in America...

As we enter the '80s, a ground swell is coming and it is coming from the grass roots and it can't be turned back. People want a change. People want to start acting like Americans again.

People want to build for the future on the solid foundations that made America great. They don't want more of the same. It is an American renaissance—that is what the new force is all about. It is a rebirth of the American character, that special something that sets this country apart from all the nations of the world.

One writer put it this way, 'France is a land and England is a people but America is more.' America, he said, 'is a willingness of the heart.'

And, that is what it is. The American character is that drive, independence, optimism, determination, grit, gumption, all those qualities wrapped up in our trust in God.

Tonight the Renaissance begins and it begins with the keynote that is more than a theme for this meeting. This is a keynote for the future and who better to give such an important address than a man who personifies our national character, a man of hope who treasures his heritage and loves his family, one who worked hard to get an education and make his way in the world. Who better to sound the keynote for our future than a man who truly understands America.

As a leader in Congress, Guy Vander Jagt has traveled to every state in this Union helping to elect almost half the members of the United States House of Representatives. He has crisscrossed this country from East to West, from North to South, and he has listened and he has learned.

Who better to start us on a new beginning than a man who loves his country and gives up so much to do his duty? Who better to call out to the American people than a man so eloquent and sincere that Americans everywhere will cling to and savor his every thought tonight?

My fellow Delegates, I ask you, do you want to hear from such a man? (A chorus of ayes.)

With one voice, do you want to hear from such a man? (A chorus of ayes.)

Do you believe there is hope? (A chorus of ayes.)

Do you want a new beginning? (A chorus of ayes.)

Do you want to hear a keynote for the future? (A chorus of ayes.)

Ladies and Gentlemen, it is my honor to present my colleague in the Congress from this beautiful and friendly state of Michigan, the keynote speaker, the Honorable Guy Vander Jagt. (Applause and standing ovation.)

The huge crowd loved it and even though it now sounds as phony as most election-year speeches, it was my high water mark in national partisan politics.

27

1980 ELECTION, REAGAN INAUGRAL

Can we solve the problems confronting us? Well, the answer is an unequivocal and emphatic "yes." To paraphrase Winston Churchill, I did not take the oath I have just taken with the intention of presiding over the dissolution of the world's strongest economy.

Ronald Reagan, First Inaugural Address, Tuesday, January 20, 1981

The 1980 election produced greater Republican gains than anyone had predicted. In the House, we did not win enough seats to take the majority, but in the Senate, Republicans picked up twelve seats and gained a fifty-three to forty-six seat majority. Portentously, the Republican party held a sizable majority of congressional representatives from a Deep South state, South Carolina, for the first time since Reconstruction.

In Arkansas, Frank White unseated Governor Bill Clinton to the surprise of everyone, including Frank. Clinton had raised the license fee for cars and mishandled the relocation of Cubans at Fort Chaffee. Frank became famous for his two-note campaign: Cubans and car tags.

There was no change in our congressional delegation but that is because I resisted the temptation to run against Dale Bumpers. My closest friends and advisors said I would look uncharacteristically opportunistic if I challenged Dale after only one term in the House. I was convinced I could win, but I was not sure we could hold the Second District seat. For those reasons, I passed up my best chance to go to the Senate. After I chose not to run, a political unknown, Bill Clark, was the only person to file for the Republican nomination for U. S. Senate. He raised almost no money and got his biggest headline by handing out miniature Clark Bars, a popular candy at the time. Clark wound up getting forty-three percent of the vote, an unbelievably strong vote for a Republican in a statewide race. I won my first re-election contest with seventy-nine percent of the vote. My Democrat opponent was Jacksonville Mayor James G. Reid. Dale Bumpers told me later that I could have beaten him had I chosen to run. I believe he was right. In politics, timing is everything.

The Reagan inaugural on January 20, 1981, was something to behold. The pageantry, orchestrated by Reagan's public relations expert Michael Deaver, set a new standard for presidential inaugurals. The Reagan era was underway, and the new president got off to a fast start. Twenty minutes after he took the oath of office, Iran released fifty-two American hostages into U.S. custody (one was released earlier). They had spent 444 days in captivity.

28

SUPPORTING DEMOCRATS FOR JUSTICE DEPARTMENT

A man must be both stupid and uncharitable who believes there is no virtue or truth but on his own side.
Joseph Addison

George Proctor, a Democrat, was United States attorney for the Eastern District of Arkansas when President Reagan came to office. Typically, all sitting U. S. attorneys will tender their resignations so that a new president can appoint members of his party to fill the positions.

Republicans in Arkansas expected me to recommend a Republican for the position, and I would have done so but for the fact that I wanted George Proctor to remain as United States attorney. George was a Democratic member of the Arkansas House of Representatives before he became United States attorney so there was no doubt that he was a member of the Democratic party. However, George was a friend and he had served as my deputy prosecuting attorney in Woodruff County in 1970. He was a good man who had done a good job as United States attorney, so I went to bat for him.

The Republican party leaders in Arkansas were furious with me, claiming I was hurting the effort to build the party by refusing to give patronage to loyal Republicans. I answered by saying that partisanship should not determine how we fill positions in our system of justice; we need to choose people based on their qualifications and their commitment to serve honorably without regard to political considerations. I had the high ground and I was determined to stand fast. The personnel people at the White House gave me a lot of static, and they sent Deputy Attorney General Rudy Giuliani over to talk to me. I gave him my line about choosing people based on qualifications, and I could tell he was not going to fight me. President Reagan reappointed George and he served with distinction for several more years.

A similar issue arose later on when Charles Gray sought to carry on as United States marshal for the Eastern District of Arkansas so that he could qualify for retirement benefits. Charles was married to the sister of Dale Bumpers, and many people thought I would oppose Charles because Dale had torpedoed my nomination to be a federal district judge in 1976. I must admit I was tempted to seek revenge, but Charles was a good U. S. marshal and he was a former FBI agent. I supported Charles, and once again, the leaders of the Arkansas Republican party gave me the business. Eventually the noise subsided and my fellow Republicans forgave me for my "odd ideas" about how to staff the justice system. Senator Dale Bumpers came to me later and told me that my support for Charles Gray was "magnanimous" given how he, Dale, had handled my nomination.

29

JACK KEMP, SUPPLY SIDE ECONOMICS

The supply-side claim is not a claim. It is empirically true and historically convincing that with lower rates of taxation on labor and capital, the factors of production, you will get a bigger economy.
Jack Kemp

Jack Kemp was an all-star professional quarterback, and in 1965, he was the Most Valuable Player in the American Football League. He won a seat in Congress in 1972 representing the district in and around Buffalo, New York. I was a fan when he played football, but I did not meet him until I began my campaign for Congress in 1978 when I attended a candidate school sponsored by the National Republican Campaign Committee. Jack came to the candidate school to explain the Kemp-Roth tax cut, and I got my first exposure to supply-side economics. I was impressed with the research Jack had done, particularly his embrace of the Laffer Curve, a new economic theory explaining how marginal tax rates that are too high can depress, rather than increase revenue.

It was obvious to me that Kemp had not spent all his time studying football playbooks. I decided to study what I had learned about the Kemp-Roth tax cut bill.

The more I studied the more I liked it. Dr. Arthur Laffer, who appeared at the candidate school with Jack, maintained there are two points at which the government will collect no revenue: 1) when the tax rate is one-hundred percent (no one will work), and 2) when the tax rate is zero percent. There is, obviously, a point on the high-end of the curve when the tax rate will produce diminishing returns for the government. Laffer and Kemp showed how President Kennedy actually increased revenues by reducing marginal tax rates in the early 1960s, and they offered other proof that lower rates generate work, savings, production, and investment. To my way of thinking, it was the quintessential American way to spur economic growth, create jobs, and reduce deficits. I endorsed the Kemp-Roth bill and made it the centerpiece of my 1978 campaign for Congress. I am convinced that Jack's tax-cutting, pro-growth ideas helped me defeat Doug Brandon, a strong Democrat nominee. As a footnote, the Democrats always belittled the Laffer Curve by making fun of Dr. Laffer's name. In retrospect, I wish his name had been Wiseman. It should have been.

When I got to Congress Jack and I became close friends. He was easy to like because he was quick to smile and never spoke ill of another man. Many politicians use *ad hominem* attacks to belittle an opponent, but Jack never did that. He debated substance, not politics or personalities. He had as many friends on the Democrat side of the aisle as he did on the Republican side. His wife, Joanne, befriended Lana as soon as we got to Washington and invited her to attend a weekly Bible study known as Joanne's Friday Group.

Our friendship with the Kemps lasted beyond the time Jack and I served as colleagues in the House. We had a lot in common with them and always enjoyed their company. It was a sad day for us when Jack got sick with cancer. A few months before his death, Jack's family started the Jack F. Kemp Institute of Political Economy to establish a public library for his papers and conduct public lectures and conferences promoting his ideas. Just days before his death, I was on a conference call with Jack and he spoke about what the institute meant to him. His voice was faint, raspier than usual, and he could only say a little, but it meant a lot to me to hear him. Jack died on May 2, 2009. His funeral service at the National Cathedral—attended by thousands of friends—was a fitting tribute for the man many of us called The Good Shepherd.

30

THE REAGAN AGENDA

Far better it is to dare mighty things, to win glorious triumphs, even though checkered by failure, than to rank with those poor souls who neither enjoy much nor suffer much, because they live in the gray twilight that knows neither victory nor defeat.
Theodore Roosevelt

Expectations were higher than usual when President Reagan and the Ninety-Seventh Congress got down to business. The 1980 election was a much-needed catharsis for the American people. President Carter's claim in 1979 that the nation was in "malaise," coupled with a poor economy and the Iranian hostage crisis had everyone down in the dumps. We needed a fresh start and that is the main reason Reagan won such a resounding victory. He made it clear that he intended to take on the Soviet Union, but first he needed to fix the economy. His prescription for that was a good dose of tax and spending cuts. Could he get his program through the Congress? The Republicans had a fifty-three to forty-six seat majority in the Senate but the Democrats still controlled the House of Representatives by a wide margin, 244-191.

When the president gave his first State of the Union speech, he directed a question to Democrats who had already indicated their unwillingness to support his plan for economic recovery. He said, "Have they an alternative? Are they suggesting we can continue on the present course without coming to a day of reckoning?"

As a new member of the House Budget Committee, I was squarely in the middle of the action. Our challenge was to make a budget that would hold every Republican vote and get the twenty-seven Democrat votes that we needed to win a vote on the floor of the House. It was a tortuous process, but we were confident that a large number of Southern Democrats, known as Boll Weevils, would vote with us. (Nowadays, those once known as Boll Weevils call themselves "Blue Dogs," and they are few in number).

We got off to a fast start and momentum was clearly on our side. Then, on March 30, 1981, just two months after the State of the Union address, a deranged young man, John Hinkley, shot President Reagan as he was leaving the Washington Hilton hotel. The president survived the assassination attempt, but the country was at a standstill for several days. It was a close call; the bullet came within a hair of hitting the president's seventy-year-old heart.

As it turned out, we were right to be confident. President Reagan came back from his near-death experience to campaign vigorously for his economic agenda. We had several strategy meetings with the president to figure out how we could build public support and get the Democrat votes we needed in the House of Representatives. One meeting in the cabinet room of the White House shortly before the vote revealed that we would actually do better if we made our package more conservative, less moderate. That was contrary to the opinions of the chattering class, the so-called sophisticates who write editorials and comments for the liberal media. They were flat wrong. We adjusted our package to make it more conservative. Public support grew and Democrat opposition crumbled. On August 4, 1981, we passed the Gramm-Latta budget and the Kemp-Roth tax cuts. We did not get all we wanted, but we got a lot. Our bill restrained the growth of spending, cut income tax rates by twenty-five percent over three years, slashed estate taxes and business taxes and indexed the rates against inflation. The indexing feature was important because inflation was pushing taxpayers into higher tax brackets. We referred to that as "bracket-creep," an unfair way to increase revenues without passing a bill to increase tax rates.

A final strategy session on the Reagan budget and tax cuts in the Cabinet Room at the White House. Summer, 1981. Clockwise from President Reagan: Del Latta (OH), Tommy Hartnett (SC), Me, Chief of Staff James Baker, OMB Director David Stockman, Counselor to the President Ed Meese, Olympia Snowe (ME), Frank Horton (NY), Bill Frenzel (MN), Vice President George Herbert Walker Bush.

A large number of Democrats, several more than we needed, voted with us.

As soon as his economic package was in place, the president redoubled his effort to end the Cold War by defeating Soviet Marxism. He was not satisfied to contain communism. He intended to transcend it by showing it to be an anomaly of history. It was a monumental decision that would bear fruit a decade later when the USSR collapsed, as did the Berlin Wall, in 1989.

Throughout my time in Congress, the Democrats and liberal media attacked our supply side theory, the rationale for the Kemp-Roth tax cuts. They relentlessly claimed that our tax cuts increased the deficit and thus starved the government's ability to fund social programs. We believed mightily in the power of supply side economics, and I believe history has proven that we were right to make the deep cuts in tax rates. Our plan incentivized work, production, savings, and investment. We knew that there might be increased deficits in the short term, but if such deficits materialized, it would at least keep pressure on the big spenders. It would, we reasoned, be better to live with an increased deficit in the short term than to take money from the American people and give it to the liberals, only to see them spend it.

It takes time for new policies to take effect in an economy as large and complicated as ours, so there was not much we could do when the country slipped into recession in 1982. The jobless rate increased and people began to question "Reaganomics," the name Democrats gave to the policies we had passed in 1981. Eventually, our tax cutting produced growth and prosperity, but that did not help us in 1982. We wound up losing twenty-six Republican members of the House even though we maintained control of the United States Senate. I had an opponent, Charles George, who hammered me hard all throughout 1982. I was urging my constituents to stay the course and give our policies time to work. But Charles George was running TV commercials saying, "Hang in there say Ed Bethune and the Republicans." His ridicule of Reaganomics was effective, but not enough to unseat me. I won re-election with fifty-four percent of the vote, a significant drop from my seventy-nine percent win in 1980, but a win nevertheless. The liberal media tried to say I barely won, but I countered by saying, "Why should I be morose? As a Republican, I just won re-election with fifty-four percent of the vote in a heavily Democrat district." They gave up trying to make light of my victory.

31

RACE AND CIVIL RIGHTS

All looks yellow to the jaundiced eye.
Alexander Pope

My experience with racial issues in Arkansas during the Rockefeller years, particularly the effort of the Old Guard Democrats to suppress voter turnout in the African American community, led me to support most of the civil rights legislation that came to the House.

In 1979, less than six months after I took the oath of office, I faced a hot issue. The opponents of busing schoolchildren to force the desegregation of public schools were trying to pass a bill proposing an amendment to the U. S. Constitution that would end court-ordered busing. The bill, H.R. 74, was stuck in the Judiciary Committee, held up by those who did not want to end court-ordered busing. The opponents of school busing were urging members to sign a Discharge Petition that would discharge H.R. 74 from the Judiciary Committee and bring it to the House floor for a vote. It takes 218 signatures to effect a discharge, any number less than that will not do the job. Typically, when the number of signatures gets close to 218, the speaker of the House will urge some who have signed the petition to remove their signatures thus frustrating the effort to discharge. The process was changed later to make it more difficult for members to play such games, but in 1979 the names of the signatories were not revealed unless and until the magic number of 218 had been reached.

On June 27, 1979, the opponents of school busing asked me to sign the Discharge Petition for H.R. 74. The opponents had gotten 210 signatures and needed only eight more to get the bill to the House floor. Their plan was for eight members to go simultaneously to the well of the House and sign the petition before the speaker could get some members to take their signatures off the petition. I was not in favor of the bill, but as a member of the minority party, I despised the idea that powerful leaders could bottle up bills they did not like. I was signature number 218. The bill would now come to the floor of the full House.

On July 24, 1979, the House debated H. R. 74. There was an intense lobbying campaign by the opponents of school busing, and I received thousands of letters and phone calls urging me to support the proposed amendment to the U. S. Constitution. I voted against H. R. 74, mainly because I abhor the idea of amending the Constitution to fix problems that should be resolved in other ways. Additionally, the poorly worded proposed amendment would have caused more problems than it solved. It took me a year to put out the firestorm in my district. I had excellent reasons to oppose the proposed constitutional amendment, but it was a hard issue to explain. Many of my constituents were sick and tired of court-ordered school busing and they let me know it, using plain language.

In 1981, I made an early commitment to support a twenty-five-year extension of the Voting Rights Act. This was an easy decision for me. The purpose of the Voting Rights Act was to stop the kind of discrimination that African Americans had experienced in Arkansas under the Old Guard Democrats. During the administration of Governor Winthrop Rockefeller we put an end to the blatant effort to suppress black voter turnout in Arkansas but the problem continued in other states. On June 29, 1982, President Ronald Reagan signed the extension of the Voting Rights Act. The reauthorization made Section 2 of the act permanent. That section of the bill prohibited the violation of voting rights by any practices that discriminated based on race, regardless whether the practices had been adopted with the intent to discriminate or not.

In 1983, a bill to create a Martin Luther King holiday came to the floor of the House of Representatives. The bill was explosively controversial, but I vowed to support it. Senator Jesse Helms of North Carolina and a number of outside groups were attacking the bill arguing that confidential FBI records would show that Dr. King had communist ties. It was a specious claim, but it was politically effective. As a former FBI agent, I countered the contention. A number of news outlets mentioned my work on the bill and *The New Republic* used the speech I made on the House floor to wrap up a 1986 analysis of how and why the bill passed. Here is a portion of what I said, as it appears in the *Congressional Record* for August 2, 1983:

> Mr. BETHUNE:
>
> Mr. Speaker, as a Republican and as a former FBI agent, I rise in strong support of the Martin Luther King holiday bill.
>
> In the 1960s we in Arkansas rallied around Winthrop Rockefeller. I was a Democrat at the time. I became a Republican because we wanted to break the stranglehold that Orval Faubus and machine politics had on our state for a long time which had suppressed not just black citizens but all citizens in our state, and we Republicans, in the finest tradition of Abraham Lincoln, brought blacks into government, and we Republicans, in the finest tradition of Abraham Lincoln, made changes in the election laws and opened up the political process for blacks in Arkansas.
>
> And do you know what we learned out of all that? The great changes are not made here in the legislative chambers or in the judicial halls. The great changes in this world are made in the hearts and minds of men and women. Attitudes are so important.

> I think that this holiday for Martin Luther King will give us an annual opportunity to recommit ourselves to the proposition that all men are created equal. It will nourish the spirit of reconciliation that we need so desperately in this country right now.
>
> Mr. Speaker, I urge all Members and I urge particularly the Members on my side of the aisle to support this bill. Let us make this a bipartisan effort, as it should be.

A significant number of blacks in the Second District supported me every time I ran for office, this in spite of the fact that I was a hard-core conservative on economic issues. I have long believed that the creation of a full-blown welfare state is an American tragedy, particularly for blacks, and I never pulled my punches on that. The trust I developed during the Rockefeller years held firm.

Two prominent black scholars, Walter Williams of George Mason University and Thomas Sowell of the Hoover Institution, have written extensively, for decades, about the plight of blacks in America. They argue powerfully that the welfare state impedes black progress and destroys black families by creating dependency. I am hopeful that a majority of blacks will soon come to realize the truth of what they say.

In 1981, my colleagues Bob Livingston of Louisiana, Mickey Edwards of Oklahoma, and I decided to bring a few prominent black leaders from our congressional districts to Washington, D.C. to meet with officials in the Reagan administration. Livingston and Edwards also had good support from blacks in their districts, and we wanted to awaken national Republicans who had just about given up on the black community. We had a series of high-level meetings at the White House, the Republican National Committee, and with leaders in the House and Senate; unfortunately, we got tepid responses and no action to promote better relationships. Our constituents were pleased that we had tried. It confirmed the trust we had with them, but the indifferent reaction we got from the people we visited was disappointing.

32

CONSERVATION AND WILDERNESS

Everybody needs beauty as well as bread, places to play in and pray in, where nature may heal and give strength to body and soul.
John Muir

My fondness for the conservation ideas of President Theodore Roosevelt led me to support wilderness and environmental issues. In my first term I spent days studying the arguments for and against the construction of a series of earthen impoundments that would dam the Cadron Creek, a free-flowing stream that starts in Cleburne County and flows south into Faulkner County. I walked, rode, canoed, and flew over all the areas covered by the project, a brainchild of the Soil Conservation Service. It was a hot issue. Most farmers, concerned about flooding, were in favor of the dams, but the environmental community was dead-set in opposition. After much thought and several public hearings, I decided to oppose the project. It was a good decision. Today, Cadron Creek is a favored, widely promoted, recreational spot in Central Arkansas. Outfitters provide tourists with canoes and provisions for floating the Cadron. The creek offers good fishing and spectacular scenery including many caves, bluffs and pinnacles.

The Arkansas Wildlife Federation, in cooperation with the National Wildlife Federation, gave me a beautiful award, a miniature bronze bear, mounted on a wooden base. It was their 1979 Legislative Conservationist of the Year Award. I love my bear—it has been on my desk ever since I got it.

In my first year in Congress, I also voted for the Alaska Lands Bill, an historic measure designating millions of acres of wilderness. The bill that I voted for in May of 1979 was adjusted in the Senate to take account of concerns about oil drilling, but overall it was a good step to take and on December 2, 1980, just before leaving office, President Carter signed the bill into law. T. H. Watkins, the noted environmentalist and author said the Alaska Lands Act "set aside more wild country than had been preserved anywhere in the world up to that time," and that it stood as a ringing validation of the best of what the conservation movement had stood for.

One of the best things I did was to support and lead the effort to pass the Arkansas Wilderness Act. In a paper delivered to the Arkansas Historical Association at Southern Arkansas University in Magnolia on April 25, 2009, Little Rock banker French Hill remembered my work:

> Public support ... came not from a Democrat, but from a Republican, Second District U. S. Representative Ed Bethune of Searcy. In April of 1983, Bethune, toured the areas and announced that he would introduce legislation to designate Flatside in Perry and Saline Counties as wilderness. Flatside (about 10,885 acres) was the only ACC [Arkansas Conservation Coalition] designated area in the Second District. He also told reporters that he would like to see all eleven areas recommended by the ACC included in a final bill.
>
> Bethune's action prompted the Arkansas delegations only other Republican, U. S. Representative John Paul Hammerschmidt (R-AR) of Harrison, to take a position. He announced that he was opposed to Bethune's effort . . . recalling that he had told his constituents a 'number of years ago that we probably had enough wilderness

areas.' However, by the end of 1983, Hammerschmidt and Bill Alexander had sided with Beryl Anthony and co-sponsored his Forest Service-backed bill. Arkansas wilderness legislation was now deadlocked in the House, and Senators Bumpers and Pryor had yet to take any action.

The *Arkansas Democrat* reported that Anthony and Bethune were applying pressure on Bumpers and Pryor and that Bumpers and Pryor were waiting on a compromise in the House. But in the 'air war,' Bethune was gaining ground. He obtained endorsements from pro-business groups such as The Little Rock Chamber, (Mack McLarty, Chairman) and the Arkansas Industrial Development Commission.

Then, a miracle of legislative courage happened. On the last day of the 1983 session, Senators Bumpers and Pryor introduced a wilderness bill, S. 2125, almost a duplicate of Bethune's. They indicated that they would hold public hearings in Arkansas despite the fact that two House subcommittees had already held extensive hearings in May 1983. Regardless of the two-year delay, proponents now had a House bill and a Senate companion. The delay also resulted in trying to legislate during the upcoming presidential election year. Indeed, it was an uncertain environment for wilderness.

On Wednesday, February 15, 1984, on the campus of UALR, Bumpers and Bethune sat side by side, allied and ready to hear 130 scheduled witnesses—the most Senator Bumpers remarked he had seen in his nine years in the Senate. Senator Pryor would have joined them, but was attending the funeral of his mother. These hearings would be followed by a second set of hearings in Washington in April 1984.

French Hill, then a legislative aide to Senator John Tower (R-Texas), enlisted the support of the senior senator and he co-sponsored the Arkansas Wilderness Bill. It was unusual for an out-of-state senator to support another state's wilderness bill, thus his endorsement helped our cause. The *Arkansas Gazette* and the *Pine Bluff Commercial* also endorsed the bill.

The U. S. Senate passed the Arkansas Wilderness Bill on August 9, 1984. Following House passage, President Reagan signed the bill into law on October 19, 1984.

The Arkansas Conservation Coalition and Don Hamilton of Little Rock, another law school classmate of mine, were indispensable allies. They worked tirelessly to pass the Arkansas Wilderness Bill. They urged Susan Morrison, a famous wildlife artist, to give me the artist's proof of her etching entitled *Flatside Wilderness.* It is a treasure and it, along with her poem of the same name, has hung in my home office ever since.

33

POLAND AND THE POPE

Before his pontificate, the world was divided into blocs.
Nobody knew how to get rid of communism.
In Warsaw, in 1979, he simply said, "Do not be afraid."
Lech Wałęsa, founder of Solidarity.

In August of 1980, Lech Walesa led Polish workers to strike the Gdansk shipyard. The strike gave rise to a wave of strikes all across Poland that forced the communist authorities to give Polish workers the right to strike and organize unions. Shortly thereafter, General Wojciech Jaruzelski took over the communist party. He imposed martial law in December of 1981, and then arrested Walesa and other union leaders. The conflict between the workers and the state was the death-knell for communism in Eastern Europe.

In 1982, I was fortunate to be a member of the first congressional delegation to visit Poland after the declaration of martial law.

Shortly after we landed in Warsaw and left the airport, someone broke into our aircraft, the kind of thing that happens in a police state. We had left no official papers or materials on the plane so it did not turn into a big deal, but we lodged an official protest because the break-in was a dastardly violation of diplomatic protocol.

Our small delegation toured many sites and visited with church leaders and others who were struggling to make the best out of a tense situation. At every stop, the Poles treated us with respect and were effusive in their praise and kindness. I concluded that the Polish people love America and love Americans. It gave me a good feeling to be on their side and to see how much they admired our country.

It was impossible to feel good about anything on our third day in Poland. We visited Auschwitz, the concentration camp where the Germans held and exterminated more than a million people, mostly Jews—men, women, and children. It is a devastating experience to hear the stories of Auschwitz and to see the collection of shoes, garments and other personal possessions of the poor souls imprisoned and murdered there.

The grisly tour brought back haunting memories of a trip that Lana and I made two years earlier to Dachau, the first concentration camp set up by the Nazis near Munich, Germany in 1933. There, the Germans abused and murdered thousands of political opponents, Christians and Jews, Gypsies and homosexuals—anyone they considered to be an enemy of the Nazi regime.

The unspeakable horrors of Auschwitz and Dachau—too extensive and painful to cover here—will haunt me forever.

Just as our visit to Poland was winding down, we received a call from the Vatican. Pope John Paul II had heard of our trip. As a Pole he was curious to hear about our visit to his homeland. He invited us to meet with him at the Vatican on our way back to the United States, so we quickly rearranged our itinerary.

When we arrived in St. Peter's Square, Vatican officials met us and led us through vast hallways and rooms to the Pope's private apartment. On our way, we passed through a large hall where hundreds of people were waiting for an audience and that made me realize that we—there were only seven in our delegation—were receiving special treatment. Eventually we were ushered into a small room that had what appeared to be a throne at one end. Within minutes, Pope John Paul II, dressed in a white cassock, entered the room through a side door. He took a seat on the throne, and began reading a prepared statement into a microphone welcoming us to the Vatican. I thought it was strange until he finished, shoved the microphone aside and stepped down to meet us. We shook hands and then, for a remarkable half hour we talked informally with the world's most important religious leader. He asked about our families, but he was most interested to learn how things were going in his homeland, Poland. His magnetic, engaging personality reminded me of President Reagan.

When our meeting was over the Pope put a maroon box containing a crucifix in my hands and gave it and me his blessing. He did the same for the other members of our small delegation and then he was gone.

His Holiness, Pope John Paul II, met with our congressional delegation in the Vatican in 1982 after we visited Poland, his homeland. We were the first delegation from Congress to enter Poland after the Soviet-controlled government declared martial law.

My trip to Poland, a country oppressed by the Soviets and suffering the heavy hand of martial law, exposed me to the hopes and dreams of the Poles, the horrors of the Holocaust, and finally, the goodness and grace of the Holy Father. Emotionally drained—having experienced the highest of highs and the lowest of lows—I hungered for home.

34

CHEMICAL WEAPONS

As we recall the unspeakable horror endured by victims of chemical weapons, let us all reaffirm our common commitment to eliminate the dangers posed by such instruments of mass destruction.
UN Secretary-General Ban Ki-moon.

In 1982, the Department of Defense declared that it wanted to spend $32 million to make 155-millimeter artillery shells and aerial Bigeye bombs that would contain binary nerve gas. Binary gas was a new development. It consisted of two agents considered harmless until mixed in flight. The new binary chemical weapons were to be produced at the Pine Bluff Arsenal in Arkansas. Many of my constituents worked at the arsenal and thousands lived nearby. In deciding whether to support or oppose the project, I had to consider economic, public safety, and national defense concerns.

I began an intensive study of chemical warfare to determine what I should do about the request to spend millions on a new age of chemical weapons. I concluded it was a mistake for America to begin the new program. We still had a supply of unitary nerve gas sufficient to provide the necessary deterrence and there were other good reasons to forego production. The more I learned about chemical warfare the less I liked the idea of producing nerve gas, especially at Pine Bluff.

Nerve gas is a terrible war weapon. One drop on the skin will send a person into rigors and painful death. I used to remind my constituents that the prevailing winds around Little Rock are south to north. When the paper mills in Pine Bluff were going strong, everyone in Little Rock had to hold their nose because the stench of a paper mill is awful. When I made the case against producing nerve gas in Pine Bluff, I used to say, "If you don't like the paper-mill smell, wait till you get a whiff of this stuff."

I also railed against the Army Chemical Corps for all the mistakes they had made in storing and developing chemical weapons over the years. The unit was moribund and useless, so much so that the Army once tried to dissolve it. I did not hesitate to point that out; consequently, I was not a favorite of the Army Chemical Corps.

When I showed up to inspect the operation at the Pine Bluff Arsenal the officer in charge told me I would have to give a blood sample before they could let me go through the facility. I think it was a rule more honored in the breach than the observance, but I did not object. I should have, because they sent in a man who reeked of whisky to draw my blood sample. I did not give them the satisfaction they were looking for. I let the man—conspicuously incompetent—poke around until he hit a vein and got his sample. Then we toured the facility, and when we were done, I wrote up the problems I had found.

The stupid confrontation with me did the Chemical Corps no good. I began calling them the "Moribund Chemical Corps," or the "MCC" for short.

In July of 1982, I joined with Wisconsin Democrat Clement Zablocki, the chairman of the House Foreign Affairs Committee, to block production of the new binary weapons. We won by a vote of 251 to 158. My opposition set off a firestorm at the Pine Bluff Arsenal and throughout the Pentagon.

In 1983, the Pentagon announced that it would try again to get funding for the production of binary nerve gas. I wrote a letter to President Reagan asking him to abandon the effort to launch a new age of chemical weapons. I urged him to restate the 1969 policy announced by President Nixon against the production of chemical and biological weapons. I argued that a restatement of the moratorium would give the United States the high ground in the struggle for world opinion because we could distinguish ourselves from the Soviet Union, a nation that was making and using chemical weapons. We could not make such a distinction regarding nuclear weapons.

Secretary of Defense Casper Weinberger came to my office and tried to get me to back off but I politely declined.

On May 25, 1983, Chairman Zablocki and I went to the White House to state our case. It was a power-packed meeting in the Oval Office with President Reagan, Vice President George H. W. Bush, Secretary of Defense Casper Weinberger, Ed Meese, Jim Baker, Mike Deaver, William Clark, and Chief of Staff Ken Duberstein. The president's command of detail was startling. Zablocki and I did not expect him to lead the discussion but he did. We had a good exchange and I eventually urged the president to show the world our good intentions by restating Nixon's moratorium. He said it was a good argument, but added, "The press wouldn't let me get away with it."

Clem and I left the meeting agreeing that we had gotten a fair hearing. Soon thereafter, I re-filed my amendment to kill the program and once again, it passed the House.

After I left Congress, the debate continued for a few years but in 1990, President George H. W. Bush met with President Mikhail S. Gorbachev and reached an historic understanding to eliminate most chemical weapons. In 1991, President Bush took it a step further. He declared that the United States would give up chemical weapons saying he expected it would lead to a worldwide ban on their production. On April 24, 1997, during the administration of President Bill Clinton, the United States Senate ratified the Chemical Weapons Convention, making illegal the production, acquisition, stockpiling, or use of chemical weapons.

35

THE PAGE SCANDAL

It is always with the best intentions that the worst work is done.
Oscar Wilde

In my second term, I put in a bid to select a young Arkansan to serve as a congressional page. Scores of young Arkansans had come to Washington to serve as pages, but none had come at the invitation of the Republican party. The Democrats, being in the majority, were entitled to twice as many pages as Republicans, but I thought I could make a good case to select at least one page for the Ninety-Seventh Congress.

I asked Marlene Thompson, my personal assistant, to gather applications from deserving students in the Second Congressional District and told her I was determined to select a page based on merit. Most pages were the children of big contributors or people with political connections. I wanted to break that mold and open the selection up to kids that might not otherwise have a chance to serve. The people of Pocahontas gave me a chance when I moved there in the eleventh grade and it changed my life. I wanted to return the favor to a deserving youngster.

Marlene did a good job. We were impressed with a young black man named Leroy Williams. He was an honor student at Hall High School, and all his teachers and friends gave him strong recommendations. I nominated Leroy and the committee selected him. He entered the page program in Washington,

D.C., and we got good reports from the managers of the program, at least for the first few months.

Then, in a shock to everyone that knew him, Leroy suddenly became unstable and alleged that a number of members of Congress were making homosexual advances to pages. It was national news for a few days until Leroy recanted his personal claims and admitted that he was lying about what he had alleged. Nevertheless, the speaker of the House launched a major investigation of the page program and it was a good thing that he did. The lead investigator, Joe Califano, quickly confirmed that Leroy's allegations were false but his investigation did reveal abuses. Gerry Studds, a Democrat of Massachusetts admitted having sexual relations with a seventeen-year-old male page and Dan Crane, a Republican of Indiana, admitted having sexual relations with a seventeen-year-old female page. The House of Representatives voted to censure both members. Speaker Tip O'Neil called them to the well of the House and read the censures. Dan Crane faced the speaker and apologized. He was defeated in the next election. Gerry Studds turned his back to the speaker and refused to apologize. His constituents re-elected him.

I was done with the page program.

36

CHINA THEN, CHINA NOW

The man who removes a mountain begins by carrying away small stones.
Chinese proverb

When I was a little boy, everyone said China was our friend and that Chiang Kai-shek was a good leader but after World War II a revolution ousted the generalissimo, the country converted to communism and China—led by a hard-liner, Mao Zedong—began a dalliance with Joseph Stalin and the Soviet Union.

Just five years later, a new war in Korea—euphemistically called a police action—was not going well for the United States. The Chinese, our allies during World War II, had intervened in support of our enemy, North Korea. On November 1, 1950 hordes of bugle-blowing Chinese infantry swarmed around the flanks and over the defensive positions of United Nations forces, mainly troops of the U. S. Army and the U. S. Marine Corps. Our troops fought extreme cold and isolation, barely avoiding disasters at Chongchon River and the Chosin Reservoir. There was talk of using atomic weapons to regain the offensive and on April 10, 1951, President Harry Truman—after a rancorous public disagreement over how best to proceed—relieved General Douglas MacArthur from his position as commander of all United Nations forces.

Truman's curt dismissal of the long-time military leader—a hero to most Americans—created a storm of controversy that led to a rare invitation for the old general to appear before a Joint Session of Congress to explain his side of things.

I was fifteen years old on April 19, 1951, the day my homeroom teacher herded our class into the school auditorium at Little Rock Senior High School to hear a radio broadcast of MacArthur's speech. The general outlined the need for a global strategy to fight communism and cautioned us not to appease Red China, but the main thing everyone remembers is his famous closing line, "Old soldiers never die—they just fade away."

Two years later, on July 27, 1953, the opposing forces in Korea signed an armistice creating a Demilitarized Zone separating North and South Korea. The tension in Korea subsided and things were relatively quiet when I boarded a troopship to go there in December of 1954, but the fear of international communist expansion—The Domino Theory—had taken deep root in America.

In 1972—the year I ran for attorney general—President Richard Nixon, a strong anti-communist made an out-of-character visit to China, met with Chairman Mao and began the process of normalizing relations. However, China did not shake off the constraints of communism and begin its ascendancy as a world economic power until Mao died in 1976 and Deng Xiaoping became the *de facto* leader of the country in 1978.

Deng opened up China to capitalist ideas, planting the seeds for a run of prosperity that continues to this day. He fought off opposition to his capitalist ideas with an old proverb from his native Sichuan: ''It doesn't matter whether a cat is black or white, as long as it catches mice."

Five years after Deng took power, in March of 1983, Lana and I were part of a congressional delegation to the mainland of China. We made two stops in communist controlled territory—Shanghai and Bejing—and ended our trip with a visit to capitalist Hong Kong when it was still under British control.

It was a rare opportunity—almost laboratory conditions—to compare communism to capitalism. Deng's reforms were just getting started, but he was confidently predicting better things to come: "When our thousands of Chinese students abroad return home, you will see how China will transform itself."

Lana recorded the stark differences of the two systems in a letter she wrote to my mother in April of 1983.

> Dear Grandmother:
>
> … when we landed in Shanghai there were only three airplanes at the airport … there were only buses, bicycles and walkers on the streets … we saw pull-carts piled high with cabbages and fresh vegetables and all the people were wearing dull grey, blue, or green Mao jackets and pants. Our stay at the hotel, the run-down Jing Jang, was as if stepping back in time—worn-out overstuffed sofas and chairs with lace shawls over them, and frazzled Chinese rugs on the floor. Even so, the hotel was upscale compared to the living conditions afforded to most Chinese … no heat, no running water or toilet facilities, only a porcelain pot … bamboo poles hanging out of windows strung with the laundry. ... It is rare to see foreigners … the faces of the people tell a story of a hard life … the lines in the old faces show sadness … it was the same in Bejing and on the road to and from the Great Wall of China …
>
> After the dismal sites of Shanghai and Bejing, we arrived in Hong Kong … what a contrast! We saw what the Chinese people can do when the yoke of communism is taken off ... bustling enterprise and colorful signs … a hubbub of commerce from street vendors … new buildings … heavy car, truck, and bus traffic … people going in and out of *haute couture* stores that were making and selling the latest western fashions. Everywhere we looked there seemed to be an endless array of fancy hotels and restaurants. Some Chinese were in traditional attire, but most were in Western dress....

When we left Hong Kong, Lana and I agreed that the entire mainland could be like Hong Kong if China continued Deng Xiaoping's reforms.

The China story—just from the time I was a child—shows how quickly things can change on the world stage. My recitation of the last sixty years is by no means complete, but it does hit the high spots. The once impoverished Chinese, subjugated for years by the Japanese, then by the heavy hand of communism, are now on the rise. They have serious issues resulting from their rapid growth and from the continued oppression of their people, but many experts predict China will surpass the United States as an economic power by the year 2020. It is instructive to note that as I write this memoir, the United States of America is nearly $14 trillion in debt, and China holds twenty percent of that.

Those who doubt the miraculous transformation should compare China's recent history with the most watched show in the history of the Olympics—the Opening Ceremony of the 2008 Olympics in Bejing. More than 15,000 proud Chinese participated in a four-hour ceremony that captivated the world. Various commentators called it "spectacular … spellbinding … a grand, unprecedented success." The rich display of Chinese culture began with the intense beating of Fao drums. A seemingly endless parade of Chinese in dazzling costumes followed the drummers and the ceremony ended with a famous Chinese gymnast, suspended by an intricate system of wires, making a full lap of the stadium high in the air.

There are excellent videos at http://en.beijing2008.cn/ceremonies.

From time to time, I pull out the photos that I took on our visit to Bejing and Shanghai in 1983 and compare them with what is going on now. Two of my old photos are worth a thousand words. One shows a Chinese peasant riding a beat-up tricycle that he had converted into a street-sweeper. The contraption had a rotating brush and a homemade catchment device, and it seemed to do the job. The other shows a very wide street with no cars but hundreds of people walking and riding bikes, a common scene throughout Bejing and Shanghai in 1983.

The very latest street-sweeping equipment. Bejing, March 1983.

37

BLUE WATER DREAM REALIZED

God gives us dreams a size too big so that we can grow in them.
Anonymous

In May of 1983, I borrowed two items from fellow sailors for our first blue water sailing trip. Congressman Stan Parris of Virginia loaned us an inflatable life raft, and Congressman Jim Martin of North Carolina loaned us his Loran receiver, a pre-GPS navigational device.

I was suffering from head and chest congestion, a persistent condition that was not responding to medication, but we were determined to get underway as soon as we had a free week. Our plan was to sail to the north end of the Chesapeake, traverse the Chesapeake & Delaware Canal, and sail down the Delaware Bay to Cape May, New Jersey where we would enter the Atlantic Ocean.

We provisioned *Salute*, mounted the life raft, rigged up the Loran, and departed in early June. We got to Cape May on the second day, but it was late at night because Delaware Bay was choppy and the wind was on our nose. The first leg of our trip was rough, but the fresh salt air did what the medicines had failed to do. My head and chest were clear of congestion, another reason to go sailing. We dropped the anchor and got a few hours sleep.

Our big moment came with the sunrise. We headed out of Cape May inlet into the Atlantic Ocean bound for Rhode Island.

Our track would take us northeast across the busy shipping lanes that lead in and out of New York Harbor. The weather forecast was good. Our little boat was slow, but with fair winds, we could make landfall in a couple of days. Everything went according to plan until midday when the wind lay down and the waves flattened out. *Salute* was pulsing up and down on a sea as slick as glass. It was stifling hot and we could do nothing about it. We were becalmed, prisoners to the odd rhythms of a sea without wind. We took down our sails and waited, and waited. Soon we saw a number of black fins slowly cutting a meandering path around our boat. The distinctive fin shape was unmistakable. It was an eerie experience but it did not frighten us. We felt safe on *Salute*. Nevertheless, we double-checked the lashings on our life raft.

It is one thing to be becalmed on the Chesapeake when you know you are only a few miles from land, but it is quite another to sit well offshore not knowing when the wind will pick up. Eventually, the sun went down so we decided to enjoy a nice dinner and go to bed.

The calm lasted all night and I awoke to a humming sound that was getting louder by the minute. I poked my head out of the hatch and saw a huge transport loaded with stacks of containers steam by us at full speed. The noise that woke me was the propeller of the transport; it came that close to us. The wake of the vessel was the next thing to hit *Salute*, and that woke Lana. We made a new resolution: When in or anywhere near the shipping lanes, someone must stay awake to keep watch.

It was late morning before the wind piped up. Waves replaced the glassy surface and the shark fins disappeared, or at least were out of sight. We hoisted the sails and got underway. It was obvious, due to the time we were becalmed, that we would have to spend another night, perhaps two more nights at sea.

The waters between Cape May and Rhode Island are heavily trafficked, but we saw only two other vessels before nightfall. One was a motor yacht heading south, and the other was what appeared to be a garbage scow headed out to sea.

Our second night at sea brought another new experience, lightning, lots of lightning. It was scary at first, but realizing there was nothing we could do about it, we enjoyed it as we would enjoy a fireworks display. When the lightning storm ended, the night was pitch-dark and there was no wind. We decided we needed to make up some time so we started up our little fifteen-horsepower Lister diesel engine. I was a little woozy so Lana took the helm and steered a course of 040°. I went below to get some sleep, and absolutely lost track of time. When I woke up five hours later, there was Lana hovered over the tiller steering 040°. I was slightly ashamed that I had left the hard work to her, but I was extremely proud of her for toughing it out. Sailing is hard work anytime, but it is doubly hard when you are on the ocean because there is no let up and you are on your own.

With daylight and a fresh breeze, we raised the sails and kept our northeast heading. The Loran was showing that we would soon reach Block Island, but at our slow pace it would be well after dark before we got there. We had hoped to make our landfall in daylight, but after two rough nights, we were eager to finish our first blue water trip. Everything was going well. When it got dark we were still twenty miles southwest of Block Island, the patch of land that guards the water between Long Island Sound and the Narragansett Bay leading into Newport, Rhode Island.

Our short trip into blue water had already taught us about tanker traffic, sharks, and lightning. Now we were about to experience the scariest hazard of all, and we were unprepared for it.

In early summer when the temperature of the sea is still cold, warm land air may move over the cold sea causing fog to form. Before we knew it, we were in fog, thick fog. The wind was gone again and there we were, in the dark, blinded, and still fifteen miles southwest of Block Island.

Salute was not equipped with radar and we had no experience sailing in fog, but we did have a radar reflector mounted on the top of the mast and we had a loud electric foghorn.

We could barely see the navigation lights on the bow of our little boat; the fog was that thick. We could do nothing but pray, turn on the foghorn, and forge ahead. I monitored the Loran and our chart every five minutes to verify our course line.

We had a scary moment as we entered the high traffic area between Montauk Point and Block Island, about five miles from the inlet to Salt Pond, the shallow protected place where we hoped to anchor. We heard the foghorn of another vessel, but we could not see a thing. The horn got louder and louder and it was impossible to tell from which direction the sound was coming. At one moment it seemed to be behind us and seconds later we were certain it was dead ahead. Finally, we thought we heard the sound of engines—maybe it was our imagination—and suddenly the foghorn seemed farther away. We turned our attention to finding the inlet with the aid of the Loran. We still could not see beyond the bow of our boat so the Loran would have to guide us to the inlet. We seemed to be on course but the figures on the Loran showed us to be only fifty yards from the inlet. We began to get nervous—where were the lights marking the entry to Salt Pond? Our depth meter indicated we were getting into shallow water, but we still could not see the lights. Were we on course? Were we about to hit bottom? Was the Loran accurate? We were about to go nuts when we saw the lights, the red was 90° to starboard and the green was 90° to port. That meant we were actually in the inlet before we saw the entrance lights on the breakwaters.

We were safe. We continued into Salt Pond and carefully maneuvered our way around and between scores of boats already at anchor. It was midnight when we found a spot and dropped our anchor. Within minutes, we were in the bunk sound asleep.

The next day we launched our dinghy and went ashore to explore Block Island. Our first blue water voyage was behind us. We had made many mistakes and were lucky to survive the hazards we encountered, but we were proud of what we had accomplished. That evening at sunset, we were sitting in a restaurant overlooking the Atlantic and I said to Lana, "You know I have been in the Marine Corps, the FBI, and Congress and I have done a number of adventurous things with men-friends, but this has been the greatest adventure of my life, and I shared it with you." We both tuned up a little bit. It was a great moment.

We spent one more night in Salt Pond and the next day we headed to nearby Newport, where we met a friend from Arkansas, Don Mehlburger, who had a thirty-eight-foot Swan sloop-rigged sailboat that he kept there. We stayed a couple of days in Newport and then we moved *Salute* to Buzzards Bay and left her on a mooring near the entry to the Cape Cod Canal. It was time to head back to Washington and a full schedule of work for the next six weeks.

The Congress takes off in August. It had been my practice to spend all that time at home tending to the needs of my constituents, but I had not taken a serious vacation since my election to Congress in 1978 and we needed a break. I decided to devote the entire month of August 1983 to a blue water exploration of the New England states. We would sail to Maine. Our daughter, Paige, decided to go with us, so as soon as Congress adjourned, the three of us headed to Buzzards Bay.

We spent a day provisioning *Salute* and checking all our systems, and then we dropped the mooring line and headed north where the top of Buzzards Bay narrows and feeds into the Cape Cod Canal, which leads to Cape Cod Bay. When we entered the canal, we had our first serious lesson with tidal currents. The tidal range and currents in the Chesapeake Bay are modest, and through sheer luck, we did not have much trouble with currents on our trip down the Delaware Bay. Our trip through Cape Cod Canal was different. The two greatest dangers facing boaters in the canal are swift currents and the high volume of recreational and large commercial traffic. The current can reach a velocity of six knots, and it changes direction every six hours. Our little fifteen horsepower engine would give us about five knots per hour in no current, but that was the best we could get her to do. It is theoretically possible for an underpowered boat to go backwards in such a current. A seasoned mariner would have checked the tide and current tables and waited for a favorable current. Had we done that, the ten-mile trip through the Canal could have been a piece of cake, but we picked a bad time. When we entered the canal, the tidal current was running against us, and it took us a little over three hours to go ten miles, the length of the canal. Ignorance is bliss; our transit of the canal could have gotten ugly, but we finally made it to the Cape Cod Bay. It was a fortunate beginning to the second leg of our blue water cruise to Maine.

As we entered Cape Cod Bay, we hoisted the sails. Now free of the canal currents, we set a direct course for Monhegan Island, off the coast of Maine, some 130 nautical miles northeast. It was late afternoon so it appeared that we would most likely spend two nights at sea before reaching port. There is a way to coastal-cruise north to Maine, stopping at various anchorages along the way thus avoiding nighttime on the open sea but that is not blue water sailing, and it is not how we wanted to do it. We planned to sail direct to Maine in the blue water and coastal-cruise our way back to the Chesapeake.

The first night was pleasant with not much wind, but we managed to cover about thirty miles. The second night was beautiful, perfectly clear skies, many stars, and a good breeze. When the sun rose, we started making plans for our landfall and decided to divert into Boothbay Harbor instead of going to Monhegan Island. We were tired and that cut a few miles off our trip. We arrived in Boothbay, picked up a mooring, put the dinghy over the side, and headed to town. Our hairy experience in the fog near Block Island, and the lesson we learned in the swift current of Cape Cod Canal would stick with us forever. The lessons you learn from experience are the ones that make you a better sailor.

We had a glorious two weeks going from one anchorage to another in Penobscot Bay and Casco Bay. We ate lobster almost every day. The best place we found was in Boothbay Harbor at the Lobsterman's Co-Op, an operation run by the families of the men who catch the lobsters. By cutting out all the middlemen, they offer steamed lobster and corn on the cob for a fantastically low price. Occasionally we would go ashore, buy three or four steamed lobsters and retreat to the cockpit of *Salute* for a lobster feast. The gulls loved us because we would throw the leftovers up as high as we could and they would pluck them out of the air and then fight over the scraps.

When it was time to leave Maine we headed southwest along the coast, managing to find a number of good anchorages before the end of most days. Our last stop in Maine was at Kennebunkport, and as we headed into the Kennebunk River, we heard someone calling our boat name on the radio so we answered. It is a good thing we did because the caller was notifying us that we were about to go aground. In the days before GPS, it was especially critical to pay close attention to the buoys and fixed markers. It is easy to confuse markers because they are often different and hard to see but I thought I had read the markers right, so at first I did not understand what the caller was trying to say. Then it hit me: We were heading straight across a rocky shallow that might not be deep enough for *Salute.* Another lesson learned, I diverted and avoided the rocks. In Maine and most northeastern waters, the bottom is not soft sand or mud like the Chesapeake bottom. In the Northeast if you hit bottom a rock is probably going to make a hole in your boat. So far, on this trip we had gathered experience with fog, currents, and now rocky bottoms that can sink a boat in a matter of minutes.

Finally, we were safely in the Kennebunk River. We put the dinghy over the side, and when we got ashore Lana saw a pay phone and said she was going to see if she could reach Vice President George Bush. The Bush family has long owned a marvelous home on Walker Point on the north side of the entrance into the river. I pooh-poohed the idea, saying he would not appreciate the interruption but Lana ignored me. Within minutes, she had Vice President Bush on the line and he told us to wait where we were.

Soon he came roaring up to Chick's Marina in a fast cigarette boat, followed by another boat full of Secret Service agents. He tied up and since the tide was out, he had to climb up a long ladder to reach the place where we were waiting. He was dressed in an old floppy hat and a suede jacket that must have been twenty years old. He was enjoying every minute of the day, a trait

I admire and Lana practices. He invited us to come to Walker Point for lunch and a swim, so Lana, Paige, and I piled into his cigarette boat and off we went. He gunned it as we left the river, dodging one lobster pot after another.

We tied up at his private dock and walked up to the house where Barbara Bush and the vice president's eighty-two-year-old mother, Dorothy, met us. We had a nice lunch with soup made from bluefish that the vice president had caught that morning. Then we sat for several hours around the pool. Mrs. Dorothy Bush asked me a lot about my congressional district and asked me about the issues that were important to me. We talked about many issues, but when I mentioned the nerve gas issue, it set her off. She was on my side and opposed to the position of the Reagan Administration. I quickly ended the discussion because her son, the vice president, had to support President Reagan's position on nerve gas. In fact, he had been in the meeting that I had with President Reagan on May 25, 1983, just three months earlier, when Clem Zablocki and I argued against the nerve gas program. (In 1989, Vice President George Bush became president of the United States. In 1990 and 1991, he took several bold steps that led to a ban on the production and use of chemical weapons.)

As we were getting ready to leave, Mrs. Dorothy Bush asked me where we were going after Kennebunkport. I told her we intended to stop in Nantucket and Martha's Vineyard and then head on to New York City via the Long Island Sound. She said, "Oh, you must see Cuttyhunk, it is magnificent. You must tell your captain to stop there." I told Mrs. Bush we would definitely stop in Cuttyhunk, but that we had no captain. She was stunned that we had sailed a thirty-one-foot boat from the Chesapeake to Maine and that we had no captain.

The Bush family has money, lots of it, so Mrs. Bush's vision of a blue water cruise was quite different from ours. I finessed my way out of the delicate moment by telling Mrs. Bush that Lana and I decided long ago that I would be captain of *Salute*, but Lana is the admiral and she makes all the strategic decisions about where to go and how long to stay. Mrs. Bush liked that division of labor and wished us well, but with characteristic feistiness, she repeated her insistence that we stop in Cuttyhunk.

Vice President Bush, Barbara Bush, Lana and me at the Vice President's Residence in Washington, D. C. in 1983.

As we were getting ready to leave Walker Point, I mentioned that I had tried to catch a fish on the way to Maine but had no luck. The vice president, claiming to be a "great bluefish fisherman" got out his tackle box. He showed me several lures, proudly explaining how each had landed a record bluefish. Then he gave me a strange looking lure and guaranteed it would catch a fish. I trolled that lure all the way from Walker Point to the Chesapeake and never got a strike. I have reminded Mr. Bush of that ever since, and he always gets a big laugh out of it and then says, "It must be the fisherman because that is a great lure."

We timed our return trip through the Cape Cod Canal to coincide with a current that was going our way. We made it through the canal in an hour, two hours less than it had taken when we transited against the current. When we entered Buzzards Bay we headed for Woods Hole, the passage that leads into Vineyard Sound and gives access to the islands of Nantucket and Martha's Vineyard. We spent three glorious days anchoring in and around the islands, including an all-important stop in Cuttyhunk, and then we headed west.

We stopped in Newport for a couple of days and then continued west into Long Island Sound. We took a slight detour to spend a day in Mystic, Connecticut. There we toured the excellent Mariner's Museum and boarded several old sailing vessels. The next morning we headed back into Long Island Sound, bound for New York City.

When we approached Oyster Bay, which lies on the south side of the Long Island Sound near New York City, we saw many little white sails going in all directions. It was a regatta sponsored by a ritzy club in upscale Oyster Bay. The day's race was about to begin and as we approached the sailboats, we saw a large motor yacht loaded with scores of finely dressed New Yorkers. It was the hoity-toity crowd in their starched white shirts and navy blazers out for a proper afternoon of yachting and race watching. We were on a course that would take us right through the middle of the racing boats and close to the big boat of observers.

No one would ever mistake *Salute* for a racing boat. She was a blue water cruising vessel and she looked like one. We had our dinghy stowed upside down on the foredeck and our life raft was lashed astern of the helm. Lana, Paige and I were not dressed in finery, we were in blue jeans, and to cut the description short, we looked like a waterborne version of the Joad family in Steinbeck's classic, *The Grapes of Wrath.*

I was not smoking at the time, but I had a pipe and some old tobacco on board so Paige and I challenged Lana to light up the pipe and put it in her mouth when we sailed past the hoity-toities. I did not think she would do it, but we kept goading her, and to my surprise, she lit up the pipe and clenched it between her teeth. We tried as hard as we could to keep a straight face as we sailed right through the racing boats and within ten yards of the motor yacht. We were so close that Paige and I could see the stunned reaction of the hoity-toities. Paige had the best take on what they must have been thinking. She said, "They were in the middle of their ritzy Oyster Bay yachting club event, and here we came, a boat load of white trash sailing right through as if we owned the place."

As soon as we were out of earshot Lana, Paige, and I laughed like crazy. It was the most memorable part of the trip, at least so far. That night we tied up on a mooring at City Island and witnessed another spectacular lightning show. Paige and I went forward in the middle of the storm to check our lines, and Lana was screaming her belief that a lightning bolt would strike us dead, but it did not. After the lightning stopped, we collapsed in our bunks and got a good night's sleep.

The next morning, having learned about currents, we timed our passage through Hell's Gate, the notorious passage from Long Island Sound into the East River. Using what we had learned about currents, we figured out when it would be slack tide, and that is when we went through.

As we headed down the East River, Paige, in a bikini, was steering *Salute*. She was standing in the cockpit with one foot on the tiller, guiding our boat down the river toward New York Harbor. As we passed the United Nations, there was a bunch of construction guys working on a building right next to the river. When they saw Paige, they stopped working and gave out with their best New York catcalls and whistles. I think Paige and Lana enjoyed it. I did not like it, but the workers on shore could do no harm. We were moving smartly down the river so I considered it a case of "no harm, no foul."

We entered New York Harbor, dodged the Circle Line tour boats, the Staten Island Ferry, and a fleet of barges. Then we headed east toward the point of Sandy Hook, New Jersey and the Atlantic Ocean. The Statue of Liberty was off to starboard, and quite a sight she was. It was a rough ride because the tide was coming in and the winds were going out. That always causes the waves to build up, but we cleared the point and headed down the coast to Cape May, New Jersey.

It was our last overnight blue water sail of the trip, but we were close enough to the coast to see the glow of the lights onshore. Just as the sun rose, we passed through the inlet into Cape May. We had only to go up the Delaware Bay, through the Chesapeake and Delaware Canal and we would be back in the safe confines of the Chesapeake. The next day as we neared Annapolis, we heard a radio broadcast with the news that a colleague, Congressman Larry McDonald, a Democrat from Georgia and a medical doctor, was a passenger on board Korean Air Lines Flight 007, the plane that was shot down by Soviet interceptors. An archconservative Democrat and a member of the John Birch Society, Larry believed powerful groups in the United States were covertly trying to bring about a socialist world government. Liberals in and out of the media ridiculed Larry then but today, major news outlets regularly debate his thesis.

Our first venture into blue water sailing was a checkered experience, but we proved we could make a voyage, even if we did have some tense moments along the way. This trip, during which we learned about fog, shipping-traffic, tidal currents, rocky bottoms, and a host of other hazards, became the foundation for a career decision we would soon make. Now, however, it was time to get back to work.

38

JIM WATT RESIGNATION

Never attribute to malice that which can
be adequately explained by stupidity.
Anonymous

In the early 1980s, The Beach Boys performed at the Independence Day concert on the National Mall in Washington, D.C. The annual concerts on the Fourth of July were popular, attracting hundreds of thousands of people. In 1983, Jim Watt, the secretary of the Interior, announced that he would not allow rock bands to participate in the annual celebration because they encouraged drug use and alcoholism and attracted "the wrong element." Watt then chose Wayne Newton to perform at the 1983 Independence Day celebration instead of the Beach Boys, and his decision created a whirlwind of criticism. The Beach Boys were offended, and said so. Nancy Reagan apologized for Watt and Vice President George H. W. Bush said, "They're my friends and I like their music."

It was a typical Jim Watt screw-up, and White House staff tried to defuse the issue by presenting Watt with a plaster foot with a hole in it, symbolizing his having shot himself in the foot.

I have always been slow to criticize people in high office for gaffes because it is easy to misspeak and, like most Americans, I am willing to forgive and forget but Jim Watt was a problem. He was an ideologue with little or no tolerance and that led to a long list of dumb, public comments. As an example, in 1982, he said, "I never use the words Democrats and Republicans. It's liberals and Americans."

In September, 1983, he crossed the line with me. Secretary Watt, in a speech to the U. S. Chamber of Commerce, mocked affirmative action by saying this about the makeup of the Interior Department's coal-leasing panel: "I have a black, a woman, two Jews and a cripple. We have talent."

When I heard what he had said I came unglued. His insensitive remarks were wrong. His gratuitous use of the word "cripple" reminded me of the time my father was looking for work and a man told him, "We don't hire cripples." Daddy, uncharacteristically, whacked that man senseless with his cane. When I asked my dad why he hit the man, he said it never bothered him for someone to say he was crippled, but it did bother him if he believed the person meant to disparage him.

I went directly to the House floor and called for Secretary Watt to resign. In my speech, I said, "The greatest man I ever knew was a cripple and he never walked a step in his life without a cane, a crutch, or an artificial leg. That man was my father." It was my way of whacking Jim Watt for Daddy. I think the secretary's comment was stupid, not malicious, but it was disparaging and unbecoming for a member of President Reagan's cabinet.

A public controversy erupted and a few weeks later Watt submitted his resignation letter.

39

CONCERNS ABOUT OUR SYSTEM OF GOVERNMENT

The historical experience of socialist countries has sadly demonstrated that collectivism does not do away with alienation but rather increases it, adding to it a lack of basic necessities and economic inefficiency.
Pope John Paul II

As my understanding of our federal government matured, I became concerned about getting something done in a system that is—more often than not—entangled in gridlock.

Our constitution, conceived and written in simpler times, is a masterpiece. The founders made it hard for the federal government to expand, fearing that expansion would take freedom from the people. They put shackles on the federal government, a few of which are these: the separation of powers, a bicameral legislature, an independent judiciary, and presidential veto power. They envisioned a union of states and reserved rights to the states. They did not contemplate the wide-ranging, all-powerful federal government that has emerged since the Great Depression. They certainly did not expect the creation of a management-hierarchy with the federal government lording it over all other polities.

The arrangement we have today is not working. The federal government is involved in every twist and turn of American life.

We need to get back to federalism, a system suited to our constitution. Otherwise, pressure will mount for us to forsake our constitution in favor of a European-style parliamentary system. Such a system would allow the current management-hierarchy, dominated by the federal government, to function quickly and with less political wrangling.

When people speak of the nation being at a crossroads, and they do it every election, it is a fair comment. We have faced the same choice—federalism or management-hierarchy—every two years, for decades. The difference now is that time is running out. The argument today is essentially the same argument framed by Harrington and Simon in the late 1970s. If we do not soon reverse the inexorable trend toward big, centralized government and get back to federalism, it will be too late. Year after year, compromises made for the sake of getting something done lead to more and bigger government at all levels. I believe there is still time, but without strong action the management-hierarchy will win by default.

Lately, proponents of a management-hierarchy are resorting to an undemocratic technique to circumvent the limits imposed by the constitution. They are using executive orders, administrative rules, official regulations, and other bureaucratic techniques to get around the complicated protections set up by our founders. The most egregious example of this occurred in late 2010 when the head of Medicare and Medicaid Services issued a regulation authorizing "end of life consultations," and "advance planning for seniors." A few months earlier the liberal Democrat Congress attempted to authorize the same concept, but when the people found out about it they saw it as an attempt to create government "death panels" that would pressure end of life decision-making. The people rose up *en masse* to register their objection to death panels. The liberals backed off, dropping the provision from the ObamaCare legislation but the bureaucrats in the Obama Administration could not have cared less. The head of the Medicare and Medicaid Services thumbed his nose at the people and issued the regulation anyway. These examples of bureaucratic insensitivity—there are many others—illustrate the urgent need to deal with the fundamental question: Are we to have a management-hierarchy or federalism?

On February 11, 2011, Federal Judge Roger Vinson declared the ObamaCare law unconstitutional. He said the case before him was not really about health care, or the wisdom of the ObamaCare entitlement. It was about the architecture of the American system. He noted how the proponents of a management-hierarchy were using their own contraption to justify an unprecedented expansion of the Commerce Clause. He embraced federalism and in so doing raised the fundamental question that has concerned me for some time. Are there any remaining limits on the reach of the federal government? To support his position Judge Vinson quoted from Federalist Paper No. 51, written by James Madison in 1788: "If men were angels, no government would be necessary. If angels were to govern men, neither external nor internal controls on government would be necessary. In framing a government which is to be administered by men over men, the great difficulty lies in this: You must first enable the government to control the governed and in the next place oblige it to control itself."

The struggle that concerned me a quarter century ago has now reached critical mass. Is it the twilight of capitalism? Has Simon's time for truth passed? The 2010 elections gave hope that the people do not want Harrington's socialism or the management-hierarchy that socialism requires, but Election Day 2012 will tell the tale. It will be our last chance to choose the road that leads back to federalism and capitalism. If we take that road, our constitution will work. The other road leads to an entirely different constitutional architecture, and an entirely different America.

40

RUNNING FOR THE SENATE

The greater danger for most of us is not that our aim is too high and we miss it, but that it is too low and we reach it.
Michelangelo

As 1983 was winding down, I began to consider a race for a seat in the United States Senate. Mitch Daniel, who later became governor of Indiana, was the executive director of the National Republican Senatorial Committee (NRSC), the organization responsible for electing Republicans to the Senate. Senator Richard Lugar, Republican of Indiana and a good friend, was chair of the committee. When they heard of my interest, they assured me that I would have the full support of the NRSC if I chose to run.

President Reagan also encouraged me to run because it appeared the Republicans might lose the majority in the Senate in 1986 if we did not pick up a few seats in 1984. I met with the president in the Oval Office to discuss the race, and he promised that if I decided to run he would come to Arkansas and campaign for me. I wanted to help the cause, but I was also tired of serving in the House of Representatives. It was simply too hard to get anything done as a junior minority member, and I had to fight every day to assure my hold on a seat in a Democrat leaning district. If I could get to the Senate, I would have more power, less political pressure, and I could actually fix things. Such thinking did not make much sense politically because it would be a difficult campaign. Nevertheless, I wanted to fix the debt and credit issues I had worked on for five years. As a member of the Senate, I could shine light on the problems and force Congress to deal with issues that had the potential to bring the country down.

President Reagan and I talk in the Oval Office about my race for a seat in the United States Senate. Late 1983.

My thinking had little to do with the fact that I would be running against my longtime friend and law school classmate, Senator David Pryor. My philosophy was driving me, particularly my strong belief in federalism and capitalism. Big-city liberals have long controlled the Democratic party. The only hope to restore federalism and save capitalism is to elect more conservative Republicans at all levels of government.

I finalized my decision during the Christmas holiday recess in 1983. Lana, Paige, Sam, and I were staying at the home of Dennis and Liz Hadden in Searcy. The Haddens were away for

Christmas, so they kindly let us stay in their house, which was in our old neighborhood near the Country Club of Searcy.

We had a fun, old-time Christmas with a focus on family and the true meaning of the season but I anguished for days thinking about the difficulties of a statewide campaign at a time when Republican was still a dirty word in Arkansas. My friend and pastor, Don Meredith, was visiting in Little Rock and we got together in my district office for a moment of prayer. I wish I could say I had a prayerful attitude but looking back, I know I had too much pride—too much focus on me and my ambitions and not enough on God. Nevertheless, I was comforted and I made my decision that afternoon. I had gone to Congress to bring important change to the country; therefore, I should and would be a candidate for the United States Senate. If elected, I could emphasize my settled belief that we needed to break the cycle of dependency—individual and corporate—that was, and is, turning our country into a welfare state.

Secondly, I wanted to highlight my argument that federally created credit programs such REA, Fannie Mae, Freddie Mac, and the Chrysler bailout, were damaging our economy. I believed, unshakably, that the federal government would rue the day that it failed to control these programs. Politicians and bureaucrats should not allocate credit; free market forces should determine such allocations. The director of the Congressional Budget Office, Alice Rivlin, and other experts including Alan Greenspan agreed with me in principle and endorsed my effort to fix the problem, but I needed more power than I had as a minority member of the House to turn my ideas into law.

Finally, I wanted to emphasize the need to scrutinize candidates for seats on the federal bench to determine their judicial philosophy. I put out a letter stating that I wanted to interview all candidates for federal judgeships in Arkansas. I wrote that I wanted to discuss a number of landmark cases to ascertain whether they really believed in strict construction, or whether they were just giving lip service to the concept.

The Arkansas Bar Association, led by liberal Democrats who were committed to my opponent, seized on the issue and tried to make it look like I wanted to get commitments on how the judges would vote on specific issues. They actually voted to censure me after a rigged, kangaroo court hearing in Fayetteville. I appeared to argue my case and was startled when Jim McLarty of Newport—one of David Pryor's supporters—made the argument that I should not make such inquiries of prospects for district court judgeships, but that it would have been all right to do so if interviewing potential nominees for the Supreme Court. He said he based his opinion on the fact that the Supreme Court is a "policymaking court." I told him, "Your position is absurd; the Supreme Court is there to interpret law, not to make policy. Making policy is the business of legislators, duly elected by the people." We need to know how nominees for district court judgeships feel about judicial activism because they might eventually become a nominee for a higher court. I put it this way at the time, "No court at any level has the right to make policy and that is why we must take greater care in the selection process up and down the line."

In the years since, the members of the United States Senate—Democrats and Republicans—have made it clear that I was simply ahead of the times. Today, members of Congress routinely grill nominees to determine their sentiments about judicial activism.

The three big ideas I had were good ideas, but my timing was bad. It would be another twenty-five years before the country would awaken to these problems. Nowadays all candidates are harping about the unbridled growth of entitlements, dependency, and the welfare state. The runaway credit problems at Fannie Mae and Freddie Mac nearly brought the country down in 2008, and the federal judiciary continues to encroach into the exclusive prerogatives of the legislative branch.

A prescient moment in the campaign occurred the day I announced my candidacy. The first question from the reporters asked why I was running against my good friend David Pryor. I quickly responded, "Look, if the people of Arkansas are looking for a warm, friendly person to be their senator then they should vote for my friend, David Pryor. On the other hand, if they are concerned about the direction of the country and are looking for real change to get back to the basics that made our country great, then they should vote for me." It was at that moment that I lost the campaign because people were not as concerned about the direction of the country as I was—they were looking for a warm, friendly person to be their senator. David, by those criteria, was the better choice.

During the race for the Senate, we had many experiences, mostly good ones. No one could have worked harder than we did. We pledged to walk across the state so we set aside several days to actually walk from town to town in various areas of the state. It was a good campaign gimmick, and we got great pictures with supporters waiving the American flag and following us along the road. Toward the end of the campaign, after we had walked for miles and miles and run TV ads promoting our campaign, we found ourselves between Walnut Ridge and Pocahontas. We had stopped for a water break in front of a little white house about fifty feet off the highway. As we drank our water and talked, I noticed two little girls and their mother peeking out from behind the front door of the house. I waved to them and the woman came out to where we were and said, "Are you the one that's walking? I heard about you on the radio." I said, "Yes, why don't you get the girls to come out and we'll make a picture with them?" She then turned toward the house and hollered, "Girls, get out here and get your picture made with him, he may be somebody, someday!" We all got a big kick out of that, but it really brought us down to earth and made us realize two things. First, not everyone thinks you are "somebody" just because you are a sitting member of the United States House of Representatives. Second, it reminded us how hard it is to spread a political message.

President Reagan honored his promise to campaign for me. He flew into the Little Rock airport on *Air Force One* on the Saturday before Election Day. An enormous crowd greeted him and an even bigger crowd turned out for a rally at the convention center. The president did a great job for me and for the indomitable Judy Petty who was running to fill the seat that I was leaving. We dominated the news that weekend. Even so, I lost the race for the Senate rather handily. Judy did better in her effort, but she also lost. It hurt, but it was not devastating. Lana and I knew when we started that it would be an uphill battle all the way. We simply could not overcome the built-in advantages of a popular incumbent Democrat senator in the state of Arkansas. I was ahead of my time on the issues, 1984 was not as good a year as 1980, and Arkansans were not quite ready to send a Republican to the U. S. Senate.

We had no regrets about making the race. We were still a young couple. We had enjoyed much success, more than we ever dreamed we would when we started our first campaign for political office. The loss would segue into a period of honest introspection about what we had done and what we should be doing in the years to come. Fortunately, we were about to take a sabbatical that would give us the time to think, distill what we had learned, and plan for our future.

41

SAILING AWAY

There is nothing more enticing, disenchanting,
and enslaving than the life at sea.
Joseph Conrad

Before getting into the Senate race, Lana and I carefully considered the options that would face us if we won or lost.

If elected, we would go to the Senate and do the best we could, most probably spending the rest of our days in the political arena.

On the other hand, if we lost the race, we could and would take at least six months off before making any decisions about our future. The sabbatical is an underused concept, particularly for someone who is leaving elective office. We believed we should put some time and distance between us and the points of reference that surround those in high office.

We did not have a lot of money, but we had enough. Besides, we had started with nothing when we married and figured we could do it again if we had to. We had no fear of being broke but we were afraid that the thoughts and friendships we developed in politics might unduly influence our decision-making. Simply put, we wanted to clear our heads before starting the rest of our life.

We sold our house in Arlington and stored our furniture in the summer of the campaign year, 1984. We planned to buy a smaller house on Capitol Hill near the Senate if we won the election.

Since we had a sailboat and loved blue water cruising we prepositioned our boat in Savannah, Georgia. Our sabbatical, if we lost, would be a sailing trip to the Bahamas to rest and think while enjoying the sun and sand. We could marshal our remaining assets, and that would give us enough money to complete our sabbatical and help our children who, at the time, were finishing college. By Election Day, we would be ready to go—to the Senate if we won or sailing if we lost. We saw it as a Win-Win situation.

A few weeks before Election Day we knew that things were not going our way. It was apparent that I was going to lose my bid to go to the Senate and the voters had their say on November 6, 1984. When it was over, we took a few days to thank our supporters, talk to media, and take calls from well-wishers. Then we headed directly to Savannah. We provisioned *Salute*, gave her a good scrub-down fore and aft, and sailed her south on the Intracoastal Waterway to Miami. There we met a number of sailors, mostly Canadians, who were also bound for the Bahamas.

The decision to run for the Senate was a bad one politically, but getting out of politics and taking a sabbatical allowed me think about my life in ways that would not have been possible had I won the race. You learn more from your losses than you do from your victories, and that was certainly true in my case. I had gone from being a guilt-ridden, incorrigible child to the big league of politics and I was puffed up with ego and false pride. It was time to figure out how and why that happened and what to do about it.

Our new environment, sailing freely from island to island, was a perfect laboratory for the hard business of self-evaluation. The contrast between sailing and politics is dramatic. We were free. Not to do anything we wanted; man is never that free. But we were free from the rules, structure, addictions, and preoccupations of political life. Our kids were pretty much out on their own, so it was a good time to break away from politics, making money, career development, building a new home—all the upward and onward stuff.

Within days, Jerry Climer called to say that the media were reporting that we had disappeared and they were spinning it to make it look like we had run away. The reporters knew we were going away for a well-deserved break, but they love to pick over the bones of defeated candidates like vultures with fresh road-kill. We were done with politics, the congressional session was over, I had no more votes to cast and my staff was busy packing my papers for donation to the University of Arkansas archives. I had given the people of Arkansas my best, and I believe they appreciated my service, but the media did not want to write that story. I deprived them of their postelection fun and they did not like it. In reprisal, they began a series of "Bethune Sighting" reports. The mini-controversy did not amount to a hill of beans in my judgment. I was leaving high office and did not care how they might portray me. Furthermore, I no longer had to answer their foolish, trite, often imbecilic questions.

We planned to cruise for six months; enough time for the natural forces that are important to sailors to sweep away the political cobwebs. No longer were we concerned about issues, polls, raising campaign funds, or personal popularity. We now had things to think about that were more important; our provisions, our water supply, the wind, the waves, the currents, and most important of all—staying afloat.

The Gulf Stream is a river within the sea. The current runs swiftly north between Miami and the Bahamas, and when the winds are blowing south, the collision of forces creates an inhospitable sea. Crossing the Gulf Stream to get to the Bahamas would be our first serious test. We were a little apprehensive, but it was a good feeling to be on our way to the islands.

As it turned out, the Gulf Stream behaved itself, and our crossing was uneventful. But our good luck was not to hold. When we arrived we anchored east of Cat Cay, which is just south of Bimini. The day was pleasant and we thoroughly enjoyed making our first landfall in a foreign country. After checking in with the local immigration officials, we settled down to enjoy a fabulous sunset. About the time our wine was gone, the wind piped up, clouds and darkness obscured the beautiful sunset, and all boats in the anchorage, fully exposed to the wind, had one thought in mind—making it through the night. Our anchor was secure on the bottom, but the chain leading from the anchor to our boat was taking a beating. When our boat rose up and down over the large waves, the anchor chain would pull taut and jerk the bow of the boat to one side or the other. A loud clank accompanied every jerk. It was too rough to think about raising the anchor, so we were at the mercy of the sea. We would just have to wait it out. Then, just as day was breaking, the chain broke and we fell back on a second anchor that I had rigged with a rope line off the stern of the boat. That put us with our stern to the wind—a position we could not hold—and to make matters worse the anchor rope had fouled around our propeller. Now we were in a real pickle, and we could do nothing about it. It reminded me of our first day off Turkey Point near the South River on the Chesapeake. Once again, I felt like a turkey, but once again a fellow sailor helped us, and we managed to get to a safe place. The new experience taught us—even when the weather is perfect—to always rig a snubber, a simple device that takes the stress off the anchor chain. It was another bit of information we added to our knowledge of fog, currents, rocky bottoms, and weather. Sailing is that way; you are always learning, and fellow sailors are always ready to lend a hand.

We made a few repairs to *Salute,* and the next day we left Cat Cay, heading farther into the Bahamas. After a couple of windy nights on the anchor, we eased our way into Nassau harbor after dark. The harbor is large, heavily populated with big cruise boats and a plethora of smaller boats at anchor and on moorings. The variety of lights and reflections on a dark night in a busy harbor make it hard to see, but we eventually found an open spot and dropped our anchor, only to discover the next morning when we tried to move to a marina that our anchor had fouled around the propeller shaft of a sunken boat. We could do nothing but laugh at ourselves. It was a mistake to come in after dark. The harbor at Nassau, which seems so inviting, is full of such hazards, but we had no way to know that. We had to dive to free the anchor, but eventually got it loose and safely tied up at a marina near the bridge to Paradise Island. Finally, after gaining this latest bit of sailing experience, we could relax and enjoy the Bahamas.

We spent a good part of each day in the old city of Nassau in quest of a new and different kind of conch chowder but our favorite thing was to buy freshly baked warm bread, fill it with butter, and devour it as we strolled through town.

Several big cruise boats arrived during our week in Nassau and thousands of passengers got off for their short walk around town. They stood out like a sore thumb. Well-dressed, well fed and pampered, they headed straight to the straw-markets then wandered around in search of something to take home as a souvenir. The cruising sailors, in contrast, were easy to spot. Well-tanned and slightly sloppy, we shied away from the souvenir shops; heading instead to an endless supply of mom-and-pop stands to bargain for fresh fish, avocados, tomatoes, and other good things to eat. Fresh vegetables are worth their weight in gold to cruising sailors, particularly in the tropics.

One day we walked across the bridge that leads to Paradise Island, a popular destination for tourists. We entered a big hotel just to look around, and as we were about to leave we decided to check out a casino connected to one end of the hotel lobby. We were almost past the blackjack tables when Lana cried out, "Bud, what in the world are you doing here?" I looked around and there sat Lana's uncle, Bud Collier from Hope, Arkansas. It is truly a small world. We caught up on family news and invited Bud to lunch, but he could not join us because his cruise boat was leaving in an hour to return to the United States. I think Bud must have told someone that he saw us, because we learned later that our connection with Bud triggered another "Bethune Sighting" report in the Arkansas papers.

After a week of easy living at the Nassau marina, we sailed to the Exuma Islands, a chain of small islands, most of which are uninhabited. Nassau was fun, but we were eager to get to the Exumas, the finest cruising grounds known to man.

Our first stop was Allen Cay, a wee island at the northern end of the island chain. There is a narrow channel where we, and most of the other sailboats, anchored. The water is so clear that in daylight you can easily see the bottom. There are no people living on Allen Cay, but there are inhabitants. We rowed our dinghy ashore and a small herd of iguanas greeted us. Iguanas, rare and scary critters, look like a cross between a gila monster and a small alligator. I cannot say the ones that met us were friendly because iguanas just naturally look mean. The iguanas on Allen Cay are borderline-domesticated because visiting sailors feed them lettuce, which they love. We fed them too, just to be on the safe side.

Just two years before we sailed into Norman Cay, our next anchorage in the Exumas, the island had been home to a Columbian drug lord who used it as a base for shipping cocaine into the United States. The history of the place reads like a movie script, and some say it was the inspiration for Hollywood to make the movie, *Blow*, starring Johnny Depp. We had heard a number of stories from other sailors about the hazards of inadvertently running into drug criminals. There were boardings, shootings, and murders of sailors who got too close to the action. It was something we had to watch out for, and we could not count on the authorities to protect us. There were plenty of stories about how the drug dealers had bought off the authorities and key political people. Extreme caution was the best policy for us to follow.

There was a submerged two-engine plane in the harbor of Norman Cay. Some say the drug lord had used the plane in his drug trafficking, that it crashed in the water, sank to the bottom and that he abandoned it there. We rowed over to it and what we saw made us wonder why no one tried to raise the aircraft. It was still in one piece, mostly.

The next day, Lana saw a low-flying airplane drop a sizeable square package about a mile offshore from Warderick Wells Cay, our first stop after Norman Cay. She said she bet it was drugs, and she was probably right. She said we should call the authorities on our VHF radio to let them know of the drop. My instincts as a former FBI agent kicked in and I said, "Are you kidding? The drug dealers can hear our radio transmissions as well as the authorities can, and they will not think of us as public-minded tourists, they will think of us as witnesses!" We maintained radio silence and it was a good thing that we did. Shortly after the package hit the water, a big, fast cigarette boat was on its way to the site. It scooped up the package and headed off in the direction of Nassau.

In the Bahamas there are many hazardous reefs, and sailors learn to avoid them by studying the shade of the water when the sun is high. One mistake and a reef can rip a hole in your boat, and it will be lying on the bottom in a matter of minutes. There were a few drawings depicting the location of some of the most dangerous reefs, but for the most part, sailors in the days before GPS were on their own to see and avoid the reefs.

A week after our brush with the drug dealers, we were at Little Farmers Cay, ready for a nice night. We anchored by two other sailboats in a well-protected cove. It was almost dark when we saw a good-sized sailboat heading in from the sea. Without sunlight, the newcomer would not see the unmarked reef that separated the main channel from the anchorage. If he knew about the reef, he might miss it, or he might anchor in another part of Little Farmers Cay. When the boat turned toward us, it was immediately apparent that the captain was going to go up on the reef. Even before he hit it, we—the captains of the boats at anchor—were lowering our dinghies and heading in his direction. It was my turn to help a sailor in distress. It was payback for the time sailors had helped us at Cat Cay when our anchor chain broke. It took the best part of an hour to get the large boat off the reef, and it was dark by the time we got back to our boats, but the distressed sailor was safe, anchored alongside us in our little cove. The incident scarred his boat and hurt his pride, but he had survived a serious grounding that could have ended his adventure. He rowed over to *Salute* and gave us a bottle of good red wine. Sailors take care of each other.

Georgetown, the capital of the Exumas, is a small place. With only a few hundred permanent residents, the little town is a beehive of activity in the winter months when sailors and tourists arriving by plane dominate the community. We sailed into Elizabeth Harbor in early February and anchored in a protected area, just across from the town's main dock. The Exuma Island chain consists of some three hundred cays and is about 120 miles long. Georgetown, situated on Great Exuma Island, is at the bottom of the chain and has been an important seaport since the seventeenth century when pirates, including the notorious Captain Kidd, made good use of its deep-water harbor. It was also a refitting base for British vessels in Revolutionary War days, and the U. S. Navy used the port in World War II. Like most sailors, we had worked our way south from cay to cay, and Georgetown was as far as we would go.

Our first few days in Georgetown were spent hauling jugs of fresh water from the town fountain to *Salute*. Good, clean, fresh water is scarce and expensive, and so are fresh vegetables. The mail boat arrives twice a week laden with crates of fresh vegetables, and sailors scurry to the main dock to get what they can before it is all gone. We just missed the mail boat when we first arrived, so we spent several days eating canned vegetables. Soon, though, we discovered the rhythm of Georgetown and spent most days snorkeling, swimming, and adventuring to nearby cays. We had been in Georgetown nearly three weeks when one night, on a whim, we decided to anchor near the town's oldest hotel, a pink-painted building on the north end of town. The building, like most architecture in the islands, was nothing special but it was functional. As the sun was setting, we heard on our radio that the prime minister of the Bahamas was attending a reception at the old hotel. When he and his entourage arrived, we were in the cockpit of our boat, roughly fifty yards from the veranda, the site of the reception. Our view of the scene, the folderol, and the colorful music brought back a flood of memories from our time in political office. It gave us a chance to contrast our best memories—trips to the White House, gala events, and exciting elections—with the simple life we were living as sailors. Soon we realized that we had not thought about or talked about politics for nearly a month, and that was a satisfying feeling. We had achieved the main purpose of our sabbatical: We had washed away the influences and persistent thoughts that consume people in public life. Our minds were clear and fresh. We were now ready to start thinking and talking about what we would do with the rest of our life together.

The sights and sounds of Georgetown are captivating, but we will always remember it as the place where we declared victory over the mind warping influences of politics. We stayed almost a month, but left in early March before the extra-heavy influx of people and boats that arrive each year for the annual Georgetown Sailing Regatta.

We stopped again in Little Farmer's Cay on the way back and dropped our anchor next to a beautiful schooner from the Virgin Islands. Just as we settled down the schooner sailors, two men and two women, all in their early eighties, jumped over the side to cool off and clean up. It amazed us that these senior citizens had sailed such a long distance. They were thoroughly enjoying life to the fullest. They were bobbing around and splashing each other like teenagers as they laughed and jabbered. It was a great lesson for us, particularly since we were sorting out what we wanted to do in the years to come. I was forty-nine and Lana was forty-seven. We felt very young as we watched the kids from the Virgin Islands.

At our next stop I decided to snorkel around in water about fifteen feet deep while Lana stayed aboard the dinghy. The sights below the surface—plant life, fish, and other critters—are stunning. The water throughout the Bahamas is crystal-clear. I dove down to look at a school of fish and as I marveled at the view, something told me to look back to my right. I could not believe what I saw. I was face to face with a big shark who was watching me watch the fish. It was my first up-close encounter with a shark, and, contrary to the local lore that I should keep my cool, I shot to the surface and in one motion hauled myself aboard the inflatable dinghy which was directly above. Gasping for air, I blubbered to Lana, "Shark! Let's get out of here!" I probably scared the shark, but I shudder to think what might have happened if Lana and the dinghy had not been right above me.

We stopped at Samson Cay, our last stop before returning to Nassau. Our daughter Paige, twenty-two at the time, joined us for the rest of our adventure. The amenities at Samson Cay are surprisingly upscale. It is one of the few inhabited places in the Exumas, and the three of us enjoyed a sit-down dinner on a patio overlooking the circular harbor where *Salute* was at anchor. We were living high on the hog for the first time since we had left Nassau.

Our trip back home was slow by design. We had mixed feelings. We hated to leave the islands, but we were eager to get back to the United States.

I had a new challenge to face. We were broke and needed to start thinking about how to make a living and how to secure our senior years. In keeping with the Vermilye maxim, I had refused to take the congressional pension because it would have produced a larcenous windfall for me, and I had railed against it in my campaigns. My benefit would have been sizeable because I had six years in Congress, three years in the Marine Corps, and four years in the FBI; a total of thirteen years federal service. I was not going to be a hypocrite; besides, my upbringing taught me that I did not need or want anything from "them."

The good news was that we had many options. We had worn ourselves out debating the career choices that were available to me, and to Lana, now that I was a former congressman. I had offers to be part of the Reagan administration, and I had offers from Washington, D. C. law firms and lobby shops. There were corporations looking for people like me, but in the end, we decided we wanted to go home to Arkansas. I wanted to go back to the practice of law. I had been a good trial lawyer before Congress, and I wanted to pick up where I had left off. I had an offer to join the Hilburn Law Firm in North Little Rock that was appealing to me. I had dated Sam Hilburn's sister, a Walnut Ridge girl, when I was in high school in Pocahontas, and his older brother and I were friends during my first hitch at the University of Arkansas in 1953. The lawyers at the firm were smart, solid, ethical practitioners. It was a natural fit.

Our voyage from Nassau took us back through Miami, down through the Florida Keys, up the west coast of Florida to Naples and eventually to Fort Myers. We left *Salute* at a marina in Fort Myers and headed to Arkansas.

Our excellent adventure, a six-month journey from Savannah, Georgia to the Exumas and back to Florida was a success. It cleared our heads, allowing us to make a good choice about our future.

Meanwhile, I was on another journey, one that was not over. After our move to Potomac Chapel, I reoriented my thinking about religious matters. I was a new Christian because I had learned, intellectually at least, that I needed to put God in the center of my life in order to make sense out of the Bible. Our years at Potomac taught me that I needed to suppress the urge to self-centeredness but learning and doing are two different things, particularly for someone so steeped in the Vermilye worldview. It also occurred to me, as an academic proposition, that the media and entertainment industry, as well as other secular forces, were making it increasingly difficult to change from secular, self-centered thinking to Biblical, God-centered thinking. I spent too much time thinking about that, probably because I loved to shuck the blame for my own shortcomings. I read and studied, as much as time would allow, in an effort to master the intellectual aspects of the challenge I faced. But I was missing something and I could not put my finger on it. My sailing trip had been successful, but my Christian voyage still had a long way to go.

42

HOME AGAIN, LAWYER AGAIN

Mid pleasures and palaces though we may roam, Be it ever so humble, there's no place like home.
Robert Louis Stevenson

My return to Little Rock and the practice of law with the Hilburn Firm gave me a chance to be a "tall building lawyer," the moniker lawyers outside of Little Rock used to describe any highfalutin lawyer with an office in a big building, in a big city. Lawyers in little towns, at least when I started practicing, were a special breed. Much of the work we did in Searcy that involved an opposing lawyer we did on a handshake. We knew a lot about every lawyer in our town and all the little towns around us. We knew more than his name and favorite areas of practice. We knew his family, his secretary, how much money he made, his style of argument, his educational background, his personal preferences, his peccadilloes. We knew it all, and we worked and played together. Because of that, we knew whom to trust.

Almost everyone followed the creed that a lawyer's word is his bond, and we knew the few who did not. It was a wonderful way to practice law. We did a good job for our clients without a lot of redundant paperwork and unnecessary court hearings. We did what we needed to do, of course, but there was no fear that we were not dotting every *i* and crossing every *t*. We served our clients, made a good living, but kept our fees at a fair level.

That era of trust and efficiency in the legal system began to fade away in the 1970s, and it started with the tall building lawyers in the big cities. Not knowing their colleagues as we did in Searcy led to an high level of distrust, hence more paperwork—more concern to cover one's ass, and bigger bills for the clients to pay. The collapse of tradition, which goes beyond the legal profession, is an old story. The city breeds a sense of anonymity that in turn breeds a lack of trust and care about colleagues and neighbors. Eventually, the lack of trust amongst lawyers in the big cities spread to the lawyers in the small towns.

I discovered upon my return to the practice of law that it is like riding a bicycle; you never forget how to do it. I had to brush up on some of the changes but almost immediately, I was back in the courtroom doing the things I had done before going to Congress. I had a successful two years at the firm.

Everything was going well, but we lost Lana's dad, George Douthit, on May 25, 1985. He was a character, self-taught and self-made. He was born in Texas, but ran away from home in his teens and started work as a copyboy for a newspaper in Texarkana.

Journalism would be his life. Like so many others his age, George went away to World War II in 1941. He served in Patton's Third Army, and as an officer in the Transportation Corps, he dealt with the great fuel shortage that threatened Patton's advance across Europe. When he returned from the war, George married Lana's mother and adopted Lana when she was nine years old. He worked his way up to be a reporter for the *Arkansas Democrat* and usually got the scoop when it concerned Governor Orval Faubus. George did not agree with Faubus on everything, but Faubus trusted him to be fair.

It was inevitable that the media would call from time to time to get a quote about some issue, but for the most part, they left me alone. I cannot say as much for the Republican Party of Arkansas. I had planned to stay out of politics for a few years, at least until I reestablished my law practice, but in 1986, as we approached the end of President Reagan's second term in office, Republicans all across Arkansas started to worry about the upcoming 1988 presidential election.

Bill Clinton had retaken the governor's office after his defeat by Frank White in 1980 and the state Democratic party was in a strong position.

A number of influential party leaders beseeched me to run for state party chairman on the theory that I could hold the party together as we scrambled to choose our best nominee for president in 1988. There was a legitimate concern that Arkansas Republicans might split up as we had in the primary contest between Ronald Reagan and Gerald Ford in 1976, a fracture that enabled Jimmy Carter to carry Arkansas on his way to the White House. Carter beat Ford by a margin of sixty-five to thirty-five percent, a drubbing that put Arkansas back in the Democrat column for the first time since 1964. I agreed to run, won the chairmanship, and served through the 1988 presidential year.

We did just fine. Vice President George Herbert Walker Bush was our nominee, and he easily defeated Michael Dukakis, the former governor of Massachusetts. Bush won Arkansas with fifty-six percent of the vote compared to forty-two percent for Dukakis. Arkansas was back in the Republican column, and my job as party chair was over. I was not suited for the incessant need to raise money or the infighting that is a healthy dynamic for a growing party. I did not run for re-election.

At the beginning of 1987, I received an offer to take a high position with First Federal, a savings and loan association in Little Rock. My ego got the better of me. I had never worked in corporate America. The job was a new and different challenge so I decided to try it. It was a mistake. I am just too independent minded and free-spirited to be a corporate man. The misfit was soon apparent to me and to the leadership of First Federal. We decided that we should dissolve our contract by mutual agreement, so that is what we did before the end of 1987. I returned to my law practice.

In December 1988, I took another trip on the blue water, but this one was quite different from our voyages on *Salute*. Our son

Sam was in his third year in the United States Navy and his ship, the *USS Carl Vinson*—a Nimitz-class aircraft carrier—was returning from a six-month tour of duty in the North Arabian Sea where it had spent eighty-two days escorting American tankers.

Sam invited me to meet the *Vinson* in Hawaii and join him for a Tiger Cruise, an official U.S. Navy program that allows family members to board the ship and go on a cruise so they can see their sons and daughters in action. The public relations program solidifies the tie between the Navy, sailors, and their extended families.

Many Tiger Cruises are of short duration, but our cruise was going to be a humdinger. Sam's ship would arrive in Pearl Harbor on December 7, to celebrate the forty-seventh anniversary of the Japanese attack in 1941. Lana flew with me to Hawaii, and we were there when the *Vinson* steamed into the harbor. Sam was in a helicopter that was flying channel guard. When the helicopter flew close to us, Lana—with a mother's eagle eye—spotted Sam in the open doorway. It was quite a thrill to see all that on such a special day. The next morning, I and all the other Tigers went onboard and the *Vinson* departed for Alameda in San Francisco Bay.

We were nine days at sea and had a chance to see a number of operations. The greatest thrill was to see my son in action. As a rescue swimmer and anti-submarine warfare specialist, he has logged thousands of hours in helicopters flying over dangerous waters. I was bursting with pride every day of the trip.

The Navy has a rule that Tigers will stay in the same quarters with their Navy relative. If your son is new to the Navy, as Sam was, then you will stay with him in a compartment populated by scores of enlisted sailors. It reminded me of my days on the troop ship when I was a lowly enlisted man in the U. S. Marine Corps. We also ate in the same mess hall and used the same heads that our Navy relatives used.

As soon as we left Hawaii, Lana flew to San Francisco to meet us. She was on a hill overlooking the Golden Gate Bridge when we passed beneath it on our way to Alameda. Sam and the other sailors were manning the rail in their whites, and the fireboats that met us shot sprays of colored water high into the sky.

When we pulled up to the dock, the Navy Band was there and they played "Anchors Aweigh" and the "Marine Corps Hymn." I was sniveling and trying to hide it, but so were many of the other Tigers, especially those who had served in the military.

We met Lana and had a grand time in San Francisco. Since then, Sam has completed twenty-three years in the Navy, rising to the rank of Lieutenant Commander. His chest is full of ribbons telling a story of brave service on the sea as well as a tour in Afghanistan. Yes, we are proud of him and thankful for what the Navy and other services do for us, every day of every year

43

BACK TO WASHINGTON, LANA SHINES

When good character adds adornment to natural charms, whoever comes near is doubly captivated.
Meander, 290 B.C.

I met George H. W. Bush when he was vice president and I was in Congress. Lana and I were on the best of terms with him and his wife, Barbara. He campaigned for me when I ran for the Senate in 1984, and we loved to talk about the time Lana and I sailed *Salute* into Kennebunkport in 1983. Our relationship was close, but not as close as the one we had with Dan and Marilyn Quayle.

Dan was a colleague of mine in the House of Representatives, and a fellow member of Chowder and Marching.

Marilyn and Lana were good friends. They were together a lot when I was in the House, and one of their favorite things to do was to shop for bargains at the outlet malls in Virginia and Maryland. In January of 1989, the Quayles were about to move into the Vice President's Residence at the Naval Observatory in Washington, D. C. They needed a social secretary and Marilyn asked Lana to take the job.

I did not want a job in the Bush administration, but I could tell that Lana wanted to help Marilyn and Dan get off to a good start. She was perfect for the job because she knew the protocol, the people, and the politics of high office. The job involved organizing event after event at the residence—sometimes three a day—for an endless stream of supporters and dignitaries, domestic and foreign. In the course of her year they entertained Charlton Heston, Israeli Prime Minister Yitzhak Shamir, King Hussein and Queen Noor of Jordan, and Prince Charles, just to name a few. The culinary issues—serving Arabs at breakfast, Israelis at lunch, and Englishmen at dinner—would stagger a normal person, but Lana thrives on such challenges. That, coupled with her easy manner and the ability to work with complete strangers made her a perfect social secretary for Vice President Quayle and Mrs. Quayle.

Her new role did mean that we would have to move back to Washington. I had just landed a new client, the FBI Agent's Association. That representation would require me to be in Washington a lot, so I decided to open my own law office in D. C. I landed a few other clients and soon I was doing well. Most importantly, Lana was having a great time with her new gig, meeting one dignitary after another. She did a great job and I was happy for her, but it was a demanding job, and she had told Marilyn and Dan at the outset that she would help them get started but did not want to make a career out of it.

In early 1990, we began to think about making another blue water cruise. By the time Lana finished her work with the vice president, our boat, *Salute,* was back on the Chesapeake and we were spending more time than ever resurrecting the good feelings we had when we sailed to Maine and especially the feelings we had on our six-month cruise to the Bahamas. We talked about it incessantly but I had a challenging legal matter that I needed to finish before we could go anywhere.

44

LAWYERING FOR NEWT

Those men who carry about and who listen to accusations, should be hanged, if so it could be at my decision—the carriers by their tongues, the listeners by their ears.
Titus Maccius Plautus

I developed a unique relationship with Newt Gingrich of Georgia from the first day we met in 1978. He had just won a seat in Congress and so had I. Our friendship would draw me into a nationally publicized struggle between Newt and the Democrats in 1989, long after I was out of Congress.

As new members of the U. S. House of Representatives, we were intellectual soul mates and our personal chemistry was good. I respected him and he respected me. I think Newt admired the fact that I had worn so many different hats before coming to Congress.

Early on, we challenged the Republican leadership in the House. I was president of the freshman class of Republican members of the House of Representatives and Newt was secretary. We led a mini-revolt by issuing a demand to the Republican party leaders in the House to come to our organizational meeting at the Marriott Hotel at Dulles International Airport to explain what they had in mind for the upcoming session of Congress. It was an audacious gambit for a bunch of rookies, but we believed the Republican leadership had developed a professional minority-member attitude.

We were determined to change things. We spoke out publicly, saying it was "Day One of the new Republican party." John Rhodes of Arizona, the minority leader, took offense at our public contentions and confronted us on the House floor shortly after we took the oath of office. He said, "I've had a bellyful of you two, you better be careful. If you live by the sword, you will die by the sword." It was a dumb approach to take with two strong-willed new members of the House. It was a blatant attempt to force us to get in line with the current Republican leadership. I told Rhodes, "John, you better put that damn sword away because we intend to press our agenda to change the House." After that, I was not a favorite of John Rhodes, and he did everything he could to hold back my progress in the Republican Conference.

We then mounted an open challenge to his leadership. Soon, John Rhodes announced he was not going to run for re-election as minority leader. We had planted a seed of reform that would, fifteen years later, enable the Republicans, under Newt's leadership, to take control of the House of Representatives.

Newt started a small caucus in 1983 called the Conservative Opportunity Society, COS for short. I, along with Newt, Dan Lungren, Henry Hyde, Bob Walker, Connie Mack, Vin Weber and a few others were charter members. We all believed that we needed to throw off the image that the Republicans were just trying to install a cheaper welfare state. We wanted people to see the Republican party as the party of growth, and opportunity. We were all disciples of Jack Kemp's mantra that a free society and a free entrepreneurial system will create the incentives for the American people to work, save, invest, and produce. Later, virtually every Republican member of the House joined the caucus and there was no need for it anymore. We had advanced the idea and that was the main purpose of COS.

In 1988, Newt went after the speaker of the House, Jim Wright, a Democrat from Texas on ethics charges. Newt alleged that Wright had wrongfully profited from a hastily thrown together manuscript that he sold as a "book." That led to an investigation that forced Jim Wright to resign as speaker. The Democrat members of the House were furious and began looking for ways to get their pound of flesh from Newt.

Shortly before Wright resigned, Congressman Bill Alexander of Arkansas took the lead for the Democrats. He filed a long, ten-count ethics charge against Newt Gingrich that listed over four hundred separate allegations. It reeked of partisanship, which Bill Alexander did not deny. He said, "I have become increasingly outraged by the pompous moralizing of Congressman Newt Gingrich ... we have all witnessed his bizarre and outrageous condemnations of individual members of Congress." Newt responded saying, "The charges come from enraged Democrats led by an almost irrational Bill Alexander."

The centerpiece of Alexander's contention was that Newt violated House rules in writing and marketing a book called *Window of Opportunity*. He tried to liken what Newt had done to what Jim Wright had done. In the spring of 1989, Newt asked me to represent him before the Ethics Committee and I did. It took a few months but we successfully disposed of all the allegations. Alexander got his headlines and managed to smear Newt, but his attempt at revenge was a conspicuous failure. Newt's book was a real book, not a contrivance as had been the case with Wright's "book." It was the first time I served as counsel for a member charged with violating the rules of the House of Representatives, but it would not be the last.

45

THE CALL OF THE SEA, AGAIN

The restless, deep, dividing sea. That flows and foams from shore to shore. Calls to its sunburned chivalry, "Push out, set sail, explore."
Henry Van Dyke

As I was winding up my representation of Newt Gingrich before the Ethics Committee, Lana and I decided to make another blue water sailing trip. Lana had completed the year that she promised the vice president and we hungered to get away on *Salute* to relive our Bahamian experience. Paige had a good job and Sam was in the Navy and doing well. My mother and Lana's mother were doing well in Little Rock. We were young and healthy; why should we not give it a go? We had the seed of a new dream but there were many questions.

Where should we go? What should we do? What could we learn? How long should we stay?

People have always given us credit for being adventurous, but one political commentator took it beyond adventurous when he said, "Bethune would walk into a buzz saw." That may be a fair description, albeit too graphic. Like my father, I have always been a dreamer. I think we all want to live a life that suits our inner needs, but often reality gets in the way. My dreaming, for some reason, includes an incessant compulsion to go beyond dreaming. I want to live out my dreams, and I have always been especially attracted to those that seem unattainable. Driven more by compulsion than bravery, I have ventured out and taken up challenges that others might pass by. It sounds extreme, even crazy, but I cannot resist the call when it comes.

Lana is a little different. She likes adventure but she can take it or leave it. She loves to see new places and explore new frontiers, but the thing that really drives her is the urge to share the rush I get from living out my dreams. Her main fear is that she will not live life to the fullest, and one who has not been to sea on a small boat has missed one of life's great experiences.

Together, we have proven—at least to ourselves—that magical things happen when two people sharing a dream embark on a great adventure.

At first, our new dream was just a desire to sail away, but it finally took shape. We would sail *Salute* across the Atlantic Ocean to the Mediterranean Sea, travel the routes of the Apostle Paul, and write a book about it.

By this time, we had compiled an extensive résumé of blue water and coastal sailing. We had sailed from the Chesapeake to Maine and back. Later we had sailed from the Chesapeake to the Bahamas where we cruised for six months in 1985. After that, we kept our boat in Fort Myers, Florida for several years and made periodic cruises through the keys and on the west coast of Florida, including trips to Fort Jefferson in the Dry Tortugas. After George Herbert Walker Bush became president, we moved back to Washington, D.C. and in 1989, we sailed *Salute* back to the Chesapeake and berthed her in Galesville, Maryland. All along the way, we met many blue water sailors and talked to them about their adventures and we avidly read every monthly bulletin from the Seven Seas Cruising Association, a compilation of voyaging reports from sailors like us. We had a lot of sailing experience and knowledge and we were physically fit.

Preparing to cross the Atlantic in a thirty-one-foot sailboat is a lot of work, but our plan to cruise extensively after the crossing created an even longer list of things we needed to do. We had committed to go, so we started working on our list. We would do our best to get it all done, but a long list of concerns was not going to deter us or cause us to delay our trip.

It is not easy to get away from the endless array of obligations and responsibilities in the workaday world; the inevitable strings of life that tie us down and steal our freedom. I am talking about licenses, registrations, memberships, insurance, maintaining property, debts, and things of that sort. I am not talking about the welcome obligations and responsibilities that we have to loved ones, family and friends.

I wound down my law practice and transferred a few pending matters to other lawyers. We moved out of our Arlington, Virginia rental house and stored our furniture and belongings in my old Searcy law office, which was vacant at the time. We sold our cars, arranged our finances and established a way to get our mail forwarded so that we could stay in touch with our family.

We took our sloop, *Salute*, to Hartge's Yacht Yard in Galesville, Maryland for painting and repairs to critical woodwork which had begun to show some wear and tear. Then we took her to a rigger in Deale, Maryland who put up all new rigging. A sail maker put on a new roller-furling genoa, which is a large foresail than can be made smaller by rolling it around the forestay. I installed a satellite navigation system and a single-sideband radio that would allow us to receive and transmit while on the high seas, a necessity in the days before cell phones and satellite phones. By the time we were done, we had spent nearly $20,000 getting the boat ready, but we were a hundred percent confident she could make the trip.

I read everything I could find about Atlantic crossings, and after studying the pilot charts that show weather trends based on information collected from sailors for as far back as six hundred years, we decided to leave Deale at the end of May 1990. There are fewer gales in the North Atlantic in June than any other month, and we had no reason to expect otherwise.

We sailed Salute on the Chesapeake Bay as often as we could. This sail was on a nice day in early 1990.

We took a few days to sail down the Chesapeake Bay to Norfolk, Virginia. Our goal was to start the first leg of our voyage as early in June as we could. We would sail the northern circle route to the Azores, a Portuguese archipelago in the North Atlantic about 900 miles from the mainland of Portugal. Our route would take advantage of the northeasterly current of the Gulf Stream, a force likened to a river in the sea.

The great current starts in the South Atlantic Ocean and flows north until trade winds push it westerly into the Caribbean. It then heads toward the east coast of Mexico, spins its way through the Yucatan Channel, and turns back to the east. It gains speed as it squeezes its way through the Florida Straits, the narrow opening between the Florida Keys and Cuba. Then the current, now powerful, warm, and swift, rejoins the Atlantic and takes the name given it by Benjamin Franklin, the Gulf Stream. The mighty current then turns north, moving fast between Florida and the Bahamas where Ponce de Leon discovered it in 1513.

For centuries mariners have taken advantage of the Gulf Stream. It serves as a moving sidewalk for boats headed north and thence east to Europe. We planned to enter the Gulf Stream north of Cape Hatteras, North Carolina where the Chesapeake opens to the sea. We could ride the current from there to the Azores.

There is a downside to riding the Gulf Stream. It can become treacherous and unforgiving if it meets a powerful wind moving in the opposite direction. The collision of southbound winds with a northbound Gulf Stream will cause huge seas with confused, unpredictable wave action. Many a sailor has lived to report the horror of being in the Gulf Stream when it is at its worst but no one knows how many have perished, overcome by enormous rogue waves.

We arrived in Little Creek, on the north side of Norfolk, on June 1. *Salute* had performed well on the trip south. We sailed most of the way, but we did motor for a small part of the trip when the wind lay down. Our little boat had a correspondingly little engine, a fifteen-horsepower Lister diesel. It had never given us a bit of trouble in eight years, but on the way to Norfolk, we noticed it was overheating on occasion, so we had it checked by a diesel mechanic. When he examined the Lister, Murphy's Law was in full force—the engine performed beautifully.

We went to the government weather station in Norfolk and talked to a meteorologist who said the weather would be good on June 6. He reviewed all the data available to him and we discussed the pilot chart predictions that gale force winds are unlikely in June. We were most concerned that we might encounter an unseasonable Nor'easter, the term often used for any storm that occurs in the northeast part of the United States. The risk looked to be small.

We rented a car and began filling our boat with provisions. We bought ten dozen eggs, rubbed each egg with Vaseline, and put them back in the cartons. They would stay fresh for a long time if we turned the cartons upside down at least once a week. We bought cans of tuna, corned beef, and chicken. We got fresh bread, crackers, muffin mixes, and citrus fruit that we hung up in nets. We filled other nets with onions, potatoes, and other vegetables that would be slow to spoil. Before we left Maryland, we had bought several tins of canned butter that came from Australia. We also found canned bacon, a product of Poland. It is packed in brine and quite salty, but if soaked overnight in water it is a good substitute for fresh bacon. We had a rainwater catchment system on *Salute* that would replenish our water supply, but to start our trip we emptied our water tanks and refilled them with fresh water.

The entire provisioning exercise was actually a lot of fun as we had endless debates about the kinds of food that would keep well, and that we would eat on our trip to the Azores, a journey that would most likely take thirty days.

After reaching the Azores, we would sail to the mainland of Portugal, rest for a few weeks and then sail into the Mediterranean Sea. Eventually we would work our way to Greece and Turkey where we would sail the routes sailed by the Apostle Paul—the coasts of Greece, Turkey, Cyprus, Crete, and Malta, the site of his famous shipwreck. Ultimately, we would return to the south coast of France, pass through the French canals to the English Channel and on to England and Scotland. We did not have a definite plan beyond that but figured, if we liked it, to be gone for as much as two or three years.

46

GETTING UNDERWAY

The secret for harvesting from existence the greatest fruitfulness and the greatest engagement is—to live dangerously! Build your cities on the slopes of Vesuvius! Send your ships into uncharted seas.
Freidrich Nietzsche

Early in the morning on June 6, 1990, we dropped our lines to the dock in Little Creek, Virginia and headed east toward the Atlantic Ocean. There is something therapeutic about sailing away. It is a special feeling to head off into the sea without having to advise the government, explain it to the media, or to anyone in the whole world. You are on your own, liberated, as free and independent from worldly influences as one can be in this modern world. Even so, the forces of the sea are powerful, so strong that newfound freedoms can vanish in a wink. If the sea gets angry, you are at its mercy, no longer in control of your destiny. Thoughts of liberation disappear, replaced by a determination to stay afloat, react as best you can, and survive. Sailors can be free one minute and humbled the next, scrambling to stay alive. This dilemma is the essence of the spell ensnaring those who go to sea.

The inlet to Little Creek faded behind us as we approached the missing section of the Chesapeake Bay Bridge, an odd-looking vacant space where the bridge becomes a tunnel allowing big, tall vessels to pass over the tunnel as they go in and out of the Chesapeake. As we passed through the opening, close to the bridge pillars I thought of our sailing trip to Maine and our attempt to enter Salt Pond Harbor in fog so thick we could not see the inlet markers until we were directly between them. This opening was wide and easy to see, but for some reason it reminded me of how quickly things can go bad. The thought passed, washed away by the sight before us, the Chesapeake Bay giving way to the open sea. We were on our way into the blue water of the Atlantic Ocean.

The weather could not have been better. An azure sky had not a single cloud or even a wisp of one, and a fair wind made for a synchronized parade of blue waves. We tasted and smelled the salt air as the seagulls screamed, diving into the sea to catch their breakfast or soaring in circles then skimming just above the wave-tops to get a better look. Beneath us, the water got deeper and deeper. Soon we were out of sight of land, and the murmur of the sea, our constant companion, settled in.

Salute, at her best, could sail five nautical miles in an hour. Allowing for slack winds or adverse currents, we hoped to average ninety to a hundred knots a day. At that pace, we would reach land in thirty days or less. Our goal for the first day was to head in a northeasterly direction toward the Gulf Stream, which once entered would give us a one-to-two-knot boost every hour.

We enjoyed every minute of our first day, and as the sun began to set, we prepared our little boat for nighttime. With each shade of darkness on the first night at sea, we feel an increasing sense of aloneness. Nighttime blue water sailing takes some getting used to. Things look and sound different. The noise of a boat slicing through the water is barely noticeable in daylight, but at night, the motion of the boat creates an eerie phosphorescent trail of disturbed ocean water and the docile daytime sound becomes a mysterious gurgle.

We were adapting and thinking about the challenge of nighttime shipping traffic or the risk of hitting a floating object when a thunderstorm came up out of the west, complete with an awesome display of lightning bolts and bursts of brightness that made it seem like day. It was spectacular, but our minds gave way to a moment of worry about lighting striking our boat. *Salute* was equipped with a grounding plate system that tied a chunk of metal on the bottom of the boat to a spider web of wires connected to important metal points throughout the interior of the boat. I installed the protective system especially for our trip, but no system is failsafe. Lana and I talked about the technical aspects of lightning strikes at sea for a few minutes, and then we lowered sail and settled down to enjoy the thunderstorm show. There is not much more you can do.

Our second day at sea was another beautiful day with fair winds. We cooked our breakfast, checked *Salute* from stem to stern and continued our northeasterly track. As the sun rose higher, I prepared to take a noon-sight with the sextant. It is the oldest and easiest way to determine latitude. We had a satellite navigation system, the forerunner of GPS, but it is good practice to have a backup method for knowing where you are. I was pleased to see that my celestial navigation exercise squared with the electronic reading on our satellite navigation device. We were on course to join the Gulf Stream and to follow a bowed route that would take us over the smaller part of the globe to our destination. I also made temperature readings of the sea. The Gulf Stream—the river in the sea—is warmer than the water through which it travels thus a significant increase in water temperature indicates you are riding the great current. My temperature readings proved we had not yet found the Gulf Stream.

We saw a few big ships as we began to cross the traffic lanes that feed into New York harbor, but none was close to us. The vessel sightings tapered off dramatically as we made our easting. The second night was uneventful, no lightning show. We took turns keeping watch, something at which Lana excels. She is not distracted, as I tend to be, with navigation, rigging, and mechanics. Her focus has the intensity of a laser and we have never gotten off course, not a single degree, when she is at the helm. We made a hundred knots, a good second day.

As we started our third day, we were well off the coast of New Jersey, bending ever northeast. The electric autopilot I had rigged to operate the tiller failed, but we had an Aries Windvane, an ingenious device that reads the wind and keeps a boat on course. We saw no other boats during the day, but we did see the lights of one after dark. Our navigation system and charts told us we were now over very deep water and right on course. As the day wound down the wind died. We decided to run our engine to generate electricity for our batteries, power we needed for our electronic gear and for our navigation lights. After a quarter-hour the engine overheated, the same problem that had hid itself from the diesel mechanic in Little Creek. We hoped it was an isolated incident similar to the one we experienced coming down the Chesapeake Bay, so we shut the engine down.

47

GETTING INTO TROUBLE

The sea, the snotgreen sea, the scrotumtightening sea.
James Joyce (Ulysses)

On the fourth day, we determined by positioning and reading water temperature that we were in the Gulf Stream and riding the current that would carry us along our chosen course. The winds began to pipe up in mid-afternoon and the sea began to show her teeth. Whitecaps are a telltale sign that conditions are changing but it is no cause for alarm. Stronger wind meant we would get a better sail, but as the wind and waves continued to build, we turned on our single-side band radio to get a current weather forecast. We learned that an unexpected Nor'easter that began in Nova Scotia might affect us. We tried the engine again hoping to recharge our batteries, but it overheated just as it had before. That was not a good development, and the winds were getting stronger and stronger with every passing hour. The sea was changing, oddly, unpredictably.

It was our first time to be in the Gulf Stream when the current was encountering a strong wind coming from the opposite direction, out of the northeast. We knew quite a bit about the Gulf Stream because we had dealt with it on our travels to the Bahamas and through the Florida Straits. We knew about Nor'easters because people in the northeast part of the United States call any strong rain or snowstorm a Nor'easter regardless of season, prevailing wind direction, where it began or how it is moving. The storms can be devastating, particularly to ships caught in the warmer ocean water of the Gulf Stream. The storm coming our way deserved its name—Nor'easter—because the wind was blowing strongly out of the northeast.

We reefed the sails, making them smaller, and pressed on into the dark but by midnight the wind forced us to reef the mainsail to its smallest size and we completely furled the foresail. We put our boat in the heave-to position and lay down to get some rest.

Edgar Allen Poe, in his *Narrative of A. Gordon Pym of Nantucket*, explained the purpose of "heaving-to," sometimes called "laying-to." Poe said it is a measure resorted to "for when it is too violent to admit of carrying sail without danger of capsizing … or … the sea is too heavy for the vessel … [and] much damage is usually done her by the shipping of water over her stern and sometimes by the violent plunges she makes forward."

Every boat has its unique way of heaving-to; ours on *Salute* was to set a reefed mainsail so that the wind would backfill it. Then we tied the tiller over so that if the boat began to inch forward the rudder would steer her back into the wind, thus causing the boat to lose forward motion and stay in the same position. It is a classic way to ride out a storm, but this storm was about to test us as we had never been tested.

It was a rough night, but *Salute* performed well.

When daylight came on the fifth day we knew we were in a precarious situation. I looked at the charts and saw that we were closer to Newport, Rhode Island than any other port, and it was a harbor familiar to us. I raised the issue of diverting to Newport to fix our engine and wait for better weather.

Lana asked the important questions, "How long will it take to get there, and can we avoid the worst part of the storm?" For the best part of an hour we discussed the idea of diverting, the direction of the winds and currents, and the trouble we were having with our diesel engine. Lana then said, "Let's press on! We have made a good start and our chance of weathering the storm is just as good as our chance of reaching Newport." It was another good example of why she has been such a good companion for me. She was gutsy enough to make the trip, and tough enough to stay the course—a rare woman. She would have been a good Marine.

We pressed on. Our reasoning was that we could—if we had to—run the engine enough to keep the batteries charged and that would allow us to operate our lights at night and sparingly use the radio for weather reports and essential communications. Most of all, we did not want to give up the good start we had made and we were convinced we could ride out the coming storm. We let out sail and forged ahead. It was rough and bouncy and we did not make much headway, but at least we were fighting back and that strengthened our resolve. In mid-afternoon, the winds picked up and we had no choice but to reduce sail and heave-to. It was going to be a long night, but we were satisfied we were doing what any other sailor would have done: Rig for heavy weather, wait for the storm to clear, and proceed on course.

When dark came *Salute* was riding fairly well, up then down, up then down. We were down below in the cabin riding it out as best we could.

Suddenly, about 10:00 p.m., Lana said, "Something has changed, I can tell by the sound of it. Listen." I could not hear or feel any difference, but Lana has the best set of ears in the Western Hemisphere. She can distinguish the walk of a big cat from that of a small cat. She has always been that way. House noises, car noises, equipment noises, all noises must stay the same or Lana will immediately notice the change. She said again, "Be still, listen." I still did not hear what she was hearing, but I could sense a different motion, a wilder motion. I said, "You're right, I'll go topside and have a look."

I threw open the hatch and climbed the ladder into the cockpit, holding on for dear life. The wind was shrieking, hammering the boat and forcing the waves to enormous heights. The noise of breaking waves and wind whistling through the rigging of *Salute* was like nothing I had ever heard. It did not take long to see why *Salute* was behaving strangely. The strong winds had blown the triple-reefed mainsail completely out of its track. The sail, now flapping uselessly over the side, left *Salute* defenseless. We were now lying-ahull, a controversial method for weathering a storm, whereby a sailor takes down all sails, battens the hatches and locks the tiller to leeward. Unlike heaving to, the boat will bob around—much like a cork—and drift freely, completely at the mercy of the storm.

It was too rough and dangerous to jury-rig the mainsail, so I just took a seat in the cockpit and told Lana we had a problem. She said, "If you can't do anything about it, then come below, it's safer."

She was right, so I went below and started kicking myself for not getting a storm tri-sail before I left port. A storm tri-sail is a small sail that fits securely in a separate track on the mainmast. It would not have blown out; it would still be working.

I spent a little too much time whining about not getting a tri-sail. Lana, a fierce opponent of negative talk, brought my self-flagellation to a halt. She said, "Hindsight is 20-20. We're where we are and we have to make the best of it." Wise woman—she should have been a federal judge.

It was going to be a long night, seven more hours to sunrise. Our little ship tossed about, left to right and up and down. She turned first one way and then another. Every five minutes or so an enormous wave would lift us skyward, and when we reached the top, perched on the crest of the wave, our boat would fall sideways off the crest of the wave and crash, and shudder, against the trough of the wave. The fall of twenty-five feet felt like a thousand. All the while, the rigging—even with the mainsail out of its track and the foresail furled—strained and creaked as if it were about to be torn away. Once *Salute* bobbed back to the upright position, we had only a minute or two to collect ourselves before we started rising up, up again to the dropping off spot. There was an unholy rhythm to our dance with the ocean, and it lasted all night.

Lana and I lay flat on our backs on the cabin floor. It is the lowest point of the boat; therefore, it is the safest and most stable place. Our feet were touching; my head was pointing aft and hers was pointing forward. We ate a bit of nourishment, got out our Bibles, and inflated our life preservers. Every so often when *Salute* settled in the low spot, one of us would turn on a flashlight and read a scripture. Then we would sit up and try to hug and kiss one another, a comical exercise given the bulk of our lifejackets.

We talked about our life together, but mostly we talked about Paige and Sam. Neither of our kids was married yet, so we speculated about them settling down and having children of their own. We talked about the grandkids that we expected to have, and we talked about our mothers, our family, and our faith. I would not say we were cool, calm, and collected but we were doing pretty well considering the circumstances. The interesting thing is we never talked about politics, business, sports, movies, or any of the things that consume people when they think they are going to live forever.

During the night, the noise and motion increased. The storm was worsening. We began to worry that the battering might cause our boat to break up. We prayed often. As the noise got louder and the battering sank into a regular beat, I thought about the morning when I was a teenager and woke up to the irritating sound of a jackhammer that was busting up concrete just below my room at Mama Lewallen's hotel. I had made a life altering decision that day by deciding to give up incorrigibility in favor of finishing high school. It was time to make another life altering decision.

I had wrestled with the idea of surrendering to a higher power all my life; first as a self-centered Vermilye descendant and later when trying to give my life to Christ. I think it is the hardest part of faith. Lana understood surrender—what it is, and what it is not. I pretended to agree with the concept, but I had never let go the way she had, the way believers should. Now we were at the mercy of the sea. Things we had stored on the boat—personal treasures—did not matter. There was no logical or emotional reason to hold back, to resist, or to deny. Our lives were in God's hands. She was remarkably calm, at peace. I was a basket case: worried, anxious, uptight, and afraid. I could do nothing. It was time for me to accept God's promise of salvation, unconditionally.

I surrendered. It was a different kind of surrender than I had ever done. Previously I had always tried to work out a deal. Just let me out of this, Lord, and I will be a good boy. Just let me out of that and I will never do it again, that sort of surrender. We lawyers would probably name it "transactional immunity," a broad but limited protection from prosecution. No, this was different. I was not looking for a deal, I was ready for full surrender, ready to recognize that salvation is God's idea, not man's, and certainly not mine. I was ready, finally, to accept God's promise, to love Him and live with the Holy Spirit.

Intercession takes many forms, some more dramatic than others. In my case it took thirty-six hours of nonstop jackhammering, and as I gave in and let go, I thought of all the times I had visited prisoners when I was practicing law and when I was a FBI agent. Prisoners—hard cases, many are barely literate—write poetry, lots of poetry. The bulletin boards, the prison newsletters, are full of poetic tributes, mostly to Jesus and mother. When the cell door slams shut behind them, they are at the end of the line, no freedom, no privacy, no hope. They turn to Jesus and mother.

I do not recommend jackhammering or prison for everyone but it does work for those who are bullheaded and stubbornly independent, even one with Vermilye blood.

At daybreak on the sixth day, we emerged from our cocoon to evaluate our situation. No sooner were we topside than a wave of greenish water crashed over the stern of *Salute*, filling the cockpit and soaking us. I had heard blue water sailors speak of "green water," but I thought it was a figment of their imagination. It is not, it is something that happens, unexplainably, when the sea is at it meanest.

The sea was wild, confused, and in total control but with daylight, we gained an understanding of how the waves lifted and dropped us. We took turns at the tiller, running before the wind, steering as best we could to keep the bow pointed forward. We learned to ride the waves up, and down without falling off the top of the wave and landing on our side in the bottom of the trough, as we had done all night long. It was a bit of progress, but soon we realized that our new technique of speeding down the wave instead of falling off sideways increased our chance of pitchpoling—the most dreaded way for a boat to capsize. Just thinking about it was scary. I imagined *Salute* sticking her nose into the water as we sped down to the bottom of a trough, then a following wave lifting her stern up and over the bow, completing the perfect pitchpole. We needed something to slow us down when we surfed down the waves, so we put out a drogue, a small cone-shaped device that trailed behind *Salute* on a long line. In theory, a drogue—working like a small parachute—will slow a boat down so that it does not speed excessively down the slope of a wave and crash into the next trough, the first step to pitchpoling.

The drogue seemed to help and our fear of pitchpoling lessened, but a new concern arose. Slowing the boat made it easier for the green water waves to catch up to us, break over our stern and fill the cockpit. We were now receiving regular instead of sporadic doses of green water. The work we were doing to steer the boat while sitting outside in the storm was so exhausting that we gave it up and returned to our spots on the cabin floor.

As I lay down, I realized that I was no longer worried, anxious, uptight, or afraid. I, like Lana, had put my life in the hands of the Lord. Surrender works. Praise God!

About nine o'clock we started the engine to see if it would run without overheating. Propulsion would give us better steerage and we could charge up our batteries. Alas, within five minutes the engine temperature gauge was in the red zone. We had no choice but to shut it down.

We tuned our single-sideband radio to a weather station. The reports said the foul weather would continue and that it might get worse but we could not get an accurate picture of how long the storm would last. Having rested for a couple of hours, I fastened a lifeline to my lifejacket, went topside, and crawled to the mast to see if I could repair the mainsail, which was still hanging over the side of the boat. After a few tries I gave up. It was too hard and too dangerous; the repair would have to wait for the end of the storm.

I could see no other problems on deck, so I went below to make a full inspection of the boat from stem to stern. We were getting water in the bilge, which was unusual for *Salute*, ordinarily a very dry boat. I needed to find out how water was getting in the bilge, so I opened every compartment and emptied its contents allowing me to see the inside of the hull. The hard work made me a little woozy but I found no holes or cracks in the hull, and the through-hull fittings and hoses appeared to be intact. Still, we had water in the bilge and it had to be coming from somewhere.

The mast on our boat did not rest on the keel at the bottom of the boat; it was stepped on top of the coach roof, so I began a careful check of the bulkheads directly under the mast. There I found several stress fractures and lots of wetness. It appeared to me that the beating we had taken during the night had damaged the foundation for the mast and that seawater was making its way into our bilge because of that. It was just a theory, but it fed our concern that the powerful storm could breakup our boat.

By late morning, I finished my survey of *Salute*, and we evaluated the risks that we faced. *Salute* was beginning to show structural damage that might lead to a breakup if we endured another night of pounding. We had electricity in our batteries, but we needed to run the bilge pump, use the radio, and keep our navigation lights burning. Our engine would not run without overheating so we had no way to recharge the batteries. We could conserve electricity by hand pumping the bilge water out of the boat, but that would not save much. Our mainsail was down and repairs to it would have to wait for the storm to pass. We had been fighting with the storm for thirty-six hours and fatigue, a sailor's greatest danger, had us in its grip. We were getting regular doses of green water, and we faced the potential of capsizing by pitch-poling or rolling over. We were in a Hell of a mess, and another night would come in eight hours.

We needed relief if we could get it. If the storm was going to last for days or get worse, any one of the challenges we faced could take us down. We would be lost forever. There would be no second chance. We needed a definitive weather forecast for our position, 210 miles south of Cape Cod.

48

GETTING OUT OF TROUBLE

A gem cannot be polished without friction,
nor a man perfected without trials.
Chinese Proverb.

Around noon on Tuesday, June 12, I called the United States Coast Guard on our single-sideband radio, told them our position, our circumstances, and asked for a reliable weather prediction. Shortly thereafter, the Coast Guard advised us by radio: "A low pressure system is expected to remain stationary leaving conditions as they are until 15 June."

That was three more days, and other radio forecasts that we heard indicated it might get worse, much worse. It was decision time. Lana and I talked about our options, which is what we always do. We balanced the real risk of catastrophe against an unknown: Could we take another three days of storm in twenty-five-foot seas with winds over forty knots. It was not a hard decision. At 2:00 p.m., I radioed the Coast Guard and told them that we were not sure we could maintain hull integrity or survive the beating we were taking for another twenty-four hours, much less three days. We did not know whether they could help us due to our distance from shore, but we requested their assistance.

The Coast Guard, Air Station Cape Cod, put us on an hourly communication schedule and told us to energize our EPIRB, an electronic positioning device, if our situation worsened or if we were unable to communicate for two successive radio checks.

Unbeknownst to us, the Coast Guard signaled one of it cutters, *Tampa*, to head in our direction. These vessels ply the waters daily, in good weather and bad, waiting for such a call. They also told a merchant vessel, *Atlantic Huron*, of our predicament. Later we learned that neither of these ships could reach us until after dark. They were twelve to eighteen hours away. Moving from a bobbing, twisting thirty-one-foot sailboat to a larger vessel at night, in rough seas was not a happy prospect but we prepared ourselves to do whatever the Coast Guard advised us to do.

The Coast Guard keeps its cards close to the vest, and they know what they are doing. They have learned it is not wise to disclose how they intend to make a rescue until they are certain they have a plan that will work. It is a good policy. Sailors in peril on the sea need honest information, not false hopes. At 4:25 p.m., the Coast Guard launched a HU-25 Falcon jet to search for us. The pilot flew to our last known position and instituted an expanding square search, but he could not see *Salute*. It is hard to see a small white sailboat against the backdrop of an unruly sea with huge waves and whitecaps. The Coast Guard launched a second Falcon jet and it headed to our area to continue the search. The pilot of the second search plane had better luck—he spotted *Salute* at 6:38 p.m., just two minutes after arriving on the scene. He established contact with us on our single-sideband radio and told us to turn our VHF radio to Channel 16, which I did. His voice came in loud and clear; it was a wonderful sound. We knew he must be close since we were talking on VHF, so we hustled up the ladder into the cockpit.

It was a sight to see! There were two jets circling and a rescue helicopter was hovering low above, just slightly behind us. Lana and I broke into a cheer and started waving. I finally saw what my angel looks like. She is big, orange and white, and the blades that circle inside her big halo make a loud *whoosh-whoosh-whoosh* beating sound. It was no surprise to me that the noisy, thumping sound had the cadence of a jackhammer.

The recorded history showing how the Coast Guard coordinated the search planes, crews, and rescue helicopter hovering above us is a testament to the competency of our men and women in uniform. Their motto, Semper Paratus, pledges that they are always ready and their hymn says they are ready to "do or die, through howling gale, shot or shell." Thank God for the United States Coast Guard.

At 4:30 p.m., before the search plane located us, the Coast Guard sent an HH-3F Helicopter with a crew that included a rescue swimmer on a short flight from Air Station Cape Cod to Nantucket Island. The helicopter topped off with fuel on Nantucket Island, which is thirty miles closer to where we were. They did that because the HH-3F helicopter has limited range. Stopping at Nantucket would give the crew more time at the rescue site and a better chance to return safely. We were 210 miles south of Nantucket. There was no way a helicopter could fly that far, search for a vessel that was hard to see, conduct a full-scale rescue operation, and then fly back to land. That is why they send search planes ahead of the helicopter, to find and pinpoint the exact location of the vessel in distress.

The HH-3F left Nantucket and headed to our last reported site *before* the second Falcon jet search plane spotted *Salute.* If the Falcon jet had not found us, the helicopter would have aborted the mission and returned to its home base. There would have been no choice but to leave us where we were to spend another night in the storm. As it was, the helicopter, benefitting from a following wind, arrived on scene at 6:40 p.m., exactly two minutes after the search plane pinpointed our position. The perfectly coordinated response meant that the helicopter would have up to forty-five minutes to make the rescue. There was no time to spare. The helicopter would have to leave the site in forty-five minutes whether we were on board or not.

Fortunately, the Coast Guard has a training program, Safety at Sea, designed to teach civilian sailors how to deal with the challenges they will face on the high seas, especially the mechanics of rescue. Lana and I had attended such a session in Annapolis before we set out on our voyage. The main feature of the program we attended was a rescue at sea by helicopter. "How fortunate is that," I thought to myself.

The wonderful sound coming through our VHF radio said: "Sailing vessel *Salute*, this is Coast Guard 2121, do you read me?" We were waving to the jets and the crew of my angel. We were ecstatic!

"Yes, Coast Guard 2121, we read you loud and clear." I had so much excitement in my voice that the pilot of CG 2121 said, "Please listen to our instructions and do exactly what we say."

"Roger that," I said, using the radio lingo I had learned in the FBI and Marine Corps. CG 2121 then said he was going to hand me off to the crew of the helicopter and immediately we heard this, "Sailing vessel *Salute*, this is Coast Guard 1475, do you read me?"

"Yes, loud and clear," I responded. Then the crew of the helicopter told us what they planned to do, and what they expected of us.

A helicopter cannot get close to a sailboat that is rolling wildly in the sea because the rotor blades might hit the sailboat's mast or rigging. Therefore, the crew told us they could not hoist us directly from *Salute*. We would have to get into the water and put some distance between the sailboat and us. They said we would need to launch our inflatable life raft, but leave it tied to the boat. The plan was for us to jump off *Salute* into the life raft. The rescue swimmer would take us one by one from the life raft to a position well away from *Salute* where we would get into a metal rescue basket that the helicopter would hoist up and through the wide-open cargo door.

I radioed that we had seen a demonstration of the operation at Annapolis, albeit in milder weather conditions, and they were pleased to hear that. Nevertheless, they wanted us to listen carefully and not get ahead of the way they wanted to do things. The crew then radioed, "Due to high seas, we might not be able to complete all or part of the rescue mission, and we have a narrow window of time we can stay here. If we cannot complete the rescue, you will have to pull the life raft back to the sailboat and wait there for further communications. Do you understand?"

The last part of the message, about having to spend another night on *Salute*, gave new meaning to the cliché: Time is of the essence.

I immediately unlashed the life raft that we had stowed on the stern of the boat and kicked it into the ocean. When it drifted as far away from *Salute* as it could the line that held it grew taut and set off a CO2 cartridge that blew off the plastic cover, and the life raft inflated automatically. The life raft was five years old, but we had taken it to Annapolis for updating and servicing just a month before we set sail. It worked perfectly, the bottom inflated first followed by a canopy designed to afford protection from the elements—so far so good.

Now it was time to jump off *Salute* onto the life raft. I pulled the life raft as close as I could and Lana climbed over the stern rail and made ready to jump. We had never used the raft, but we had seen demonstrations of how to deploy and use them. The recommended technique for getting onto a life raft is to dive right on top of it instead of trying to climb into it. Lana, now in position, executed a beautiful swan dive, a perfect ten.

The impact pulled the line from my hands, but once inside the life raft, Lana pulled it back close to *Salute* and I made my dive, complicated a little by the fact that Lana was already in the life raft and I needed to miss her. I did not get a perfect ten; maybe a six-point-five, but it worked. Now we were both in the life raft, and it had drifted to the end of its lanyard. We were ready for the next step.

While we were getting into the life raft, the helicopter crew lowered a rescue swimmer, Petty Officer Rod Parker, into the raging sea. From our new perspective, right on the water with a helicopter hovering close and low, we got a new appreciation for the men and women of the Coast Guard. The waves were twenty-five to thirty feet high with no pattern to their rise and fall. The howling wind was blowing the top of the waves sideways as they crested. It takes real courage to be a Coast Guard rescue team, in the air or in the water. The bravery of Petty Officer Parker was special to us because our son, Sam, was for ten years a rescue swimmer in the United States Navy.

When Parker reached the life raft, he was all business. Dark haired and good-looking, Parker was in a black wetsuit and had an air of authority about him even though he was quite young. He quickly took charge, telling us we would need to get out of the raft, one at a time so that he could take us over to where the helicopter was hovering. He said, "Ladies first." Lana did not hesitate; there was no time for idle chatter, no time to waste. I gave Lana a quick kiss, she slipped out of the raft and they were off, headed to the area about thirty yards away where the helicopter was waiting. The crew had lowered a rescue basket on a cable, and it was dangling just above the water. As Parker and Lana got close, the crew lowered the stainless steel basket, which is five feet long and two feet wide, into the water. Parker helped Lana into it, making sure she was secure. Then he signaled to the helicopter crew and the hoist started up. I waved to Lana but she did not see me, she was hanging on for dear life. It was 6:55 p.m. So far, the entire operation had taken fifteen minutes, which left twenty to thirty minutes for Parker to swim back to me, get me out of the life raft, and hoisted to safety. Things were looking good, but if equipment failed, or something went wrong, something that would use too much time, the Coast Guard might have to leave me and come back for me later. If that happened, I would need to pull the life raft back to *Salute*, climb on board the sailboat and wait for another opportunity to get off. I did not relish the idea of spending another night on *Salute* but at least Lana was safe.

Something did go wrong. It was not my fault; it was not the Coast Guard's fault. It was the fault of Joyce's "snotgreen sea, the scrotumtightening sea." During the time Parker was taking Lana to the rescue basket, *Salute* and the life raft, with me in it, had drifted almost the length of a football field from the rescue site. To reach me Parker would have to swim a long way through heavy, confused seas. He tried valiantly, but it was obvious that he was not making much progress in my direction. It was a strange sight. He was at least seventy-five yards away. At one moment, I, in a trough would be looking up the bank of a colossal wave where Parker, at the top, was swimming furiously in my direction but in a blink, we would change positions. I would be high on top of a wave looking down at Parker who, still seventy-five yards away, was now in the trough. This odd exchange, up and down, kept repeating itself, but Parker was getting no closer to me. There was little hope that he could reach me by swimming, so the helicopter crew decided to hoist Parker up and carry him to where I had drifted. Time was running out. The plan to hoist Parker, move him to my location, and then get both of us back into the helicopter would have to work perfectly or I was going to spend another night on *Salute.*

Miracles do happen. I know that to be true. As the helicopter neared Parker to lift and move him, he was on the crest of a wave looking way down to where I was at the bottom of a trough, now at least a hundred yards away. Suddenly, as if he were on a surfboard in Hawaii, Parker surfed down the wave. In seconds, he was with me, holding onto the life raft. He was coughing and spitting, choked with seawater and conspicuously fatigued. He had fought the unruly sea for almost half an hour. When he caught his breath, I said to him, "My son is a rescue swimmer in the United States Navy, and I love you both." He smiled, just a little, and said, "Alright! Let me rest a minute then I will get you out of here." The helicopter moved closer to where we were and in a few minutes, Parker took me to the rescue basket and got me settled into it.

Up. The hoist was lifting me up. Thank God! I was on my way to safety.

Then I was going down, down under the water, I opened my eyes, green water. What was happening? What was going on? I thought I was sinking, but then I was going up again.

I was out of the water and going up. Thank God, again. Wait, I was going down again, down under the water, green water again.

I held my breath until the basket got out of the water and this time, thank God, it kept going up. I looked down, saw Parker in the water, and looked up to see the crew getting ready to receive me. When they pulled me into the helicopter, I plunged into the seat next to Lana. We hugged and kissed each other, and thanked the crew for saving us, but they were busy lifting Parker out of the water and into the helicopter. When they got Parker inside the helicopter, he collapsed on the floor and scarcely moved for the next half hour.

It was 7:28 p.m.; the entire operation had taken forty-eight minutes, the outer limit for an HH-3F Helicopter that was still 210 miles from home. The pilots turned north, into the wind, heading for their home base, Air Station Cape Cod. The Falcon jet, Coast Guard 2121, escorted us back to base. The first search jet, Coast Guard 2116, had already gone home.

As we flew away, I saw *Salute*, with the life raft attached. She was still rolling violently with her mainsail collapsed over the side, hanging into the water. I felt sad that we were leaving her, but it was the right decision. We lost everything that was on the boat. Lana had tied a waterproof pouch around her waist that held our cash, our credit cards, and our driver's licenses. That, and the clothes on our back were all we salvaged. *Salute* was now just another speck of white in a sea of large whitecaps; she blended in and soon was lost to sight. It was easy to see why it is so hard for search pilots to find a small sailing vessel in a stormy sea, even when they have exact coordinates fixing the position. Our dream of sailing across the Atlantic was also gone, but we took it in stride; after all, we were safe. We would live to see our children and loved ones once again.

As darkness engulfed us, the crew wired us up with earphones and microphones enabling us to talk to the pilots and crew on the long flight to land. We, of course, were effusive in our praise and thankful for what they had just done. I wasted no time telling them that I had served as a member of the United States House of Representatives, and that I intended to tell all my friends and former colleagues of my respect and admiration for the United States Coast Guard. It did not matter that I had served in Congress but it did matter that they had rescued us without regard to who we were, who we knew, or what we might do for them or the Coast Guard. That is how things ought to work.

It took almost two hours to fly to Air Station Cape Cod, and we saw the lights of Nantucket, Martha's Vineyard, and Cape Cod as we neared land. It was enchanting. We would live to get another sailboat and sail again in the blue water, but land and civilization looked good to us at that moment. When the HH-23 Helicopter landed, Coast Guard 1475 and crew had been in the air for four hours. The aircraft may have been able to fly for another half hour, or forty-five minutes, but then it would have been running on fumes.

The commanding officer of Air Station Cape Cod met us as we got off the helicopter. We thanked him and praised the crew. He simply said, "It is our duty; it is what we do." He turned us over to a medical officer who gave us a quick but thorough examination. He concluded we suffered from exhaustion but nothing more. Someone asked if we would be agreeable to a news conference about the rescue because there had been reports of it along with other local news about the storm, and the damage it had done ashore. I said I would be happy to tell about our rescue, so the news conference was set for 9:00 a.m. the next morning.

The pilots and crew invited us to spend the night on base, and as we were on our way to the officer's quarters, the commanding officer whispered to me that the rescue crews love to visit with the survivors. It is good for their morale, but they also learn things that may help them in the future. We were dead tired, but nothing was going to keep us from visiting with our rescuers, for as long as they wanted.

First, we called our children and parents and gave a short version of our misadventure. We played it down as no big deal and told them we would give them the whole story soon enough. Then we plopped down in the officer's lounge to sip coffee, eat snacks, and talk with our rescuers. Parker was too tired to do anything but go to bed, but the others were there. We talked about the entire operation, and they filled us in on how they planned and coordinated our rescue. We learned that most Coastguardsmen are in the service because it is a calling to serve and protect the United States, and to help people in the process. It is different from conventional military service, and the difference is what attracts them to the Coast Guard. It was a fascinating visit but I was itching to ask the question that had been on my mind since they hoisted me from the water to the helicopter.

I directed my question to the pilot of the helicopter, Lieutenant Commander Robert Hughes. I said, "When I was being hoisted I was going up out of the water and then down underwater, over and over again." All the rescuers started giggling, and Lana and I giggled too, because it was a funny sight to see. Finally, the pilot said, "We call that teabagging." That broke up the room and we all had a good laugh. Lieutenant Commander Hughes then explained the challenge of getting a smooth lift in a helicopter when the sea is rising and falling and the winds are blowing hard. He explained the physics of it and it made sense, but I have long since forgotten the technical aspects of teabagging. My explanation is shorter. Getting teabagged may have an ugly connotation in today's world, but getting teabagged by the Coast Guard in 1990 in the course of a difficult rescue mission beats perishing at sea.

We got to bed about 10:45 p.m. Lana, as usual, fell asleep right away. I expected to because I was tired, but I could not stop thinking about what we had just gone through. We lost our boat and we were not going to live out our dream to sail the routes of the Apostle Paul. Our dream was gone, but we were alive and safe, and it occurred to me that I had taken a step that I might not have taken otherwise. The hammering we took for thirty-six hours in the middle of a wild and stormy sea worked on me as a jackhammer works on solid concrete. The constant pounding shattered my rock-solid mindset, the one that had always told me that I—me, the big enchilada—could will my way out of any predicament. I was nearing fifty-five years of age but I finally "got it." When I was at the mercy of the sea, I accepted, for the first time in my life that man is never in total control. There are times when no amount of logic, emotion or willpower can save you. All my life I have misunderstood, perhaps intentionally, the concept of Christian surrender. I saw it as an intellectual proposition. Surrender, I reckoned, was the ongoing business of obeying the Father, the Son, and the Holy Ghost. I figured, this being the modern world, that God would judge my obedience and my faith by reference to my behavior, my service, and my works. I thought that by believing in the Trinity and being good I was surrendering. I had accepted the wise teaching I learned at Potomac Chapel, that we must put God in the center of our lives, not man. Nevertheless, I saw the concepts of surrender, obedience, and faith as a complex business. That was a misunderstanding. Honest, total surrender is not complicated it is simple. Obedience is simple, and faith is simple. The parable of the fig tree teaches that we all need pruning from time to time. Pruning is good, and it works for most people but it takes a powerful force—a jackhammer—to bust up a mindset as tough as mine. The disaster on the high seas changed my life. The experience opened my mind. Now I had to figure out what I needed to do next. I began to ask myself questions, "If I scrub away the last vestiges of Vermilyeism, what then will I be? How then shall I live?" I fell asleep realizing that I had more to learn, more to understand, more to …

We got up early and went to the Coast Guard Exchange as soon as it opened. We needed to buy some clothes for the news conference but we also needed to get toiletries, shoes, socks, underwear, and other necessities. The list was long, and it got longer when we added brushes, lipstick, mascara, facial crème and other indispensable items for Lana's new purse. We did not have much time because we needed to change clothes and get to the news conference at 9:00 a.m. We sped through the aisles grabbing one item after another. Our escapade reminded us of an old TV game show that let contestants keep whatever they could stuff into a grocery basket in fifteen minutes. At 8:50 a.m., we stopped shopping, put on our new duds, and headed to the site of the news conference. I was surprised to see the big turnout of media. The commanding officer and public relations people opened the conference by describing the rescue then they asked me to speak about our experience.

Wearing a brand-new Air Station Cape Cod ball cap, I said, "I have just three things to say. The Coast Guard is great! The Coast Guard is great! The Coast Guard is great!" There were other questions, but my opening lines became the lead in most of the stories. There is a small advantage to serving in high political office: You learn the art of coining irresistible sound bites. Our story was the top story locally and the wire services spread it all across the country.

As the news conference broke up, I asked the commanding officer if it would be appropriate for me to buy several cases of Moosehead beer for the men in his unit. He could not say yes officially, but I got the distinct impression that the beer would find its way to the right place if I had it delivered to the base. That afternoon a truck driver offloaded case after case of Moosehead beer, and it was gone the next day. It was our way of saying thanks for a job well done.

There was one more thing we had to do to wind up business with the Coast Guard. *Tampa*, the Coast Guard cutter steaming in the area near the site of our rescue had located *Salute*. She was foundering, a hazard to navigation. We authorized the captain of *Tampa* to sink her, and he did. It was a painful decision, but it was the only thing to do. It would have been irresponsible to leave a hazard that might put other sailors in harm's way. We closed the book on *Salute* and our dream to sail the routes of the Apostle Paul. What should we do next? We had arranged our affairs so that we could be gone for a long time, but we had no boat. Should we go home and start over, or should we take time to think deeply, introspectively about our near-death experience? We needed a new plan.

49

OUR NEW PLAN, BACKPACKING IN EUROPE

Be happy while y'er leevin', For y'er a lang time dead.
Anonymous (Scotland)

Not everyone has looked death in the eye and lived to tell about it. If we returned to conventional life in the work-a-day world, there would be time for introspection, but we would have to squeeze it into a schedule dominated by the events and obligations that often cause us to say, "I wonder where the day went? I had the best plans but never got around to doing what I intended to do." We wanted to cloister ourselves from such distractions to the extent we could. We knew how to find the right environment for good thinking. We learned that lesson when we sailed *Salute* to the Bahamas for a six-month sabbatical.

It was an easy decision. We would take another sabbatical. We had set aside the time, and while we did not have a lot of money, we had enough for a few months even though touring on land is more expensive than traveling and living on a sailboat. Our kids and parents were doing fine and we were still young. We decided to seize the moment and worry about the future later. If it meant starting over from scratch, we had no fear of that; we had done it many times and we could do it again.

The second decision we made was to stay away from Portugal, the Mediterranean, and countries we had intended to visit on

Salute. Visiting those ports would remind us of our failure to sail across the Atlantic. Dwelling on the past, particularly adventures that did not work out as planned, is not our thing.

We took a room at The Falmouth Square Inn, a quaint Cape Cod inn near Air Station Cape Cod, to flesh out a new plan. We walked to the library and scoured the travel section. After hours and hours of reading, thinking, and talking we decided to go to England, Scotland, and the north of France. Our family roots reach deep into those places. A long visit would let us learn more about our European heritage, something we had talked about for years.

Having chosen our destination, we next agreed that we would travel unconventionally. Most people our age take too much baggage, rent too many cars, hire too many taxis, and eat in too many restaurants. We had prepared ourselves for a long, low budget sailing voyage on a small boat. Now we wanted to travel over land similar to the way sailors travel the seas. We decided to backpack and spend our nights in B&B's, or *gites* when in France. We made a commitment to hike when we could and take public busses and trains when we were going too far to walk. We vowed to stay out of restaurants except for an occasional lunch. Our rules would save money, force us to mix and mingle with the locals, better understand the culture, and give us plenty of exercise. That is how it is for sailors, and that is what we wanted.

Our plan was too austere and vigorous for most couples in their early fifties, but it was perfect for us. We have long admired G. K. Chesterton's essay, "On Running after One's Hat." Chesterton compares the image of a man chasing a hat that has blown off his head and is tumbling down the street with the image of a man chasing a bouncing football. The man chasing the hat is grumbling and upset, but the man chasing the football is excited and happy. Chesterton wisely concludes, "An adventure is an inconvenience rightly considered; whereas an inconvenience is an adventure wrongly considered."

We booked a flight to Glasgow, Scotland to leave on Monday, June 18, 1990 but we had much to do before taking off. First, we needed new passports. Ours had gone down with the ship. I called Newt Gingrich's office in D.C. and got his staff to set up an expedited passport process with the Boston Passport Agency of the Department of State. I had done the same for many constituents when I was in Congress. Everything worked like clockwork and we picked up our new passports on Friday, June 15.

We found backpacks small enough to carry but big enough to hold our clothes and toiletries. We were ready to go.

When we were researching our travel plans at the Falmouth Library, Lana met a nice man who soon figured out that we were the couple he had just read about in the Falmouth newspaper. He invited us to attend his church on Sunday and then join him and his wife for lunch afterward. We did, and it was then that we told the fullness of our story for the first time. It was good to get it off our chests, but we could see from the way it affected our hosts that our tale had a meaning larger than the mechanics of the rescue. When we told our new friends that we were going to Glasgow, they said they had dear friends living there, Ian and Anne Grant. They called the Grants and Anne said she would pick us up at the Glasgow airport. She insisted that we stay a few nights with them. Our new adventure was off to a good start.

We arrived in Glasgow early Tuesday morning, June 19. Anne met us and was astounded that we had only two backpacks for a three-month tour of Europe. We explained our theory, that unconventionality would yield a better experience. She said she understood but I think she thought we were slightly crazy. Perhaps we were, perhaps we are, but it works for us.

That night we told our story for the second time and Ian, a tenderhearted man, cried openly. Since then we have told our story only a few times. It affects people in different ways. It moves those who dream of getting away to share a great adventure with a loved one, and it speaks to the heart of those who have faced death or those who struggle with the idea of surrendering their will to God's will.

On Thursday, we put on our backpacks, bid Ian and Anne goodbye, and caught the train to Edinburgh to begin our tour of Scotland, England, and France.

We saw all the well-known sights, but mostly we imbedded ourselves with the people. We did not plan to write a travelogue. Our new purpose was to learn about the people and trace the life journey of our ancestors. We wanted to know as much as we could about our family names. In my case, it was Bethune, Lewallen, and Vermilye. For Lana, it was Collier, and Prewitt. We lost ourselves in our quest, and the telling of it could fill another book. Even so, there are a few memories that give a sense of our month-long adventure in Scotland.

On a day trip by train from Inverness to Kyle of Lockhalsh, one of the world's most scenic rides, an old gentleman told us that on the Isle of Skye we would find the headquarters of Clan Donald in a town called Armadale. It fascinated us to learn from him that Bethune, frequently interchanged with the name Beaton, is a widely known name in Scotland, as is my middle name, Ruthvin. He told us of two blood brothers on Skye, one who used the name Bethune while the other used the name Beaton. He urged us to go there because he was certain that the Bethune family was part of Clan Donald. We could see Skye from Kyle of Lockhalsh, but we had to go back to Inverness to get our things.

A day later, we headed south to the town of Mallaig, a mainland town directly across a small bay from the town of Armadale. The beautiful Isle of Skye, easily visible from Mallaig, is irresistible. We caught the Caledonian MacBrayne ferryboat, and in less than thirty minutes we were on Skye looking for the B&B operator we had called earlier to arrange a room for the night.

She, plumpish and red-faced, spotted us and waved us over to a tiny, two-door, beat-up economy car. It would have been a challenge to get in the car if it had been empty, but there were two big dogs in it, barking and jumping from the front seat to the back. We were not surprised because almost every Scot has a dog or two, and they take them everywhere they go, even into the grocery markets. We had no choice because it was late in the day and we needed a place to sleep. We climbed in with the dogs, the fleshy woman, the smell, and the dog hairs and set off for her place in Armadale. It turned out that the B&B she advertised was nothing more than an extra bedroom in her small house. Lana and I gave each other a familiar look of resignation; it was another chance for us to follow G. K. Chesterton's counsel. We would rightly consider this inconvenience, thus turning it into an adventure. We managed to sleep, but our adventure ended abruptly at breakfast. Our hostess fed the dogs and us at the same time, their bowls being in the breakfast room. We ate a piece of toast, pulled on our backpacks, bid the dogs and the woman goodbye, and hiked to the Clan Donald Center.

The library at the center contains thousands of books covering all aspects of Scot culture, Highland history, and clan genealogies. Donald was the grandson of a medieval Gaelic hero. He gave his descendants and followers the name of MacDonald, and the clan exercised a powerful influence on Highland history. It is the largest clan in Scotland and Bethune descendants, including those who immigrated to the United States, are members of the clan.

When we introduced ourselves to an elderly attendant in the library, he said, "Ah, Bethune, a famous name." Then he pulled an ancient book from the shelf and showed it to us. Even though printed in 1778, the book—*The Bethunes of the Isle of Skye*—was in excellent condition. As we perused it and talked about my family the librarian confirmed the story the old man on the train told us about the two blood brothers, one using Bethune as his surname and the other using Beaton.

It intrigued me to hear about my ancestors. We also learned that the Bethune family ranged from the Isle of Skye to County Fife near Edinburgh, specifically Markinch Parish, where there stands a famous cottage built in 1837 by two Bethune brothers, Alexander and John.

The man then told the interesting story, well known to Scots, of Cardinal David Bethune, presumably an ancestor, who was born in Markinch. He played a large role as a Catholic leader in the history of sixteenth century Scotland when religious tensions gripped the land. In 1539, he became archbishop and took up residence in St. Andrew's Castle, the official residence of Scotland's leading prelates throughout the Middle Ages. His uncle, James Bethune, preceded him as archbishop and lived in the castle from 1521 to 1539. Cardinal David Bethune, with full backing from King James V, vehemently opposed the burgeoning Protestant Reformation. He had broad authority as papal legate of Scotland to stop the Reformation, and to that end he ordered the burning of a Protestant preacher, George Wishart on March 1, 1546.

Cardinal Bethune was widely despised for his arrogant and unrelenting method of governing and that led Wishart's sympathizers to knife him to death on May 28, 1546 in his chambers at St. Andrews castle. David Bethune's successor also opposed the Protestant Reformation, and for that and his support of Mary Queen of Scots, he went to the gallows. Soon thereafter, the episcopacy collapsed and the castle had no resident. It fell into disrepair and a big part of it fell into the ocean. A seawall constructed in 1886 saved the rest of the castle, which today is a huge tourist attraction.

I had never had much interest in genealogy, but our visit to the Clan Donald Center changed my mind. I vowed to learn more about my ancestors; the Bethunes were proving to be an interesting cast of characters.

The talk of religious turmoil and the Protestant Reformation led me to ask the old gentleman at the library what he thought about the declining influence of religion in Scotland and in Europe; a subject of lively debate in the United States. He just shook his head and said, "I know, I know, the churches are empty." He did not seem interested in pursuing the subject, so I did not ask more but promised myself to give more thought to the question as we continued our travels.

The old man changed the subject from religion to something near and dear to his heart, sheepdogs and sheepdog trials. The

Scots are famous for breeding, rearing and training sheepdogs, and several important trials occur annually on the Isle of Skye. He was excited about a trial that was taking place that day, not too far from the Clan Donald Center, and he invited us to go with him. We quickly accepted. It did not look too promising when we first arrived at the hillside field, but soon trucks and cars began to arrive and the Scots offloaded their dogs and took their positions. Just as the trials were about to begin, a cold rain started to fall, but no one complained. We watched in awe as the Highland shepherds put their dogs to work. It is a sight to see a herd of sheep brought a quarter of a mile from the top of a hill to a pen at the bottom. The shepherds will occasionally shout, but for the most part the dogs skillfully herd the sheep around a series of obstacles and into the pen in response to individualized whistling.

Shepherding is a traditional livelihood for Scots so deeply imbedded in the culture that today it is a beloved sport, and the Scots have their own special way to enhance the fun. We discovered the enhancement when we retreated to the only shelter, a dilapidated, unlighted wood shack with a leaky tin roof and a dirt floor. Inside the shack, no surprise, two men were pouring shots of single malt scotch whiskey for a nominal fee. There were about twenty wet Scots in the shack when we entered, and they were having a grand time. Several of them were wearing dark green, waxy looking raincoats with matching fedoras and they seemed to be the driest. Double doors swung open to the field, thus providing a little light for the bartenders and a view of the trials. It was the place to be. We joined in the fun and stayed for a few more trials but then it was time for us to leave. It was a stroke of luck to hear about the sheepdog trials and our good fortune turned into an afternoon of precious memories.

We said goodbye to the old Scot and headed to a small hotel, The Old Manse, for afternoon tea. The ancient hotel overlooks Loch Snizort Beag and has wonderful views of the mountains of the Isle of Skye. While there, we heard about a nearby graveyard with Bethune markers. We walked there and found several flat, full-length stones carved to look like knights in armor, inscribed with the name Bethune. Some dated back to the 1500s. It was spooky so we made a mental note of our findings and left after a few minutes.

We took a bus to the north end of the Isle of Skye to a town named Uig. There we caught the Caledonian MacBrayne ferry-boat for an hour and forty-five minute trip to Lochmaddy on the Island of North Uist, in the Outer Hebrides. The trip across the channel known as Little Minch was rough, cold, and wet. It was nearing dark when we got off the ferry and we asked the few people we could find if there was a B&B in the town. As it turned out, there was one woman in the town who occasionally rented rooms to strangers, but her place was full. We begged her to let us stay the night. Seeing our desperation, she set up a rollaway bed and we got a good night's sleep. The next morning our host served us a full Scot breakfast, complete with a serving of blood pudding. It was the first time anyone had put it on our plate, even though it is a staple for the Scots. I ate mine, but Lana did not eat hers. She later told me she would rather take a whipping than to take a single bite of blood pudding.

Later that day we made our way south by bus from North Uist to the island of South Uist. We saw workers cutting chunks of soil and the air was full of a sweet and pungent aroma. We consulted our guidebooks and learned that Outer Hebridians use peat for fuel. They go into a bog and cut out big chunks of peat. Then they cut the chunks into slices and set them out to dry naturally. When dry, the peat is ready to burn. They have been cutting, drying, and burning peat for centuries. The process typifies the hard life faced by the residents of the Outer Hebrides, where the wind blows so strongly that mothers tether little children to keep them from blowing into the sea.

It was mid-summer, cold and blustery, as our bus continued on south. I wondered if it was a typical summer day in the Outer Hebrides and soon got my answer. The bus stopped at an isolated place about half way down the island to pick up a single passenger who waved to the driver to stop. The new passenger was a lady who appeared to be eighty-five years old. She struggled on board, paid her fare and hung on for dear life as the driver started up, bouncing his way on down the road. The old lady worked her way down the aisle to a seat across from us, and plopped into it. Once settled, she let out a heavy sigh, looked at us, wiped her runny eyes, and in a sharp but finely tuned Hebridian brogue rolled out the words, "Rough day!" That is all she said. I turned to Lana and said, "That is one tough lady, if she says it is a rough day, it is a rough day!"

Later on, in Edinburgh, we climbed onto a crowded bus after a pleasant day at Princes Street Gardens. A young girl, perhaps fourteen years old, jumped up to give her seat to Lana. It was a new experience for Lana, who was only a few months from her fifty-third birthday. The good news was that the young Scot was respecting an elder but when it happened, Lana turned to look me in the eye and with a bit of pain said, "Oh dear."

We met interesting, friendly Scots everywhere we went, especially in the pubs and parks, but the best way to meet them is at a ceilidh (kay'-lay). These traditional, evening gatherings are usually informal, and we attended a lot of them. There may be a band, but those we attended, particularly in the smaller towns, featured two or three musicians who just wanted a place to play. People would dance or sing if the spirit moved them. Occasionally a piper would play a local tune or an old Scot would rise to recite a poem or tell a story. Some ceilidhs, those held on special occasions, are big and structured, but the best ones are not, they happen spontaneously for no particular reason. The Scots love a hometown ceilidh. It is their way to pass traditions and folklore to the next generation through storytelling and song. We loved them too.

In mid-July, we treated ourselves to a week of golf watching at The Open at the Old Course in St. Andrews. The best part of the week was our daily train trip to Dundee where we connected to a bus that took us to the course. There is nothing to compare with a trainload of Scots on their way to The Open. They jabber endlessly about the history of the game, recite statistics, and try to outdo each other with trivia. The discussions get louder as the beer and scotch disappear and reach crescendo when nearing the course. We watched all the practice rounds, and on the final day we followed Payne Stewart who was playing in the last twosome with Nick Faldo. When Stewart showed up to start play, a loud buzz ran through the big crowd seated in the bleachers next to the first tee. Payne was wearing his trademark four-plus knickers and country cap. They were blue, but his shirt was a replica of the American flag. He looked great to us, but a Brit seated near us said to his companion, "Hrrrrrumph! Slightly garish, don't you think?" We laughed and stood to cheer Payne Stewart. Payne matched Faldo shot for shot until he hit his ball into the Coffin Bunkers on the twelfth hole. It was his downfall. Faldo won by five strokes.

We left Scotland to visit England on our way to France. We spent most of our time in London tracking the Collier and Prewitt lineages, Lana's ancestral names. We learned the usual things you learn about surnames, but we did not hit pay dirt as we had at the Clan Donald Center on the Isle of Skye. We had the same poor result when we checked into my Lewallen and Vermilye lineages. We decided to shelve the genealogy project and come back to it later when we had more time.

We took the train to the coast and boarded a ferry that took us to the mainland of France. We went directly to Bayeux, a good-size town in Normandy, and made it our headquarters for ten days. On the first day, we saw the ancient Bayeux Tapestry, an embroidered scroll two-thirds the length of a football field that tells the story of the Norman Conquest of England led by William the Conqueror in 1066. Some historians say the conquest resulted in the spread of Norman families and French culture to England, Scotland, Ireland, and Wales. We had already planned, out of curiosity, to visit the town of Bethune near the northern border of Normandy. Our latest finding about the effect of the Norman Conquest gave us reason to think we might find a French connection to what we had learned about the Bethune family at the Clan Donald Center on the Isle of Skye.

We decided to resurrect our genealogy project long enough to investigate this new lead but first we would shift our focus to the main reason we came to Bayeux.

Bayeux is located near the beaches where Allied Forces stormed ashore on D-Day, June 6, 1944. On our third day in Bayeux, we hiked eleven kilometers to Arromanches-les-Bains, the place where British forces landed. A few days later, we caught a bus to the American Military Cemetery at Colleville-Sur-Mer. Seeing the rows and rows of white marble Crosses and Stars of David marking the graves of 9,387 American soldiers brought tears to our eyes and took us back to our childhood days when we heard reports of the D-Day invasion. We also visited Point du Hoc where 225 American Rangers scaled the cliffs to capture German guns that were a threat to our troops on Omaha Beach. The battle on the Point was so intense that we lost two-thirds of our troops. President Ronald Reagan called the Rangers "the boys of Point du Hoc," in a 1984 D-Day memorial speech. It is nearly impossible to write a proper tribute to those who give life and limb in a great cause but President Reagan found a way to do it. His touching remembrance, perfect in every way, captured the enormous sacrifice our American troops made to free Europe from the grip of Nazi Germany.

Exhausted from the emotion of our visit to the cemetery and Point du Hoc, we returned to Bayeux. We intended to get a bite to eat and then go to bed, but a small traveling circus had come to town while we were visiting the Normandy beaches. The newly erected circus tent was not as big as the ones I remember from my childhood, but it took up a good part of a wide intersection right in the middle of town. A barker was hustling up a crowd, and the colorful posters promised clowns, animals, and acrobats. It was all in French but we got the picture. It looked like fun and we could not resist. We bought tickets, entered the tent and found a place to sit. The tent quickly filled up with French men, women, and kids. A five-piece band played lively tunes and the clowns were doing what clowns do, making people laugh. A one-ring oval area, centered beneath the highest point of the tent, took up half the available space. Portable bleachers with ten rows of seats, enough for three hundred people, surrounded the oval performance area. The barker had done a good job; the place was full of screaming kids and grownups. It was loud, but cozy.

At the perfect moment, before excitement turned to restlessness, the ringmaster entered and commenced his introductory pitch. The band and clowns continued their work, complimenting the ringmaster's effort to bring the audience to a fevered pitch. He introduced the first act and the circus was underway. In came a horse with a standing rider followed by the monkeys, the trained dogs and the acrobats marching and preening themselves. It was a grand beginning and we soon realized that it did not matter that the performers and the audience were speaking French. A circus is a circus wherever it plays. The sights, smells, and sounds of a circus are universal.

As the performance progressed, we realized that this circus was a family operation. The ringmaster was the barker who hustled the crowd. He doubled as the dog trainer and elephant tender. The equestrians doubled as acrobats and we recognized one of the acrobats as the woman who had sold us our ticket to the circus. The clowns and band members doubled as stagehands, removing and setting up props for the next act. The same familiar faces kept showing up in different roles, and the same animals showed up in all the acts. Lana and I noticed familial resemblances and figured there were no more than eighteen people in the entourage. The funny thing is we enjoyed the little French circus more than the big name extravaganzas—Barnum & Bailey and Ringling Brothers—that came to Little Rock when we were kids.

We left Bayeux with warm memories and caught a train to Béthune, France. We seldom booked ahead, so when we got off the train we went to the first small hotel that looked presentable. The man who greeted us spoke no English so we had a bit of trouble with the formalities. He seemed to be asking me for my name so I kept saying, "Bethune. My name is Bethune." He, exasperated, kept responding, "No—not city—nom!" It finally occurred to me that he thought I was giving him the name of the town instead of giving him my name. I dug out my passport and showed it to him and he laughed. "Ah, Béthune (Bay-Tune) is nom," he said in broken English. We all laughed, and to humor him I pointed to myself and said my name as he had, "Ed Bay-Tune." He seemed pleased that he had taught me how to pronounce my own name, so we quickly finished the checking-in process. It was the second time in a month a stranger told me I did not know how to say my own name. The Scots told me I mispronounced Ruthvin, my middle name. It is a common name in Scotland. They put a heavy, guttural emphasis on the first syllable making it sound like "Rough." My parents taught me to make the first syllable sound like "Ruth." I liked the manly sound that the Scots give to Ruthvin. I might have used my middle name more if I had known how to pronounce it.

I am not especially fond of the French pronunciation of Béthune, but I used "Bay-Tune" for the rest of our time there because the French like it that way. *Que Sera, Sera.*

All roads lead to Paris, but before going there we took a brief detour to Neufchâtel-en-Bray, a town famous for its French Neufchâtel, a soft, crumbly, mold-ripened cheese that dates back to the sixth century. We tried the cheese and it was fantastic but the main reason for our visit was to see the Béthune River, a quaint stream that runs through the town. We had lunch by the river and I collected a few river rocks to take home as a reminder of the day.

Finally, we arrived in Paris. We stayed on Ile Saint-Louis a few blocks from Quai de Béthune, a waterfront street where Madam Marie Curie lived when she developed her theory of radioactivity. We now had three French connections to my surname: Quai de Béthune in Paris, the Béthune River in Neufchatel, and the city of Béthune in Normandy. We began to think there might be something to the belief that the Bethune lineage started in France and migrated to Scotland after the Norman Conquest in 1066. The possibility was interesting, but it would take a lot of research to prove, or disprove, the connection.

Our Paris visit started with the obligatory tours: Musée Louvre, Musée d'Orsay, Musée Rodin, Musée Orangerie, and other Paris treasures. In most cases, we were going over ground we had covered many times before, but who tires of seeing the magnificent artworks, the Eiffel Tower, the Arc de Triomphe, or strolling along the Champs-Elysée? These marvels always stir the passion and warm the heart. But we soon ended the sightseeing and turned our attention to the parks of Paris.

Going to any park in Paris is a wonderful experience, but we did it as young French lovers do. First you choose a park, and on the way you stop at a delicatessen-style shop, known to the French as a *charcuterie,* to choose a fancy sandwich or salad or a cut of cheese. Upon entering the park, you scout around, take possession of a nice grassy spot and spread your blanket. Then, you lie down and open a bottle of good French wine. When the spirit moves you, you dig into your sack of gastronomical delights. There is no greater joy on the face of the earth, although it helps to add a sweet from a *boulangerie* to the menu, and take a nap after lunch. We adopted the young lover technique as our own.

Much of our talk as we lounged about Paris was about our near-death experience on the high seas, especially the thirty-six hour jackhammering that finally caused me to surrender and adopt a God-centered worldview. I was finally on the right road with Lana, but ironically we kept running into Europeans headed in the *opposite* direction, toward a man-centered, secular worldview. The irony disturbed us. I wanted to scream at them in the way that Sergeant Lorres, my drill instructor in boot camp used to scream at me, "You people are going the wrong way—you should have been with us on *Salute.*"

I doubt it would have slowed them down. When we were on the Isle of Skye I had tried to discuss the issue of empty European churches with the old Scot at Clan Donald Center. It seemed to bother him but he did not want to talk about it, so he changed the subject to sheep dogs and sheep dog trials.

The subject of conflicting worldviews—sacred versus secular—intrigued us, perhaps because we had just been through a harrowing experience. We spent hours talking about our family and our future—all of which we would have missed if we had been lost at sea—but the empty church issue kept coming up. As a newly surrendered Christian, I was puzzled and I wanted answers. Fortunately, Lana was way ahead of me. She had studied the works of Francis Schaefer at Friday Group, Joanne Kemp's weekly Bible study, and her understanding of the subject kept us on track. During our Paris visit, we found attitudes ranging from total adoption of a secular worldview, to total indifference. Only a few seemed determined to reverse the obvious trend. Beyond that, when we tried to pin down the cause for the trend, we stumbled. There were too many factors at play. The question would take more time and study.

Two decades later, the picture is clearer. The secular trend has escalated and so has our understanding of it. The great cathedrals of Europe still stand, the laws and culture still recognize the long history of Christianity, but the congregations are shrinking and organized religion has lost its power and influence. Many people, particularly young Europeans, say they are religious, but it is something they are doing on their own. Their preference is to treat religion as a personal matter because that allows them to choose what they wish to believe, a sure formula for self-centeredness. In any cathedral, on any given Sunday, there are few people in the pews, and those who are there have grey hair. It is not a good sign for the future. Scholars propound a range of explanations. Secularists argue that religion gives way when society advances. They contend that the spiritual basis of organized religion cannot stand against the logic of modern intellectual and scientific developments. Other thinkers agree that something is happening but deny that religion is failing, pointing to places where organized religions, not necessarily Christianity, are growing and prospering, the clearest example being the spread of Islam in Europe.

The differing theories are interesting but the big picture is undeniable: Christianity is facing serious challenges from secular forces that are determined to push religion into a corner.

The secularists have made greater headway in Europe but their contentions are taking root in America, gaining ground on many fronts. The secular mindset has insinuated itself into our politics, movies, schools, music, television—virtually every aspect of modern life. Consider, for example, the widespread practice of scheduling sports activities for children on Sunday morning—soccer matches, swim meets, track meets, and other secular events. It is the modern way and, regrettably, very few parents resist. Left-wing politicians openly attack the "Christian Right" and "Religious Fundamentalists," spreading demeaning messages with mass mailings, and on television and radio with paid advertising. A more troublesome assault occurs when a religious issue is the subject of a news story. The media, always searching for controversy, report the Christian view and then report a contrary, secular view. Then, all too often, the media—professing fairness—will bias the report in favor of secularism.

Christians have the tools to compete and win this struggle, but we must remember our mission is not to win intellectual arguments. We have a higher calling. It is our duty—in all seasons, fair and foul—to spread the Gospel. It is a simple story. The logic of it, the ultimate proof of it, comes from the way believers live, by the example we set.

Long before the birth of Christ, the Chinese general, Sun Tzu said, "Know the enemy and know yourself; in a hundred battles you will never be in peril. When you are ignorant of the enemy but know yourself, your chances of winning or losing are equal. If ignorant both of your enemy and of yourself, you are certain in every battle to be in peril." We have had fair warning.

We are always sad when it is time to leave Paris but we wanted to stop in Edinburgh on our way back to Arkansas. When we were there in June, we learned that Edinburgh is the place to be in August.

In the wake of World War II, the Scots decided to hold an annual festival in August to enliven and enrich cultural life in Europe. In the beginning, The Edinburgh International Festival promoted opera, classical music, dance and theatre and participation was by invitation only. It was a huge success but as the years went by, free-spirited artists began to present unofficial performances. The public loved the impromptu unofficial events, referring to them as the "Fringe" events. By the time we attended the Edinburgh International Festival, the unofficial Fringe performances were organized and immensely popular. Nowadays, due to popular demand, there is a third tier of performances called, "Beyond the Fringe."

On any given day in August, there are hundreds of performances—Official, Fringe, and Beyond the Fringe. In a three-week period, we saw the Bolshoi ballet, the opera *Faust,* an all-Scot performance of *Treasure Island,* and the *Military Tattoo* at Edinburgh Castle. We also saw scores of Fringe events, most of which were good. We took in some events Beyond the Fringe, some great and some not so great. To complete our overdose of festival, we attended several pipe-band competitions in Princes Street Gardens, a beautiful park in the shadow of Edinburgh Castle.

The festival ended on September 2, and we headed back to Glasgow to spend two nights with Ian and Anne Grant before catching our return flight to the United States. Our sabbatical was over. Our European odyssey through Scotland, England, and France gave us a chance to sort out our experiences and get ready for our return to Searcy, where we hoped to rekindle the life we had before my election to Congress.

50

GOING HOME TO SEARCY

East and West, Home is best.
Charles Haddon Spurgeon

The rule of thumb in the modern world seems to be onward and upward. It is a good rule but we were tired of the rat race. We hungered to go back to Searcy, to be with our friends and close to our extended family. I wanted to reopen my old law office, hang out my shingle, and be the country-lawyer I was before providence took me to Washington, D.C. I had no clients and we were just about out of money, but none of that scared us. We had started from scratch before and we could do it again.

On September 10, 1990, we arrived in Searcy, home at last. We used the back room of my law office building as a temporary residence, and set up the front rooms for my law practice. I was open for business on September 12, 1990. I did everything I could to get the word out that we were back home and that I was ready to take new clients. The local paper and radio station ran stories of our return and I spent several days going to all the coffee shops and lunch places telling everyone that I was open for business and that I intended to handle all cases, large and small, just as I had before I went to Congress. I had high expectations. People knew me because I had represented them in Congress for six years, and I had a good reputation due to my successful record as a prosecuting attorney and general practitioner. I figured it would only take a couple of weeks to rebuild my practice and develop a positive cash flow. To my great surprise, it took much longer. The other lawyers in town were getting many new cases that would have come to me in the old days. That puzzled me so I began asking people why they did not ask me to handle their cases. I got a variety of answers, but the most common response was, "Gee, Ed, I didn't think you would handle anything that small." I readjusted my expectations. The only way I could overcome the mindset that I was not interested in the small stuff was to be patient and let the people see me handling run-of-the-mill legal work. Soon people saw that I was not "too good" to take their case and my business flourished. By December, we were confident enough that we bought a house that backed up to the Searcy Country Club golf course. We were back. All was well.

Returning was, for us, the right thing to do. We wanted to sort out all we had learned and experienced in high politics and on the high seas. Living in Searcy and rekindling the shared memories we had with old friends would give us that perspective. By the spring of 1991 we were back in the groove; we were ordinary Searcians once again.

We rejoined the First United Methodist Church of Searcy and settled into the comfortable routines of small town life.

As a newly surrendered Christian, I was amazed to discover that I was like a newborn baby. Before I surrendered my will—*really surrendered*—I thought I had a fair understanding of the Gospel and how it applied to my life. What a fool I was. Surrender is just the first step of a long journey. For much of my life I was so self-centered that I could only see the Bible as an important collection of beautiful stories and poetic thoughts, just a roadmap showing a good way to live. Now, with God in the center of my life, the same Bible was making perfect sense to me. I now saw Christianity as a comprehensive, consistent way to live, a worldview for the ages.

Nevertheless, it was apparent that I had a lot to learn, so it was good that we were home. I would have time for learning and introspection and I was close to Mother. It was time for the two of us to talk.

I had reached a new and different place in my life, and I was excited to tell Mother about it. I was also eager to go back in time and learn more about her childhood, her life with my father, and my own childhood. Seldom had we talked about our spiritual lives, our beliefs—it was not the Vermilye way.

51

MOTHER

A mother's love is indeed the golden link that binds youth to age; and he is still but a child, however time may have furrowed his cheek, or silvered his brow, who can yet recall, with a softened heart, the fond devotion or the gentle chidings of the best friend that God ever gives us.

Christian Nestell Bovee

In the 1980s, Mother became a celebrity. She first attracted attention when I was in Congress and we were dealing with the energy issue. There were long lines for gasoline at the filling stations, energy prices were climbing, and I was deeply engaged in formulating a national energy policy.

Energy conservation became a big political issue, so I decided to take a team of energy experts to Mother's house so that they could look it over and propose ways for her to lower her gas and electric bills. My idea for the well-publicized event was to help people in the Second District understand that there are many ways to conserve energy.

The experts spent an entire morning going from the attic to the cellar making notes about insulation, appliance use, caulking, lighting, heating and cooling. As they worked, they interacted with Mother to find out what she was doing to save energy. Soon, she was telling them more than they were telling her. She told them that she had never had air conditioning and showed them how she used a low energy attic fan and a variety of window openings to create a strong draft, pulling air from cool shady spots into the house. She told them how she did not have a clothes-dryer because she had always hung her laundry out to dry in the sun and she did not own a dishwasher because she washed her dishes in the sink. She told them how she always turned out the lights when she left a room, and so on. She was putting on a show and the media loved it. Then, caught up in the excitement, Mother started bragging that her most recent electric bill was only $16 and her gas bill was $6.80. Alarms went off in my politically attuned head. If she was exaggerating, it could be embarrassing. I pulled her aside and suggested she find her latest bills so we could correct the record if necessary. She said it would take too much time, but I insisted. She was not pleased with me, but she did locate the gas bill. It was $6.80. I asked if it was low because the prior month's bill had been too high, or something like that. By now, Mother was upset with me, and said, "No, Edwin! It was lower." She then showed me the previous month's bill. It was for $6.20. The experts were astounded, I was mad at myself for doubting her, and the media was lapping it up. Mother's tricks for saving energy got more coverage than the recommendations of the experts, although they had much good advice for people who were not as frugal as Mother.

In 1989, Ned Perme, the weather reporter at Channel 7, KATV, heard that Mother was an extraordinary gardener. I do not know how the word got around about Mother's green thumb, but I am not surprised that it did. Mother could grow anything, and she seldom did it in a conventional way. She was always inventing a new arbor, a new technique for planting, watering, fertilizing, weeding, or harvesting. She occasionally planted flowers, but her focus was vegetables. It was the Vermilye way, the practical way. Each winter, she would make what she called, "My schematic," a drawing of what she intended to do for her next garden. She could pack more information into her schematic than one could find in the *Farmer's Almanac.* She loved to talk about her garden, and using her schematic, she would tell about the "1990 model Big Boy Tomato," or the "1991 model butterbean," or "the Burpee Speckled Lima." Her garden was a work of art, perfect in every respect. On the side closest to her house, there was a small plaque with the verse: "He who works in a garden, works hand in hand with God."

Ned contacted Mother and quickly realized that she was a unique, interesting woman. He decided to do a weather report from her garden with the hope that it would add spice to his show. It did, so Ned and Mother worked out a plan for him to give his Wednesday weather reports from her garden. KATV called the segment, The Weather Garden, and a star was born. Mother loved every minute of the show, and she loved Ned Perme and the television crews who came to her house once a week. And they loved her. She made their work fun and surprised them each week with an eclectic array of newly baked treats such as her Jelly Bean Cake, or Broccoli Cornbread. The station managers were pleased, the viewers liked the chemistry of Ned and Mother, and the ratings for the Weather Garden were strong. All had a good time.

When I was in Congress people would ask Mother, "Are you Ed Bethune's mother?" It made her proud to say yes, but after I left Congress my celebrity status began to fade, and she did not get the question as often as she had when I was making news on a regular basis. When Mother started the Weather Garden show, I had been back in the private sector for several years. One day I went to the grocery store for Mother, and when I was checking out a woman said, "You look familiar, what is your name?" I said, "Ed Bethune," and she said, "Oh, are you Delta Bethune's son?" I was proud to say yes. How quickly things can change in the world of celebrity.

All during this time, Mother was living in the house where I grew up, 2309 State Street in Little Rock. Two young white men shared the house next door, but the residents in the rest of the neighborhood, for blocks around, were all black. Mother, no shrinking violet, was well known and respected by all her neighbors because she stayed when other whites fled to the suburbs.

She had a strong relationship with the black family that lived at 2305. When they barbequed meat they would give her some, and she gave them vegetables from her garden. When she spent a few days at St. Vincent's Hospital in 1991 her good neighbor, an elderly gentleman from 2305, was the first to visit her, and she got cards and calls from several other friends in the neighborhood.

Mother, with a few of her best tomatoes, getting ready for the Weather Garden show on Channel 7 with Meteorologist Ned Perme in 1991.

Mother's garden took up a large portion of the backyard where I used to play ping-pong-ball and work on my A-Model car, and to save on utilities she had closed off the upstairs. Otherwise, the place looked pretty much like it did when I was a little boy. Familiar paintings and photographs filled every wall and her masterpiece, an oil painting of two birddogs that she did in the 1920s, was still hanging next to her favorite sitting spot in the parlor. Every table and unused chair held at least one of her ongoing projects. Mother was always in the middle of knitting a sweater or an afghan, crocheting a doily, sewing something, or exploring some new way to paint. She always finished whatever she started, with one exception.

When she was seventy-five, she covered the north wall of the parlor with a huge piece of black velvet and began painting a landscape with fluorescent colors that would glow when illuminated by an invisible ultraviolet black light. Illuminated, the colors exploded. Un-illuminated the colors were drab. Either way it was hideous. Mother knew it was hideous, but she would never admit it. She just quit working on it, ignored it, and never took it down. She was no fan of failure.

Mother's projects always had a purpose. Piddling around to kill time was not her way; purpose was her way, the Vermilye way. If she knitted a small knickknack and liked it, she would fill it with candy and give it to a friend. If the friend liked it, Mother would knit a hundred duplicates, fill them with candy, and give them to friends and neighbors. I watched her do this, or similar projects, year in and year out, especially at Christmastime. She would knit or crochet for hours on end until she finished the project. She never ran short of determination and perseverance. Waste not, want not; where there is a will, there is a way—the good Vermilye traits came to perfection in Delta Bethune. She was predictably practical, a little standoffish, and you could never tell what she might say. Once, our daughter Paige brought a young man to meet Mother. When she opened the door, Mother grabbed his hand, enthusiastically shook it, and said, "Hi, Chip. How're you percolating?" The young man, stunned speechless, was not her first victim.

When I ran for Congress, Mother was working for the U. S. Department of Agriculture at the federal building on Capitol Avenue. The elevators were usually crowded, particularly in the morning. Mother saw it as a great opportunity to give each person on the elevator one of my colorful campaign brochures, featuring a photo of me and a list of my accomplishments. Her zealous method soon attracted the attention of a longtime Democrat who also worked at the federal building. He challenged Mother one day on the elevator, saying, "Mrs. Bethune, this is a federal building and you cannot hand out political cards; it is against the law." There was a moment of silence and a gasp or two from others in the crowded elevator. They empathized with Mother and the confrontation made them uncomfortable. The slight hesitation was all the time Mother needed. She gave a defiant look to the Democrat and said, "I'm not handing out political cards, I am handing out pictures of my son." With that, Mother continued to hand out my brochures. It was a perfect squelch, and such a good story that it spread throughout the federal building which, of course, is the best thing that can happen in a political campaign.

For me growing up, Mother was an enigma. She loved me, but she was a tough taskmaster, and the Vermilye credo all too often got the best of her. On those occasions, it was best to stand clear and wait for a better time but as she aged Mother changed, and it was a change for the better. She jettisoned the bad parts of the Vermilye worldview and adopted many of the softhearted Bethune family traits.

I had also changed. I was a difficult kid and took a torturous path to manhood, but in my fifties I began to mellow. The time had come for us to talk about our spiritual lives, our beliefs—better late than never.

Within days of our return from Europe in 1990, I drove to Little Rock to see Mother. I was eager to tell her about my sailing experience and my surrender to Jesus. I wanted to tell her how it happened and what it meant to me. I also wanted to go back in time and talk about her childhood, her life with Daddy, and my early years.

When I got to her house, I gave her a hug and we sat down in the parlor. The big black, hideous velvet landscape was still there, but the thing that got my attention was the television set. Mother was watching Pat Robertson's *700 Club*, something I had never known her to do. What a perfect entrée to start a conversation about faith. I asked her if it was a regular thing, and before

I could use the occasion to tell of my commitment to Jesus, she told me of hers. I laughed and said, "Well, we are finally on the same wave length." I told how it had taken thirty-six hours of jackhammering on the high seas, but I finally made the decision to surrender my will to God's will. She said her decision was incremental. Her interest in the *700 Club* led her to attend services at Quapaw Quarter United Methodist Church, the same church she sent my sister and me to when we were kids. Back then, it was Winfield Methodist Church, but Winfield had moved to West Little Rock. Mother told me she was happy at Quapaw, but she made it clear that Pat Robertson was the one who got through to her, and she took a friendly poke at me, saying, "He didn't need a jackhammer to do it." She said it was surprisingly easy for her, even after years of resistance. Once she got on the right road, she realized she was ready to surrender her powerful, Vermilye will to The Almighty. I expect health issues and the mellowing that comes with old age set the stage for her surrender, as it does with so many people. But in the end Mother, the strongest willed woman I ever met, surrendered her will to the will of God.

Our witness to each other that day was a magical moment. Many times after that we talked about her childhood, her life with Daddy, and my early years, the things I wanted to know more about. Our talks were happy moments, but there were some painful moments. We talked about the Vermilye way and how it differed from the Bethune way, and, yes, we talked about the divorce, and we talked about Daddy. Mother loved Daddy and she knew that he loved her. We had a good laugh about the time when Daddy hired a maid to help Mother and she said it made her feel like the "Queen of Sheba." Mother respected his intellect and his good heart but she could not handle Daddy's tendency to dream and do the impractical. In the end, we realized these things no longer mattered. It was a new day for both of us, a time to understand and forgive.

Mother held back in one area. She still could not talk about the death of her younger brother, Little Gerle. When I asked her about it, she clammed up. She just repeated what she had always said, "Little Gerle died of diphtheria when I was nine." His death was still too painful to discuss. Before she died, Mama Lewallen told me how Little Gerle's death caused Mother—a warm, loving little girl—to surround herself with a shell as hard as steel. Mother's unwillingness to talk about it convinced me that Mama was right; the gruesome death had hurt Mother deeply. It definitely changed her, but now she was back to where she started, warm and loving. Her hard shell dissolved completely when she surrendered her will to God. I never again asked her about Little Gerle; there was no need to.

I also held back a little. I told Mother that I had visited Daddy's grave many times and that I had wonderful memories of him and our life as a family, but I never said how much it hurt me when they separated and later divorced. I did not need to, nor did I want to. I think she knew and it did not matter, now that we had forgiven all and moved on.

My lifelong attempt to reconcile the many conflicts between the Vermilye worldview and the Bethune worldview vanished. My struggle to choose between the two was over the instant I surrendered my will and adopted a God-centered worldview. I was making real progress, getting square with Mother, better understanding her and myself. I was beginning to think I had solved the great riddle of my life, but then I discovered that I had only just begun. There was more for me to do. The path to salvation is free and simple, but there is a cost to being a good disciple. New duties and challenges come with that territory. Once again, G. K. Chesterton challenged me from the grave: An inconvenience is an adventure wrongly considered, and an adventure is an inconvenience rightly considered. All my life I have been a dreamer and an adventurer. Why stop now, I asked myself. The Christian walk would be the greatest adventure of my life.

❧

52

FAMILY HAPPY, FAMILY SAD

Man is fond of counting his troubles, but he does not count his joys. If he counted them up as he ought to, he would see that every lot has enough happiness provided for it.
Fyodor Dostoevsky

In May of 1990, just before we left on our ill-starred sailing trip, Chris Nassetta, a fine young man, came to me and asked for my daughter's hand in marriage. It was not a surprise. He had had his eye on Paige from the moment we moved to Arlington, Virginia in 1978.

Paige made quite a splash when she transferred to Yorktown High School from Searcy High School. The boys at Yorktown were talking about her good looks, but before any of the students had a chance to get to know her, a huge snowstorm piled deep banks of snow and ice around our new house. We could not get out of our driveway, and we were so new to the area that we did not know who to call for help. As soon as the snow stopped, a seventeen-year-old kid turned into our driveway with a snowplow on the front of his Jeep. It was Chris Nassetta. He rang our doorbell and told Lana that he was "just in the neighborhood and saw that we needed someone to plow our driveway." Lana, not knowing him, naturally asked how much he would charge, and he said, "Oh, nothing, I just wanted to help out." He did not fool Lana. It took only a couple of questions for her to figure out that Chris wanted to meet Paige, and that is how it started. They dated off and on for several years, and on May 11, 1991, they were married and we could not have been happier. Chris was the fourth child in a family of three boys, and three girls. His mother and father are our dear friends, and have been since we first met them. At the wedding in St. Michaels, Maryland, I gave my daughter's hand to Chris. Later at the reception Paige and I danced the first dance as the band played "Wind Beneath My Wings," the song she chose.

After the wedding Lana and I hustled back to Arkansas. I was busy being a country lawyer and she was selling real estate in and around Searcy. Lana always made time to visit her mother who was retired and living alone in Little Rock, and I had many good visits with Mother, but she was not well, her heart was getting weaker by the day.

It was only a question of time. Mother—the Queen of Sheba, the predominant influence in my life, the Vermilye to Bethune convert, the television star, the fully surrendered Christian—died June 7, 1992.

She slipped away on a Sunday morning. Only God knows her last thoughts, but I know what was on her mind as my sister and I sat with her through the night at St. Vincent's Hospital. Mother was in and out of consciousness, sometimes she would be out for as much as half an hour, but it was usually less. Her moments of consciousness never lasted long, but when they came, Delta Lew and I would listen and then tell her, "We're right here, Mother. We love you." She would squeeze our hands and say she loved us too. Then, without fail, she would say, "There's a little white fence with a gate, and there is Little Gerle." Throughout the long night, the three of us repeated the same script—over and over—and toward morning, we all got louder and louder as if Mother was moving away from us, which she was.

As Mother lay dying, I thought of what Mama Lewallen had told me about Mother and Little Gerle, how they were so close, and how his gruesome death was so painful for her.

My sister and I knew Mother's vision of Little Gerle was a vital step for her to take. Since 1919, Mother would say Little Gerle's name as part of her rote response that he died when she was nine, but she never ever brought his name up in any other way. It was as if he never existed. It was her way to defend against the painful memory of that day when the strangling angel of children filled his throat with the thick, gray membrane of diphtheria.

Never again will I question the extent to which a traumatic event can warp a child's mind. In Mother's case, the damage and pain stayed with her from 1919 to 1992, frozen in place.

Now, my dying Mother was making her final surrender, and as her life ebbed away, she was seeing her little brother. In her mind she and Little Gerle were together again. Soon, they would play again in Marr Creek, run helter-skelter through the carnival, and watch Baseball Man put up the World Series scores on the square in Pocahontas.

Mother rallied for a little while on Sunday morning before she died. It was a fine moment. Most of the family was there in her room and Ned Perme came by too. We all knew it was time to say our goodbyes and Mother knew it too. She sat up in bed, put on a cheerful face and "held court" for a few minutes, determined to see a smile on our faces, to see us happy. It was a brave and fitting finish. The nurse came in and asked if she was ready for a shot of pain medicine. Mother said yes and soon she was asleep, never to awake.

It was a comfort to Delta Lew and me to see Mother remembering and talking about Little Gerle. It told us that the long spell was broken; she was finally free of the demons that had haunted her from childhood. It was also significant that Mother told Delta Lew to be sure that her obituary explained that she was the widow of Edwin R. Bethune, Senior. She wanted to say, we preferred to believe, that she loved and respected Daddy and she wanted people to remember her as a softhearted Bethune, not a hardheaded Vermilye.

KATV ran a special on the evening news telling how Mother had built up a loyal following for her weekly visits with Ned

Perme in her backyard garden. They told how her garden was crammed to capacity with just about every vegetable that will grow in the Central Arkansas climate. They had fun reporting how Mother and Ned Perme had made a running joke out of her determination to get Ned to eat exotic vegetables he had never tried before.

Ned Perme made a touching personal tribute to Mother that brought tears to the eyes of her loyal fans. He ended up saying, "Delta is now helping the Good Lord tend the ultimate garden."

Delta Lew and I talked often about Mother after she was gone, and we talked about Daddy just as much. Never has there been a sister as loyal, loving and dedicated as Delta Lew was to me. She put her life on hold to mother me. After she graduated from Little Rock Senior High School, she moved to Pocahontas, took an entry-level job, and devoted herself to helping me morph from an incorrigible child to a kid with promise. Little did we know, as we talked after Mother's death in 1992, that Delta Lew did not have long to live. It was a blessing, however, that she was here long enough to enjoy a few more happy family events.

Lana and I worried after my election to Congress in 1978 that our children would have a hard time making the move from Searcy to Arlington, Virginia. They had gone through all the grades of school in Searcy. Paige was in the middle of the eleventh grade and Sam was in the middle of the tenth. It would not be an easy transition. Fortunately, they had new Arkansas friends who were in the same boat with them. Beryl Anthony had just won the Fourth District seat in Congress, and David Pryor had just won a seat in the United States Senate. Beryl, David, and I had been classmates in college and law school at the University of Arkansas in Fayetteville. We were a lot alike except for the fact that I was a Republican and Beryl and David were Democrats. Beryl had two daughters, David had two sons who were school age, and we were all moving to the Washington, D.C. area at the same time.

The kids got together often for marathon-length games of Monopoly. They were inseparable for the first few months, and that gave them time to make new friendship and acclimate to their new surroundings.

It was quickly apparent that Beryl's daughter Alison had a crush on Sam. He was ahead of her in school, but that did not slow her down. Soon she and Sam were dating and they developed an on and off relationship that continued for years.

Eventually, the time was ripe for Sam and Alison. Sam proposed marriage, Alison said, "Yes," and a wedding date, October 10, 1992 was set. A happy ceremony at St. Luke's Episcopal Church in Hot Springs, Arkansas, preceded a gala reception at the Arlington Hotel.

When Lana and I got to the church, the young ushers were having entirely too much fun. We quickly determined why that was so. Ordinarily, ushers will ask guests whether they wish to sit on the bride's side of the church or the groom's side of the church. Since this was a bipartisan wedding, the ushers had stopped asking, "Bride or Groom?" Instead, they asked the arriving guests, "Republican or Democrat?" It turned out to be a good way to welcome folks, and everyone seemed to enjoy it.

A large number of Democrat and Republican notables attended the wedding ceremony and the reception but most of those who came could have cared less about politics. They were longtime friends and family. Governor Bill Clinton was not in attendance because he was running for president and it was only three weeks to Election Day. His mother, Virginia, did come and when I saw her at the reception, I pulled her aside and said, "You are three weeks away from every mother's dream." It was clear at that time that Clinton was going to win the election, thanks to the candidacy of Ross Perot, an independent who siphoned votes from George H.W. Bush. She beamed, and we talked for a few minutes about the wedding and our hope that Sam and Alison would have a good and happy marriage.

Three weeks later Bill Clinton won the election. He would be the forty-second president of the United States.

I was somewhat concerned that Clinton's election was a setback for the Republican party, but for the most part I was determined to keep my focus on taking care of my law practice in Searcy. My first responsibility was to my clients, and I was happy to focus on something other than politics.

No one outside of Arkansas paid much attention when Lieutenant Governor Jim Guy Tucker moved up to be governor of Arkansas the day Clinton vacated the seat to take the office of president. They paid less attention when a political unknown, Mike Huckabee, won a special election to fill the seat vacated by Tucker. In winning the race for lieutenant governor, Huckabee became only the fourth Republican to win a statewide race since Reconstruction. His victory would matter later.

As 1993 rolled around, Lana and I bought a thirty-three-foot sailboat, *Greensleeves*, and immediately sailed her into the Atlantic Ocean on a blue water trip from Fort Lauderdale to Charleston, South Carolina. It was a belated application of the hair of the dog that bit you remedy. A few months later, my son Sam and I made another blue water trip on *Greensleeves*. It was exciting to be back on the high seas but it did not compare with our next adventure.

We were about to become grandparents! Our daughter Paige was pregnant and the baby was due in May, the birth month of Paige and Sam. Everything went smoothly and on *Cinco de Mayo*—May 5, 1993—Bailey Alexandra Nassetta was born. We were there, of course.

Then, on October 25, 1993, Sam and Alison became the parents of a baby girl, Amy Nicole Bethune. We drove all night from Searcy in an effort to be on hand for the delivery, but Nicole would not wait on us. We got to the hospital in St. Mary's County, Maryland a few hours after she was born. Now we had two granddaughters. It never occurred to us that we might wind up with eight granddaughters, but that is exactly what happened over the course of the next ten years.

The joy of witnessing new life occurred against a backdrop of sadness, of sickness, and death. My sister, Delta Lew, died on December 23, 1993, a victim of lung cancer. It was painful to watch the chemotherapy take her hair, the sickness from it take her flesh, and the cancer take her life. She, the most beautiful girl ever, the one who sacrificed so much to help me, just wasted away.

Delta Lew did not live to see her own grandchildren, but she did get to see our first granddaughter, Bailey, who she lovingly called, "Chunk." When she died, her husband, Bill, arranged a private family burial in Little Rock because that is what she wanted. It was her way to live inconspicuously, devoting herself to family first, last, and always.

Throughout the joy and sadness of the early 1990s, I was doing my best to learn and grow as a believer and disciple of Christ. The first part, believing and surrendering may take longer, as it did in my case, but it is simple compared to the second part, discipleship.

Once I was in the fold, I learned that I had to get rid of the idea that I could figure out, on my own, how to conform to God's purpose. That is nothing more than ego, self, and pride. I would have to be patient and let God explain things to me as I was able to understand them, and that does not come all at once. I was going to have to study and pray to get to where God wanted me to be. Some call it the "process" of sanctification to illustrate that it is not an overnight thing, and that is a good description. Sanctification is a lifelong effort that comes to a screeching halt every time pride shows up. I was learning, the hard way (my specialty) that Jesus cannot teach me a thing until I get rid of those barriers.

53

POLITICAL UPHEAVAL AND GRANDDAUGHTERS

A revolution is an idea which has found its bayonets.
Napoleon Bonaparte

Clinton's popularity as the newly elected president of the United States was not to last. He misread his mandate and overreached, just as he had done when he, at age thirty-two, became governor of Arkansas. As the youngest governor in the country, he surrounded himself with liberals, made some unpopular decisions, and the people of Arkansas booted him out of office after only two years.

It was a mistake for President Clinton to empower his wife, Hillary Clinton, to head up an effort to reform healthcare. Opponents called it a big-government, liberal takeover of healthcare. The brand stuck and Clinton's initiative became known as HillaryCare. The effort failed, the voters were upset, and Clinton paid for it in the next election.

There were other reasons for what was about to happen. The Republican party united conservative and independent voters behind their Contract with America, a pledge that panned HillaryCare and argued, among other things, that the House of Representatives was under the control of corrupt leaders.

On Election Day, 1994 the Republican party gained a majority of seats in the House of Representatives for the first time since 1954. There was a fifty-four-seat swing in membership from Democrats to Republicans. The Democrats had run the House of Representatives for all but four of the preceding sixty-two years.

Virtually overnight Lana and I found ourselves questioning the wisdom of staying in Searcy. My law practice was going well, and we were thoroughly happy with life in small town Arkansas, but now there were new factors to consider.

We had two granddaughters living in the Washington, D. C. area, and more were on the way.

The Republican takeover of the House, with Newt Gingrich scheduled to be speaker, created a real opportunity for me and I had an outstanding offer to join the Washington office of a prestigious Texas law firm as a partner.

For us, it came down to this: If I could make a living in Washington and we could be close to our grandchildren, why not go?

Once again, we pulled up stakes. I became a partner at Bracewell & Patterson (later Bracewell & Giuliani) and handed my Arkansas law practice over to Russ Hunt, a former FBI agent, who had joined my practice a year earlier.

We moved into a condominium that gave us an inspirational view of the Potomac River and all the major monuments. I worked at the law firm and Lana began to sell real estate in the Northern Virginia area. We were not getting any younger, and since I had refused to take the congressional retirement benefit, we needed to start preparing financially for our retirement years.

Our move to Washington got us there just in time to witness the birth of our third granddaughter, Mason Ellis Nassetta, on January 31, 1995, an event that confirmed the wisdom of our decision to return.

On Easter Sunday, April 7, 1996 our daughter, Paige converted to Catholicism. All Nassetta family members are Roman Catholics and have been for eons. Paige wanted to raise her children in the Christian faith, and she did not want them distracted by debates over which church has the best approach.

Christians have debated the differences between one church and another for centuries, and in spite of the violent opposition to Protestantism of our presumed ancestor, Cardinal David Bethune, the Bethune family switched to Protestant somewhere along the way. The arguments about church doctrine continue, but for me there is but one concern: Is the church—Catholic or Protestant—united and is there a shared love of Jesus Christ?

Lana and I attended the service that Easter Sunday. When it was over, I placed in my daughter's hands the crucifix that Pope John Paul II had blessed when he placed it in my hands at the Vatican in 1982. It was a special moment.

The granddaughters kept coming. On May 21, 1996, Alison gave birth to Olivia Lee Bethune. Our son's second daughter was born on his birthday, the best birthday present a father could ever have.

Then it was Paige's turn again. Kirby Marie Nassetta was born on November 27, 1997. Sydney Paige Nassetta was born on November 25, 1999 and Peyton Lynley Nassetta was born on March 21, 2001. Fittingly, our son-in-law, Chris Nassetta, got a new boat and named her *Another Girl.*

Life is not all joy, there are always moments of sadness. Lana's mother, Mary Lou Douthit passed away on October 9, 2002. She did not live to see her eighth great-granddaughter, Avery Frances Nassetta, born August 15, 2003.

Meanwhile, the Republican Party of Arkansas was growing, but not as fast as in other southern states. Bill Clinton's remarkable victory over President George H. W. Bush in 1992 created what I called the "Clinton Interregnum." His election to the presidency brought a natural outpouring of state pride and provincialism that slowed but did not stop Republican progress in Arkansas.

Republicans Tim Hutchinson and Jay Dickey won seats in the United States House of Representatives in 1992. Dickey's amazing victory was the first for a Republican in the Fourth District since Reconstruction. Then in 1996, Tim Hutchinson won a seat in the United States Senate. His brother, Asa, won the House seat that Tim vacated to run for the Senate.

On July 15, 1996, Lieutenant Governor Mike Huckabee, a Republican, became governor of Arkansas. He moved into the position when Governor Jim Guy Tucker resigned due to a criminal conviction arising out of the Whitewater investigations. The unexpected turn of events was embarrassing for the state, but Huckabee handled the sad moment with dignity.

On November 5, 1996 in a special election to fill the seat vacated by Huckabee, Arkansans elected Win Paul Rockefeller, the son of Governor Winthrop Rockefeller. He served with distinction as lieutenant governor until July 16, 2006 when he tragically succumbed to a fatal blood disorder.

Huckabee proved to be a popular governor, so much so that the people elected him to a full four-year term as governor in 1998. In that election he got the largest percentage of the vote ever received by a Republican gubernatorial nominee in Arkansas. He was re-elected to another four-year term in November 2002.

In all, Mike Huckabee served ten years and six months as governor. The Republican Party of Arkansas gained stature and strength during his tenure.

On August 6, 2001, Congressman Asa Hutchinson vacated his seat in the House to become administrator of the Drug Enforcement Administration. John Boozman, who would later win a seat in the United States Senate, succeeded Asa.

Elsewhere in the political sphere, Arkansas Republicans were winning hundreds of positions at the county and state legislative level. Hard working volunteers and financial supporters from all walks of life were growing the party. The newcomers took over for the intrepid few—most are gone, but not forgotten—who worked so hard to build the party when the political ground was hard as a brickbat.

We were not in the state for most of Huckabee's governorship, but he and all the others who joined the Republican effort made us proud. It was extremely satisfying to see the growth of a two-party system in Arkansas.

Finally, in 2010, the maturity of the Arkansas Republican party reached new levels and everyone, even partisan Democrats, conceded that Arkansas had become a legitimate two-party state. Tim Griffin of Little Rock won the congressional seat I once held, the Second District of Arkansas. Steve Womack of Rogers won the Third District seat in Congress. And, for the first time since Reconstruction a Republican, Rick Crawford of Jonesboro won the First District seat in Congress.

Speaker-to-be John Boehner came to Little Rock during the 2010 campaign to help our candidates for Congress.

Statewide, Congressman John Boozman defeated incumbent Senator Blanche Lincoln. We had a fine candidate for governor, Jim Keet. I chaired his campaign but he came up short in a gallant effort to oust the incumbent Democrat, Mike Beebe. Mark Darr became lieutenant governor; Mark Martin became secretary of state and John Thurston became land commissioner. To top off the stunning political upheaval, Republicans reached historic highs in the state Senate and the state House of Representatives.

54

ANOTHER NEW CAREER

Damn with faint praise, assent with civil leer, and without sneering teach the rest to sneer. Willing to wound and yet afraid to strike, just hint a fault, and hesitate dislike.
Alexander Pope

When I first joined the Washington, D.C. office of Bracewell & Giuliani in 1995, I worked on a number of government relations issues. I represented Alltel, a Little Rock-based telephone company, and I continued my work for the FBI Agents Association. There were other clients, but it was not long before I took on a new role, one that would continue for more than a decade. Members of Congress started retaining me to represent them when someone accused them of violating a law or ethical code of conduct.

I was a natural for this work because of my background as an FBI agent, a prosecutor, a defense attorney, and a recognized expert in criminal procedure but most importantly, I was a trusted former colleague with Ethics Committee experience.

Members knew that I had represented Newt Gingrich in 1989 when Bill Alexander, the Arkansas Democrat, filed a ten-count ethics complaint against Newt alleging over four hundred instances of misbehavior. It took a few months, but the bipartisan committee found no violations and dismissed Alexander's complaint saying it did not warrant a formal inquiry. It was a shameless attempt to use the ethics process for revenge and to belittle Newt, solely because he had instigated an ethics investigation that ultimately forced Speaker Jim Wright, a Democrat, to resign. Alexander's ethics charge failed miserably, but he and the Democrats fed story after story to the media to get what they wanted; headlines suggesting Newt had done something wrong when he had not.

There is a serious fault in the congressional ethics process. It derives from the disingenuous nature of political warfare. The rotten, devious attitude permeating our current system is like that described in 1734 by Alexander Pope (see quote above) in his "Epistle to Dr. Arbuthnot." There are many examples to prove my assertion that the congressional ethics process has degenerated into a partisan tool, but one sordid episode stands above all others.

The Democrats went after Newt Gingrich again in 1994, this time alleging that he violated campaign finance and tax laws by establishing a college course called "Renewing American Civilization." He had not, and that was the ultimate finding of the Ethics Committee.

In the course of the protracted inquiry the top Democrat on the Ethics Committee, Congressman Jim McDermott, a Democrat from the state of Washington, was doing everything he could to hurt Newt. His conduct got so bad that Jim Bunning of Kentucky, a Republican member, resigned from the committee saying, "He [McDermott] has poisoned the well for that committee forever."

An example of McDermott's poison showed up in the first days of January 1997. Congressman John Boehner was traveling in Florida and used his cell phone to join a telephone conference call for Republican leaders of the House of Representatives. The purpose of the private conference was to discuss what Republican leaders could do and not do in connection with Newt's campaign for reelection as speaker of the U. S. House of Representatives.

A Florida couple—monitoring transmissions from a nearby cell phone tower—intercepted Boehner's connection and tape-recorded the conference call. They soon realized that the call involved Speaker Newt Gingrich, me as the speaker's lawyer, and other Republican leaders and we were discussing the heavily publicized ethics case. At that point, they gave the tape recording to a Democrat member of Congress from Florida.

The ill-gotten tape eventually found its way to McDermott who released it to *The New York Times* for the express purpose of biasing the case that he, as the top Democrat on the Ethics Committee, had sworn to judge fairly.

On January 10, 1997, *The New York Times* ran a front-page story reporting verbatim excerpts of the telephone conference call. The story said a Democrat congressman hostile to Newt Gingrich had given a transcript of the tape recording to the newspaper.

During the conference call, I was explaining what the leaders could say and not say about the pending ethics case while Newt was running for reelection as speaker of the House. My guidance to the Republican leaders was all about how to obey the rules. It was perfectly appropriate, but the Democrats tried (unsuccessfully) to spin our conference call as a nefarious violation of the committee process. The incident backfired on the Democrats because it showed how partisan Jim McDermott had become. His breach of duty revealed his willingness to deprive an accused of a fair and impartial trial. The incident forced McDermott to resign four days later from the Ethics Committee. Later on, John Boehner sued McDermott and recovered a sizeable judgment. The Ethics Committee then found McDermott to be in violation of the rules, but did nothing about it.

In the early stages of the ethics case, Newt signed a letter to the Ethics Committee that omitted a fact that should have been included. The omission was the fault of another lawyer Newt had hired to prepare the letter. Other documents proved that Newt was not personally trying to keep anything from the committee; nevertheless, he took responsibility for the lawyer's error and agreed to accept a reprimand and reimburse the committee for the cost it incurred. That ended the matter.

Congress needs a way to deal with members who have violated laws or codes of conduct, but the current system is failing. It is too ponderous and subject to manipulation. Most of all it is hard for a member of Congress accused of an ethics violation to get a fair hearing. The incident involving Congressman Jim McDermott is an egregious example of how partisanship can infect the ethics process, but there are other reasons the system is not working.

In the real world if a person has committed a civil or criminal wrong, a trial is held in a court, and the lawyers and litigants are bound to follow rules of procedure and evidence that are designed to produce a fair trial, one that is unbiased by irrelevant, prejudicial information.

A congressional ethics proceeding, on the other hand, is wide open to bias. It can come from partisans, on both sides of the aisle, who make public comments designed to stoke hatred and prejudice. In the extreme, bias can come from the likes of Jim McDermott, a partisan willing to bias a case even though he is sitting in judgment of a colleague with an express duty to be fair and impartial. It can come from the media, who seem ever eager to write stories full of innuendo but short on facts. It can come from organized outside groups that claim to be nonpartisan, but which are led by people with long records of partisanship. All these forces, usually obvious, occasionally subtle, are at play when someone files an ethics complaint against a member of Congress.

All told, I spent twelve years representing members of Congress in matters subject to the jurisdiction of the Ethics Committee. While in that position, I had a rare chance, as the Republican "Go-to-Guy" for ethics issues, to view it from a unique perspective. I saw how partisans, locked in a great struggle for political power, are willing to use the ethics process to portray colleagues as criminals when they are not. More often than not, they exaggerate and distort the way politicians raise campaign funds alleging that a member of Congress has sold out to special interests. This pharisaic twist occurs even though the U.S.

Supreme Court has repeatedly recognized that raising campaign money is—whether we like it or not—part of the American political process.

My friend and client Tom DeLay was the victim of such hypocrisy. He went through two years of Hell with the partisan Democrats doing everything they could to make him look bad. In the end, the Ethics Committee found that he had not violated a single law or House rule but doing what it does best, the committee invented a new procedure and issued a fifty-six page, carefully worded report attempting to justify its recommendation that Tom deserved admonishment. The report proved only that Tom was doing the same kind of things that many members do. In a fitting touch of irony, the Ethics Committee concluded that Chris Bell, the disgruntled member of Congress who had filed the charges against Tom, *did* violate a rule of the House because he knowingly made false and exaggerated allegations in his complaint.

Tom, as I write this memoir, is still the subject of a political prosecution in Texas that also concerns campaign fundraising. Texas lawyers have represented Tom in that case, and I hope it will ultimately be resolved in his favor by the Texas Appeals Court. Meanwhile, the entire episode has destroyed his career and ruined his reputation.

55

THE GOLDEN YEARS

The first half of life consists of the capacity to enjoy life without the chance; the last half consists of the chance without the capacity.
Mark Twain

Lana and I have tried to turn Mark Twain's quote upside down. We created chances to enjoy life when we were young, and we have refused to be scared out of taking chances now that we are older. Why should we—young or old—not live life to the fullest?

On December 19, 2005, my seventieth birthday, we made another dramatic change, this time in our work. I left Bracewell & Giuliani and the law practice to devote my energy to writing and political matters. At the same time, Lana left the real estate business to focus on her emerging career as an artist (her latest work, *The Snotgreen Sea*, adorns the cover of this book).

Our new ventures would also give us more time to enjoy our eight granddaughters. I could always go back to the practice of law if we needed money or if an interesting case came along.

The first thing we did was no surprise to our family, our friends, or us. We took a cruise to Fort Lauderdale, Florida. In a small concession to advancing age, we swapped our second sailboat, *Greensleeves*, for a forty-foot trawler, a slow moving motor vessel that averages about seven knots an hour.

It is a twelve hundred mile trip on the Intracoastal Waterway so—to beat the cold weather—we moved our boat from the Chesapeake to Fernandina Beach on the Georgia-Florida border in September before I left the law firm in December.

True sailors mock the transition from a sailboat to a "stinkpot" as "going over to the dark side." In spite of that, we figured to live on board *Coaster* and cruise the East Coast for four months, making stops at interesting places on the trip south as well as on our return to the Chesapeake.

The Intracoastal Waterway is a national treasure, a navigable waterway that uses a few well placed manmade canals to connect natural inlets, saltwater rivers, bays, and sounds. It gives mariners an inside, protected route up and down the East Coast. The waterway allows boats to avoid many of the hazards of travel on the open sea, but that is not to say that travel on the waterway is a piece of cake.

In North Carolina, the Albemarle Sound and the Cape Fear River can turn a pleasant cruise into a nightmare in a matter of hours. The same is true for the swift tidal currents and narrow channels in South Carolina and Georgia. We have traveled these dangerous waters many times, and we long ago concluded that the reward is worth the risk.

Our travel on *Coaster*, was easier than our earlier waterway trips on *Salute* and *Greensleeves*. There is less work on a motor vessel and the accommodations on board are similar to those in a tiny studio apartment. We have a motorized dinghy that we use to get to and from shore when we anchor out and we carry two bicycles that get us around town when we tie up at a dock.

We left Fernandina Beach and motored slowly down the waterway to the city of Fort Pierce, Florida. Many boaters pass by Fort Pierce in a hurry to get farther south. We did not make that mistake. The old city is a beauty, remarkably well preserved. There is a Farmer's Market every Saturday morning at the entry to the City Marina and the local preservation association has refurbished the historic Sunrise Theatre, now an attraction for theatre lovers. We arrived there in time to enjoy the extensive

Christmas decorations and musical celebrations along the waterfront. We had planned to stay only a day or two, but once there we found it hard to leave.

A month later we reluctantly left Fort Pierce and headed to Fort Lauderdale and our slip at the International Swimming Hall of Fame Marina.

The beautiful Hall of Fame Marina is on the narrow spit of land that separates the ocean from the Intracoastal Waterway. Our slip put us in such a position that while sitting on our aft-deck we could see scores of megayachts—worth millions—berthed directly behind us at Bahia Mar, the fanciest marina in Florida. By looking to the right we could watch boats going up and down the waterway and to our left, we could see the ocean and the beachgoers. At night, we opened all the windows and hatches on *Coaster* and slept to the rhythm of surf crashing against sand. We were definitely in the high-rent district of Fort Lauderdale.

Throughout our stay at the Hall of Fame Marina we watched hundreds of people come and go to the megayachts. Most of them were renting the huge yachts for two or three days. They would live high on the hog, pampered around the clock by a crew of uniformed young people. It was fun to watch them, especially since we were enjoying the same fun for five percent of what they were paying.

We made daily treks to the beach and rode our bikes all over Fort Lauderdale, but occasionally we took the city transit, buses numbers 40 and 01, to Gulfstream Park where we enjoyed thoroughbred racing at its finest.

Our new approach to life gave us a good feeling, we had gone from boom to bust so many times in our life that it was odd to think that we did not plan to go back to conventional work at the end of our cruise to Florida.

Many people shift to an overly conservative lifestyle as they grow older. We believe that is a sure formula for shriveling up, mentally and physically. It is important to stay active, to run risks, to be bold, to dare. Risk and fear lie at the heart of Mark Twain's quote. If we, as we age, still have the physical capacity to enjoy life, then the biggest obstacle to a full life is fear itself.

Lana and I are not immune to fear and ailments, we have had our share of both.

I had to deal with one such challenge in 1997, when I was sixty-two. I went in for my annual physical and the doctor told me that my PSA was too high. I asked him, “What is PSA?” I had always enjoyed good health and was surprised to learn that my laboratory results were not perfect. He sent me to the urologist, and soon I was on the operating table at Georgetown University Medical Center. I had prostate cancer and the best option was to take it out, so that is what they did.

After the operation, I was on the fast track to recovery but then I encountered one of the great ironies of my life. My body did not like the surgery and in a few months, scar tissue began to block my ability to pee. It got to the point that I could only pee by inserting a disposable catheter each time my bladder filled up. This is not a fun exercise, but I mused at the irony of getting up in the middle of the night to force myself to pee. For the first fourteen years of my life, I wet the bed every night and tried everything I could to keep from peeing. Now, at age sixty-two I could not pee at all. This went on for three months until the doctor put me back on the operating table and removed the scar tissue using a medical procedure similar to what the plumbers do when they open up a sewer line with a roto-rooter. The roto-rootering worked and so did the original surgery. The prostate cancer has been gone for fifteen years and I pee freely, but not in bed.

Such challenges lurk around as we get older, but we do not intend to let them slow us down. As long as we are physically able, we are determined to enjoy the gift of life.

Lana was worried that I would be bored without the practice of law to keep me focused, and we talked about that a lot. As it turned out I spent a good part of the next three years gathering material and writing this memoir and I spent the rest getting to know my eight granddaughters and letting them get to know me. I have seen more soccer games, swim meets, gymnastic contests, basketball games, track meets, cross-country races, tennis matches, dance recitals, ice skating shows, school graduations, plays, musicals, and piano rehearsals than I can count.

Our eight granddaughters and their parents with Lana and me in Maine. Summer, 2011.

I am busier than ever in this new phase of my life and to complete my days, I rekindled an old love, baseball. I have been a Baltimore Orioles fan since Brooks Robinson joined the team in 1955. Baseball has been the one constant in my life since childhood, and after I left the law firm, I have seen at least a dozen games each year at Oriole Park at Camden Yards in Baltimore. I watch at least twenty-five Oriole games each year on television. Ask me anything about the Orioles—or say anything about them—and you will have my full attention.

Lana and I are blessed. As we neared the end of 2008, we began to give a lot of thought to how we have managed to stay married for fifty years and do as many things as we have done. Antoine de Saint-Exupery, a French writer and aviator, said, "Love does not consist of gazing at each other, but in looking together in the same direction," and that has been a key to our success. Throughout the years, we have been open with each other, never holding back our innermost thoughts. It is perilous, we believe, for a husband or a wife to have a hidden agenda. That approach undermines the ability to plan for the future and dream great dreams.

We have had as much fun planning and dreaming as we have had in doing, and honest teamwork has kept us looking in the same direction.

Most people get the family and friends together for a Golden Anniversary celebration, but as we approached our special day, we had to face facts. Paige and Chris at that time lived in Bel Air, California and their six girls would be in school in late January. Sam and Alison lived in Virginia Beach, Virginia and their two girls were in school there. We needed a celebration plan that would work for everyone, one that would memorialize the day and be special for all the kids and us.

Lana and I decided to celebrate by flying out west to a secluded place, and we developed a plan that turned out to be a masterstroke. We landed in Montana on January 18, 2009. We had arranged to stay on a ranch near Ennis, Montana, a spread owned jointly by Chris Nassetta's father and his uncle, Leland Phillips. It is a beautiful place, particularly in January when the Madison River freezes over and snow blankets the entire valley and continues up to the mountaintops. The sturdy cabin where we stayed has a great room with an enormous fireplace that supplants an entire wall. Big stacks of wood for the fireplace are easy to reach. Outside, just across from the cabin stands a small, beautiful chapel that is empty most of the time because it is for the exclusive use of those who stay on the ranch. There are horses to ride, trails to walk, and lots of scenery and wildlife to photograph.

Our plan for the anniversary was simple. We would go to the chapel alone at 10:30 a.m. on the twenty-fourth and repeat our vows. That was the exact moment of our wedding, fifty years earlier.

On the day before our ceremony, we emailed copies of our wedding vows to all our children and grandchildren and told them what we planned to do. We asked them to read the vows and think about us at the exact moment we would be in the chapel.

Next, we arranged a conference call for 11:00 a.m. so we could all talk about the vows and celebrate the occasion.

Everything went off like clockwork. At 10:25 a.m., we entered the chapel and walked to the altar that is in front of a large window with a magnificent panorama of pastureland backed by snow-covered mountains. Soon we tore ourselves away from the view and turned to each other. It was time to repeat our vows and reconcile our thoughts and feelings with those of fifty years ago. For a second it seemed clumsy since we were all alone but as I looked into Lana's eyes, it became easy, as natural as our relationship has become over the years. The eyes and the soul are the same forever. The face around the eyes may crease and weather, and the body may age, but none of that can change all that has gone before. That is what I saw in her eyes—her tender hazel eyes that had the sparkle and freshness of yesterday.

Lana felt the same—I know she did—as we repeated the marriage vows. The words are so familiar: "In the presence of God … to live together in holy marriage … to have and to hold from this day forward, for better, for worse, for richer, for poorer, in sickness and in health, to love and to cherish, until we are parted by death … in the name of the Father, and of the Son, and of the Holy Spirit."

We kissed to seal the special moment and turned to leave the altar. As we walked back up the aisle the stained glass window over the door, glowing from the light outside, told the story of our life together. A rainbow of many colors—arched from one side of the window to the other over a chalice and loaves—bespoke the story of God's love, and our love for each other. Our life story has been and is a story of blessed love, not a pot of gold.

As soon as we got back to the cabin we began the conference call. All eight granddaughters got on the line along with Paige and Chris and Sam and Alison. The girls had read the vows and we talked to each of them and answered their many questions about our long marriage. We told them about our visit with Dr. Kenneth Shamblin, the preacher who married us in 1959, and our special pledge to be loyal to each other. We also told them how, after our first argument, we made a rule that we would never go to bed without first making up. I am convinced the girls learned more from the way we celebrated our anniversary than they would ever have learned if we had done it in the conventional way.

The next day Lana and I got up early and drove a couple of hours from Ennis to West Yellowstone, Montana where we caught a snowcoach—a big van with skis on the front and tractor-style tracks on the rear—for a trip into Yellowstone National Park.

It was a perfect day, a perfect place, and a perfect time to reminisce and think deeply about how we should live the rest of our lives.

The winter-blue sky, deep snow, and waterfalls with cones of ice set against the mountains and valleys were in sharp contrast with the evergreen trees and the endless supply of steam rising from hundreds of springs and geysers. The earth is God's work—there can be no doubt.

The winter-critters of Yellowstone, big and small, forage for food. The slow-moving bison were in clusters, using their large heads like plows to push aside the snow so they could get to the food below. The elk herds were scattered, mainly in the valleys along the rivers, but they stood out against ground that was thick-layered with snow. There are bears, wolves, and bobcats, and hundreds of smaller creatures in the park, but they like to hide and they are hard to spot. The birdlife, in winter, is scarcer than in summer and hard to see but we saw the king of the sky, the bald eagle, nesting in a large tree close to water. The magnificence of the animal kingdom is always inspiring and it leaves no doubt: This too is God's work.

God also made man, but he gave him the ability to think and choose how he wants to live. All too often, man forgets who is in charge and puts himself in the center.

In the preface of this memoir, I said, "On our life journey, we see right and wrong, good and evil, fair and foul, love and hate. Sometimes the path is easy to see, sometimes not. We struggle, we succeed, we err, and we go on. Eventually, we encounter an inescapable truth. We are not the center of the universe. Our destiny hinges upon acceptance of that truth."

My path through life has been complicated, particularly in the early years, but I have had a great companion to help me find my way. There is still much to do and we are off in search of yet another adventure. It is our way. When we have done all we can, then and only then will it be time to say: "I have fought a good fight, I have finished the course, and I have kept the faith."

EPILOGUE

Pearls do not lie on the seashore.
If you desire one, you must dive for it.
Oriental Proverb

I began this memoir thinking it would end with telling about our granddaughters and our fiftieth wedding anniversary. That is how life usually works, but my life is nothing if not unusual.

In August of 1915, the Black River crested at 27.9 feet, flooding the bottomlands in and around Pocahontas—my mother was five going on six years old and her brother, Little Gerle, was four.

The 1915 flood was the worst until April 28, 2011 when the Black River rose to the highest level she has ever reached, 28.4 feet. The recurring floods bear witness that we, like those who came before, are forever vulnerable to the natural forces, a lesson I have learned and relearned when sailing on the high seas.

I have been back to Pocahontas many times since graduating from high school in 1953, and I was there again in 2011 to see old friends. When I am there, I always go down to the river—for old times' sake. The town has changed over the years but the river is unchanged. She is, as she has always been, a source of prosperity as well as devastation. She brought the settlers and the steamboats and yielded the fish and mussels that supported the River Rats and the button factory. She has provided irrigation for the farmers and water for the people and days of pleasure when she behaves. Her mystique draws me close.

When I stand in my favorite spot on the bank of the river down from the town square, I always think of Toni, the River Rat girl who was my friend when I was a little boy. She was a good girl, smart and tenderhearted. I think of the times we sat on the side of her tarpapered houseboat, our bare feet dangling in the current, our heels rubbing up against the mossy scum on the side of the boat. More than sixty-five years have passed since Toni told me about the River Rat who found a pearl worth $500. She said, "That-un got him and his'n off the river." It was her dream that she would one day find a big, well-shaped Black River pearl, a windfall that would change her life.

I do not know if Toni ever found her pearl because I never saw her after she and the other River Rats moved on, but I remember the determined look in her eyes when she said, "We're not 'bout to quit lookin', or give up." I know she kept trying to find a big pearl, but I wonder if she found God, a bigger prize. I hope she found both, but if she only found one, I pray it was God.

Since finishing my memoir, I have thought a lot about my adventures and the good things that have happened to me and I have wondered why blessings come to those who are undeserving.

There is no logic to it, at least in this world. If I had gotten what I deserved, my life would have been dramatically different. The only possible explanation is that God keeps the door open for everyone, and He gets a real kick out of it when those who are flawed find their way into His Kingdom.

The Good Book says it like this: "God saved you by his grace when you believed. And you can't take credit for this; it is a gift from God." Ephesians 2:8 NLT

I believe He wants me, having finally surrendered my will to his, to learn and grow, and be a good witness to others who need help and are still searching for it. He does not want me, or Lana, or anyone to stop or slow down.

There is plenty to do—there is always plenty to do. Our nation is facing severe economic and political challenges that will affect life at home and abroad. There are young people and troubled grownups hungry for counsel and guidance from those of us who have been through the crucible. Our children and grandchildren and the generations to come will live in a world where the culture changes day by day. These challenges call for the best we have to offer and we must face them as adventures, not inconveniences.

Stories do not end until you close the book, and life does not end until you are unable or unwilling to accept the next challenge, the next adventure. God wants all of us to keep looking for the big pearl, but He wants us to do it His way.